An International Legal Framework for Geoengineering

T0331454

Geoengineering provides new possibilities for humans to deal with dangerous climate change and its effects but at the same time creates new risks to the planet. This book responds to the challenges geoengineering poses to international law by identifying and developing the rules and principles that are aimed at controlling the risks to the environment and human health arising from geoengineering activities, without neglecting the contribution that geoengineering could make in preventing dangerous climate change and its impacts. This book first investigates international laws and principles that apply to geoengineering in general and to six specific geoengineering techniques respectively. Then, this book compares different governance approaches and predicts the short-, mid- and long-term scenarios of the international governance of geoengineering. In the end, in order to balance the positive and negative dimensions of geoengineering, this book proposes an assessment framework and a tailored implementation of the precautionary approach.

Haomiao Du is a post-doctoral researcher at the University of Twente, the Netherlands.

Routledge Research in International Environmental Law

www.routledge.com/Routledge-Research-in-International-Environmental-Law/book-series/INTENVLAW

An International
Legal Framework
for Geoengineering
Managing the Risks of an Emerging Technology

Haomiao Du

Routledge
Taylor & Francis Group

LONDON AND NEW YORK

First published 2018 by Routledge

2 Park Square, Milton Park, Abingdon, Oxfordshire OX14 4RN
52 Vanderbilt Avenue, New York, NY 10017

Routledge is an imprint of the Taylor & Francis Group, an informa business

First issued in paperback 2019

British Library Cataloguing-in-Publication Data
A catalogue record for this book is available from the British Library

Library of Congress Cataloging-in-Publication Data
Names: Du, Haomiao, author.
Title: An international legal framework for geoengineering : managing
    the risks of an emerging technology / Haomiao Du.
Description: New York, NY : Routledge, 2018. | Series: Routledge
    research in international environmental law | Includes bibliographical
    references and index.
Identifiers: LCCN 2017031665 | ISBN 9781138744615 (hbk)
Subjects: LCSH: Environmental geotechnology—Law and legislation. |
    Global warming—Law and legislation. | Environmental engineering—
    Law and legislation. | Technology and law. | Climatology.
Classification: LCC K3585.5 .D8 2018 | DDC 344.04/63—dc23
LC record available at https://lccn.loc.gov/2017031665

ISBN: 978-1-138-74461-5 (hbk)
ISBN: 978-0-367-88878-7 (pbk)

Typeset in Galliard
by Apex CoVantage, LLC

Contents

List of figures and tables

Figures

Tables

Acronyms

AR5	Fifth Assessment Report of the Intergovernmental Panel on Climate Change
ASEAN	Association of Southeast Asian Nations
BECCS	Bioenergy with Carbon Capture and Sequestration
CBD	Convention on Biological Diversity
CCAMLR	Convention on the Conservation of Antarctic Marine Living Resources
CDR	Carbon Dioxide Removal
CLRTAP	Convention on Long-Range Transboundary Air Pollution
CMA	Conference of Parties serving as the meeting of the Parties to the Paris Agreement
CMP	Conference of the Parties serving as the meeting of the Parties to the Kyoto Protocol
CMS	Convention on the Conservation of Migratory Species of Wild Animals
COP	Conference of the Parties
DAC	Direct Air Capture
EEC	Exclusive Economic Zone
ENMOD	Convention on the Prohibition of Military or Any Hostile Use of Environmental Modification Techniques
FECCS	Fossil-fuel Energy with Carbon Capture and Storage
ILA	International Law Association
ILC	International Law Commission
IMO	International Maritime Organization
INDC	Intended Nationally Determined Contribution
IOC	Intergovernmental Oceanographic Commission
IPCC	Intergovernmental Panel on Climate Change
ITLOS	International Tribunal for the Law of the Sea
KP	Kyoto Protocol
LC	London Convention, namely Convention on the Prevention of Marine pollution by Dumping of Wastes and Other Matter
LP	Protocol of the London Convention
MCW	Marine Cloud Whitening

MEA	Multilateral Environmental Agreement
MODUs	Mobile Offshore Drilling Units
NDC	Nationally Determined Contribution
NETs	Negative Emissions Technologies
OSPAR	Convention for the Protection of the Marine Environment of the North-East Atlantic
PA	Paris Agreement
SAI	Sulphate Aerosol Injection
SAR	IPCC Second Assessment Report
SBI	Subsidiary Body for Implementation
SBSTA	Subsidiary Body for Scientific and Technological Advices
SRM	Solar Radiation Management
TAR	IPCC Third Assessment Report
UNCED	United Nations Conference on Environment and Development
UNCLOS	United Nations Convention on the Law of the Sea
UNEA	United Nations Environmental Assembly
UNECE	United Nations Economic Commission for Europe
UNEP	United Nations Environment Programme
UNESCO	United Nations Educational, Science and Cultural Organization
UNFCCC	United Nations Framework Convention on Climate Change
WG	IPCC Working Group
WMO	World Meteorological Organization

Preface

The present book titled *An International Legal Framework for Geoengineering – Managing the Risks of an Emerging Technology* is a revised version of my dissertation. Geoengineering, or climate engineering, has been exposed to the international community as an emerging technology to deal with anthropogenic climate change and its impact. Geoengineering provides new possibilities for humans to deal with dangerous climate change and its effects, on the one hand, and creates new risks to the planet, on the other hand. Scientific uncertainties contained in such novel techniques and their impacts bring challenges to environmentalists, politicians as well as lawyers.

In response to the challenges posed by geoengineering to international law, this book aims to identify and develop international rules and principles that minimize or control the risks arising from geoengineering activities to the environmental and human health without neglecting the contribution that some geoengineering techniques could make in preventing serious or irreversible climate change and its impacts.

I would not have completed this book without support from great people. First and foremost, my PhD supervisor René Lefeber has been the most significant guide. I feel so grateful that he never restricts my thoughts, and always quickly clears up my confusions and points out my mistakes, preventing me from going astray. I also appreciate very much the supervision from my co-supervisor Jesse Reynolds. His expertise on geoengineering, in particular from the perspective of political science and international relations, broadened my horizon and effectively complemented my legal research.

Also, I would like to express my gratitude to my internship supervisor Maria Socorro Manguiat, the former legal officer at the secretariat of the United Nations Framework Convention on Climate Change (UNFCCC), for her kindness, patience and strictness. I learned from her how to transfer my ivory-tower ideas to realistic proposals and to present them in a professional manner.

Special appreciation goes to Alexander Proelß, professor of public international and European law from Trier University, Germany, for his valuable comments on my dissertation as well as the present book.

Haomiao Du
March 2017 in Eindhoven, The Netherlands

Introduction

Since the beginning of the Industrial Revolution, the world has entered into the epoch of the Anthropocene, in which the traditional relationship between nature and humankind has shifted. A man-made world challenges the natural environment as well as human society. Geoengineering has emerged in the Anthropocene: human beings are attempting to counter anthropogenic global warming and its effects by manipulating the planetary environment. Main geoengineering methods can be divided into two categories: sequestering CO_2 from the atmosphere (carbon dioxide removal, CDR) and modifying solar radiation coming to the atmosphere and land surface (solar radiation management, SRM). The emerging ideas include, for instance, injecting a layer of sulphate aerosols in the upper atmosphere to reflect more solar radiation, adding iron particles into the ocean to increase the rate of photosynthesis, and installing huge mirrors in outer space to block sunlight. These novel techniques provide new possibilities for humans to deal with dangerous climate change and its effects, on the one hand, and create new risks to the planet, on the other hand. It may be the first time for humankind to think about this question: can we and should we save the planet by intervening/manipulating it?

Geoengineering has raised debates in various disciplines. Environmentalists have identified the adverse impacts arising from different geoengineering methods on the environment as well as on human health. The knowledge about the feasibility of these novel methods and the potential impacts on the environment and human health are far from fully available; Ethicists have identified the problem called "moral hazards", which implies that geoengineering would entice people to maintain their high-carbon lifestyle; Politicians have identified potential conflicts in geopolitics: the focus of climate negotiations would be deviated from emissions reduction, and there would be a risk that some developed countries use geoengineering as a means to escape from their mitigation obligations. More problematically, the implementation of geoengineering techniques can be exercised by one single country or a small group of countries, but the impacts, both beneficial and adverse ones, would be uneven and affect a wide range of countries.

Geoengineering also poses challenges to the development, interpretation and application of international environmental law. First, SRM techniques may force legal scholars to examine the implication of new responses more than mitigation and adaption to combating global warming on the climate change regime, *inter alia*, the United Nations Framework Convention on Climate Change (UNFCCC). Second, as geoengineering can bring both opportunities and challenges to the environment, international environmental law needs to provide methods to balance the benefits and risks. Third, geoengineering is not a single technique; different techniques and different scales of activities contain different types and levels of risks and uncertainties. Were geoengineering to be implemented, either for research studies or real deployment, international law needs to govern different geoengineering techniques in a tailored manner. The specific challenge would be: how to properly, sufficiently and proportionately govern the implementation of geoengineering by, among others, choosing the proper governing institutions and applying rules and mechanisms under treaties, customary international law and non-binding legal instruments.

The main body of this book consists of five chapters:

Chapter 1 introduces the political and scientific aspects of geoengineering techniques, attempting to find out which geoengineering techniques need to be addressed in an international context. The priority of international legal analysis should be given to the techniques that are designed to be deployed transnationally or in the areas of global commons, and the techniques of which the deployment may cause transboundary interferences to environmental media and the climate system. In view of this, six geoengineering methods merit further examination in subsequent chapters. Four CDR techniques (ocean fertilization, ocean upwelling, ocean alkalinity addition, bioenergy and carbon capture and storage (BECCS)) and two SRM techniques (sulphate aerosol injection (SAI) and marine cloud whitening (MCW)) are selected.

Chapter 2 examines contemporary international legal rules and principles that are applicable to the six geoengineering techniques. This chapter first examines the climate change regime, including the UNFCCC, the Kyoto Protocol, the Paris Agreement and several decisions made by the Conference of Parties (COP) and the Conference of Parties serving as the meeting of the Parties to the Kyoto Protocol (CMP). This chapter then examines the Convention on the Prohibition of Military or Any Hostile Use of Environmental Modification Techniques (the ENMOD Convention). Regarding customary international law, the prevention principle is applicable to geoengineering activity for the purpose of preventing significant harm or controlling the risk of significant harm to another state or in the global commons. In addition, the precautionary approach, taking into account the controversy with respect to its customary legal status, serves as a significant tool to deal with scientific uncertainties contained in geoengineering techniques and their impacts on the environment.

Chapter 3 addresses contemporary international rules and principles that are applicable to each of the six geoengineering techniques. Via a technique-by-technique approach, two main issues are examined: one is the lawfulness of undertaking a geoengineering activity or the use of materials in a technique; the other is whether a technique breaches the obligations to protect the environment and to preserve natural resources due to the resulting adverse impacts and, consequently, whether such a technique is allowed or largely restricted. When examining the lawfulness of conducting a marine geoengineering activity, the analysis is divided based on the location of the activity – i.e. the territorial sea, the exclusive economic zone (EEZ) and the high seas.

Chapter 4 attempts to find the most appropriate approach to regulate geoengineering techniques. The criteria for the most appropriate approach are applied: such an approach should be able to provide inclusive, transparent, responsive, adaptive and effective governance of various geoengineering techniques. It should also avoid over- and under-governance of geoengineering. While responding to the risk of causing significant harm resulting from geoengineering to the environment and human health, it should also avoid impeding the appropriate development of geoengineering technology.

Chapter 5 attempts to deal with the issue of balancing the risk of climate change against the risk created by the implementation of geoengineering techniques. This chapter proposes an assessment framework by applying the procedural obligations under the prevention principle, among others, the obligation to conduct an environmental impact assessment. This chapter also proposes a mechanism to implement the precautionary approach for each proposed geoengineering project in a tailored manner by establishing flexible thresholds for triggering the precautionary approach and applying proportionate precautionary measures.

Part I

Background

1 Political and scientific aspects of geoengineering

1.1 Introduction

On 8 November 2013, three days before the opening of the Warsaw Climate Change Conference (UNFCCC COP19/CMP9), Super Typhoon Haiyan slammed into the Philippines, killing 6,021 individuals, destroying more than one million houses, and resulting in colossal damages to agriculture and infrastructure.[1] Haiyan was reported as the strongest typhoon that has ever made landfall in recorded history. On 11 November 2013, at the COP 19 opening ceremony, the emotional speech from the Philippines' chief negotiator, Yeb Sano, moved the plenary to tears and reminded the international community of the great urgency to tackle climate change.

There is a broad scientific consensus on the link between typhoon strength and sea temperature: When the temperatures of surface water and deep sea water rise, huge quantities of energy are stored up and integrated with the water column fuelling the storm.

The Fifth Assessment Report (AR5) of the Intergovernmental Panel on Climate Change (IPCC) Working Group I concludes that "it is *extremely likely* that human influence has been the dominant cause of the observed warming since the mid-20th century". Climate scientists assert that anthropogenic global warming causes rising ocean temperatures, which may increase energy in oceans and create stronger and more frequently extreme climate events. Although no clear causal relationship between global warming and extreme climate events has yet been built, the disaster from Haiyan could be seen as a reminder for the parties to take actions on controlling anthropogenic climate change.

This chapter begins by describing anthropogenic climate change, which leads to discussions on geoengineering. The projection of a dangerous peaking point of global average temperature has urged humans to find a rapid solution. At the crucial point, geoengineering may be a set of promising technologies to efficiently and effectively cope with global warming. This chapter then addresses the definition of geoengineering, emphasizing that geoengineering cannot be simply categorized into either of the two primary and fundamental options to combat global warming: mitigation or adaptation.

Then, this chapter briefly demonstrates the science of each geoengineering technique,[2] in particular elucidating the adverse transboundary impacts of them on environmental media, including the oceans, the land, the atmosphere and the biosphere, as well as the adverse impacts on the climate. Finally, this chapter provides an overview of the current development of different geoengineering methods.

1.2 International background of geoengineering

1.2.1 Changes in the climate system

"Climate change is no longer an environmental or political issue; it is a borderless human security issue", said Deputy Prime Minister Vete Palakua Sakaio of Tuvalu, a low-lying country of atolls in the direct line of threats from rising oceans.[3] Regardless of whether it is called an environmental, political or a security issue, climate change has been a globally significant topic for several decades. This significance is reflected in the establishment of the IPCC, the publishing of reports related to climate change, and more importantly, the UN Conference on Environment and Development and its resulting documents.

In 1988, the IPCC was established by the United Nations Environment Programme (UNEP) and the World Meteorological Organization (WMO) to provide the world with a clear scientific view on the current state of knowledge relevant to climate change as well as its potential and socio-economic impacts.[4] The IPCC is the leading scientific and intergovernmental body for the assessment of climate change. Thousands of scientists from all over the world voluntarily contribute to the work of the IPCC; 195 countries are currently members. Its special nature has enabled the IPCC to provide rigorous, neutral and thus authoritative reports.

Since 1990, the IPCC has published five assessment reports. The latest one is the AR5, comprising Working Group (WGI II and III) Assessment Reports and the Synthesis Report approved by the IPCC in 2013 and 2014.[5] According to the AR5, warming of the climate system is unequivocal. From 1880 to 2012, the globally averaged combined land and ocean surface temperature data, as calculated by a linear trend, show a warming of 0.85 °C. Since 1950, a wide range of climate changes have been observed: the atmosphere and oceans have been warmed, ice sheets and snow cover have diminished, the sea level has risen, and the atmospheric concentration of carbon dioxide, methane and nitrous oxide have increased to unprecedented levels. Due to these changes, oceans have been acidified, and biodiversity is under threat.

In 1992, the UN Conference on Environment and Development, known as the Earth Summit, was unprecedented for a UN conference and notably a milestone for the international governance of climate change.[6] The Earth Summit resulted in five documents,[7] among which was the UN Framework Convention on Climate Change (UNFCCC), which symbolized the commencement of international cooperation on limiting the on-going increase in global average temperature and the resulting changes to the climate. The ultimate objective of the UNFCCC is to stabilize greenhouse gas concentrations in the atmosphere at a level that would prevent dangerous anthropogenic interference with the climate system.[8] Based on the UNFCCC, the annual climate change conferences have become the most important event for international climate change negotiation.

In 2015, the UN General Assembly adopted the 2030 Agenda for Sustainable Development, which includes taking urgent action to combat climate change and its impacts as one of the seventeen sustainable development goals.[9] Paragraph 31 of the agenda "calls for the widest possible international cooperation aimed at accelerating the reduction of global greenhouse gas emissions and addressing adaptation to the adverse impacts of climate change".

A host of intergovernmental and non-governmental organizations concerned about climate change issues have produced various reports as well. For instance, the UNEP Emissions Gap Report has been published annually since 2010. This report highlights the emissions gap between the ambition of reduction and the reality, and suggests options to bridge the gap. Moreover, the World Economic Forum began to publish the Global Risk Network Report in 2006. In the Global Risks Report of 2006, risks stemming from climate change were considered an "emerging risk" and were predicted to be moved to the global agenda.[10] One year later in the Global Risks Report of 2007, climate change was identified as one of the core environmental risks.[11] More recently, in the Global Risks Report of 2014, "failure of climate change mitigation and adaptation" was ranked as the fifth-highest concerned global risk. Another influential report concerning climate change, *Turn Down the Heat: Why a 4°C Warmer World Must be Avoided*, was published by the World Bank in 2012. This report provides a devastating scenario of a 4 °C warmer world, including extreme weather and climate events, a dramatic change in landscape and profound consequences for food, water, ecosystems and human health.

1.2.2 Attribution of climate change

Both natural and anthropogenic substances and processes can alter Earth's radiation budget, producing a radiative forcing (RF) that brings about changes in the climate.[12] RF is a measure of the net change in the energy balance in response to an external perturbation. Positive RF leads to surface warming, while negative RF leads to surface cooling. Some drivers of RF alteration are changes in the solar irradiance and changes in atmospheric trace gases and aerosol concentrations.[13] Observational and model studies show that the total RF since 1750 is positive, and the increase in CO_2 concentration by anthropogenic carbon emissions makes the largest contribution to the total RF production. Thus, the increase in anthropogenic CO_2 concentration, or the growth of carbon emissions, results in global warming as well as other changes in climate.[14]

Pursuant to AR5, it is *extremely likely* that human influence has been the dominant cause of the observed warming since the mid-20th century.[15] Human activities have contributed to the increase of the global average temperature, the shrinking of glaciers, the rise of the mean sea level and perhaps stronger extreme weather events. The necessity of controlling global warming from anthropogenic sources is beyond scientific doubt, which requires substantial and sustained strategies.

1.2.3 Emission reduction – target and gap

In 2010, the parties to the UNFCCC agreed to a concrete target of limiting the increase in global average temperature to 2 °C compared to pre-industrial levels.[16] In 2015, the Paris Agreement reiterated the 2 °C target and recognized that the efforts to limit the temperature increase to 1.5 °C above pre-industrial levels would significantly reduce the risks and impacts of climate change.[17][18] In 2014, total GHG emissions amounted to about 52.7 $GtCO_2e$ (range: 47.9–57.5), and the amount of GHG emissions is not expected to peak before 2020.[19] The median emission level in 2030 in scenarios that have a >66% chance of keeping global mean temperature increase below 2 °C by the end of the century is 42 $GtCO_2e$ (range: 37–44).[20] The similar level for a 1.5 °C target is 39 $GtCO_2e$ (range: 31–44) per year.[21]

In order to accomplish at least the 2 °C goal, pledges and commitments should be made by every state. Taking enhanced early actions (pre-2020), as compared to the current pledges by 2020, would facilitate the transition to the stringent, long-term emission reductions required for the 2 °C and 1.5 °C targets, and would reduce the costs of emission reductions, avoid lock-in of carbon and energy intensive infrastructure, and decrease the risks associated with climate change.[22] Regarding the post-2020 commitments, the implementation of intended nationally determined contributions (INDCs) will be the new approach to close the emissions gap.[23] As of 12 December 2015, 160 INDCs were submitted, covering emissions of 187 parties to the UNFCCC. However, the emissions gap between the full implementation of the conditional INDCs[24] and the least-cost emission level[25] for a pathway to stay below 2 °C is estimated to be 12 $GtCO_2e$ in 2030.[26]

1.2.4 A complement to traditional mitigation methods

In addition to the initiatives in the areas of energy efficiency and renewable energy, negative emission technologies are required to bridge the emissions gap.[27] It is estimated that scenarios in line with the 2 °C target require net zero CO_2 emissions around 2075, and the scenarios that keep global warming to below 1.5 °C require net zero CO_2 emissions around 2050.[28] In most scenarios, global net zero and negative emissions are achieved by the use of negative emissions technologies on a large scale. Such technologies and methods, including massive afforestation and reforestation, bioenergy with carbon capture and storage (BECCS), and carbon capture and storage (CCS) in combination with direct air capture, have the potential in contributing to closing the emission gap.[29]

In contrast to carbon dioxide removal (CDR), which tackles the root cause of global warming, the aim of solar radiation management (SRM) techniques[30] is to decrease the average temperature of the Earth's surface by reducing solar radiation. The proposal that has generated the most concerns and interest is stratospheric aerosol injection (SAI).

Inspired by volcanic eruptions,[31] scientists proposed the idea of deliberately injecting sulphate aerosol into the stratosphere to block sunlight and cool the planet.[32] SAI is expected to substantially offset global warming and win time for mitigation.[33]

The emergence of the geoengineering debate in the IPCC is a very good example to reflect the historical development of geoengineering as a suite of new options to counteract climate change.[34] Since the IPCC Second Assessment Report (SAR) of 1995, geoengineering options have been assessed as conceptual approaches for counterbalancing anthropogenic climate change.[35] The IPCC noticed that these approaches have important adverse environmental consequences. However, most of these approaches were "poorly understood" at that time.[36] Five years later, the Third Assessment Report (TAR) briefly introduced the concept of geoengineering and summarized the concerns from a host of papers about the feasibility of using this novel technology, *inter alia*, about the environmental risks, knowledge gaps, and the legal and ethical implications.[37] In the Fourth Assessment Report (AR4), two examples – iron ocean fertilization from CDR and sulphate aerosol injection from SRM – were particularly mentioned.[38] Still, "little is known about effectiveness, costs or potential side effects of the options".[39] In the AR5 of 2013, geoengineering options have been much more extensively assessed than in the previous reports. The AR5 identifies the science, the benefits and risks, costs, and the socio-economic implications of some CDR and SRM methods.[40] In particular, IPCC Working Group III assessed large-scale afforestation and BECCS in the assessment of mitigation scenarios.

1.3 Definitions

1.3.1 The definition of geoengineering

There is currently no universal or uniform use for the term "geoengineering". The old and broad usage of "geoengineering" refers to a contraction of geotechnical engineering, which concerns the alteration of the Earth's environment through engineering. In etymology, "geo-" from the Greek root *geō-* means Earth and "engineering" means "the application of science to the optimum conversion of the resources of nature to the uses of humankind".[41] The oldest activity of geotechnical engineering can be dated back to ancient times (around 3,000–2,000 BC) when human beings first used soil to build dams or canals for flood control and irrigation. The novel meaning of "geoengineering", as manipulations to the global climate, emerged much later, due to the increasingly serious undesired climate change in the last half century. The novel meaning of geoengineering is not wholly unrelated to the conventional one since the manipulation of the climate system is also the alteration of the Earth's systems. Note that the definition discussed hereafter is only associated with climate-related geoengineering.

The first use of the term geoengineering to counter global warming can be traced back to 1977, when one of the earliest papers by Marchetti illustrated the idea of geoengineering by dividing it into three phases – CO_2 collection, CO_2 transportation and CO_2 disposal.[42] This research concluded that the large equilibrium capacity of the deep ocean should be taken into consideration, and Marchetti proposed a CO_2 management system whereby CO_2 would be collected by suitable transformation points, disposed of by injecting it into sinking thermohaline currents and stored in deep oceans.[43]

Since the 1990s, academic researchers, as well as national and multilateral bodies, have defined the term geoengineering differently.[44] An early example of a definition came from David Keith in 2000: geoengineering is the deliberate manipulation of the planetary environment to counteract anthropogenic climate change. In 2009, the Royal Society[45] proposed a definition of geoengineering, which has become one of the most widely cited definitions in the literature: "Geoengineering is the *deliberate large-scale* manipulation of the planetary environment to counteract anthropogenic climate change [. . .]. [T]hey have been classified into two main groups: i. carbon dioxide removal (CDR) [. . .]; ii. solar radiation management (SRM)".[46]

Unlike all of the previous definitions from academic or political documents, marine geoengineering was for the first time defined in a legally binding document (not yet into force), the 2013 Amendment to the 1996 Protocol to the London Convention (2013 Amendment to the LP), as "a deliberate intervention in the marine environment to manipulate natural processes, including to counteract anthropogenic climate change and/or its impacts, and that has the potential to result in deleterious effects, especially where those effects may be widespread, long-lasting or severe".

Even though different scholars or bodies formulate geoengineering differently, most of the existing definitions share four common elements: intent, scale, action(s) and purpose.[47] The element of "intent" differentiates geoengineering from other activities that impact the climate inadvertently. The "scale" element relates to the size of action which should be "large",[48] or the magnitude of impact, which should be "widespread" or "long-lasting".[49]

The elements of "action" or "actions" are phrased differently, for instance, as "manipulation", "interventions", or "methods and technologies".[50] In many definitions, actions are further divided into CDR and SRM methods.[51] The "purpose" is to counter climate change and/or alleviate its impacts.[52] Among the four elements, intent and scale are of central significance.[53] Geoengineering methods "*use* or *affect* the climate system (e.g. atmosphere, land or ocean) *globally* or *regionally*, and/or could have *substantive* unintended effects that cross national boundaries".[54]

Any definition, if used for regulatory purposes, needs to be complemented by further details on the four elements. The first consideration relates to scientific research activities.

To date, SRM techniques are in the stage of computer modelling and ocean fertilization is in the stage of field tests. The purpose of scientific research activities is to gain human knowledge of these geoengineering techniques and their potential impacts on the climate system rather than counteracting climate change *per se*. In some cases, it is difficult to draw the line between small-scale scientific research activities and large-scale deployment on the basis of the size of the area of implementation or the amount of materials, because the likely unexpected impacts of a small-scale field trial may be more than a small scale. It remains to be determined how to address scientific research activities in the definition of geoengineering.[55] The second consideration relates to the identification of techniques and methods. One approach would be to complement the definition with a positive list of techniques and methods that qualify as geoengineering. Such a list could be comprehensive or allow room for new methods and advances.[56]

1.3.2 The definition of CDR

The Royal Society defines CDR as methods "which reduce the levels of carbon dioxide in the atmosphere, allowing outgoing long-wave (thermal infrared) heat radiation to escape more easily".[57] CDR methods refer to a set of techniques or methods that aim to remove CO_2 directly from the atmosphere by either increasing natural sinks for carbon or using chemical engineering to remove atmospheric CO_2, with the intent of reducing the atmospheric CO_2 concentration.[58] CDR methods include chemical techniques to accelerate weathering over land or ocean, biological techniques to fertilize the ocean through particles to augment the primary productivity, and "biological + physical" techniques to produce bioenergy and store the captured carbon in oceans or geological formations. The proposal of global forestation, though not strictly an engineering intervention, could also be viewed as a long-term method to increase carbon sinks and thus belongs to CDR methods.[59] Note that not all levels of CDR activities fall under geoengineering activities; the distinction is based on the magnitude, scale and impact of a particular CDR activity.[60] Such an activity can be considered as geoengineering only if it is implemented on a climate-moderating scale.

According to the science of CDR methods and the location of their implementation, they are categorized as chemical, physical or biological methods, deployed on land or in the ocean. Table 1.1 demonstrates a brief categorization of the main CDR methods.[61]

This categorization will be the basis of the technique-based analysis in Chapter 3. The methods listed in this table are indicative; similar methods can be merged into corresponding categories. For instance, non-till agriculture and creation of wetlands belong to the category of "land use management".

Table 1.1 Carbon dioxide removal methods

CDR technique	Method	Location
Ocean fertilization	Biological	Ocean
Ocean upwelling and downwelling	Physical & biological	Ocean
Enhanced weathering	Chemical	Ocean or land
Ambient air capture	Chemical & physical	CO_2 Capture: land CO_2 sequestration: ocean or land
Afforestation, reforestation and land-use management	Biological	Land
Biochar/ biomass burial	Biological	Land
BECCS	Biological & physical	Bioenergy production: land; CO_2 sequestration: ocean or land

In fact, physical methods are not independent, but are associated with chemical or biological methods. As shown in Table 1.1, physical storage (in the seabed or on land) is the second step following CO_2 removal in order to store the inorganic carbon absorbed from ambient air or captured by BECCS. With regard to ocean upwelling and downwelling, the overturning circulation transports the CO_2 in the deep ocean to the surface ocean, thereby increasing biological pumping[62] in surface water.

Chemical techniques refer to enhanced weathering over land via spreading silicate minerals and enhanced weathering over oceans via dissolving alkaline rocks. Ambient air capture absorbing CO_2 via "artificial trees" or "wet scrubbers" is a chemical technique as well.

Essentially, biological methods artificially promote photosynthesis or avert oxygenated decomposition in order to remove CO_2 either from land or the ocean. Afforestation, reforestation and land-use management consume CO_2 via photosynthesis by trees or other kinds of vegetation. Ocean fertilization increases the absorption of CO_2 by stimulating primary productivity in the oceans. Other biological methods are biomass burial and biochar burial, which deposit carbon in anoxic conditions and prevent the release of CO_2 from oxygenated decomposition.

1.3.3 The definition of SRM

The incoming sunlight to the Earth is either absorbed or reflected. On average, 30% of the energy from sunlight is reflected back into space while 70% is absorbed. Scientists have estimated that SRM methods are capable of offsetting a doubling of CO_2 concentration from pre-industrial levels with just 2% more sunlight reflection.[63] SRM methods aim at reducing the net incoming solar radiation by deflecting a small percentage of sunlight back into space or by increasing the reflectivity of the atmosphere, clouds or the Earth's surface.[64] The core

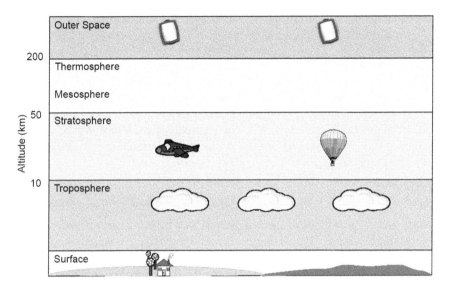

Figure 1.1 Solar radiation management techniques

difference between CDR and SRM is that CDR methods cope with the cause of global warming (CO_2 and other greenhouse gases), whereas SRM methods just manage some symptoms of global warming, notably lowering the global average temperature. SRM would do nothing with CO_2 *per se*, so it cannot solve other problems arising from CO_2 emission, such as ocean acidification.[65]

Depending on the location of implementation, from low to high altitudes, SRM techniques can be classified as space-based, stratosphere-based, troposphere-based and surface-based techniques.[66] Figure 1.1 sketches the main SRM techniques and the location where they are deployed. Space-based reflectors (simplified as mirrors in Figure 1.1) are designed to be placed in outer space 200 km or more above the surface of the Earth. The technique of SAI aims to inject sulphates into the stratosphere between altitudes of about 10 km and 50 km. Two main methods of transporting sulphates into the stratosphere are airplane and balloon (as simplified in Figure 1.1). The troposphere is the lowest atmospheric layer with the majority of water vapour and all weather phenomena, and therefore the best location for cloud whitening (simplified as clouds in Figure 1.1). Below the troposphere is the land and ocean surface. A host of surface-based methods have been proposed, such as planting grassland and reflective roofs (simplified as a green base and house in Figure 1.1).

1.3.4 Difference between CCS and geoengineering

Carbon capture and storage (CCS) deals with CO_2 emissions and attempts to store the captured carbon permanently. In a broad sense, CCS can be understood as the capture and storage phases of some CDR techniques, such as bioenergy with CCS (BECCS) (see Section 1.4.1.4) and direct air capture (see Section 1.4.1.5). In a narrow sense, CCS refers to the "conventional" CCS technology, which combines fossil-fuel energy with carbon capture and storage (FECCS). FECCS is a process consisting of the separation of CO_2 from industrial and energy-related sources, transport to a storage location and long-term isolation from the atmosphere.[67] FECCS is not considered a geoengineering technique because FECCS captures CO_2 before it is released into the atmosphere.[68] In comparison, BECCS or direct air capture removes CO_2 from the atmosphere, reducing pre-existing atmospheric CO_2 concentration.[69]

1.3.5 *Difference between geoengineering and mitigation and adaptation*

Mitigation and adaptation are two primary and fundamental options to combat global warming. The definitions of the two terms are stated in TAR and reiterated in AR4 and AR5. Mitigation refers to an anthropogenic intervention to reduce the sources or enhance the sinks of greenhouse gases. Climate adaptation is the adjustment in natural or human systems in response to experienced or future climatic conditions or their effects.[70]

Due to the distinct attributes of CDR and SRM, they should be discussed separately for the clarity of comparison. Pursuant to the definition of mitigation, the methods that "reduce the sources" or "enhance the sinks" of greenhouse gases belong to mitigation. CDR methods remove atmospheric CO_2 by either enlarging natural sinks or providing new forms of sink for carbon. Biological CDR methods are anthropogenic interventions to enhance the sinks (either ocean or land) of CO_2 and thus pertain to mitigation options. Chemical CDR techniques use chemical processes to create new forms of sink, such as "artificial trees" in ambient air capture. Therefore, CDR is a sub-category of mitigation.[71] By contrast, SRM techniques, which aim to deflect a small percentage of the sunlight or enhance the albedo of the Earth's surface or clouds, do not affect the concentration of CO_2. Therefore, SRM techniques do not belong to mitigation methods.

With regard to the relationship between adaptation and geoengineering, it is apparent that CDR methods are distinguished from adaptation because CDR belongs to mitigation. It is worth discussing whether SRM belongs to adaption. Adaptation focuses on adjustments to deal with irreversible consequences arising from past emissions. In this sense, SRM is not a subset of adaptation because SRM is used to prevent sustained temperature rise rather than endure the rise and try to minimize damages to core interests.[72] However, according to the definition of adaption from the IPCC, adaptation is the adjustment in response to not only "experienced" but also "future" climatic conditions or their effects. It might be reasonable to suggest that SRM could be understood as responsive and adaptive to "future" climate conditions, viz. global average temperature increase, and thus partly belongs to adaptation.

1.4 Scientific aspects of CDR and SRM techniques

1.4.1 CDR

1.4.1.1 Ocean fertilization

Thanks to their massive volume, oceans have a great capacity to sequester a large quantity of CO_2.[73] Covering approximately 70% of the Earth's surface,[74] oceans are a vast greenhouse gas sink, which can absorb 50 times more inorganic carbon than the atmosphere can.[75] Carbon cycles into the ocean through two mechanisms: the "biological pump" and the "solubility pump".[76] The idea of ocean fertilization is to artificially increase one of the "pumps" in order to sequester more atmospheric CO_2 into the oceans. In this section, direct fertilization and indirect fertilization will be introduced individually based on the theories of the "biological pump" and the "solubility pump".

(I) DIRECT FERTILIZATION – IRON, NITROGEN OR PHOSPHORUS FERTILIZATION

Direction fertilization means the direct addition of nutrients including iron, nitrogen or phosphorus into the ocean to enhance the biological pump. The biological pump is driven by photosynthesis of phytoplankton within the surface water layers.[77] The sunlight provides energy for photosynthesis, in which the phytoplankton converts carbonic acid into organic carbon. Most of the organic carbon is consumed by zooplankton and converted back to CO_2 and released to the atmosphere. However, some of the organic carbon finds a way to sink in the deep ocean before being consumed; in doing so, CO_2 is "fixed" in the deep ocean. Based on this theory, increasing phytoplankton photosynthesis would be a potential method to promote drawdown of photosynthesized carbon into the deep ocean.[78]

The growth of phytoplankton is restricted by several factors, including light, temperature and the supply of inorganic nutrients, such as iron, nitrogen and phosphorus.[79] These nutrients are essential for the synthesis of chlorophyll and for other functions in the photosynthetic process.[80] In 1988, the oceanographer John Martin observed that the amount of chlorophyll in phytoplankton increased in proportion to the amount of iron added.[81] Two years later, Martin observed that the higher concentration of atmospheric iron dust during the last glacial period resulted in a large enhancement of phytoplankton growth, and the stimulation of new productivity may have contributed to the drawdown of atmospheric CO_2 concentration.[82] Martin hypothesized that iron deficiency was responsible for the small quantities of phytoplankton in major-nutrient-rich (PO_4, NO_3, SiO_3) waters, such as the northern and equatorial Pacific Ocean and the Southern Ocean.[83] This "iron hypothesis" indicates that iron availability can influence the rate of phytoplankton productivity in the ocean in "high-nitrate, low chlorophyll (HNLC)"[84] ocean areas, such as the equatorial and subarctic Pacific Ocean areas, and therefore would stimulate phytoplankton blooms capable of increasing the uptake of CO_2 in those ocean areas.

However, the efficacy of ocean fertilization is limited by local conditions. First, ocean fertilization will only work in areas where there are underutilized major nutrients in the euphotic zone,[85] and the deficiency of certain micronutrients, such as iron, is the main factor limiting phytoplankton growth.[86] Second, even in areas generally suitable for ocean fertilization, the physical and biochemical conditions vary with factors.[87]

Other variations of ocean fertilization involve adding nitrogen or phosphorus. Nitrogen fertilization is suitable to the ocean areas in which the lack of sufficient nitrogen is the main factor limiting phytoplankton growth. It is disputable whether nitrogen alone would lead to long-term carbon fixation because nitrogen fixation[88] requires an ample supply of energy, iron and phosphorus.[89] Compared to iron (and nitrogen) fertilization, phosphorus fertilization requires much larger quantities to be added to the ocean, making phosphorus fertilization much more costly.

The effectiveness of direct fertilization is doubted. It is uncertain how much organic carbon really sinks to deeper waters. The *in-situ* experiments reflect an overestimate of the effectiveness of iron fertilization from the previous bottle experiments and models.[90] Laboratory experiments suggest that every tonne of iron added to the ocean could remove 0.0001 to 0.0004 $GtCO_2$ from the atmosphere.[91] Early climate models show that intentional iron fertilization across the entire Southern Ocean could remove 3.33 to 6.66 $GtCO_2$ from the air, which would offset 10–25% of the world's annual total emissions.[92] Since 1993, 13 ocean experiments have taken place in different ocean regions.[93] Unlike the projection of 0.0001 to 0.0004 $GtCO_2$ resulting from adding one tonne of iron to the ocean, recent experiments indicate that only 3.67^{-6} $GtCO_2$ is sequestered for every tonne of iron added.[94] It has proven to be extremely difficult and highly uncertain to quantify the actual amount of organic carbon that sinks from the surface and is sequestered in the deep ocean.[95] Actually, most of the phytoplankton is consumed by zooplankton and the sequestered carbon goes back to the air due to zooplankton's respiration.[96] With respect to the sinking carbon, only a small percentage reaches the deep ocean and a tiny fraction is buried in seafloor sediments for millennia; a higher percentage of carbon (between 5% and 50%) deposits in middle-depth waters and will remain there for decades,[97] which means that the carbon will be recycled back to the surface in a relatively short time-frame. The results from the experiments have led scientists to believe that ocean fertilization is likely to be less efficient in permanently removing atmospheric CO_2 than earlier expected.[98]

(II) INDIRECT FERTILIZATION – UPWELLING AND DOWNWELLING

As discussed earlier, the biological pump can only be accelerated in the euphotic zone due to the limited penetration of sunlight in the ocean. In the deeper ocean (200–1000 m), the transfer of dissolved CO_2 to the deep ocean can be achieved by upwelling and downwelling of ocean water.

Ocean upwelling transfers deep, cold and often nutrient-rich waters from the deep ocean to the surface layer thereby fertilizing phytoplankton. In this way, phytoplankton photosynthesis accelerates without external fertilization. Ocean upwelling, as a geoengineering technique, aims to artificially increase the upward movement of water by introducing ocean pipes. One approach to achieve ocean upwelling is to use free-floating or tethered vertical pipes. One-way valves inside the pipes would then force water to circulate, transporting nutrient-rich waters up to the ocean surface.[99]

Upwelling in one area must lead to downwelling at another location. Ocean downwelling occurs naturally in high-latitude regions of the northern and southern hemisphere where surface waters are cooled by winds. Wind cools the surface waters and increases evaporation. The evaporation results in an increase of the salinity and thus makes the surface water denser. The colder and denser water sinks into the depths. As CO_2 solubility is greater in colder water, more dissolved CO_2 is transferred to the deep ocean during the downwelling of the cold and dense water (i.e. solubility pump).[100] Hence, solubility pump enhancement is an approach to sediment CO_2 in the deep ocean.

However, the effectiveness of manipulating upwelling and downwelling is questionable. In addition to the scientific difficulty of modifying ocean current circulation, some inherent problems are involved in this approach. First, the upwelling of the nutrient-rich cold water brings decomposed organic materials to the ocean surface. The CO_2 respired from organic materials is released into the atmosphere and thus decreases the net drawdown of atmospheric CO_2 from the phytoplankton fertilization.[101] Second, downwelling cannot permanently fix CO_2 due to the change of solubility of CO_2 in the ocean. When water temperature rises, CO_2 solubility falls and thus CO_2 is released back to the atmosphere.[102] In addition, the artificial cooling of surface waters at high latitudes does not appear to be energetically feasible.[103] Given the infeasibility and the lack of scientific research, the legal examination of ocean downwelling will not be addressed in next chapters.

1.4.1.2 Enhanced weathering

CO_2 can be removed from the atmosphere by the chemical process of weathering, which is a very slow natural process, breaking down carbonate and silicate rocks by the actions of rain, snow and wind over thousands of years. The weathering process on Earth is based on the reaction between silicate minerals and CO_2 to form carbonate, thereby consuming CO_2 ($CaSiO_3 + CO_2 \rightarrow CaCO_3 + SiO_2$). Enhanced weathering is aimed at artificially accelerating the weathering of rocks to absorb more CO_2.

(I) ADDING ALKALINE TO THE OCEAN

Adding alkaline to the ocean refers to ocean liming or ocean-based enhanced weathering, aiming at chemically increasing CO_2 removal by adding alkaline minerals into the ocean. One proposal suggests the addition of lime into surface waters, whereby calcium hydroxide would react with CO_2 to form calcium carbonate ($CaCO_3$) and water.[104] In this way, CO_2 is captured and stored in minerals. Note that if limestone is used to create lime, the net amount of captured CO_2 would be partly offset by the CO_2 released in the process of burning limestone.[105]

Other proposals of ocean-based enhanced weathering suggest the use of carbonate or silicate rocks. The weathering process could be artificially accelerated by enlarging the surface of the rock, such as by grinding it. The rock powder could be directly spread or transported through pipelines to the sea, reacting with CO_2 to create an alkaline bicarbonate solution.[106] The potential to reduce atmospheric CO_2 through enhanced weathering is expected to be very high. However, the deployment of enhanced weathering on a geoengineering level requires vast quantities of rock powder. The rock-grinding process requires an extensive energy supply and thus would offset the climate benefits of weathering.

(II) SPREADING SILICATE MINERALS

One proposal to enhance the speed of land weathering is spreading silicate minerals, such as olivine (Mg_2SiO_4), over the soil. The basic chemical reaction is as follows:

$$Mg_2SiO_4 + 4CO_2 + 4H_2O \rightarrow 2Mg^{2+} + 4HCO_3^- + H_4SiO_4 \quad [107]$$

This method needs large quantities of olivine, transported and spread over arable land. Crushed olivine weathers rather quickly in a wet and temperate climate.[108] Hence, it is more effective to spread olivine on moist soil. Spreading olivine can offset acid and thus is beneficial to areas with acid rain or acid sulphate soils.[109] However, this positive effect is not suitable for all soil types, and worse, the excess alkalinity may change soil properties. More importantly, in agriculture, olivine doses must remain within limits to avoid imbalances in plant nutrition.[110]

1.4.1.3 Afforestation, reforestation and land-use management

Afforestation, reforestation and land-use management are traditional means of ecosystem management. Afforestation refers to planting or seeding on lands that have not been forested for a period of at least 50 years.[111] By contrast, reforestation refers to the reestablishment of forest cover on lands that were forested but that have been converted to non-forested land.[112] Land-use management aims at enhancement of soil CO_2 sequestration. This aim is achieved by, for example, a change of planting types, alteration of grazing patterns, and rehydrating and restoration of wetlands.[113] Normally, afforestation, reforestation and land-use management are not always labelled geoengineering, because they are seen as natural ways of enhancing land-based carbon sinks instead of *engineering* the climate.

Terrestrial ecosystems remove nearly three billion tonnes of anthropogenic carbon annually, absorbing around 30% of all CO_2 emissions from fossil fuel burning and net deforestation.[114] Forests are currently the major contributors of carbon mitigation in terrestrial ecosystems and can store more than twice the carbon as is in the atmosphere.[115] Agricultural soils normally contain much less organic carbon than equivalent soils under pasture or forest, because the clearance of crops or other vegetation leads to a decrease in aboveground carbon stocks and soil carbon stocks.[116]

1.4.1.4 Biomass-related techniques

Terrestrial vegetation removes large amounts of atmospheric CO_2 through photosynthesis, but most of the stored CO_2 returns to the atmosphere after the death and decay of the vegetation. Biomass-related techniques are a range of alternatives that sequester the CO_2 released from decomposed terrestrial organisms.[117] Biomass, biochar and bioenergy are three key concepts in this section that merit distinction. Biomass is a broad term applied to any non-fossil material of biological origin that can be used as a source of energy, including agricultural waste, livestock manure and forest residues.[118] Biomass can be used either directly to heat or generate electricity, or can be converted into biofuels (in gas, liquid or solid form). Biochar is one kind of solid biofuels produced from land-plant biomass. Bioenergy refers to all forms of biomass and biofuels that are used as sources of energy.

(I) BIOENERGY WITH CARBON CAPTURE AND SEQUESTRATION (BECCS)

BECCS is a technique that integrates three steps: planting and harvesting biomass, utilizing biomass to produce energy, and sequestering the resulting CO_2 by using CCS facilities. The first two steps belong to bioenergy source preparation while the third step belongs to CCS. BECCS moves CO_2 from the atmosphere into the ground. CO_2 is absorbed through photosynthesis as biomass grows. Normally, CO_2 is released back to the atmosphere when biomass is combusted or broken down through natural processes. In the application of BECCS, the CO_2 in biomass is captured instead of released and the CO_2 is stored permanently.[119] BECCS systems can be created by using bioenergy plants to provide energy for CCS facilities in the form of power plants, pulp and paper industries, ethanol plants, etc.[120]

As mentioned in Section 1.3.4, fossil-fuel energy with carbon capture and storage (FECCS) is not within the scope of CDR techniques because it does not remove atmospheric CO_2 (see Figure 1.2 left below). However, BECCS lies somewhere between conventional emission reduction and a CDR technique in geoengineering, depending on the scale of use.[121] BECCS is considered a typical technique of "negative emissions technologies (NETs)" (see Figure 1.2). First, plants extract CO_2 from the air to form biomass. Then, the biomass used for generating energy results in CO_2 emissions. As the CO_2 emissions released from energy use are approximately the same quantity as consumed during the biomass growth ("zero emissions"), the capture and long-term storage of those emissions remove *additional* CO_2 from the atmosphere.[122] The captured CO_2 will be stored in geological formations, such as depleted oil or gas wells and saline aquifers, as well as in oceans or rocks.

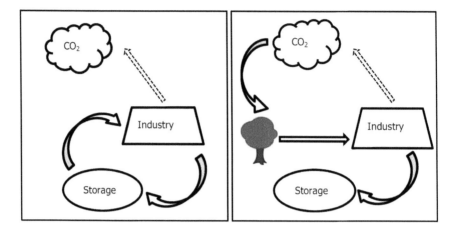

Figure 1.2 FECCS and BECCS[123]

The left figure above illustrates the carbon cycle based on fossil-fuel energy with carbon capture and sequestration (FECCS). Industries would use fossil fuel as energy, then transmit the majority of the emitted CO_2 into an underground geologic formation; a small amount of CO_2 may be released to the atmosphere. The right figure illustrates the carbon cycle based on BECCS. Biomass extracts CO_2 for growth. Industries use biomass as energy, and then transmit the majority of the emitted CO_2 to the geologic formation; a small amount of CO_2 may be released to the atmosphere.

(II) BIOCHAR

Biochar refers to the carbon-rich product made from biomass when it is heated in a closed container with little or no oxygen.[124] This term emphasizes the organic origin, distinguishing the charcoal from charred non-biological material. The life cycle of biochar comprises three stages: biomass feedstock supply, conversion technology and biochar product utilization. First, the production of biochar requires a sustainable supply of biomass. Second, pyrolysis and gasification are the technologies to produce biochar.[125] Third, the traditional motivation of using biochar is to improve soil properties and sometimes also to manage wastes and produce energy.[126]

Originally, biochar was only produced with the intent to improve soil quality. Later, the application of biochar technology was expanded for the purpose of waste management, energy production and climate change mitigation. It has become a new trend that national governments and international organizations recognize the potential of biochar in carbon sequestration and are attempting to utilize biochar on a climate-changing scale.[127] Utilizing biochar as a geoengineering solution is different from combusting some wood and burying it in the backyard; it should be on a large scale.

(III) BIOMASS BURIAL

Biomass burial refers to an alternative to biochar to deal with biomass – i.e. burying the biomass in anoxic conditions, such as the soil or the seabed. Biomass burial is an alternative to depositing the biomass to decelerate decomposition, normally through burying the biomass in an anoxic condition, such as in deep soil or the seabed. CO_2 is converted into methane via anaerobic biological reactions. Biomass burial seems to be less efficient than biochar in carbon sequestration. As the carbon atoms in charcoal are bound together much more strongly than in vegetation, biochar is resistant to decomposition and locks the carbon for much longer than biomass burial.

1.4.1.5 CO_2 capture from ambient air

The CDR technique of direct air capture (DAC) is an industrial process that adsorbs CO_2 directly from the atmosphere.[128] Whereas air capture is more expensive than capture from large point sources, it remains a valuable technique, because it can capture dispersed CO_2, such as that from means of transportation. To date, there are two main alternatives to capture CO_2 from the air:

- Adsorption of CO_2 onto solid sorbents (e.g. resin).[129]

A famous example of this technique is the use of "artificial trees" to soak up CO_2 from the ambient air. The "leaves" of these "artificial trees" are made from plastic resin-based material that adsorb CO_2 from the air when they are dry and then release the CO_2 when they are exposed to moisture.[130]

- Absorption of CO_2 in an alkaline solution.[131]

This technique is called the "wet scrubbing technique", because it "scrubs" CO_2 in an alkaline adsorbent.[132] The process takes four steps:[133] first, a sodium hydroxide (NaOH) solution is used to remove the CO_2 from ambient air; second, the resultant sodium carbonate (Na_2CO_3) solution reacts with calcium hydroxide ($Ca(OH)_2$) to regenerate the sodium hydroxide solution and precipitate calcite ($CaCO_3$); third, calcite thermally decomposes to produce lime (CaO) and CO_2; and, last, the lime reacting with water to complete the process.[134]

After capturing CO_2 from the ambient air, the captured CO_2 will be stored. The process of CO_2 storage is the same as the last step of BECCS, and thus will not be separately discussed in this section. Removing and sequestering carbon directly from the air would be very straightforward and rapid to deal with the emission problem and it will be easy to measure the captured carbon. However, current technologies are inefficient for directly separating CO_2 from the air. It is much more difficult to capture CO_2 from ambient air (with an extremely low concentration of CO_2 of about 390 ppm) than from a coal-fired stack (about 120,000 ppm). Large-scale implementation is currently neither cost-effective nor thermodynamically efficient.[135] This situation may be changed in the future when the cost decreases and DAC becomes competitive with other traditional mitigation methods.

1.4.2 SRM

1.4.2.1 Space-based reflectors

Basically, space-based reflectors refer to the artificial "sunshades" placed in outer space to deflect sunlight. There are two main options for the placement of reflectors: the one is lifting a thin film like a ring into orbit around the Earth, and the other is placing a shade into solar orbit. The shade would then function as a "space parasol"[136] or a metallic scatterer.[137]

Existing studies on space-based reflectors are only in the stage of computer modelling. Even though the launching of sunshade materials may be technically feasible (via rockets), the relevant studies including investigating and controlling systems for maintaining the sunshades in position are inchoate.[138] In addition, the implementation of space-based reflectors appears to be very expensive. As a result, the technology of space-based reflectors is unlikely to be given priority in the research and development of SRM geoengineering. Spaced-based reflectors will not be further discussed in this book.

1.4.2.2 Stratospheric Aerosols Injection (SAI)

The idea of SAI is derived from volcanic eruptions. In 1784, Benjamin Franklin found that volcanic aerosols could reflect sunlight to space and thus reduce solar heating of the Earth.[139] On June 15, 1991, the eruption of the Philippine volcano Mt. Pinatubo spewed huge quantities of gas and ash (primarily SO_2) into the atmosphere, reaching a height of 40 km.[140] More than 17 megatons of SO_2 formed sulphate aerosols in the stratosphere and spread rapidly around the Earth in the subsequent months. These stratospheric sulphate aerosols decreased the global average temperature by approximately 0.4 °C in 1992, but in 1995 the temperature returned to the value before the Pinatubo eruption.[141] The scientific findings of how a volcanic eruption affects the climate system provide a natural analogy to SAI. This event showed that an injection of 15–20 megatons of SO_2 into the stratosphere could produce a sulphate aerosol layer to reflect sunlight into space and thus cool the planet for a period of 2–3 years.[142]

Compared to CO_2 mitigation, the advantages of SAI include easiness, cheapness and rapidness.

- *Easiness*: Rather than building any infrastructure, aerosols can be injected to the stratosphere simply by a few high-altitude aircraft, stratospheric balloons,[143] or artillery shells.
- *Cheapness*: Modelling studies show that the annual cost of injecting 1 Tg[144] of sulphur gas by aircraft varies from approximately USD

200 million to USD 4 billion depending on the type of aircraft.[145] So, the annual cost of injecting 15 Tg of sulphate gas by aircraft is between USD 3–60 billion. It is a small amount in comparison with the annual cost of CO_2 reduction worldwide or the annual global military budget.[146]

- *Rapidness*: As shown in the observation of the Mt. Pinatubo eruption, the global temperature decreased a few months after the volcanic eruption. Although artificial SAI cannot affect the climate system as rapidly as instantaneous volcanic eruptions, the efficiency of SAI in global cooling would be still much higher than mitigation methods.

1.4.2.3 Marine cloud whitening

The idea of marine cloud whitening (MCW) is that the enhancement of marine cloud albedo in the lower atmosphere can reflect more solar radiation and thus ameliorate global warming.[147] The basic principle is to seed marine stratocumulus clouds[148] with fine seawater droplets to enhance the cloud droplet concentration, and thereby enhancing the cloud albedo.[149] Increasing the cloud droplet concentration is also likely to prolong the longevity of clouds, because the salt particles ensure that the cloud droplets are not so large as to form precipitation.[150]

Scientists have designed a fleet of rotor ships[151] that could pump seawater out of the ocean and spray seawater droplets into clouds.[152] The wind-powered unmanned ships can be remotely guided to favourable regions for cloud whitening. In order to provide a cooling effect, around 1,000 ships would be required and each needs to spray seawater droplets continuously at a rate of 50 cubic metres per second over a substantial fraction of the world's oceanic surface.[153]

1.4.2.4 Enhanced surface albedo

The aim of surface albedo enhancement is to make the Earth's surface more reflective. This method consists of a host of approaches depending on different surface types: painting roofs in urban areas white, planting grassland and more reflective crops, covering deserts with reflective material, etc.[154] These approaches will not be addressed further as they would be implemented locally and hardly raise international concerns.

1.5 A description of adverse impacts of geoengineering activities on the environment and the climate

The attributes as well as the potential effectiveness and efficiency of various geoengineering techniques have been addressed in Section 1.4. In this section, a categorized description of adverse transboundary impacts serves as a scientific basis for the corresponding legal examination in Chapters 2 and 3. This section addresses the impacts that geoengineering techniques and methods (may) have on environmental media, focusing on adverse impacts occurring beyond the jurisdiction or control of the state of origin. Potential adverse impacts arising from geoengineering activities on the environment, including the ocean, the land, the atmosphere and the biosphere as well as the adverse impacts that SAI and MCW activities may have on the climate system will be described in this section.[155] Note that this section does not address the "net effects" which concerns the balancing between the benefits brought by geoengineering in preventing dangerous climate change and the adverse impacts arising from geoengineering activities. The issue of "net effects" will be addressed in later chapters, because it is beyond a scientific description as criteria of balancing are required.

1.5.1 *The ocean*

The ocean is the biggest carbon reservoir on the Earth and thus plays a significant role in sequestering CO_2 to counteract global clime change. Geoengineering may impact the ocean in several ways. First, as mentioned in the previous section, ocean-based techniques may disturb the marine ecosystems and pose a threat to the marine biodiversity. Second, some activities may threaten the marine environment, leading to marine pollution and increased ocean acidity. This section will examine marine pollution and acidification arising from geoengineering.

1.5.1.1 *Marine pollution*

Marine pollution is defined in the United Nations Convention on the Law of the Sea (UNCLOS):

> "[P]ollution of the marine environment" means the introduction by man, directly or indirectly, of substances or energy into the marine environment, including estuaries, which results or is likely to result in such deleterious effects as harm to living resources and marine life, hazards to human health, hindrance to marine activities, including fishing and other legitimate uses of the sea, impairment of quality for use of sea water and reduction of amenities.[156]

Toxic algal bloom that might arise from iron fertilization may result in deleterious effects to surface-dwelling organisms. Pursuant to the definition of the UNCLOS, iron fertilization may introduce indirect pollution to the ocean because toxic substances impair not only the ocean ecosystem, but also the quality of seawater.

1.5.1.2 *Ocean acidification*

Ocean acidification is a special kind of ocean pollution. The "pollutant" is CO_2 or another greenhouse gas. The term ocean acidification refers to the process of increasing ocean acidity. When CO_2 is absorbed by seawater, the chemical reaction produces carbonic acid, which can increase the acidity of seawater and reduce its pH.[157] A consequence of the oceans becoming more acid is the binding up of carbonate ions, which would otherwise be used by marine creatures to make their calcium carbonate shells and skeletons.[158] As free carbonate ions decrease, more marine organisms would have problems building their calcium carbonate structures. In particular, increasing ocean acidification significantly impedes the building up of coral reefs, which are highly valued marine ecosystems.

Since the start of the Industrial Revolution (approximately 1750), the ocean has absorbed large amounts of CO_2. The pH of the ocean surface has already fallen 0.1 units, representing a 30% increase in acidity.[159] Anthropogenic CO_2 release is the main cause of ocean acidification. Human activities (e.g. burning fossil fuels) have dramatically increased the release of CO_2 in the atmosphere and contributes to ocean acidification since the ocean absorbs approximately a quarter of all CO_2 released into the atmosphere by human beings.[160]

The adverse impacts from ocean acidification are substantial in several ways: Ocean acidification limits the capacity of the ocean to absorb CO_2 from emissions; it changes ecosystems and marine biodiversity; and it has the potential to affect food security.[161] The only effective way of addressing the problem of ocean acidification is to decrease CO_2 emissions. However, the deployment of ocean fertilization and marine carbon storage is not able to reduce ocean acidification. With respect to the techniques of direct air capture and BECCS, while the uptake of atmospheric CO_2 would reduce ocean acidification of surface seawaters, this positive impact might be compromised by CO_2 leakage into the ocean from geological storage sites or as a result of the decomposition of the stored organic materials.[162] The net effect on ocean acidity would depend on the difference between the benefit of removing atmospheric CO_2 by carbon storage in the ocean and the accidental leakage of CO_2 in the ocean.

1.5.2 The land

The term "land" in this section refers to Earth surface areas that are not covered by oceans. This section will first examine the potential soil acidification caused by BECCS and SAI, and then briefly touch upon watercourse pollution resulting from soil pollution due to geological closeness.

1.5.2.1 Soil

SAI might cause soil acidification if significant amounts of additional acid particles from SO_2 injection deposit in the soil. The leakage of transported or stored CO_2 is a main concern associated with carbon capture and storage.[163] Risks of CO_2 leakage include but are not limited to: CO_2 leaking from pipelines during the transport of captured CO_2, fugitive emissions from injection processes, and large leakage from storage sites. The release of CO_2 into the soil could result in the formation of carbonic acid (H_2CO_3) as CO_2 reacts with water in the soil's pores.[164]

1.5.2.2 Watercourses

Watercourse pollution is not directly connected to geoengineering activities, because no technique is directly applied to fresh surface waters or underground waters. Instead, watercourse pollution results from soil pollution due to geological closeness, or from air pollutants washed down into watercourses. For instance, in biomass burial, bio-wastes accumulate and could cause serious pollution to watercourses because of the escape of hazardous materials.[165] SO_2 aerosols may be washed down with the rain or snow into watercourses.

1.5.3 The atmosphere

The injection of sulphate aerosols into the stratosphere may adversely affect the atmosphere in various ways. First and foremost, sulphate aerosols provide surfaces for the heterogeneous chemical reaction that may destroy ozone in the lower stratosphere.[166] The aerosols themselves do not increase ozone depletion, but they could increase chlorine's effectiveness at destroying ozone.[167] The ozone layer plays a crucial role in the atmosphere, because it absorbs a portion of ultraviolet radiation (UV) from the sun, preventing excessive radiation from reaching the Earth's surface. Most importantly, the ozone layer absorbs large amount of UVB,[168] which is dangerous to the health and life of humans, animals and plants.[169,170]Hence, as long as the concentration of ozone-depletion substances (mainly referring to chlorofluorocarbons, or CFCs) is high in the stratosphere, SAI could contribute to increasing chlorine's effectiveness at destroying ozone.[171] Second, significant amounts of additional sulphate particles, in the form of gas, dust or rain, will decrease the air quality in the lower atmosphere.[172] The amount of additional sulphate particles caused by SAI, if significant, would lead to more respiratory diseases. Third, the sky would become whiter since the aerosols block more sunlight. This is not "pollution", but may be serious for psychological reasons, namely whether humans are willing to live on the Earth without a blue sky.

Ocean fertilization is expected to cause undesired impacts on the atmosphere in two aspects. One such aspect is that ocean fertilization may increase the production of methane and nitrous oxide, which make the second- and third-greatest contributions respectively to the increase in global radiative forcing caused by all long-lived greenhouse gases since 1750.[173] Methane and nitrous oxide tend to form in deeper water when organic matter decomposes. Then, with ocean circulation, these gases move to the surface and are ultimately released into the atmosphere. As a greenhouse gas, methane is about 20 times as potent as CO_2.[174] Considering the trade-off between burying CO_2 and generating a new greenhouse gas, the harmful emission of methane could counteract any benefit from CO_2 removal from iron fertilization. The other aspect is that ocean fertilization may release dimethylsulfide

(DMS), which is another kind of gas related to climate change. DMS is a volatile sulphur compound produced by oceanic microbial communities and is the largest natural source of atmospheric sulphate aerosol, which is relevant in cloud formation.[175] Some scientists fear that the increase of DMS could increase the amount of cloud in the atmosphere and thus cool the planet in a highly undesirable manner.[176] Interestingly, proponents of ocean fertilization consider this effect as a benefit in terms of reducing global warming.[177]

High CO_2 concentrations create the risk of accidental CO_2 leakage from BECCS activities. Any sudden large release could be extremely dangerous for human and animal health, because exposure to elevated concentrations of CO_2 can be lethal. While the normal atmospheric concentration (0.037%) is not toxic, concentrations of 3% or higher may result in serious health problems, such as hearing loss, visual disturbances and laboured breathing. CO_2 concentrations of 20% may be fatal, as a result of asphyxiation.[178]

1.5.4 The biosphere

The biosphere is the global ecosystem that integrates all plants, animals, microorganisms, and the habitats on which they depend. Biological diversity of species, habitats and ecosystems is significant for evolution and for maintaining the life-sustaining systems of the biosphere.[179] As biological diversity is directly and adversely affected by habitat conversion, invasive species, over-exploitation, pollution and climate change, it is important to address factors that negatively impact biodiversity.[180] All of the geoengineering techniques may result in unintended impacts on biological diversity.

Depending on the features of different techniques, they may harm marine and/or territorial biological diversity. With respect to ocean fertilization, when iron, nitrogen or phosphorus is dumped into the ocean, photosynthesis of phytoplankton accelerates, thereby absorbing more dissolved CO_2. This process significantly changes the natural species' abundance of phytoplankton, the base of the marine food chain, and consequently impacts all species that depend on phytoplankton.[181] Studies reveal that enhanced phytoplankton productivity will lead to an increase in food supply for larger predators, such as fish and jellyfish, and correspondingly an increase in fish stocks. However, scientists fear that fertilization may disrupt the basic marine food chain and affect the population of marine species. They especially fear harmful algal blooms, which could impact fish, birds, and mammals further up the food web.[182] A more extreme effect of large-scale ocean fertilization is that fertilization may reduce oxygen levels in deeper waters. When plankton die, they begin to decompose and sink to deeper waters. The decomposition of the dead plankton may deplete oxygen in deeper water, and sometimes creates anoxic "dead zones" where fish cannot survive.[183] In addition, iron fertilization resulting in the proliferation of harmful species of phytoplankton could damage surface ocean ecosystems.[184] Scientific research has revealed that species of diatom communities belonging to the *Pseudonitzschia* genus produce a toxin domoic acid, which has led to massive toxic algal blooms in coastal waters.[185] This finding indicates that toxic phytoplankton might increase in response to iron fertilization, and large-scale iron fertilization projects could produce ecologically harmful levels of domoic acid.[186]

Ocean alkalinity enhancement may trigger both beneficial and adverse impacts on marine biological diversity. On the one hand, large-scale and long-term alkalinity addition increases the ocean pH and therefore would be effective in counteracting ocean acidification. In particular, ocean alkalinity addition would be beneficial in protecting coral reefs. On the other hand, local spatial and temporal pH spikes would bring about side effects on marine ecosystems, albeit with largely unknown effect thus far.[187] Other unknown effects include the toxic effects of the rock dust involved and mineral impurities.[188] In addition, large-scale mining may lead to terrestrial habitat destruction and degradation of river or groundwater quality.[189]

Albedo enhancement may also harm ecosystems. As for SAI, one assertion is that sulphate injection, although it takes place in the stratosphere, will increase acid deposits in the lower atmosphere (acid rain) and the Earth's surface (acidic particles). The additional amount of acid, if significant, would harm the ecosystem.[190] Another assertion is that the enhanced stratospheric albedo reduces the total solar radiation to the Earth's surface. Less sunlight means less efficient photosynthesis in plants and consequently, fewer carbon sinks.[191] The injection of seawater into the troposphere for cloud whitening raises a similar problem of less solar radiation, resulting in less efficient photosynthesis in phytoplankton.

Normally, afforestation, reforestation and land-use management bring tremendous benefits to the environment.[192] However, in special situations, they may adversely affect the biosphere. For instance, a very large-scale increase in forest or other types of vegetation will likely increase the scramble for land, water, and other resources, and conflicts may arise related to food security, soil and water conservation.[193] Moreover, if managed poorly, land-use change may exacerbate the risk of losing species and habitats.[194] Also, in special situations, large-scale production of biomass for carbon sequestration may lead to habitat loss (because of land-use change), and may even bring about the loss of species.[195]

In sum, ocean fertilization, ocean alkalinity enhancement, SAI and MCW may lead to unintended impacts on the biosphere. Land geoengineering activities do not result in transboundary adverse impacts on the land ecosystem except for under very special circumstances. For instance, were Amazon rain forests to be replaced by other types of land use, it would undoubtedly cause transboundary adverse effect on the ecosystem and the climate in Latin America and possibly beyond.

1.5.5 The climate

It is important to differentiate the weather from the climate. Weather describes the condition of the atmosphere at a certain place at a certain time, while climate is usually defined as the average weather, or "as the statistical description in terms of the mean and variability of relevant quantities over a period of time".[196] SAI and MCW could affect both the weather and the climate. These techniques might be used as weather modification techniques, because the injection of sulphate aerosols or seawater droplets could be rapidly effective.[197] In the context of geoengineering, these techniques are continuously deployed to achieve the purpose of global cooling, and the subsequent changes of temperature and precipitation persist for an extended period, thereby affecting the climate. For this reason, this section is titled "Climate".

SAI would have both the short-term and long-term impacts on the climate system. An injection of 15–20 megatons of SO_2 can only maintain the cooling effect for 2–3 years, which means aerosols must be continuously injected into the stratosphere. Should SAI be terminated, it would lead to a rapid increase of temperature, with a much higher rate of global warming than the current rate.[198] In addition, SAI will have far-reaching impacts on the planet. For example, the surface of aerosols interacts with ozone molecules in heterogeneous chemical reactions. Sulphate aerosols therefore contribute to the depletion of the ozone layer.[199] The aerosols could also change the global radiation budget, cloud formation mechanisms, and subsequently, regional weather patterns, including the precipitation.[200] Historical observations of volcanic eruptions have shown that stratospheric aerosol injection could change regional hydrologic and temperature responses. The simulation of the climate response to tropical and polar SO_2 injections further demonstrates that continuously injecting SO_2 into the lower stratosphere would affect summer wind and precipitation patterns in Asia and Africa. It means that SO_2 injection could disrupt Asian and African summer monsoons, reducing precipitation, which will affect the food supply for billions of people.[201]

It is far from fully known how the global climate would respond to long-term MCW. Preliminary climate modelling studies have shown that MCW over the ocean would alter precipitation patterns and precipitation amounts on land. Early studies hypothesized that MCW would decrease precipitation, because the increased number of seawater droplets would prolong the lifespan of clouds and suppress the formation of rainfall.[202] More recent studies have indicated that either an increase or decrease of precipitation could occur, largely depending on regional characteristics.[203] For instance, precipitation in the Amazon is expected to increase when clouds are whitened in the North and South Pacific, while precipitation would decline when MCW is carried out in the South Atlantic. The results from scientific research studies are still far from providing scientific certainty in predicting the climate responses in different regions with a high degree of accuracy.

1.6 The status of research on and testing of different geoengineering methods

The status of research and tests of different geoengineering methods varies greatly. Some methods are mature and have been carried out extensively for a long time, such as afforestation, reforestation, and land-use change. Some have only recently been developed and implemented in field trails. BECCS projects or biomass/fossil-fuel (combined) CCS projects have become increasingly tested at different scales. Ocean fertilization experiments have drawn the most international attention. Thirteen small-scale ocean fertilization projects have been undertaken in northern and southern ocean regions since 1993.[204] Small-scale experiments of ocean fertilization may confirm the finding that iron can enhance algae productivity in the ocean and thereby absorb more atmospheric CO_2. However, unintended adverse impacts on the environment and people occur simultaneously. SAI is at the stage of computer modelling studies and no successful field trail has yet taken place.[205] MCW is at the stage of computer modelling and preparation for field trails.[206]

There are varied reasons why some geoengineering techniques have remained in the early stages of research, and others have not. The technique of launching space-based reflectors is slowly developing, mainly because the technological difficulties and financial infeasibility has led to a lack of incentives for the relevant researches. However, the slow development of SAI and ocean fertilization techniques finds its origin more in environmental, political and ethical reasons. Theoretically, SAI technique is not complex and could be deployed at a large scale very soon. The crucial issue is the unclear dangerous impacts that SAI may bring to the Earth. It is therefore very difficult to say whether, when, how and who is to carry out hazardous geoengineering techniques. In view of the opposing voices with respect to an ocean fertilization experiment off the west coast of Canada in 2012,[207] any step forward on SAI, even if just a small batch of SO_2 in one field trial, would spur academic, political and public debates.

1.7 Conclusion

This chapter provided a political and scientific background of the emergence of geoengineering. Anthropogenic global warming and a series of subsequent changes in the climate system threaten the Earth. Taking into account a wide range of mitigation methods that have been implemented, there is still an emission gap between the status quo and the 2 °C and 1.5 °C targets. Rather than entirely focusing on emission reduction, scientists and engineers have begun to consider a planetary manipulation of the environment to remove the atmospheric CO_2 and cool the Earth, namely geoengineering.

Geoengineering consists of a series of methods, which are generally divided into two modalities: CDR and SRM. In Section 1.4, the description of geoengineering methods via a technique-by-technique approach demonstrated that there is a wide diversity between those methods, in terms of location, material, principle, feasibility and effectiveness. Geographically, some methods may take place in the global commons, such as SAI in the common atmosphere and MCW over the oceans; while some methods may take place transnationally, such as the transnational movement of removed CO_2

in BECCS and ambient air capture. In contrast, most land-based methods are carried out domestically, such as biomass burial and biochar. As a result, some geoengineering methods are much more likely to raise international concerns, whereas some others are less likely to do so, mainly due to the location of implementation or effects.

As this book concentrates on how international environmental law regulates geoengineering, the scope of discussion accordingly narrows down to the techniques that are designed to be deployed transnationally or in the areas beyond national jurisdiction, as well as techniques designed to be deployed in the territorial area of one state but which may cause interferences to the environment of another state or to areas beyond national jurisdiction. Section 1.5 shows that the various geoengineering techniques do not result in identical adverse transboundary impacts on the environment and the climate. Six geoengineering methods merit further consideration. Four CDR techniques are selected: ocean fertilization and ocean upwelling (see Section 1.4.1.1(i) & (ii)), ocean-based enhanced weathering (see Section 1.4.1.2(i)) and BECCS (see Section 1.4.1.4(i)). Two SRM techniques are selected: SAI (see Section 1.4.2.2) and MCW (see Section 1.4.2.3). Although designed to be deployed in the global commons, space-based reflectors will not be further discussed due to their technical and financial unfeasibility in the near future.[208]

The main reason for excluding afforestation, reforestation and land-use management, biomass burial, biochar, land-based enhanced weathering, ambient air capture[209] and enhanced surface albedo is that they are generally deployed within the territorial jurisdiction of one state and are thus unlikely to result in transboundary interferences. As the deployment of these methods and the environmental impacts would largely be at the local level, the regulation of them would primarily fall within national rather than international law. However, it cannot be excluded that these methods may also draw international concerns, mainly because: a) They may also result in transboundary interference in very extreme situations;[210] b) All local-level activities, if broadly practised, would have large-scale impacts; c) It is an international concern for states to protect and preserve the environment and resources within their jurisdiction and control;[211] and d) These techniques still seek to alter the climate. Nevertheless, the focus of research on international law governing geoengineering should be on the techniques that are most likely to have transboundary features.

Sections 1.4 and 1.5, though not a legal analysis, are very important for the legal analysis in Chapter 3. Based on the technique-sorted description in Section 1.4, Chapter 3 will identify applicable treaties as well as non-binding instruments regulating the six selected techniques via a technique-sorted approach. The legal examination of each selected technique will be based on the categorized description of the adverse transboundary impacts on the environment in Section 1.5.

The status of research projects and trials of different geoengineering methods in this section (together with the Appendix) reflects the main issues that should be addressed in the analysis of international law regulating geoengineering. The stages of utilizing different geoengineering methods depend on a host of factors: the state of scientific knowledge, the level of harms and risks, costs and effectiveness, as well as ethical and political concerns. From the perspective of international law, Chapter 5 will seek to find norms for balancing the expected risks and the benefits brought by geoengineering, taking into account scientific uncertainties.

Notes

1 Republic of Philippines National Disaster Risk Reduction and Management Council. (January 14, 2014). SitRep No. 92 Effects of Typhoon "Yolanda" (Haiyan). Retrieved from http://reliefweb.int/sites/reliefweb.int/files/resources/NDRRMC%20Update%20re%20Sit%20Rep% 2092%20Effects%20of%20 TY%20%20YOLANDA.pdf
2 It is important to mention that, due to the rapid development of researches on geoengineering, the scope of geoengineering techniques may be expanded along with time. As a result, this chapter is not able to cover the recently proposed ideas of geoengineering techniques. An example is cirrus clouding thinning as a SRM technique.
3 UN News Centre. (2013). Asia-Pacific Nations at UN Call for Urgent Global Approach to Mitigate Climate Change. Retrieved from www.un.org/apps/news/story.asp?NewsID=46125&Cr=climate+change&Cr1=#.Um4lf3AyLjY
4 IPCC. Organization. Retrieved from www.ipcc.ch/organization/organization.shtml
5 IPCC AR5 WGI was approved by the IPCC in September 2013; Other three reports were approved by the IPCC in 2014.
6 United Nations. Earth summit. Retrieved from www.un.org/geninfo/bp/enviro.html
7 Three agreements aimed at changing the traditional approach to development were adopted: Agenda 21, Rio Declaration on Environment and Development, and Non-legally Binding Authoritative Statement of Principles for a Global Consensus on the Management, Conservation and Sustainable Development of All Types of Forests. See UNGA, Report of the United Nations Conference on Environment and Development, UN Doc. A/CONF.151/26 (Vol. I) (12 August 1992), Annexes I, II & III.
Two legally binding documents aimed at preventing global climate change and the eradication of the diversity of biological species were opened for signature: United Nations Framework Convention on Climate Change (UNFCCC) and the United Nations Convention on Biological Diversity (CBD). United Nations Framework Convention on Climate Change, New York, adopted 9 May 1992, entered into force 31 March 1994, *United Nations Treaty Series* (2000), vol. 1771, no. 30822, p. 107. Convention on Biological Diversity, Rio de Janeiro, adopted 5 June 1992, entered into force 29 December 1993, *United Nations Treaty Series* (2001), vol. 1760, no. 30619, p. 79.
8 UNFCCC, Art. 2.
9 UNGA Resolution 70/1. Transforming Our World: The 2030 Agenda for Sustainable Development, UN Doc. A/RES/70/1(21 October 2015), para. 31.
10 World Economic Forum. (2006). Global Risks 2006, 3. Retrieved from www.circleofblue.org/wp-content/uploads/2015/01/WEF_Global_Risk_Report2006.pdf
11 All six sections are economic, environmental, geopolitical, societal and technological.
12 IPCC (2013). Climate Change 2013: The Physical Science Basis. Contribution of Working Group I to the Fifth Assessment Report of the Intergovernmental

Panel on Climate Change, Stocker, T. F., Qin, D., Plattner, G. K., Tignor, M., Allen, S. K., Boschung, J., Nauels, A., Xia, Y., Bex, V., & Midgley, P. M. (eds.), Cambridge, United Kingdom and New York, NY: Cambridge University Press, 62 (hereafter "IPCC AR5 WGI").

13 Ibid.
14 Ibid.
15 IPCC. (2013). Summary for Policymakers. In: IPCC AR5 WGI, 15.
16 UNFCCC Decision 1/CP.16, The Cancun Agreements: Outcome of the work of the Ad Hoc Working Group on Long-Term Cooperative Action Under the Convention, UN Doc. FCCC/CP/2010/7/Add.1 (15 March 2011), para. 4 (hereafter "Cancun Agreements").
17 Paris Agreement, adopted 12 December 2015, entered into force 4 November 2016, (UNTS volume number not available), Art. 2.1(a). Retrieved from https://treaties.un.org/Pages/showDetails.aspx?objid=0800000280458f37
18 UNEP, The Emissions Gap Report 2015, xvi. Retrieved from http://uneplive.unep.org/media/docs/theme/13/EGR_2015_301115_lores.pdf
19 For instance, Emissions from Mexico, Brazil and South Korea are expected to peak before 2025; emissions from China and India are expected to peak in 2030 later.
20 UNEP, The Emissions Gap Report 2015, xvii.
21 Ibid.
22 Ibid., 5–7 & 30.
23 Intended nationally determined contribution (INDC) refers to submissions by parties which identify actions each national government intends to take under the future UNFCCC climate agreement, due to be negotiated in Paris in December 2015. UNEP, The Emission Gap Report 2015, ix. Under the Paris Agreement, future mitigation contributions will be referred to as National Determined Contributions (NDC), without the "Intended".
24 Conditional INDCs refers to INDCs proposed by some countries that are contingent on a range of possible conditions, such as the ability of national legislatures to enact the necessary laws, ambitious action from other countries, realization of finance and technical support, or other factors, see UNEP, The Emissions Gap Report 2015, viii. Unconditional INDCs refers to INDCs proposed by countries without conditions attached, see UNEP, The Emissions Gap Report 2015, xi.
25 Least-cost emission level refers to emission reductions start immediately after the model base year, and are distributed optimally over time, sectors and regions, such that aggregate costs of reaching the climate target are minimized. The Emissions Gap Report 2015, x.
26 The Emissions Gap Report 2015, xviii. See also, The Emissions Gap Report 2016, 16.
27 The Emissions Gap Report 2016, xv.
28 The Emissions Gap Report 2016, xv. See also, The Emissions Gap Report 2015, 5.
29 See Section 1.3.
30 See definition in Section 1.4.2.
31 For instance, volcanic eruption of Mount Pinatubo in June 1991 injected large amount of SO_2 into the stratosphere and cooled the earth's surface temperature on average by 0.5 °C in the year after eruption.
32 Crutzen, P. (2006). Albedo enhancement by stratospheric sulphur injections: A contribution to resolve a policy dilemma? *Climate Change*, *77*, 211–219.
33 Wigley, T. (2006). A combined mitigation/ geoengineering approach to climate stabilization. *Science*, *314*, 452–454. doi:10.1126/science.1131728.
34 Petersen, A. (2014). The Emergence of the Geoengineering Debate Within the IPCC. Case Study, Geoengineering Our Climate Working Paper and Opinion Article Series. Retrieved from http://wp.me/p2zsRk-bp

35   IPCC (1995). Climate Change 1995: Impacts, Adaptations and Mitigation of Climate Change: Scientific-Technical Analyses, Contribution of Working Group II to the Second Assessment Report of the Intergovernmental Panel on Climate Change, New York, NY, USA: Cambridge University Press, 813.

36   Ibid.

37   IPCC. (2001). Climate Change 2001: Working Group III: Mitigation, Section 4.7 (hereafter "IPCC TAR WGIII"). Retrieved from www.grida.no/publications/other/ipcc_tar/?src=/climate/ipcc_tar/

38   IPCC. (2007). Climate Change 2007: Contribution of Working Group III to the Fourth Assessment Report of the Intergovernmental Panel on Climate Change, Metz, B., Davidson, O. R., Bosch, P. R., Dave, R., & Meyer, L. A. (Eds.), Cambridge, United Kingdom and New York, NY: Cambridge University Press, Section 11.2.2.

39   Ibid., Section 11, Executive Summary.

40   IPCC. (2014). Climate Change 2014: Mitigation of Climate Change. Contribution of Working Group III to the Fifth Assessment Report of the Intergovernmental Panel on Climate Change, Edenhofer, O., Pichs-Madruga, R., Sokona, Y., Farahani, E., et al. (eds.), Cambridge, United Kingdom and New York, NY, USA: Cambridge University Press, Section 3.3.7, 219.

41   Gove P. B. (Ed.). (1986). *Webster's third new international dictionary of the English language unabridged.* Springfield, MA: Merriam-Webster; Keith, D. (2000). Geoengineering the climate: History and prospect. *Annual Reviews of Energy Environment*, 25(1), 245–284, at 248.

42   Marchetti, C. (1977). On the geoengineering and the CO_2 problem. *Climate Change*, 1, 59–68.

43   Ibid.

44   See ten examples of definitions from: Secretariat of the Convention on Biological Diversity. (2012). Geoengineering in Relation to the Convention on Biological Diversity: Technical and Regulatory Matters, Technical Series No. 66 (hereafter "CBD Technical Series No. 66"), Annex I. Retrieved from www.cbd.int/doc/publications/cbd-ts-66-en.pdf

45   The Royal Society is the National Academy of Science in the UK.

46   Shepherd, J. G., et al. (2009). *Geoengineering the climate: science, governance and uncertainty.* London, UK: Royal Society, 1.

47   Bodle, R., Oberthür, S., et al. (2013). Options and proposals for the international governance of geoengineering (No. (UBA-FB) 001886/E). Dessau-Roßlau: Umweltbundesamt, 40–48.

48   Shepherd, J., et al. (2009), supra note 46, 1.

49   Resolution LP.4(8) on the Amendment to the London Protocol to Regulate the Placement of Matter for Ocean Fertilization and other Maine Geoengineering Activities, IMO Report of the Thirty-fifth Consultative Meeting and the Eighth meeting of Contracting Parties, IMO DOCS LC 35/15 (21 October 2013), Annex: Amendments to Article 1 and new Article 6bis and new Annexes 4 and 5, Article 6bis. (the Annex will be shortened as "2013 Amendments to the LP" below).

50   Shepherd, J., et al. (2009), supra note 46, x & 1; 2013 Amendment to the LP; IPCC AR5 WGIII, Glossary.

51   E.g. Shepherd, J., et al. (2009), supra note 46, ix; CBD Technical Series No. 66, supra note 44, 23.

52   Resolution LP.4(8), 2013 Amendments to the LP; IPCC AR5 WGIII, Glossary.

53   Keith, D. W. (2000). Geoengineering the climate: History and prospect. *Annual Review of Energy and the Environment*, 25(1), 245–284; IPCC AR5 WGIII, Glossary.

54   IPCC AR5 WGIII, Glossary. Italic added.

55   See Chapter 5.

56   Bodle, R., Oberthür, S., et al. (2013), supra note 47, 48.

57 Shepherd, J., et al. (2009), supra note 46, 1.
58 IPCC AR5 WGI, Annex III: Glossary, 1449.
59 Corner, A., & Pidgeon, N. (2010). Geoengineering the climate: The social and ethical implications. *Environment: Science and Policy for Sustainable Development*, *52*(1), 24–37. Summary of the Synthesis Session: IPCC Expert Meeting Report on Geoengineering, 2011, 2. There are also some other CDR methods, such as non-till agriculture, creation of wetlands, conservation agriculture and fertilization of land plants. Given that those methods are similar in nature – increasing carbon storage in ecosystems, they are not separately presented but rather being represented by the method of land-use management.
60 IPCC AR5 WGI, Annex III: Glossary, 1449.
61 As different reports classify CDR techniques in different ways and also name them differently, this categorization synthesizes views from several reports, including: IPCC AR5 WGI; Shepherd, J., et al. (2009), supra note 46, p. 9; Negatonnes – An Initial Assessment of the Potential for Negative Emission Techniques to Contribute Safely and Fairly to Meeting Carbon Budgets in the 21st Century (p. 11–22); and CBD Technical Series No. 66, supra note 44, p. 55.
62 "Biological pump" means ocean fertilization, see Section 1.4.1.1.
63 Goodell, J. (2010). *How to cool the planet: Geoengineering and the audacious quest to fix Earth's climate* (1st ed.). New York: Houghton Mifflin Harcourt Publishing Company, 17; Lenton, T. M., & Vaughan, N. E. (2009). The radiative forcing potential of different climate geoengineering options. *Atmospheric Chemistry and Physics*, *9*(15), 5539–5561.
64 Shepherd, J., et al. (2009), supra note 46, 1.
65 Goodell, J. (2010). *How to cool the planet: Geoengineering and the audacious quest to fix earth's climate* (1st ed.). New York: Houghton Mifflin Harcourt Publishing Company, 17.
66 Shepherd, J., et al. (2009), supra note 46, 1; Corner, A., & Pidgeon, N. (2010), supra note 59, 27.
67 Metz, B., Davidson, O., De Coninck, H. C., Loos, M., & Meyer, L. A. (2005). IPCC special report on carbon dioxide capture and storage. Prepared by Working Group III of the Intergovernmental Panel on Climate Change. IPCC, Cambridge, United Kingdom and New York: Cambridge University Press, 3.
68 Bracmort, K., Lattanzio, R. K., & Barbour, E. C. (2010, August). Geoengineering: Governance and technology policy. Congressional Research Service, Library of Congress, 10–11. Retrieved from www.fas.org/sgp/crs/misc/R41371.pdf
69 CBD Technical Series No. 66, supra note 44, 23. See also Additional Information on Options for Definitions of Climate-related Geoengineering, Annex. UNEP/CBD/COP/11/INF/26, 14 August 2012.
70 IPCC TAR WGIII, Annex II: Glossary.
71 Heyward, C. (2013). Situating and abandoning geoengineering: a typology of five responses to dangerous climate change. *PS: Political Science & Politics*, *46*(1), 23–27, at 25.
72 Ibid.
73 Approximately 1.37 billion cubic kilometres. See Garrison, T. S. (2005). *Oceanography: An invitation to marine science*. Canada: Thompson Brooks/Cole, 2.
74 Earth's oceans: An introduction. Retrieved from www.enchantedlearning.com/subjects/ocean/; NOAA. Ocean. Retrieved from www.noaa.gov/ocean.html
75 IPCC AR5 WGI, 103.
76 Secretariat of the Convention on Biological Diversity. (2009). Scientific Synthesis of the Impact of Ocean Fertilization on Marine Biodiversity. Montreal, Technical Series No. 45, 15 (hereafter "CBD Technical Series No. 45"). Retrieved from www.cbd.int/doc/publications/cbd-ts-45-en.pdf; Rayfuse, R., Lawrence, M. G., & Gjerde, K. M. (2008). Ocean fertilization and climate change: The

need to regulate emerging high seas uses. *The International Journal of Marine and Coastal Law, 23*, 297–326, at 302.

77 Namely sunlit ocean, or "euphotic zone", a few tens of metres up to 200 metres.

78 Warner, R. (2007). Preserving a balanced ocean: Regulating climate change mitigation activities in marine areas beyond national jurisdiction. *Australia International Law Journal, 14*, 103.

79 Rayfuse, R., Lawrence, M. G., & Gjerde, K. M. (2008), supra note 76, 303.

80 Bardach, J. E., & Lewis, J. (1993). *The oceans, Algae, and the Greenhouse effect, Ocean Yearbook* (Vol. 10), Chicago: University of Chicago Press, 184.

81 Martin, J. H., & Fitzwater, S. E. (1988). Iron deficiency limits phytoplankton growth in the north-east Pacific subarctic. *Nature, 331*, 341–343; Martin, J. H. (1990). Glacial-interglacial CO_2 change: The iron hypothesis. *Paleoceanography, 5*(1), 1–13. (mentioning that "iron is essential for all life on the earth and is especially important in oceanic plant nutrition because chlorophyll cannot be synthesized, not can nitrate be reduced, nor atmospheric N fixed, without it").

82 Martin, J. H. (1990). Glacial-interglacial CO_2 change: The iron hypothesis. *Paleoceanography, 5*(1), 1–13.

83 Martin, J. H., Gordon, R. M., & Fitzwater, S. E. (1991). Iron limitation? *Limnology and Oceanography, 36*(8), 1793–1802.

84 "HNLC areas are observed in the equatorial and subarctic Pacific Ocean, the Southern Ocean and in some strong upwelling regimes, such as in the equatorial pacific". CBD Technical Series No. 45, supra note 76, 19.

85 Euphotic zone, or sunlit zone, refers to the ocean layer that is exposed to sunlight. The depth of this zone depends on the clarity of the water. The average depth is approximately 200 metres.

86 CBD Technical Series No. 45, supra note 76, 45.

87 Ibid.

88 CBD Technical Series No. 45, supra note 76, 31.

89 Nitrogen fixation means the microorganisms utilize dissolved organic nitrogen or dissolved N_2 as a source of cellular N. Karl, D. M., & Letelier, R. M. (2008). Nitrogen fixation-enhanced carbon sequestration in low nitrate, low chlorophyll seascapes. *Marine Ecology Progress Series, 364*, 257–268, at 257.

90 Dean, J. (2009). Iron fertilization: A scientific review with international policy recommendations. *Environs: Environmental Law and Policy Journal, 32*(2), 321–344, at 332.

91 Powell, H. (2008). Fertilizing the ocean with iron. *Oceanus Magazine, 46*(1), 4–9. The unit has been converted from tonnes carbon to $GtCO_2$. One tonne of carbon equals $44/12 \approx 3.67$ tonnes of CO_2. 1 Gt= 109 tonnes.

92 Ibid.

93 See four examples of ocean iron fertilization experiments in the Appendix. Except for ocean fertilization experiments, unauthorized and commercially-based ocean fertilization study took place in July 2012 off the west coast of Canada. Williamson, P., Wallace, D. W., Law, C. S., Boyd, P. W., Collos, Y., Croot, P., . . . Vivian, C. (2012). Ocean fertilization for geoengineering: A review of effectiveness, environmental impacts and emerging governance. *Process Safety and Environmental Protection, 90*(6), 475–488 (Williamson, P., et al. (2012) below).

94 Powell, H. (2008). supra note 91, 4–9.

95 De Baar, H. J. W., et al. (2005). Synthesis of iron fertilization experiments: From the iron age in the age of enlightenment. *Journal of Geophysical Research, 110*, 1–24. doi:10,1029/2004JC002601.

96 Zooplankton refers to small organisms in waters such as jellyfish and krill.

97 Powell, H. (2008), supra note 91, 6.

98 Rayfuse, R., Lawrence, M. G., & Gjerde, K. M. (2008), supra note 76, 305.

99 Lovelock, J. E., & Rapley, C. G. (2007). Ocean pipes could help the earth to cure itself. *Nature, 449*(7161), 403. doi:10.1038/449403a

100 Shepherd, J., et al. (2009), supra note 46, 19.

101 CBD Technical Series No. 66, supra note 44, 60.

102 CBD Technical Series No. 45, supra note 76, 18.

103 Rickels, W., Klepper, G., et al. (2011). *Large-scale intentional interventions into the climate system? Assessing the climate engineering debate.* Scoping report conducted on behalf of the German Federal Ministry of Education and Research (BMBF), Kiel: Kiel Earth Institute, 45.

104 $Ca(OH)_2 + CO_2 \rightarrow CaCO_3\downarrow + H_2O$

105 Rickels, W., Klepper, G., et al. (2011), supra note 103, 46.

106 Basic chemical reactions in the sea: Calcium carbonates: $CaCO_3 + CO_2 + H_2O \rightarrow Ca_2+ + 2\ HCO_3^-$; Calcium silicates: $CaSiO_3 + 2CO_2 + H_2O \rightarrow Ca_2+ + 2\ HCO_3^- + SiO_2$

107 Schuiling, R. D., & Krijgsman, P. (2006). Enhanced weathering: An effective and cheap tool to sequester CO_2. *Climatic Change, 74*(1–3), 349–354, at 351.

108 Ibid., 350.

109 Ibid.

110 Berge, Hein F. M. ten, Meer, Hugo G. van der, et al. (2012). Olivine weathering in soil, and its effects on growth and nutrient uptake in ryegrass (Lolium Perenne L.): A pot experiment. *PLOS One.* doi: 10.1371/journal.pone.0042098.

111 UNFCCC Decision 11/CP.7, Land use, Land-use Change and Forestry, Annex: Definitions, Modalities, Rules and Guidelines Relating to Land Use, Land-use Change and Forestry Activities under the Kyoto Protocol, Para. A(1). UN Doc. UNFCCC/CP/2001/13/Add.1, 58.

112 Ibid.; See also IPCC. (2000). Land use, land-use change and forestry, Watson, R. T., Noble, I. R., Bolin, B., Ravindranath, N. H., Verardo, D. J., & Dokken, D. J. (Eds.). London, United Kingdom: Cambridge University Press, Section 2.2.3. Retrieved from www.ipcc.ch

113 CBD Technical Series No. 66, supra note 44, 63; Secretariat of the Convention on Biological Diversity. (2012). Biofuels and Biodiversity, CBD Technical Series No. 65, 35. Retrieved from www.cbd.int/doc/publications/cbd-ts-65-en.pdf

114 Canadell, J. G., & Raupach, M. R. (2008). Managing forests for climate change mitigation. *Science, 320*, 1456–1457; Canadell, J. G., et al. (2007). Contributions to accelerating atmospheric CO_2 growth from economic activity, carbon intensity, and efficiency of natural sinks. *Proceedings of the National Academy of Sciences, 104*, 18866–18870.

115 Ibid.

116 Shepherd, J., et al. (2009), supra note 46, 11; Royal Society. (2001). The Role of Land Carbon Sink in Mitigating Global Climate Change, 8. Retrieved from https://royalsociety.org/~/media/Royal_Society_Content/policy/publications/2001/9996.pdf

117 Keith, D. W. (2000), supra note 53.

118 Gough, C., & Upham, P. (2010). Biomass energy with carbon capture and storage (BECCS): A review. Tyndall Centre for Climate Change Research, Working Paper 147, December 2010, 6. Retrieved from www.tyndall.ac.uk/publications/tyndall-working-paper/2010/biomass-energy-carbon-capture-and-storage-beccs-review

119 Global CCS Institute & Biorecro. (2011). *Global status of BECCS projects 2010*, 10. Retrieved from www.globalccsinstitute.com/publications/global-status-beccs-projects-2010

120 Ibid.

121 Gough, C., & Upham, P. (2010), supra note 118, 6.
122 McLauren, D. (2011). Negatonnes – An Initial Assessment of the Potential for Negative Emission Techniques to Contribute Safely and Fairly to Meeting Carbon Budgets in the 21st Century, 10. Retrieved from www.foe.co.uk/resource/ reports/negatonnes.pdf; IPCC Special Report on Carbon Dioxide Capture and Storage, 2005, 100; Smolker, R., & Ernsting, A. (2012). BECCS: Climate Saviour or Dangerous Hype? 1 & 6. Retrieved from www.biofuelwatch.net
123 Figure 1.2 is adapted from Gough, C., & Upham, P. (2010), supra note 118, 5.
124 Lehmann, J., & Joseph, S. (2009). Biochar for environmental management: an introduction. In Lehmann, J. & Joseph, S. (Eds.), *Biochar for environmental management: Science and technology and implementation* (2nd ed.). London: Earthscan Publishers Ltd, 1–13.
125 The term "pyrolysis" refers to the process of heating biomass in a non-oxygen environment (like the remaining wood of a match continues to bake after flaming combustion). The term "gasification" refers to a directly-heated reaction in a low-oxygen environment. Pyrolysis is preferable to gasification because biochar production is optimized in the absence of oxygen.
126 For instance, biochar is used in Haiti and North Viet Nam as a more sustainable cooking charcoal, but in Sri Lanka to improve soil health and to fertilize planation. International Biochar Initiative. www.biochar-international.org/ technology/production; Downie, A. et al. (2012). Biochar as a geoengineering climate solution: Hazard identification and risk management. *Critical Reviews in Environmental Science and Technology*, *42*(3), 225–250.
127 Lehmann, J., & Joseph, S. (Eds.). (2009), supra note 124.
128 Mahmoudkhani, M., & Keith, D. W. (2009). Low-energy Sodium Hyroxide Recovery for CO_2 capture from atmospheric air – thermodynamic analysis. *International Journal of Greenhouse Gas Control*, 376–384.
129 Lackner, K. S. (2009). Capture of carbon dioxide from ambient air. *The European Physical Journal Special Topics*, *176*, 93–106.
130 About the scientific updates of the "artificial tree", see Lenfest Center for Sustainable Energy. Retrieved from http://energy.columbia.edu/
131 Mahmoudkhani, M., & Keith, D. W. (2009), supra note 128; Shepherd, J., et al. (2009), supra note 46, 15.
132 Mahmoudkhani, M., & Keith, D. W. (2009), supra note 128.
133 Step 1: $2NaOH + CO_2 \rightarrow Na_2CO_3 + H_2O$; Step 2: $Ca(OH)_2 + Na_2CO_3 \rightarrow 2NaOH + CaCO_3 \downarrow$; Step 3: $CaCO_3 \rightarrow CaO + CO_2 \uparrow$; Step 4: $CaO + H_2O \rightarrow Ca(OH)_2 +$ heat
134 Zeman, F. S., & Lackner, K. S. (2004). Capturing carbon dioxide directly from the atmosphere. *World Resource Review*, *16*(2), 157–172.
135 U.S. Government Accountability Office. (2011). *Technology assessment: Climate engineering technical status, future directions, and potential responses* (No. GAO-11-71), 29.
136 Hudson, H. S. (1991). A space parasol as a countermeasure against the greenhouse effect. *Journal of the British Interplanetary Society*, *44*, 139.
137 McInnes, C. R. (2002). Minimum mass solar shield for terrestrial climate control. *Journal of the British Interplanetary Society*, *55*, 307–311.
138 Ibid.
139 Hansen, J., Lacis, A., Ruedy, R., & Sato, M. (1992). Potential climate impact of mount Pinatubo eruption. *Geophysical Research Letters*, *19*(2), 215–218, referring to Franklin, B. (1784, December). Meteorological imaginations and conjectures. In *Manchester Literary and Philosophical Society Memoirs and Proceedings* (Vol. 2, No. 122, p. 1784).
140 Self, S., Zhao, J. X., Holasek, R. E., Torres, R. C., & King, A. J. (1996). The atmospheric impact of the 1991 Mount Pinatubo eruption. In Newhall, C. G. & Punongbayan, R. S. (Eds.). *Fire and mud: Eruptions and Lahars of Mount Pinatubo, Philippines*. Seattle and London: University of Washington Press ("Self, S., et al. (1996)" below).

141 Gomes, M. S. d. P., & de Araújo, M. S. M. (2011). Artificial cooling of the atmosphere – a discussion on the environmental effects. *Renewable and Sustainable Energy Reviews*, *15*(1), 780–786. doi:http://dx.doi.org/10.1016/j.rser.2010.07.045

142 Self, S., et al. (1996), supra note 140.

143 Stratospheric balloon refers to a long-hose tethered balloon floating in the stratosphere, pumping aerosols upwards. See e.g. Davidson, P., Burgoyne, C., Hunt, H., & Causier, M. (2012). Lifting options for stratospheric aerosol geoengineering: Advantages of tethered balloon systems. *Philosophical Transactions of the Royal Society A: Mathematical, Physical and Engineering Sciences*, *370*(1974), 4263–4300.

144 Tg is the short form for Teragram (or megaton). 1Tg = 1012 gram.

145 Robock, A., Marquardt, A., Kravitz, B., & Stenchikov, G. (2009). Benefits, risks, and costs of stratospheric geoengineering. *Geophysical Research Letters*, *36*(19), L19703. doi:10.1029/2009GL039209

146 Morgan, M. G., & Ricke, K. (2010). Cooling the earth through solar radiation management: The need for research and an approach to its governance, 13. Retrieved from http:// www.irgc.com; Crutzen, P. (2006), supra note 32.

147 Latham, J. (1990). Control of global warming? *Nature, 347*, 339–340; Latham, J. (2002). Amelioration of global warming by controlled enhancement of the albedo and longevity of low-level maritime clouds. *Atmospheric Science Letters*, *3*(2–4), 52–58. doi:10.1006/asle.2002.0099

148 Stratocumulus clouds cover more than 30% of the ocean and have a high reflectance.

149 Latham, J., Bower, K., Choularton, T., Coe, H., Connolly, P., et al. (2012). Marine cloud brightening. *Philosophical Transactions of the Royal Society A: Mathematical, Physical and Engineering Sciences*, *370*(1974), 4217–4262. doi:10.1098/rsta.2012.0086

150 Ibid.

151 Rotor ship, or Flettner rotor (name after it inventor, Anton Flettner) is a ship powered by vertically mounted cylinders. The rotor plays the same role as the sails but provides greater power than a sail. See Latham, J., Bower, K., Choularton, T., Coe, H., Connolly, P., Cooper, et al. (2012), supra note 149, 4242.

152 Latham, J. (2007, 15 February). Futuristic fleet of "cloudseeders". BBC News. Retrieved from http://news.bbc.co.uk/2/hi/programmes/6354759.stm

153 Ibid.

154 Shepherd. J., et al. (2009), supra note 46, 25–26.

155 Lithosphere will not be discussed because biomass/biochar and olivine spreading mostly have local impacts on the soil.

156 United Nations Convention on the Law of the Sea, Montego Bay, adopted 10 December 1982, entered into force 16 November 1994, *United Nations Treaty Series* (1998), vol. 1833, no. 31363, p. 3, Art.1.

157 OCEANA. Ocean pollution and climate change. Retrieved from http://oceana.org/en/our-work/climate-energy/ocean-acidification/learn-act/what-is-ocean-acidificat ion

158 Ibid.

159 NOAA Pacific Marine Environmental Laboratory. What Is Ocean Acidification? Retrieved from www.pmel.noaa.gov/co2/story/What+is+Ocean+Acidification%3F

160 IPCC. (2013). Summary for Policymakers. In: IPCC AR5 WGI.

161 IGBP, IOC, & SCOR. (2013). Ocean Acidification Summary for Policymakers – Third Symposium on the Ocean in a High-CO_2 World. International Geosphere – Biosphere Programme, Stockholm, Sweden. Retrieved from www.igbp.net/download/18.30566fc6142425d6c91140a/1385975160621/OA_spm2-FULL-lorez.pdf

162 CBD Technical Series No. 66, supra note 44, 56. European Environmental Agency. (2011). Air pollution impacts from carbon capture and storage (CCS),

EEA Technical Report No 14/2011, 23. Retrieved from www.eea.europa.eu/publications/carbon-capture-and-storage

163 European Environmental Agency. (2011), supra note 162.

164 Ibid.

165 Pimentel, D., Lal, R., & Singmaster, J. (2010). Carbon capture by biomass and soil are sound: CO_2 burial wastes energy. *Environment, development and sustainability*, *12*(4), 447–448, at 448; Robock, A. (2000). Volcanic eruptions and climate. *Reviews of Geophysics*, *38*(2), 191–219, at 191. doi:10.1029/1998RG000054

166 Robock, A. (2000), supra note 165, 191.

167 U.S. Environmental Protection Agency. (2010). Ozone Science: The Facts Behind the Phaseout. Retrieved from www.epa.gov/ozone/science/sc_fact.html

168 Ozone can completely absorb UVC, which is a band of ultraviolet radiation with wavelengths shorter than 280 nm.

169 UVB is a band of solar radiation with wavelengths between 280 and 320 nm.

170 U.S. Environmental Protection Agency. (2011). Health and Environmental Effects of Ozone Layer Depletion. Retrieved from www.epa.gov/ozone/science/effects/index.html

171 Robock, A. (2008). 20 reasons why geoengineering may be a bad idea. *Bulletin of the Atomic Scientists*, *64*, 14–18. doi: 10.2968/064002006

172 Ibid.

173 CO_2 contributes to 65% to radiative forcing caused by Long-lived GHGs, whereas methane and nitrous oxide contribute to 17% and 6% respectively. WMO. (2015). *WMO greenhouse gas bulletin: The state of greenhouse gases in the atmosphere based on global observations through 2014* (No.11).

174 Lovett, R. (2008, 3 May). Burying Biomass to Fight Climate Change. Retrieved from http://science.org.au/nova/newscientist/108ns_006.htm

175 Fisheries and Oceans Canada. (2010). Ocean fertilization: Mitigating environmental impacts of future scientific research. Canadian Science Advisory Secretariat Science Advisory Report No. 2010/012, 8. Retrieved from www.dfo-mpo.gc.ca/csas-sccs/publications/sar-as/2010/2010_012_e.pdf

176 Abate, R. S., & Greenlee, A. B. (2009–2010). Sowing seeds uncertain: Ocean iron fertilization, climate change, and the international environmental law framework. *Pace International Law Review*, *27*, 555–598, at 569.

177 Dean, J. (2009), supra note 90, 328.

178 Gough, C., & Upham, P. (2010), supra note 118, 10.

179 CBD, Preamble.

180 CBD Technical Series No. 66, supra note 44, 16.

181 Abate, R. S., & Greenlee, A. B. (2009–2010), supra note 176, 566; Rayfuse, R., Lawrence, M. G., & Gjerde, K. M. (2008), supra note 76, 306.

182 Powell, H. (2008). What are the possible side effects? The uncertainties and unintended consequences of manipulating ecosystems. *Oceanus Magazine*, *46*(1), 14.

183 Ibid.

184 Abate, R. S., & Greenlee, A. B. (2009–2010), supra note 176, 568.

185 Ibid. Citing from Charles G. Trick et al. (2010). Processing of the National Acid of Scientific Iron Enrichment Stimulates Toxic Diatom Production in High-nitrate, Low-Chlorophyll Areas. Retrieved from http: www.pnas.org

186 Ibid.

187 Köhler, P., Hartmann, J., & Wolf-Gladrow, D. A. (2010). Geoengineering potential of artificially enhanced silicate weathering of olivine. *Proceedings of the National Academy of Sciences*, *107*(47), 20228–20233, 24.

188 Rickels, W., Klepper, G., et al. (2011), supra note 103, 47.

189 Bodle, R., Oberthür, S., et al. (2013), supra note 47, 94. It has been argued that adding the lime to seawater absorbs almost twice as much CO_2 generated in the process of making lime. The overall process is therefore 'carbon negative'. See Society of Chemical Industry. (2008, July 22). Adding lime to seawater may cut carbon dioxide levels back to pre-industrial levels. *Science Daily*. Retrieved from www.sciencedaily.com/releases/2008/07/080721001742.htm

190 Robock, A. (2008), supra note 171.

191 Ibid. This finding is suspected by the evidence that SRM in a high CO_2 climate causes crop yield to increase, because the effect of diffuse light, which increases photosynthesis, would be stronger. See e.g. Pongratz, J., Lobell, D. B., Cao, L., & Caldeira, K. (2012). Crop yields in a geoengineered climate. *Nature Climate Change*, 2(2), 101–105.

192 Forests provide protective habitats for animals, plants and micro-organisms and thereby play a vital role in conserving biodiversity. (12% of the world's forests are designated for the conservation of biological diversity.) See: Food and Agriculture Organization of the United Nations. (2010). *Global forest resources assessment, key findings*, 6. Forests also perform important functions in wood or non-wood production and social-economic services. Enhanced soil carbon can retain more water in the soil and may increase plant productivity. Food and Agriculture Organization of the United Nations. (2010). *Global forest resources assessment, key findings*. 7–8.

193 IPCC WGIII AR5, 6–7.

194 CBD Technical Series No. 65, supra note 113, 30; CBD Technical Series No. 66, supra note 44, 63.

195 Ibid., 65.

196 IPCC WGI AR5, 125–126.

197 Weather modification refers to the act of intentionally manipulating the weather. Mostly, weather modification is used for changing precipitation or hail/fog suppression.

198 Robock, A., Bunzl, M., Kravitz, B., & Stenchikov, G. L. (2010). A test for geoengineering? *Science*, 327(5965), 530–531; Matthews, H. D., & Caldeira, K. (2007). Transient climate – carbon simulations of planetary geoengineering. *Proceedings of the National Academy of Sciences*, 104(24), 9949–9954. doi:10.1073/pnas.0700419104.

199 Robock, A. (2000), supra note 165.

200 Gomes, M. S. d. P., & de Araújo, M. S. M. (2011), supra note 141, 783.

201 Robock, A., Oman, L., & Stenchikov, G. L. (2008). Regional climate responses to geoengineering with tropical and arctic SO_2 injections. *Journal of Geophysical Research: Atmospheres (1984–2012)*, 113, D16101. doi:10.1029/2008JD010050

202 Albrecht, B. A. (1989). Aerosols, cloud microphysics, and fractional cloudiness. *Science (New York, N.Y.)*, 245(4923), 1227–1230. doi:245/4923/1227

203 Latham, J., Bower, K., Choularton, T., Coe, H., Connolly, P., Cooper, et al. (2012), supra note 149; Rasch, P. J., Latham, J., & Chen, C. C. J. (2009). Geoengineering by cloud seeding: influence on sea ice and climate system. *Environmental Research Letters*, 4(4), 045112.

204 An overview of ocean fertilization experiments and examples of biochar projects and different types of BECCS experiments can be found in the Appendix of this book.

205 See Appendix.

206 See Appendix.

207 See Appendix.

208 Shepherd, J., et al. (2009), supra note 46, 32.

209 Note that after capturing CO_2 from the ambient air, the captured CO_2 will be stored. The process of CO_2 storage is same as the last step of BECCS. CO_2 sequestration may be a transboundary activity and may cause transboundary adverse effects. This will be further discussed in sections in later chapters relating to BECCS. Ambient air capture will not be separately discussed on this point in later chapters.

210 For instance, should the amazon rain forests be replaced by other types of land use, it would undoubtedly cause transboundary adverse effect.

211 Birnie, P., Boyle, A., & Redgwell, C. (2009). *International law & the environment* (3rd ed.). Oxford: Oxford University Press, 128 below.

Part II

Applying contemporary international law to geoengineering

2 Contemporary international law and geoengineering – a general approach

2.1 Introduction

To date, there is no single international legal framework governing geoengineering. However, a number of treaties are applicable to geoengineering in a wide range of fields. For instance, the United Nations Framework Convention on Climate Change (UNFCCC) and its Kyoto Protocol (KP)[1] and Paris Agreement (PA) encourage the development of new methods to increase carbon sinks; the Convention on Biological Diversity (CBD) aims to prevent species loss and habitats degradation; the London Convention on the Prevention of Marine pollution by Dumping of Wastes and Other Matter (LC) and its 1996 Protocol (LP) prevent marine pollution from dumping wastes and other matters;[2] and the 1982 Convention on the Law of the Sea (UNCLOS) regulates activities in different zones at sea and controls marine pollution.[3] Part II addresses contemporary international laws applicable to geoengineering by examining general rules and principles applicable to all techniques in this chapter and specific rules applicable to each individual technique in Chapter 3.[4]

As concluded in Chapter 1, not all geoengineering techniques need to be governed at the international level; instead, only the techniques for which the implementation[5] thereof may cause interference in the areas beyond the limits of national jurisdiction or control of the acting state require to be governed at the international level. This chapter and Chapter 3 concentrate on the six geoengineering techniques selected in Chapter 1.

This chapter examines the contemporary international legal rules and principles that apply to all geoengineering techniques. The international climate change regime and the Convention on the Prohibition of Military or Any Hostile Use of Environmental Modification Techniques (ENMOD Convention) are the main treaties that will be examined in this chapter. Regarding customary international law and general principles of international law, the obligation to prevent and abate significant transboundary harm or the harm to the global commons as well as the precautionary approach will be addressed in Sections 2.4.1 and 2.4.2 respectively. Note that the CBD, also as a treaty that applies to all geoengineering techniques, will be examined in Section 2.4.2.4 concerning the moratorium on geoengineering.

2.2 The international climate change regime

2.2.1 UNFCCC

Article 2 of the UNFCCC stipulates that the ultimate objective of the convention is to achieve "stabilization of greenhouse gas concentration in the atmosphere at a level that would prevent dangerous anthropogenic interference with the climate system". The UNFCCC is applicable to geoengineering primarily because the implementation of geoengineering is consistent with the ultimate objective of the UNFCCC. The manner in which the ultimate objective of the UNFCCC applies to CDR techniques and to SRM techniques varies because of the distinct attributes of the two modalities. Actions aiming at stabilizing greenhouse gas concentrations do not exclude CO_2 removal activities aiming at reducing *in situ* CO_2 concentrations in the atmosphere.[6] Hence, the implementation of CDR techniques contributes to achieving the ultimate objective of the UNFCCC. Besides, the UNFCCC encourages state parties to take measures to mitigate climate change by protecting and enhancing sinks and reservoirs, which include biological CDR methods.[7]

The aim of implementing SRM techniques is not explicitly in line with the ultimate objective of the UNFCCC of stabilizing greenhouse gas concentration, but the ultimate objective might not necessarily limit states' implementation of SRM techniques. Although the implementation of SRM techniques does not aim at "stabilization of greenhouse gas concentrations in the atmosphere", such novel techniques are able to "prevent dangerous anthropogenic interference with the climate system" – i.e. preventing dangerous global warming by reducing solar radiation. At the very least, the UNFCCC encourages new technological and technical research to combat climate change, which means research activities regarding the feasibility and potential effects of SRM techniques could be logically included therein.[8]

In addition, the UNFCCC is applicable to geoengineering in terms of three principles. First, the UNFCCC incorporates the prevention principle that aims to prevent transboundary environmental harm. Although the prevention principle is contained in the Preamble rather than in an operative provision, some procedural obligations relating to the prevention principle, including cooperation, information exchange and impact assessments, are addressed among the commitments of parties.[9] In particular, the UNFCCC requires all parties to employ appropriate methods to minimize adverse effects of "projects or measures undertaken by them to mitigate or adapt to climate change".[10] To the extent that some geoengineering techniques are considered measures that mitigate or adapt to climate change, all parties should also minimize adverse effects caused by such geoengineering techniques.

Second, the UNFCCC incorporates the precautionary principle: "The parties should take precautionary measures to anticipate, prevent or minimize the cause of climate change and mitigate its adverse effects. Where there are threats of serious or irreversible damage, lack of full scientific certainty should not be used as a reason for postponing such measures".[11] It has been argued that geoengineering would make a great contribution in counteracting the cause of climate change and mitigate its adverse impacts, given that CDR can "minimize the cause of climate change" and SRM has the potential to "mitigate its adverse effects".[12] In this context, scientific uncertainty is not a reason to postpone geoengineering if "threats of serious or irreversible damage" of climate change exists. However, taking into account the significant environmental risk created by or scientific uncertainty contained in some techniques, it might still not be appropriate to treat geoengineering techniques as precautionary measures to deal with global warming. If an activity that may threaten the climate should be undertaken with precaution, why not the risky measure *per se*?[13]

Third, developed countries and developing countries should make efforts to prevent dangerous anthropogenic climate change in accordance with their common but differentiated responsibilities and respective capabilities:[14] "The parties should protect the climate system [. . .] on the basis of equity and in accordance with their common but differentiated responsibilities and respective capabilities".[15] This principle underpins that developed countries should take the lead in modifying longer-term trends in anthropogenic emissions and combating climate change,[16] which means that developed countries should make greater contributions to developing new technologies to counteract climate change and the adverse effects thereof. Developing countries *might* also benefit from the increased knowledge of new possibilities in response to climate change.[17]

The last point that merits attention is the UNFCCC's prioritization of mitigation by addressing anthropogenic emissions by sources and removals by sinks. It remains to be answered by the policymakers whether the deployment and even the research of SRM techniques would be permitted due to the risk of "moral hazard". In other words, whether geoengineering, as Plan B, would weaken the commitment of mitigation as Plan A if SRM were to be addressed in the UNFCCC.[18] It has been argued that the UNFCCC prohibits a policy approach that would lessen the parties' main commitments.[19]

2.2.2 *Kyoto Protocol*

The KP is aimed at facilitating the achievement of the ultimate objective of the UNFCCC. Article 2(1)(a)(ii) and (iv) of the KP could be considered as a legal impetus for developing CDR techniques: each party included in Annex I to the UNFCCC, in achieving its quantified emission limitation and reduction commitments under Article 3 of the KP, shall "implement and/or further elaborate policies and measures in accordance with its national circumstances, such as: (ii) protection and enhancement of sinks and reservoirs of greenhouse gases [. . .]; promotion of sustainable forest management practices, afforestation and reforestation"; "(iv) Research on, and promotion, development and increased use of [. . .] carbon dioxide sequestration technologies and of advanced and innovative environmentally sound technologies[.]" It is notable that the Kyoto Protocol calls on parties to develop research on "advanced and innovative environmentally sound technologies", thus excluding "unsound" techniques.[20]

One limitation of applying the KP to CDR is that, although the KP calls on parties to protect and enhance sinks and reservoirs of greenhouse gases (GHGs), only the changes in GHGs resulting from afforestation and reforestation can be measured as verifiable changes to meet parties' commitments of GHG emissions reduction.[21] Another limitation concerns the fact that the KP may be terminated at some point in the next decade.[22] In light of this, the KP might not play a significant role in the governance of CDR techniques in the long run.

2.2.3 Decisions of COP and CMP

Numerous decisions of the Conference of the Parties (COP) and Conference of the Parties serving as the meeting of the Parties to the Kyoto Protocol (CMP) directly or indirectly touch upon issues within the scope of CDR techniques. In 2007, COP 13 adopted the Bali Road Map, which includes the Bali Action Plan. In the Action Plan, parties agreed to cooperate long term and enhanced national/international actions on mitigation of climate change, especially considering differentiated appropriate mitigation actions in developed and developing countries.[23]

In addition, the Cancun Agreements adopted by COP 16 made a reference to keeping the increase of the global average temperature below 2 °C and could be seen as catalysing the proposition of geoengineering. As introduced in Chapter 1, the main background of proposing geoengineering is the emission gap between the 2 °C goal and the reality, which cannot be filled by conventional mitigation methods. The Cancun Agreements recognize the need for deep cuts in global greenhouse gas emissions to meet this long-term goal of holding the increase in global average temperature below 2 °C above pre-industrial levels, and also recognize the need to consider strengthening the long-term global goal, including in relation to a maximum temperature rise of 1.5 °C.[24]

The CMP approved carbon capture and storage (CCS) projects for greenhouse-gas offsets under the Clean Development Mechanism (CDM). As explained in Chapter 1, CCS is different from CDR techniques, but the modalities and procedures of carbon sequestration are similar. Hence, the CMP decisions concerning CCS could provide a reference notwithstanding that they are not directly applicable to CDR techniques under the KP.[25]

2.2.4 Paris Agreement

The Paris Agreement (PA) adopted at the 21st session of the Conference of the Parties to the UNFCCC in December 2015 opens a new chapter in the global governance of climate change. The PA does not explicitly warrant the implementation of any specific mitigation technologies or techniques, but the PA encourages parties to take actions on conserving and enhancing sinks and reservoirs of GHGs.[26] Such a general character of the PA implies that it would be possible to implement CDR techniques when discussing how to achieve the long-term temperature goal and how to undertake intended nationally determined contributions (INDCs)[27] and nationally determined contributions (NDCs).[28]

The long-term temperature goal set out in the PA can be traced back to the Cancun Agreements in 2010.[29] The long-term temperature goal under the Cancun Agreements has been incorporated into the PA as a means towards the achievement of the ultimate objective of the UNFCCC. Although not in the language of a commitment or an obligation, Article 2(a) of the PA has reiterated the long-term temperature goal through strengthened wording. In enhancing the implementation of the convention, the PA aims to hold "the increase in the global average temperature to well below 2 °C above pre-industrial levels and pursuing efforts to limit the temperature increase to 1.5 °C above pre-industrial levels, recognizing that this would significantly reduce the risks and impacts of climate change". Compared to the long-term goal formulated in the Cancun Agreements, the word "well" has been added before "below 2 °C" and the significance of strengthening the goal to 1.5 °C above pre-industrial level has been confirmed. The goal of limiting global temperature rise under the PA entails enhanced emission reductions before 2020 and ambitious and stringent emission reductions over later decades.[30]

Considerable efforts will be required to achieve the 2 °C goal. As described in the Synthesis Report on the Aggregate Effect of the Intended Nationally Determined Contributions, *several* parties to the convention have indicated in their submitted INDCs that their expected level of emissions in the future would fall within a global emission pathway that is consistent with the 2 °C goal, while *a few* parties referred to 1.5 °C as the objective that they were aiming for with their INDCs.[31] The achievement of the 2 °C goal depends on how ambitious the parties' mitigation efforts are. It has been widely pointed out that achieving the 2 °C goal would rely heavily on the large-scale use of negative emission technologies – i.e. CDR techniques.[32] Article 5 of the PA requires parties to take actions to enhance, as appropriate, sinks and reservoirs of GHGs. The implementation of CDR techniques seems to echo the encouragement of enhancing sinks under the PA, as biological CDR methods (e.g. large-scale afforestation and ocean fertilization), chemical CDR techniques (e.g. enhanced weathering) or a combination of biological and physical methods (e.g. BECCS) would enhance either natural or artificial carbon sinks. Notably, adverse impacts on the environment arising from some CDR techniques, *inter alia*, ocean fertilization[33] and remaining scientific uncertainties in such techniques should not be ignored when assessing the feasibility of implementing such techniques.

Substantively, the main connection between the PA and the governance of CDR is NDCs made by all parties.[34] Under the PA, all parties are to undertake and communicate ambitious NDCs to the global response to climate change.[35] Parties are free to choose the methods of mitigation to be counted as their NDCs and there is no obligatory amount of emission reductions. As the PA encourages all parties to include all categories of removals in their NDCs,[36] it is reasonable to infer that parties have the freedom to implement any CDR technique as part of its NDC in order to strengthen the global response to the threat of the climate change unless the Conference of Parties serving as the meeting of the Parties to the Paris Agreement (CMA) provides otherwise in the future.[37] It is unclear whether the PA is applicable to SRM. Pursuing efforts to limit the temperature increase to 1.5 °C above pre-industrial levels would be more challenging.[38] For every state, such efforts entail considerable investment in decarbonisation of its economy, rapid development of low-emission and even zero-emission technologies as well as intensive collaboration with other states. Notably, the PA also aims to achieve a *balance* between anthropogenic emissions by sources and removals by sinks of greenhouse gas in the second half of this century, on the basis of equity, and in the context of sustainable development and efforts to eradicate poverty.[39] This aim encompasses both the ambitious mitigation efforts required and the practical limitations due to states' distinct capacities. At first sight, it seems to be reasonable to assume that the temperature goal under the PA may require the implementation of SRM: when extraordinarily ambitious mitigation efforts are not realistic, a compromise could be to limit the temperature increase by implementing SRM in order to achieve the temperature goal. However, limiting the temperature increase to 1.5 °C above pre-industrial levels is not so much an objective by itself, but a means to achieve the ultimate objective of the UNFCCC, i.e. limiting the concentration of greenhouse gas emissions at a level that would prevent dangerous climate change. As a result, whether the PA is applicable to SRM depends on the interpretation of the ultimate objective of the UNFCCC.[40]

2.3 The ENMOD Convention

In the 1970s, weather modification techniques raised particular concern. In the Vietnam War, the U.S. military used cloud seeding over the Ho Chi Minh Trail, increasing the rainfall and thereby impeding traffic along the trail. The concern about weather warfare led to the adoption of the Convention on the Prohibition of Military or Any Hostile Use of Environmental Modification Techniques (ENMOD Convention) in 1977.[41] The ENMOD Convention restricts the use of geoengineering for military or hostile use. Article II of the ENMOD Convention defines the term "environmental modification techniques" as "any techniques for changing – through the deliberate manipulation of natural processes – the dynamics, composition or structure of the Earth, including its biota, lithosphere, hydrosphere and atmosphere, or of outer space". Several examples are provided by the ENMOD to better explain the phenomena that could be caused by the use of environmental modification techniques: earthquake, change of weather patterns (clouds, precipitation, cyclones of various types and tornadic storms), changes in climate patterns, changes in ocean currents and changes in the state of the ozone layer.[42] Pursuant to the definition, and in view of the examples, the characteristics of SAI, MCW and ocean upwelling fall within the term "environmental modification techniques".[43] Article I of the ENMOD Convention stipulates that parties to this convention undertake not to engage in and not to assist, encourage or induce any state, group of states or international organization to engage in military or any other hostile use of environmental modification techniques having "widespread, long-lasting or severe effects as the means of destruction, damage or injury to any other State Party".[44] Consequently, the ENMOD Convention prohibits any climate intervention with a military or hostile purpose if it is has long-lasting, widespread or severe effects.

However, the ENMOD Convention stipulates that parties "shall not hinder the use of environmental modification techniques for peaceful purposes".[45] Activities carried out for peaceful purposes that cause "widespread, long-lasting or severe effects" are allowed by the ENMOD Convention if they are in accordance with generally recognized principles and applicable rules of public international law.[46] Furthermore, the ENMOD Convention requires parties to exchange scientific and technological information on the peaceful use of environmental modification techniques.[47] Therefore, geoengineering techniques for peaceful uses are allowed, as long as they are in accordance with applicable international rules and principles, notably the prevention principle. This mandate is of particular significance in terms of sharing information about negative consequences with other states.[48]

In sum, the ENMOD Convention applies to geoengineering in terms of exchanging information on the peaceful uses of SAI, MCW and ocean upwelling. The prohibition to make use of environmental modification techniques under the ENMOD Convention is not applicable to geoengineering unless SAI, MCW and ocean upwelling were applied for hostile purposes and would have widespread, long-lasting or severe effects.

2.4 Prevention and precaution – coping with environmental harm, the risk of harm and uncertainty

2.4.1 Coping with environmental harm and the risk of harm – the prevention principle

When conducting geoengineering activities, states are required to comply with the obligation to prevent significant transboundary harm or to minimize the risk thereof. In a broad sense, the prevention principle, or the obligation to prevent transboundary harm, refers to the rule that one state must ensure that an activity undertaken within its jurisdiction or control does not cause significant harm beyond its national jurisdiction or control. The harm may occur under the jurisdiction or control of another state or beyond the limits of national jurisdiction or control (the global commons).[49] In some legal instruments, "transboundary harm" may merely refer to the harm occurring in areas under the jurisdiction or control of another state.[50] For the convenience of discussion, this book uses the term "transboundary harm" in a narrow sense, viz. the harm to the environment of other states, as opposed to the harm to the global commons.

The prevention principle is one of the fundamental principles in contemporary customary international law pursuant to which states have the responsibility to prevent damage to the environment of other states or of areas beyond national jurisdiction. Since the prevention principle was first enunciated in the *Trail Smelter* arbitration[51] in 1938, it has gradually evolved into customary international law after the reiterations in international and regional conventions,[52] declarations, and judicial and arbitral decisions.

Originally, the prevention principle applied only to acts within one state's territory that cause transboundary harm to the territory of another state. In the *Trail Smelter* arbitration, the tribunal held that

> no State has the right to use or permit the use of its territory in such a manner as to cause injury by fumes in or to the territory of another or the properties or persons therein, when the case is of serious consequence and the injury is established by clear and convincing evidence.[53]

In 1949, the ICJ judgement in the *Corfu Channel* case concluded that "the laying of the minefield which caused the explosions [. . .] could not have been accomplished without the knowledge of the Albanian government".[54] Therefore, every state has "[the] obligation not to allow knowingly its territory to be used for acts contrary to the rights of other States".[55] Furthermore, in 1957, the *Lac Lanoux* arbitration confirmed that France should take Spanish interests into sufficient consideration in the utilization of the water of Lake Lanoux.[56]

Principle 21 of the 1972 Stockholm Declaration broadens the scope of the prevention principle, providing that states must ensure that activities within their jurisdiction or control do not cause damage not only to "the environment of other States" but also to the environment of "areas beyond the limit of national jurisdiction".[57] Principle 21 of the 1972 Stockholm Declaration has become a classic formulation of the prevention principle and is incorporated in conventions as well as cited in academic literature.[58] Later, the ICJ endorsed the prevention principle as a rule of customary international law in the *Nuclear Weapon Advisory Opinion*: "The existence of the general obligation of States to ensure that activities within their jurisdiction and control respect the environment of other states or of areas beyond national control is now part of the corpus of international law relating to the environment."[59] More recently, in 2013, *Indus Waters Kishenganga* arbitration, an arbitral tribunal looked back upon the development of this fundamental principle of customary international environmental law when it acknowledged India's commitment to ensure a minimum environmental flow downstream of the Kishenganga hydro-electric project.[60]

In contrast to the aforementioned cases, which refer to this principle as a general norm, the ICJ judgment in the *Pulp Mills* case translated the prevention principle into a series of procedural and substantive obligations.[61] The *Pulp Mills* case, between Argentina and Uruguay, concerns the obligations related to two pulp mills constructed in Uruguay on the River Uruguay.

The procedural obligations include, but are not limited to: the obligation to inform CARU (Administrative Committee of the River Uruguay) (paras. 94–111) and Uruguay's obligation to notify the other party about their plans (paras. 112–122). With respect to the substantive obligations, the judgment examined four aspects, *viz.* the obligation to the optimum and rational utilization of the river (paras. 170–177); the obligation to ensure that the management of the soil and woodland loss does not impair the regime of the river or the quality of its waters (paras. 178–180); the obligation to co-ordinate measures to avoid changes in the ecological balance (paras. 181–189); and the obligation to prevent pollution and preserve the aquatic environment (paras. 190–266).

2.4.1.1 *The threshold of harm*

The prevention principle does not imply that *any* environmental harm is prohibited.[62] Instead, the principle entails a legal obligation when activities "could *significantly* diminish the enjoyment" of the environment by others.[63] The term "significant" has been formulated in different ways. For instance, in the *Trail Smelter Case*, the tribunal was of the opinion that a claim is justified when "the case is of *serious* consequence"[64] and the threatened impairment of rights is of "serious magnitude and it must be established by clear and convincing evidence".[65] The 1992 Convention on the Transboundary Effects of Industrial Accidents also uses "*serious* effect" to describe the "transboundary effects" resulting from an industrial accident.[66] The 2001 Draft Articles on Prevention of Transboundary Harm from Hazardous Activities (hereafter 2001 Draft Articles on Prevention), adopted by the International Law Commission (ILC) elaborates the term "significant" as "something more than 'detectable' but the harm need not be at the level of 'serious' or 'substantial'".[67] However, the ILC also notes that a number of conventions have used "significant", "serious" or "substantial" to describe the threshold. Considering that the vague threshold may hinder the application of the prevention principle to specific cases, an authoritative interpretation of the words used to determine the threshold, such as "significant", "substantial" and "serious", is required. Those words could be either interchangeable or refer to differing levels of harm.[68]

The measurement of "significant harm" is not "without ambiguity".[69] On the one hand, the obligation excludes "de minimis" harm. The United Nations Environmental Programme (UNEP) defines the term "significantly effect" as "any appreciable effects on a shared natural resource and excludes 'de minimis' effects",[70] which means that "significant effects" contain a level of risk that must be more than too small to be concerned with. On the other hand, in the 2001 Draft Articles on Prevention, the ILC defined the "risk of causing significant transboundary harm" as "risks taking the form of a high probability of causing significant transboundary harm and a low probability of causing disastrous transboundary harm".[71] The definition provided by the UNEP addresses the minimum limitation, whereas the definition provided by the 2001 Draft Articles on Prevention addresses both maximum and minimum limits. However, the abovementioned definitions of "significant harm" still have not answered the question of how to determine "significant harm", because adjectives, such as "serious" and "substantial", are still abstract and fail to provide a clear and practical threshold. In view of this, some concrete criteria function as complements to the threshold of "significant harm". First, certain types of transboundary effects involving, for instance, radiological, toxic, or other highly dangerous substances, or harm to human health and safety, are likely to be *a priori* deemed significantly harmful.[72] Second, technical standards are established for assessing the significance of adverse impacts on, for instance, air and water quality.[73] Third, geographical markers, such as the proximity of an activity to the border, are used to indicate the "significance" of the transboundary effects.[74] In addition, the determination of "significant harm" involves "more factual considerations than legal determination, which means comprehensive consideration should also cover scientific knowledge and social-economic conditions.[75]

2.4.1.2 Due diligence

The concept of due diligence was discussed in 1999 by the International Law Commission in the context of the topic of prevention of transboundary damage from hazardous activities. The special rapporteur Pemmaraju Sreenivasa Rao stated that "[t]he duty of prevention, which is an obligation of conduct, is essentially regarded as a duty of due diligence".[76] In order to prevent significant transboundary harm or minimize its risk, the state shall exercise due diligence through the adoption of all appropriate methods. The 1997 Convention on the Law of the Non-navigational Use of International Watercourses implies an obligation of due diligence by referring to "appropriate measures" to be taken by states to prevent the causing of significant harm to other watercourse states.[77] In the *Pulp Mills* case, the ICJ stated that parties have the obligation to ensure that the management of the soil and woodland does not impair the regime of the River Uruguay or the quality of its waters.[78] Hence, both parties are called upon to exercise due diligence to preserve the ecological balance of the river.[79] The necessity of conducting an environmental impact assessment is particularly emphasized: "the duty of due diligence would not be considered to have been exercised if a state planning activities liable to affect the river or the quality of its waters did not undertake an environmental impact assessment upon such activities".[80]

The duty of due diligence has been interpreted differently in accordance with the standard of care involved. The duty of due diligence is not intended to guarantee the total prevention of significant harm "if it is not possible to do so".[81] The intension of due diligence offers a "flexibility"[82] that the standard of adequate care should be determined with due regard to various *technological, regulatory* and *economic* capacities and the *nature* of the activity. The Advisory Opinion of the International Tribunal for the Law of the Sea (ITLOS) points to the variability of the standard of due diligence: "[i]t may change over time as measures considered sufficiently diligent at a certain moment may become not diligent enough in light, for instance, of new scientific or technological knowledge".[83]

Pertaining to technological standards, in the *Pulp Mills* case, Argentina claimed that Uruguay had failed to take all appropriate measures to prevent harm because Uruguay had not required one of the pulp mills to use the "best available techniques".[84] However, Uruguay asserted that the Orion (Botnia) Mill, one of the mills, was in compliance with the 1975 Statute of the River Uruguay between Uruguay and Argentina, because the mill is, "by virtue of the technology employed there, one of the best pulp mills in the world, applying best available techniques and complying with European Union standards, among others, in the area".[85] The standard of "best available techniques" has been included in many conventions, *inter alia*, the 1982 UNCLOS and the Convention for the Protection of the Marine Environment of the North-East Atlantic (OSPAR Convention).[86] With respect to regulatory standards, according to the judgment in the *Pulp Mills* case, even though the pollutants discharged by the Orion (Botnia) Mill exceeded a maximum limit according to the environmental impact assessment, "Uruguay has taken action in its Regulation on Water Quality and in relation to the Orion (Botnia) mill in the conditions stipulated in the authorization issued by MVOTMA".[87] This implies that Uruguay had fulfilled its due diligence obligation in terms of best available techniques, including both regulatory and technological aspects. As regards economic viability, "the degree of care expected of a state with well-developed economic human and material resources [. . .] is not the same as for states which are not in such a position".[88] In addition, the required degree of care is commensurate with the degree of hazard of the activity involved. The more hazardous an activity is, the greater duty of care is required to prevent and abate significant transboundary harm.[89]

The due diligence obligation also closely relates to the precautionary approach.[90] In the *Advisory Opinion on Activities in the Area*, the tribunal pointed out that the precautionary approach is an integral part of the general obligation of due diligence of sponsoring states.[91] The obligation of due diligence applies in situations where scientific evidence concerning the scope and potential adverse impacts of an activity is insufficient, but where there is a plausible indication of potential risks. Disregarding such "potential risks" would constitute a failure to fulfil the obligation of due diligence and amount to a failure to comply with the precautionary approach. In the *Southern Bluefin Tuna* case, the obligation of due diligence and the precautionary approach were combined to deal with uncertain risks. The tribunal first declared that "the parties should in the circumstances act with prudence and caution to ensure that effective conservation measures are taken to prevent serious harm to the stock of southern Bluefin tuna".[92] This sentence implied that due diligence, namely "prudence and caution", should be exercised by the parties. The tribunal then considered the scientific uncertainty regarding conservation measures to be taken to conserve the stock of southern Bluefin tuna. "Although the tribunal cannot conclusively assess the scientific evidence presented by the parties, it finds that measures should be taken as a matter of urgency to preserve the rights of the parties and to avert further deterioration of the southern Bluefin tuna stock".[93]

2.4.1.3 Activities that cause significant harm

(I) SIGNIFICANT HARM BETWEEN STATES

Theoretically, the obligation to prevent transboundary harm encompasses the obligation to prevent or minimize transboundary environmental interference causing significant harm, and the obligation to prevent the materialization of a significant risk that may cause transboundary harm.[94] For some activities, the harm to the environment is technically or economically unavoidable in their normal operation.[95] In such circumstances, an activity that causes transboundary harm to an area within the jurisdiction or control of other states is unlawful, unless the affected state consents to it.

With the affected state's consent, the transboundary interference would still violate international law if the activities "transgressed" the limit of admissible behaviour agreed by the potentially affected states.[96] In the case of the *Gabčíkovo-Nagymaros Project*, the ICJ concluded that the operation of Variant C on the Danube constituted an internationally wrongful act, because Variant C is essential for Czechoslovakia's use and benefit, despite the fact that the Danube is a shared international watercourse. "Hungary had agreed to the damming of the Danube and the diversion of its waters into the bypass canal. But it was only in the context of a joint operation and sharing of its benefits that Hungary had given its consent".[97] The court considered that "the fact that Hungary had agreed in the context of the original project to the diversion of the Danube [. . .] cannot be understood as having authorized Czechoslovakia to proceed with a unilateral diversion of this magnitude without Hungary's consent".[98] Consequently, Czechoslovakia, in putting Variant C into operation, violated the 1977 Treaty between Czechoslovakia and Hungary and this constituted an internationally wrongful act.

The rule of "consent" could be broken by invoking the "interest balancing" approach to assess the activities that cause significant transboundary harm. In cases where significant transboundary harm is unavoidable despite the exercise of due diligence by the state of origin, the states concerned should carry out bilateral or multilateral negotiations on the equitable conditions under which the activity can be undertaken after balancing all interests at stake. When transboundary harm arising from an activity is significant, but far less than the cost of preventing the harm or the socio-economic benefits that the activity could bring to the affected state, the activity is lawful and does not have to be subject to consent from the affected state.[99] In this case, the state of origin has the obligation to provide reparation and compensation to the affected state.[100]

However, the rule of "consent" and the "interest balancing" approach are mainly applicable to activities that cause transboundary harm to an area within the jurisdiction or control of another state or a few states. For activities in areas covering a number of states, it is almost impossible to get consent from all affected countries. The balancing of interests becomes complex as well, as interests vary from state to state. This would be case for some geoengineering activities.[101]

(II) SIGNIFICANT HARM IN THE GLOBAL COMMONS

The term "global commons" is a "relative term, in juxtaposition with national territories or domains under state control".[102] Geographically, it refers to the high seas, the atmosphere, outer space, and arguably the polar regions. As stated in the previous section, an activity that causes transboundary harm between states may still be lawful, if the affected state consents to it or the requirement for invoking the "interest balancing" approach can be met.

However, these two exceptions do not exist in the case of significant harm to the global commons. Neither the rule of "consent" nor the approach of "interest balancing" between states is applicable to the activities undertaken in the global commons, because neither the high seas nor the common atmosphere[103] generally can act as a party[104] to negotiate with states. A practical question arises as to whether any state or institution has the right to take measures in response to an activity that may cause significant harm to the areas beyond national jurisdiction. The discussion starts with examining the term "collective interest".[105]

As Judge Weeramantry commented in the case of the *Gabčíkovo-Nagymaros Project*, contemporary international environmental law sub-serves not only the interests of individual states, but looks beyond to "the greater interests of humanity and planetary welfare".[106] Judge Weeramantry observed that

> [w]hen we enter the arena of obligations which operate *erga omnes* rather than *inter partes*, rules based on individual fairness and procedural compliance may be inadequate [. . .] International environmental law will need to proceed beyond weighing the rights and obligations of parties within a closed compartment of individual State self-interest, unrelated to the global concerns of humanity as a whole.

Prima facie, all states have access to common areas and have the freedom to use common resources. However, the use of common areas and resources must be peaceful, and no state may carry out activities in the common areas or exploit common resources without due regard for the interests of other states. In addition, the freedom to use common resources must be subject to the general rule of not causing significant harm to the environment, which has been included in many multilateral environmental agreements (MEAs).[107]

To date, it is still a matter of controversy in international law whether every state has standing to invoke the responsibility of another state for breaches of obligations owed to the international community.[108] In the *Nuclear Tests* case between Australia and France, Australia claimed that the carrying out of further atmospheric nuclear weapon tests by France in the South Pacific Ocean infringes the freedom of the high seas. Several judges of the ICJ elaborated, in dissenting opinions, on "collective interests". Some judges opined that states have individual as well as common rights with respect to the freedoms of the high seas; such rights are "implicit in the very concept of such freedoms which involve rights of use possessed by every State".[109] In contrast, Judge de Castro noted that Australia has "no legal title authorizing it to act as spokesman for the international community and the court cannot determine in a general way what France's duties are with regard to the freedoms of the sea.[110]

According to the Draft Articles on Responsibility of States for Internationally Wrongful Acts, any state other than the injured state is entitled, to invoke the responsibility of the state of origin, to take lawful measures against the responsible state to ensure cessation of the breach and reparation of the interest of the injured state or of the beneficiaries of the obligation breached.[111] However, at present, there appears to be no clearly recognized entitlement of states other than the injured state to take countermeasures in favour of the collective interest.[112] The resolution of this matter is left to further development in international law.[113]

No legal rule, so far, entitles a state to representatively consent to an activity that causes significant environmental harm in the global commons, or to have the right to balance the risk between benefits and loss from such an activity. The International Seabed Authority (ISA) is the only example of an institution that may act to represent the global commons (in this case, the deep seabed). Should there be special conditions for geoengineering activities that cause significant harm in global commons to be exempted from a breach of international law? Take SAI as an example. Injecting sulphate aerosols to the stratosphere may be beneficial in terms of controlling the global temperature while also being hazardous to the atmosphere. There might be a time when air quality and the blue sky need to give way to climate stability, due to, for instance, the dangerous tipping point of temperature increase. Can such an emergent dangerous tipping point warrant significant harm to the atmosphere beyond national jurisdiction?[114]

2.4.1.4 Activities that create a risk of causing significant transboundary harm or harm to the global commons

The ILC defines "hazardous activities" as activities creating a risk of causing significant harm.[115] All of the six geoengineering techniques selected to be examined in this book contain risks of causing transboundary harm or the harm to the global commons, Thus, the implementation of those techniques fall under "hazardous activities". The concept of the risk of causing significant transboundary harm encompasses "a low probability of causing disastrous transboundary harm or a high probability of causing significant transboundary harm". "Risk" combines the probability of occurrence of an accident and the magnitude of its injurious impact.[116] The probability that an activity causes transboundary harm depends on various elements, for instance, the character of the source of energy, the location of the activity and its proximity to a border area.[117]

Pursuant to the definition of risk, the question arises as to whether a state may carry out or permit another to carry out an activity that creates a risk of causing significant transboundary harm. Lefeber had summarized the two opposing opinions: The dominate one is that the existence of a mere risk does not itself cause significant harm, thus the carrying out of the activities may be permitted by the source state. But the risk must be minimized, taking into account the probability of occurrence of the harm and the magnitude of the harm as well as the "cost of risk-reduction".[118] The other opinion, the minority one, is that activities that create a significant risk are not admissible, unless the consent from the potentially affected states is obtained.[119] According to the former opinion, the "consent" of potentially affected states, which is necessary if activities cause significant transboundary harm, is not necessary if activities create a mere risk of causing such harm. This opinion is reflected in the *Lac Lanoux Arbitration*. Spain and France had opposite opinions on the necessity of prior agreement. The Arbitral Tribunal examined the "essence" of the "necessity of prior agreement" and analysed the legality of France's work based on "reason" and "good faith". The Arbitral Tribunal stated that, "[i]n order to appreciate in its essence the necessity of prior agreement, one must envisage the hypothesis in which the interested States cannot reach agreement".[120] "France alone is the judge of works of public utility which are to be executed on her own territory", and "Spain should not demand that other works in conformity with her wishes should be carried out".[121] Since France has taken Spanish interests into sufficient consideration "either in the course of the dealings or in her proposals", France did not commit a breach when it acted without prior agreement.[122] Consequently, a prior agreement is not necessary when an activity undertaken in one state's jurisdiction or control contains merely a risk of causing significant harm.

In order to prevent the materialization of a significant risk that may cause significant transboundary harm, states are required to comply with procedural obligations to eliminate or minimize risks. In the *Pulp Mills* case, procedural obligations were breached by Uruguay, including but not limited to: The obligation of cooperation between parties to jointly manage the risks of damage to the environment; the obligation of Uruguay to inform CARU of the pulp mill project; and the obligation to notify the plan to other parties, particularly notifying the result of a full environmental impact assessment. In the *Lac Lanoux Arbitration*, the tribunal held that the conflicting interests in the use of the river must be reconciled by mutual concessions.[123] Consultations, information exchange and negotiations must comply with the rule of reason and good faith, and must not be mere formalities.[124] The deployment of a project with a significant risk of creating significant transboundary harm must be subject to a thorough prior assessment of the potential impacts on the environment. The *MOX Plant* case dealt with a facility designed to recycle the plutonium that had been produced during the reprocessing of nuclear fuel. In order to avoid the international movement of radioactive materials and to protect the marine environment of the Irish Sea, the United Kingdom has the obligation to fully and properly assess the potential effects of the operation of the MOX Plant on the marine environment of the Irish Sea. Apart from monitoring the risks, Ireland and the United Kingdom should cooperate in exchanging information concerning the risks or effects of the MOX plant; and they should devise appropriate measures to prevent pollution and other harm.[125]

In practice, it is sometimes impossible to separate activities that cause significant transboundary harm from the activities that create risks of causing transboundary harm, because the likelihood of harm and the seriousness of the impacts on the environment are often very uncertain in advance. Generally, owing to the nature and scientific uncertainty of the six geoengineering techniques, it is very difficult if to tell one particular geoengineering activity will cause significant transboundary harm or merely create a risk of causing significant transboundary harm.

With regard to activities that create a risk of causing significant harm to the global commons, a similar problem as stated in Section 2.4.1.3(ii) arises, namely the lack of an institution to communicate with the implementing state. This problem brings challenges to the implementation of procedural obligations to minimize and control significant risks.

2.4.1.5 Procedural obligations

(I) PLANNING PHASE

(a) Obligation to assess transboundary environmental impacts The obligation to assess transboundary environmental impacts is the first part of the procedural obligations to minimize and control risks of causing significant environmental harm. Environmental impact assessment (EIA) was initially used as a tool in environmental management in domestic law to identify environmental risks, integrate environmental considerations into social-economic development and promote sustainable development.[126] Later, the obligation to conduct an EIA in the transboundary context was explicitly recognized as part of customary international law by the ICJ in the *Pulp Mills* case and the ITLOS in its *Advisory Opinion on Activities in the Area*.[127] In the *Pulp Mills* case, the ICJ recognized a requirement under general international law to undertake an environmental impact assessment of an industrial activity posing a risk of a significant adverse impact in a transboundary context, in particular on a shared resource. The ITLOS confirmed the customary rule mentioned by the ICJ with particular reference to the detrimental impacts of certain activities on the environment in an area beyond the limits of national jurisdiction, including the common heritage of mankind. More recently, in 2015, two cases in front of the ICJ between Costa Rica and Nicaragua touched upon the obligation to conduct an EIA in the transboundary context.[128] The court found that, although the obligation to undertake an EIA

in the *Pulp Mills* case "refers to industrial activities, the underlying principle applies generally to proposed activities which may have a significant adverse impact in a transboundary context".[129]

Moreover, this obligation has also been solidified in a considerable number of conventions and non-binding legal instruments.[130] The most notable and concrete one is the Convention on Environmental Impact Assessment in a Transboundary Context (Espoo Convention) which was adopted under the auspices of the United Nations Economic Commission for Europe (UNECE). Pursuant to the Espoo Convention, EIA is a "procedure to evaluate the likely impact of a proposed activity on the environment".[131]

There are several sectoral legal instruments that are relevant to geoengineering insofar as certain types of environmental impacts that geoengineering techniques may cause are under their mandates. The CBD requires its contracting parties to undertake an EIA for any projects that are likely to have significant adverse effects on biological diversity in order to avoid or minimize such effects.[132] CBD COP Decision VI/7 provides guidelines for incorporating biodiversity-related issues into environmental-impact-assessment legislation or processes.[133] According to CBD COP Decision X/33, one of the requirements to end the moratorium on geoengineering is that the projects are "subject to a thorough prior assessment of the potential impacts on the environment".

Regarding ocean-based geoengineering techniques, Article 206 of the UNCLOS is applicable: "When States have reasonable grounds for believing that planned activities under their jurisdiction or control may cause substantial pollution of or significant and harmful changes to the marine environment, they shall, as far as practicable, assess the potential effects of such activities on the marine environment". In addition, an EIA should also be undertaken if an ocean-based geoengineering activity impacts the environment in an area beyond the limit of national jurisdiction. The Seabed Disputes Chamber of the ITLOS extends the applicability of transboundary EIAs to an area beyond the limits of national jurisdiction and to resources that are the common heritage of mankind.[134] Parties to the LC and LP have adopted Resolution LC-LP.2 (2010) on the "Assessment Framework for Scientific Research Involving Ocean Fertilization" which guides parties on how to assess proposals for ocean fertilization research and provides detailed steps for completing an environmental impact assessment, including risk management and monitoring.[135]

With respect to a SAI project that may create a risk of harm to the ozone layer, the Vienna Convention for the Protection of the Ozone Layer contains provisions on conducting an EIA.[136] Article 2.2(a) stipulates "the parties shall assess the effects of human activities on the ozone layer and the effects on human health and the environment from modification of the ozone layer". However, detailed rules regarding EIAs are neither provided for in the Vienna Convention nor in its Montreal Protocol.

Even though specific contents and procedures of an EIA vary from case to case, the fundamental components of an EIA would involve the following stages.[137] First, the state of origin should take necessary measures to ensure the establishment of an EIA for a proposed activity that meets the threshold of proceeding an EIA. How is one to judge the necessity of triggering an EIA? Principle 17 of the Rio Declaration clearly stipulates that an EIA, "as a national instrument, shall be undertaken for proposed activities that are likely to have a significant adverse impact on the environment". Article 7 of the 2001 Draft Articles on Prevention uses the term "assessment of risk", which is broader than "environmental impact assessment" as a prerequisite for the authorization of an activity that may have the risk of causing transboundary harm. One consideration must be the examination of the "significance" of the risk in an activity. The "extent, nature or location" of a proposed activity should be considered in the examination of "significance".[138] For instance, the type of the source of energy used, the location of the activity and its proximity to the border.[139] As risk combines the magnitude of harm and the probability of occurrence, activities that have a low probability of serious harm may meet the threshold for conducting an EIA as well.

Notably, the threshold of triggering an EIA is lowered if an activity is proposed to take place in the Antarctic Treaty area. The Protocol on Environmental Protection to the Antarctic Treaty provides procedures for prior assessment of the impacts of those activities on the Antarctic environment or on dependent or associated ecosystems.[140] A proposed activity may proceed only if it is determined as having less than a minor or transitory impact. An initial environmental evaluation should be prepared when the activity has a minor or transitory impact; a comprehensive environmental evaluation should be prepared when the activity is likely to have more than a minor or transitory impact. The lower threshold under the Antarctic Environmental Protocol is reasonable, considering the intrinsic value of Antarctica and the fragile Antarctic environment.

Second, the proponent of the proposed project together with relevant experts and authorities determine the key issues for assessment and prepare all relevant information. Principle 4 of the UNEP Goals and Principles of Environmental Impact Assessment provides for the minimum documentation needed, encompassing descriptions and indications of the proposed activity or alternatives, the potentially affected environment, the available mitigating measures as well as an assessment of the likely or potential impacts. A similar but more comprehensive list of EIA documentation is formulated in Appendix II of the Espoo Convention.[141]

Third, competent bodies that have the relevant expertise assess and evaluate the impacts of the proposed project and its alternatives, and report their results. The competent authority should ensure public access to the resulting documents and provides opportunities of public participation. Throughout the assessment process, the state of origin should notify, consult and exchange information with potentially affected states.[142] Often, the environmental assessment results should be subject to peer review, and the result of peer review should be publicly available.

Fourth, the competent decision-making body makes a decision upon the outcome of the EIA as well as the comments collected from the public and the outcome of consultation. In addition to the final decision of authorizing or refusing the proposed project, decision-making also takes place throughout the process of an EIA from the early stage of determining whether a project should be subject to an EIA to making choice between the proposed project and the alternatives.[143]

Fifth, the competent authority should monitor whether the predicted impacts and mitigating measures occur as indicated in the environmental assessment report.[144]

The abovementioned obligation to conduct an EIA refers to a project-based EIA that is aimed to minimize and control the risk of causing significant environmental harm at an early stage of project-planning and design. In addition to the traditional project-based EIA process, another type of impact assessment, systematic environmental assessment (SEA), has rapidly developed in the last two decades.

SEA refers to the formalized, systematic and comprehensive evaluation of the likely significant environmental effects of proposed plans, programmes and other strategic initiatives in order to identify and evaluate the environmental consequences at the earliest possible stage of decision-making.[145] The 2001 EU SEA Directive and the Protocol on Strategic Environmental Assessment to the Espoo Convention are two examples of practices in SEA.[146] According to the SEA Protocol to the Espoo Convention, SEA comprises a three-stage framework: screening, scoping and in-depth EIA assessments. The process starts with "screening", which determines whether plans and programmes are likely to have significant environmental effects either through a case-by-case examination or by specifying types of plans and programmes or by combining both approaches.[147] Unless a project is determined not requiring an SEA by "screening", "scoping" will follow to define the focus of the assessment and to identify key issues of the assessment.[148]

Compared to EIA, SEA is carried out on a policy, plan and programme level, and thus, by its nature, covers a wider range of activities, a broader area and over a longer time span. SEA extends the aims and principles of EIA to the higher levels of decision-making when major alternatives are still open, various uncertainties still remain and there is much greater scope than at the project level to integrate environmental considerations into development goals.[149] In addition, SEA can be undertaken to assess the cumulative impacts of multiple implementation of a specific technology in a systematic and anticipatory way.[150] Such attributes of SEA would bring added value to the assessment framework for geoengineering activities at the level of policies and plans. The possible application of SEA to geoengineering will be addressed in Chapter 5.

(b) Obligation to notify the risks, exchange information, consult and negotiate with potentially affected states

NOTIFYING THE RISKS   If a plan is likely to cause significant transboundary harm, the party of origin shall notify the affected party about the plan.[151] Article 8 of the 2001 Draft Articles on Prevention states that:

> If the assessment referred to in article 7 indicates a risk of causing significant transboundary harm, the State of origin shall provide the State likely to be affected with timely notification of the risk and the assessment and shall transmit to it the available technical and all other relevant information on which the assessment is based.

Principle 19 of the Rio Declaration provides the time requirement for the notification. Pursuant to this Principle, the notification with all relevant information shall be provided timely. The 1992 Convention on the Protection of the Marine Environment of the Baltic Sea Area expresses the time requirement as notification "without delay".[152] In the *Pulp Mills* case, the ICJ observes that "if the CARU decides that the plan might cause significant damage to the other party or if a decision cannot be reached in that regard, 'the party concerned shall notify the other party of this plan' ", and the notification must take place "[*before*] the State concerned decides on the environmental viability of the plan".[153] Uruguay breached its obligation to notify Argentina about its plans, because it did not transmit the environmental assessments to Argentina prior to having issued the initial environmental authorizations.

The time requirement seems to be more significant in situations of emergency in the operational phase.[154] An example of an emergency situation in geoengineering is CO_2 leakage during the process of CO_2 injection or transport. States have the obligation to notify relevant states the emergency and to take action in cases of accidental transboundary environmental impact. This obligation is addressed in several legal instruments. For instance, Principle 18 of the Rio Declaration provides that "any natural disasters or other emergencies that are likely to produce sudden harmful effects on the environment" lead to an obligation to immediately notify the likely affected states. This notification shall be "without delay and by the most expeditious means".[155] In *the Corfu Channel* case, Albania had the obligation to provide notice to other states and specifically, an obligation to warn approaching British warships of the danger of explosion after a minefield had been laid in Albanian territory. Although a "general notification" might be impossible because of the short time between the minelaying and the explosion, Albania had no excuse for omitting to notify the British warship to prevent the disaster.[156]

EXCHANGING INFORMATION   Exchanging information is an important means of furnishing initial information to as well as updating potentially affected states with new knowledge, as well as receiving receive feedback from these states in order to control or minimize significant transboundary harm at an early stage. Available information and data with regard to,[157] *inter alia*, the plan of the proposed activity, the condition of the natural surroundings or resources, the possible impacts on the environment and all measures taken for fear of significant transboundary harm or the risks thereof, should be exchanged widely and in a timely manner. The information related to biological diversity, for instance, contains results from technical, scientific and socio-economic research, as well as specialized, indigenous and traditional knowledge.[158] The requirement to exchange data and information can also be found in the regulation of using transboundary watercourses.[159] The condition of the watercourse, including a hydrological, meteorological, hydrogeological and ecological nature, and the water quality is the basic information to be exchanged.[160] In addition, riparian states must also exchange the results of research, experience from the application and operation, emission and monitoring data, and measures to prevent, control and reduce transboundary impacts.[161] One more example of the obligation to exchange information can be found in the 1979 Convention on Long-range Transboundary Air Pollution (CLRTAP). Pursuant to the CLRTAP, parties shall exchange available information on, among other things, data on emissions, control technologies for reducing air pollution, and physic-chemical and biological data relating to the effects of land-range transboundary air pollution.[162]

The "best available technology" standard mentioned in Section 2.4.1.2 is applicable to the obligation to exchange information. The quality of the information provided should not be less than the best available technology standard, particularly through commercial exchange of available technology, technical assistance as well as industrial contacts and cooperation.[163]

Actually, the obligation to provide information should be fulfilled not only in the planning phase but also during the whole process of a project, including the post-operational phase. Article 12 of the 2001 Draft Articles on Prevention provides that the exchange of information "shall continue until such time as the States concerned consider it appropriate even after the activity is terminated". It is important to continue to exchange information even after the termination of geoengineering projects, because some adverse impacts might not occur until decades later. A typical example is the leakage of CO_2 after the closure of the storage site.

CONSULTATION AND NEGOTIATION   Once the environmental impact assessment as well as notification and information exchange has taken place, the source state shall enter into consultations with potentially affected states regarding the potential transboundary impacts arising from the proposed activity as well as regarding measures to prevent the transboundary harm or minimize the risks of causing significant transboundary harm.[164] There is a time requirement for the consultation that the consultation must be conducted without "undue delay" after the assessment and must be prior to the authorization of the proposed activity.[165] Such consultation may be conducted in a "joint body", which is established by neighbouring states for cooperatively preventing significant transboundary harm or the creation of risks.[166] Under the obligation to negotiate, parties enter into negotiations with a view to arriving at an agreement, or at least to contemplating some modification to their previous position. The negotiation is not merely a "formal process [. . .] as a sort of prior condition for the automatic application of a certain method of delimitation in the absence of agreement"; the negotiation should be conducted meaningfully and in good faith.[167]

The obligation of prior consultation and negotiation is discussed in the *Lac Lanoux* Arbitration with respect to a shared watercourse. The tribunal held that "consultation and negotiations between the two States must be genuine, must comply with the rules of good faith and must not be mere formalities".[168] The rule of good faith negotiation is indispensable to the obligation of consultation and negotiation. In order to prevent significant transboundary harm or the risk thereof, the party of origin must consult with the potentially affected states faithfully and explore mutually acceptable solutions. During the process of consultation and negotiation, the extent of agreement achieved by the states depends on an equitable balance of interests.[169] States concerned shall take into account all relevant factors and circumstances, including the degree of risk of significant transboundary harm and the means of preventing such harm or minimizing the risk, the importance of the activity, the risk of significant harm to the environment, the means of preventing that harm or minimizing the risk, magnitude of the likely lost benefits, and the willingness of the source state and states likely to be affected to contribute to the cost of preventive measures.[170] The factors that are taken into account for the balance of interests in the planning phase are not identical with the factors for the balance of interests in the operational phase. In the planning phase, states consider the risks of significant harm. In contrast, the materialization of significant harm, if it occurs, should be taken into consideration in the operational phase.

However, negotiations do not imply that an agreement must be achieved, and consultations do not mean that neighbouring states are given a veto over the potentially harmful activity.[171] As discussed in Section 2.4.1.4, it is not necessary to obtain the "consent" of the potentially affected state if the activity creates a risk of causing such harm. The state of origin can implement its activity even if the potentially affected state is against the activity. Of course, the state of origin should take into full account of the interests of the neighbouring states. Pursuant to the decision in the *Lac Lanoux* Arbitration, France must consult with Spain over the project and its potential effects on Spain. France should give reasonable weight to Spanish interests, but considering Spanish interests does not mean that France cannot act without consent from Spain on the work on Lake Lanoux.

(II) OPERATIONAL PHASE

(a) Obligation to authorize activities and monitor their environmental impacts   Referring to the definition of authorization in the 2001 Draft Articles on Prevention, the term 'authorization' in this context means the granting of permission by governmental authorities to conduct geoengineering

activities.[172] The authorization should take into account the result of the risk assessment, particularly the environmental impact assessment.[173]

The state government or the competent authority should not authorize any activity that may significantly harm another state. The state of origin shall adjust or terminate the activity if the transboundary environmental impact appears to be significant. In the *MOX Plant* case, Ireland took the view that United Kingdom breached its obligations in relation to the authorization of the MOX Plant, because the United Kingdom failed to take the necessary measures to prevent, reduce and control pollution of the marine environment of the Irish Sea.[174] The tribunal opined that the United Kingdom was required to monitor the risks of the operation of the MOX Plant for the Irish Sea.[175]

An example of an authorization related to CDR activities is the EU Directive on the geological storage of carbon dioxide. Chapter 2 and Chapter 3 of the Directive address exploration permits and storage permits, respectively. The provisions encompass the application procedure, conditions for storage permits, contents of storage permits as well as changes, review, update and withdrawal of the permits.[176] Note that prior authorization is required not only at the commencement of a CO_2 storage operation but also for any proposed changes. The competent authority must be informed of any changes planned in the operation. The operation as adjusted cannot be implemented until a new or updated permit is issued.

Environmental standards and monitoring are set as a general principle for environmental protection and sustainable development. "States shall establish adequate environmental protection standards and monitor changes in and publish relevant data on environmental quality and resource use".[177] States shall notify the potentially affected states about the dangerous changes and shall adjust or even terminate the ongoing operation if the transboundary environmental impact appears to be significant.

(b) Obligation to balance interests   In a broad sense, the balancing of interests is an element of "sustainable development", i.e. to integrate environmental considerations into the development process and to equitably treat economical or other social needs and environmental needs.[178] In the *Gabčíkovo-Nagymaros Project* case, the court referred to the concept of "sustainable development". The court was mindful that the growing risks from the interference with nature prompt mankind to develop new norms and standards that "reconcile economic development with protection of the environment".[179]

To be more specific, regarding the prevention of significant transboundary harm, the obligation to balance interests concentrates more on various interests between states, such as balancing the interests between economic benefits from industrial operations in one state and environmental interests in the other. In the *Trail Smelter Arbitration*, in order to "reach a solution just to all parties concerned", the tribunal endeavoured to adjust the conflicting interests by some "just solution" that would allow the continuance of the operation of the Trail Smelter but under such restrictions and limitations as would prevent damage in the United States, and as would enable indemnify the United States if damage occurs in the future.[180]A similar approach can be found in the *Lac Lanoux* arbitration, in which the tribunal indicated that a just balance between French interests of the work on Lake Lanoux and Spanish interests in agriculture and environment should be maintained.[181]

States should enter into consultations and seek solutions on the basis of an equitable balance of interests.[182] Various factors should be taken into consideration so as to achieve an equitable balance of interests: the severity of the harm (if it were to occur), the degree of the risk of significant harm, the significant harm or the risk of significant harm to the environment, the magnitude of the lost benefit or the likely lost benefit, the importance of the activity, and the cost of the preventive measures.[183]

(III) POST-OPERATIONAL PHASE

Sometimes, the implementation of procedural obligations may continue after the termination of operation. The "post-operational" phase, as called in most legal instruments, is formulated as the "post project" phase. However, the present book prefers the term "post-operational" because this stage is an integral part of the project instead of a stage thereafter. The Espoo Convention provides that a post-project EIA shall be carried out if any concerned party requests it and the post-project analysis is determined to be necessary.[184] Any post-project analysis undertaken shall include particularly surveillance of the activity and a determination of any adverse transboundary impact.[185] Appendix V of the Espoo Convention provides three objectives of post-project analysis, viz. monitoring compliance with the authorization or approval of the activity and the effectiveness of mitigation measures, review of an impact for proper management, and verification of past predictions.

In addition, the obligation to monitor the occurrence of adverse environmental impacts may also continue after the termination of an activity. Besides, states concerned should cooperate with respect to monitoring and information exchange in the post-operational phase and may continuously exchange information if necessary.

2.4.2 *Addressing uncertain risks – the precautionary approach*

Precaution is a strategy for addressing future risks.[186] Essentially, precaution entails thinking ahead and taking pre-emptive actions to avoid the materialization of uncertain future risks. Since the 1970s, the idea of precaution has been incorporated into regulations and policies at the national level in relation to human activities that may threaten human health (food safety, medication, nuclear power, terrorism, weapons, etc.), natural resources (fisheries), and the environment.[187] In international environmental law, the precautionary principle has been adopted in a growing number of treaties dealing with climate change, marine pollution, air pollution, biodiversity degradation, biosafety, etc.[188] As has been argued, the precautionary principle may be the most innovative, persuasive, and significant new concept in international environmental law in the latest two decades; meanwhile, it is also "the most reckless, arbitrary and ill-advised" one due to its unclear legal status.[189] Some assert that the wide endorsement of the precautionary principle is an indication that it is emerging as a principle of customary international law.[190] Others argue that the precautionary principle is not ripe to be a tenet of customary international law, because state practice in different instances is diverse and inconsistent, and the precautionary principle has not yet been incorporated into legal instruments with uniform formulation and unequivocal connotation.[191] Main disagreements include:

- What is the distinction between the "precautionary principle" and the "precautionary approach", and is one more appropriate than the other?
- Does the precautionary principle belong to the traditional risk management process which is a procedural obligation of the prevention principle or, alternatively, is it an independent principle in international environmental law?
- What degree of risk is necessary to invoke the precautionary principle? It may vary from "possible risk" to "serious" or "irreversible" risk.[192]
- What is the exact meaning of "full scientific certainty"? When is the appropriate time to start and terminate a precautionary action?[193]
- What kind of action should be taken in the face of uncertainty? Some documents impose no affirmative duty on states, but merely indicate that the precautionary principle is not an excuse to postpone precautionary measures.[194] Other documents formulate the precautionary principle as an affirmative duty that states should take actions to tackle environmental risk.[195] A few instruments formulate the precautionary approach as shifting the burden of proof, *viz.* prohibiting risky activities until the proponents of the activity prove that the activity poses no significant risk.[196]

All the disagreements above reflect the present ambiguity of the precautionary principle, and the ambiguity may hinder the operationalization of the precautionary principle. Regardless of the ongoing debate surrounding its formal legal status, the precautionary principle has been widely incorporated into national, regional and international regulations and policies, and has increasingly precise legal implications in international law.[197] As suggested by Bodansky, it would be better to spend less time debating a norm's legal status and more time attempting to translate general norms into concrete and enforceable treaties and actions.[198] In this view, this section will not examine the legal status of the precautionary principle in detail, but rather, will seek to figure out why the precautionary principle has not yet been effectively operationalized to govern geoengineering.

Despite the lack of a clear, consistent and commonly agreed-upon definition, three common elements can be extracted from diverse formulations of the precautionary approach in a wide range of legal documents as well as academic publications: risk of harm, scientific uncertainty and precautionary action.[199] As noted earlier, the debate on the precautionary approach surrounds the degree of risk, the meaning of uncertainty and the types of actions. The degree of risk varies from "possible", "significant" to "serious or irreversible". The meaning of scientific uncertainty is still imprecise and is associated with a question of time, namely the time to wait or act. With respect to the element "action", it varies largely in terms of strength, range of application and form. Some commentators have identified more elements than the three here. For instance, Sandin has found substantial variations along four different dimensions, which are formulated as threat, uncertainty, action and command.[200] Cameron and Abouchar have summarized the key elements as the evidentiary threshold of serious or irreversible of damage, the burden of proof, the positive obligation to establish principles and procedures to avoid environmental degradation, and a policy for action in the face of uncertainty.[201]

This section starts with clarifying the difference between the "precautionary approach" and the "precautionary principle", and the reason for using the "precautionary approach" in this book. Then this section briefly analyses the three elements of the precautionary approach: risk of harm, scientific uncertainty and precautionary actions. Among them, the first two elements are seen as the trigger of the precautionary approach whereas the third acts as the response. At last, the moratorium incorporated by international institutions, as an application of the precautionary approach to geoengineering, is analysed.

2.4.2.1 Use of terms

There is no uniform formulation of the precautionary approach, which is also referred to as the term "precautionary principle" or "precautionary measures". An early example of expressing the "precautionary principle" is Paragraph 7 of the 1990 Bergen Ministerial Declaration on Sustainable Development (Bergen Declaration):

> In order to achieve sustainable development, policies must be based on the precautionary principle. Environmental measures must anticipate, prevent and attack the cause of environmental degradation. Where there are threats of serious or irreversible damage, lack of full scientific certainty should not be used as a reason for postponing measures to prevent environmental degradation.

Principle 15 of the 1992 Rio Declaration is considered the global endorsement of the precautionary principle. Although it uses the wording "precautionary approach", Principle 15 presents a similar stipulation as Article 7 of the Bergen Declaration, only limiting the measures to "cost-effective" ones. The 1995 Agreement on Straddling and Highly Migratory Fish Stocks addresses the precautionary *approach* as one of the general *principles* for the conservation and management of straddling fish stocks and highly migratory fish stocks.[202] Similarly, the Protocol to the 1979 Convention on Long-range Transboundary Air Pollution on Persistent Organic Pollutants refers in its Preamble to the precautionary approach and in Annex V to "the principle of precaution".[203] All the examples above indicate that the term "precautionary principle" and "precautionary approach" may be interchangeable. Some scholars therefore regard the two terms as equivalents,[204] or view that the distinction in terminology is insignificant.[205]

On the contrary, others perceive these two terms differently in terms of the legal status and triggers for applying the "approach" or "principle". Typical examples can be found in the fisheries arena. In the separate opinion to the Order in the *Southern Bluefin Tuna Case*, Judge Laing opined that the tribunal "adopting an *approach*, rather than a principle, appropriately imports a certain degree of flexibility and tends, though not dispositively, to underscore reticence about making premature pronouncements about desirable normative structures". In contrast, the term "principle" offers less flexibility and refers to widely recognized legal practices. Another distinction is that the precautionary approach applies to activities that may lead to adverse impacts that are mostly reversible, and the level of uncertainty and potential costs of such activities are significant, whereas the term "principle" is more restrictive, applying merely in situations of high uncertainty with a risk of irreversible harm entailing high costs.[206]

This book does not use the two terms as equivalents, and prefers the more neutral term "approach". First, as long as the divergence in the interpretation of the "precautionary approach" and the "precautionary principle" still exists, the distinction in terminology should not be ignored. Second, regardless of the legal status of the precautionary principle or approach, it indeed plays a significant role in contemporary international environmental law and has great potential on making a contribution to the governance of geoengineering. The strict interpretation of the precautionary principle may impede its application. In view of this, it is more meaningful to set aside the ambiguity of the legal status, and to concentrate on operationalizing the precautionary approach in the context of geoengineering. More importantly, taking into account the huge differences between geoengineering techniques, the triggers of applying the precautionary approach to each technique may be different as well. The term "precautionary approach" therefore can be more flexibly applicable to each technique by setting up diverse thresholds.[207]

2.4.2.2 *The trigger of the precautionary approach*

In the Communication of the European Commission on the Precautionary Principle, two constituent aspects are identified: the factors triggering recourse to the precautionary approach and the measures resulting from the application of the precautionary approach.[208] In this communication, scientific uncertainty, identification of potentially negative effects and scientific evaluation are "three factors triggering recourse to the precautionary principle". Considering the three core elements of the precautionary approach noted earlier, this section will examine the risk of harm and the uncertainty that trigger the recourse to the precautionary approach, and Section 2.4.2.3 will examine various types of action in terms of strength and form.

(1) THE RISK OF HARM

What degree of risk is necessary to invoke the precautionary approach? The common way of describing the risk is through the magnitude of adverse impacts: non-negligible,[209][210] significant,[211] serious or irreversible.[212] Some descriptions are from the perspective of probability: potentially damaging[213] or possibly damaging.[214] Cameron and Wade-Gery have noted that not all environment impacts should be mitigated by the imposition of environmental regulation; the recourse to the precautionary approach requires a threshold of non-negligible risk.[215] Trouwborst has identified that under customary international law the precautionary approach is applicable only when the risk of harm is, at minimum, significant.[216] According to the dictionary definition, "significant" means "not insignificant or negligible".[217] Therefore, the term "non-negligible" as used by Cameron and Wade-Gery is regarded as equivalent to "significant".[218] The meaning of the term "significant" that has been discussed in Section 2.4.1.1 regarding the threshold of harm under the prevention principle is also applicable here. Basically, the term "significant" refers to the degree of harm that is "appreciable", "tangible" or "measurable", as opposed to "trivial".[219] By contrast, the term "serious" or "irreversible" embodies a higher threshold than "significant".[220] Because risk can be defined as a unity that integrates the magnitude of harm and the probability of occurrence,[221] the term "potentially damaging" or "possibly damaging" implies the degree of risk that combines a non-trivial level[222] (could be significant or serious) of harm and the uncertain likelihood of a given effect.[223] Trouwborst submitted that the precautionary approach is applicable when the adverse effects of an activity are significant, but it would then merely create a *right* for a state to take such measures; it would only create a *duty* for a state to take precautionary measures if an activity poses a risk of serious or irreversible harm.[224]

There is also a minority view that a "probable" risk, without expressing the severity of risk, may trigger the precautionary approach.[225] In order to find an appropriate role of the precautionary approach in the protection of the North Sea, Gündling submitted that environmental impacts should be reduced or prevented "even before the threshold of risks is reached".[226] Interestingly, Article 3 of the LP describes the risk as "likely to cause harm" and does not address the severity of harm either. It might be inferred that, in some situations, the threshold of risks could be lower than "significant". Arguably, the smaller the threat that triggers the precautionary approach, the more cautious the principle is.[227]

In sum, three categories will be discussed in this book: potential risk (regardless of the magnitude), the risk of causing significant/non-negligible harm,[228] and the risk of causing serious/irreversible harm.[229] Taking into account the different degrees of risk between geoengineering techniques, and also taking into account the different degrees of risk in the phases of research, fieldwork and large-scale deployment of geoengineering, a preliminary hypothesis is that there is no single threshold to invoke the precautionary approach in every geoengineering activity; a multi-threshold mechanism would be appropriate.[230]

Regarding the certainty of the risk that may invoke the precautionary approach, the risk need not be "certain", but rather reasonably foreseeable, which means the existence has not been conclusively proved by science but it is not unthinkable.[231] Otherwise, a certain risk should be eliminated or minimized by the prevention principle. Note that a hypothetical risk resting on purely speculative considerations without any scientific foundation should be excluded from the precautionary approach.[232]

Another question that merits consideration is whether the precautionary approach aims at zero risk, which means that strong and strict precautionary measures, such as a ban, should be taken until full scientific proof is established. The European Commission explicitly objects to the search for zero risk, because it is rarely to be found in reality.[233] However, in some cases, a standard of (almost) zero risk might be necessary due to the inherent irreversible harm. This standard would lead to a (temporary) ban on activities that pose any uncertain risk.

(II) UNCERTAINTY

From almost all formulations of the precautionary approach, it is clear that the uncertainty in question refers to scientific uncertainty, which expresses our lack of knowledge of the state of the world.[234] Typical phrases of scientific uncertainty are "the lack of scientific certainty"[235] or "the inconclusive evidence of a causal link between an activity and adverse consequences".[236]

Before examining the types of uncertainty, the distinction between prevention and precaution needs to be briefly clarified. The mainstream view on the distinction is that uncertainty is the core element that distinguishes the precautionary approach from the prevention principle. If an activity results in pollution or is known to create a pollution risk, the prevention principle applies to controlling and regulating the substances that cause pollution; the precautionary approach is not applicable because no element of uncertainty is involved. As stated previously, the risk could be defined as the combination of the magnitude of the adverse consequence and its probability of occurrence. Risks are always quantifiable because both the magnitude and the probability are certain or can be estimated. If either the magnitude or the probability or both are unknown, the risk becomes unknown and thus the precautionary approach is applicable. In contrast, Trouwborst submits that the precautionary approach has absorbed the prevention principle, or, alternatively, should be seen as its most developed form.[237] He argues that the presence of uncertainty is not the precondition for the application of the precautionary approach but rather acting as a reasonable ground to trigger proportionally precautionary measures that correspond to the risk. In other words, the action is taken in spite of uncertainty, not because of it.

Typologically, uncertainty can be categorized as epistemological and onto-logical uncertainty in terms of cause.[238][239] The Commission of the European Communities describes scientific uncertainty as follows:

> Scientific uncertainty results usually from five characteristics of the scien-tific methods: the variable chosen, the measurements made, the samples drawn, the models used and the causal relationship employed. Scientific uncertainty may also arise from a controversy on existing data or lack of some relevant data. Uncertainty may relate to qualitative or quantitative elements of the analysis.

Epistemological uncertainty corresponds to lack of knowledge, such as lack of measurements, scientific theories, or historical records.[240] It is sometimes referred to as parameter uncertainty. For instance, climate change can hardly be measured if the information of baseline conditions is absent. Likewise, it is impossible to estimate the loss of species if the number of the total amount of species is uncertain.[241] The lack of information may result from the limi-tation of available tools for measurement and calculation or the limitation of analysis capability.[242] Gathering more information or improving research techniques can diminish some epistemological uncertainties; however, some knowledge deficiencies cannot be made up due to infeasibility of research, such as counting the number of phytoplankton in the ocean.

Ontological uncertainty refers to the uncertainty due to complexity and variability. Complexity of nature stems from the properties and function-ing of each component of nature – biosphere, hydrosphere, atmosphere and lithosphere as well as the intricate web that all these components interrelate. Variability is the other cause of ontological uncertainty, as nature is capricious rather than linear, regular and periodical.[243] The uncertainty due to complex-ity and variability might not ever be overcome.[244]

In reality, very often, it is impossible to attain conclusive scientific proof of the likelihood or the severity of a risk. It is also hardly possible to conclusively establish the cause-effect relationship between an activity or a substance and any feared consequences. In other words, decisions are rarely made under full certainty.

2.4.2.3 Precautionary actions

Among the three elements of the precautionary approach, risk and uncer-tainty are collectively considered the trigger for the precautionary approach, whereas action is the response to the risk of harm in spite of the uncer-tainty. Actions are taken in accordance with the integrated consideration of the severity of harm and uncertainty as to the likelihood of harm. Actions are formulated in various ways in different instruments: "cost-effective mea-sures",[245] "preventive measures",[246] "conservation and management mea-sures",[247] etc. Based on the strength of the action, scholars have summarized different versions of the precautionary approach.

Wiener categorized the precautionary approach into three main versions.[248] The weak version of the precautionary approach suggests that the absence of complete evidence about a particular risk scenario does not preclude regulation. The common phrasing of this version is that "the lack of full scientific certainty shall not be used as reason for postponing (cost-effective) measures to prevent environmental degradation".[249] The second version suggests that uncertainty justifies action. This is a stronger version of the precautionary approach insofar as it impels proactive actions rather than that it merely rebuts the inaction. The common phrasing of this version is that the precautionary approach should be followed to avoid potentially damaging impacts even before a conclusive causal link between emissions and effects has been established.[250] Proactive actions are, for instance, taken to avoid or reduce potentially damaging impacts of hazardous chemicals.[251] The strong version of the precautionary approach suggests that uncertainty requires shifting the burden and standard of proof. It requires prohibiting the potentially risky activity until the proponents of the activity can prove that it poses no significant risk. Wiener pointed out that, in the first and second versions of the precautionary approach, it is not clear what kind of action should be taken, given the uncertainty.[252]

Sunstein differentiated the precautionary approach into weak and strong versions.[253] The weak version also suggests that a lack of decisive evidence of harm should not be grounds for refusing to regulate. Sunstein referred to the assertion from the Wingspread Consensus Statement on the Precautionary Principle[254] and identified that the strong version of the precautionary approach impels both pre-emptive measures and the reversal of the burden of proof.[255] "When an activity raises threats of harm to human health or the environment, precautionary measures should be taken even if some cause and effect relationships are not fully established scientifically. In this context the proponent of an activity, rather than the public, should bear the burden of proof".[256]

Stewart summarized four versions of the precautionary approach:

1   *Non-preclusion.* Regulation should not be precluded by the absence of scientific certainty about activities that pose a risk of substantial harm.
2   *Margin of Safety.* Regulation should incorporate the maximum "safe" level of an activity (the margin of safety), limiting activities to those below the level at which no adverse effect has been found or predicted.[257]
3   *Best Available Technology.* Activities that present an uncertain potential for significant harm should be subject to best-available technology requirements to minimize the risk of harm, unless the proponents of the activity can show that they present no appreciable risk of harm.
4   *Prohibitions and the Reversal of the Burden of Proof.* This version is the same as Wiener's strong version.

Versions 1 and 2 are weak versions because, unlike Versions 3 and 4, "they do not mandate regulatory action and do not make uncertainty regarding risks an affirmative justification for such regulation".[258]

All the previous regulations and commentaries provide guidance on the applicability of the precautionary approach. First, in the case of potentially irreversible harm to the environment and human health, a (temporary) ban may be necessary. Take some examples from state practice. When commercial whaling posed a risk of causing serious or irreversible harm to living resources, a provisional ban was imposed on it.[259] In order to avoid the further depletion of the ozone layer, precautionary actions have been taken in the form of the phase-out of CFCs "with the ultimate objective of their elimination".[260] In European practices of regulating genetically modified organisms (GMOs), "decisions should be made so as to prevent such activities from being conducted unless and until scientific evidence shows that the damage will not occur".[261] In the case of a worst-case scenario, "even a small amount of doubt as to the safety of that activity is sufficient to stop it taking place" in order to protect the marine environment.[262] The reversal of the burden of proof is always required in such a scenario.

Second, in a context where the risk is less serious or reversible, a ban is not necessary; less restrictive alternatives would be more proportionate. They could be "best available techniques" or "best environmental techniques" to minimize or control the risk of pollution.[263] Measures could be even weaker, such as in the case of new or exploratory activities, where states should adopt cautious conservation and management measures, among others, setting up limits under which the activities are allowed.[264] More frequently, precautionary actions comprise a portfolio of several measures, including environmental impact assessment, economic evaluation, scientific and socio-economic research, and monitoring.[265]

Third, the weak version of the precautionary approach is not without significance.[266] This version is most widely adopted in international environmental conventions and non-binding documents.[267] In some cases, "the right answer may be not to act or at least not to introduce binding legal measures. A wide range of initiatives are available in the case of action, going from a legally binding measure to a research project or a recommendation".[268]

However, both versions of the precautionary approach have been criticized about their utilities in practice. In Sunstein's view, the weak version of the precautionary principle lacks clear guidance for society to respond to threats, and the strong version "stands as an obstacle to regulation and non-regulation, and to everything in between".[269] As regards the weak version, the position that "a lack of decisive evidence of harm should not be ground for refusing to regulate" fails to provide any clear guidance for regulators to decide whether to regulate a risky activity or the use of a hazardous substance with the absence of decisive scientific evidence. As regards the strong version of the precautionary approach, it simultaneously prohibits and permits an activity or the use of a substance, as long as such an activity or a substance may bring both benefits and threats to the society. Well-discussed examples include genetically modified food, nuclear power, pesticides, new medicines and the use of arsenic in drinking water.[270] The strong version of the precautionary approach is therefore considered paralyzing: the restriction of a new technology prevents new risks created by the technology but deprives the society of significant benefit (opportunity benefits); the promotion of a new technology is helpful to ameliorate the target risk but creates substitute risks.[271]

Geoengineering techniques provide another example to which the application of the precautionary approach is problematic. Sections 2.4.2.4 and 2.4.2.5 will address the current application of the precautionary approach to geoengineering addressed by the LP and the CBD, and the problems contained in such a manner of application.

2.4.2.4 *The current application of the precautionary approach to geoengineering*

A temporary ban, or moratorium, was introduced by the LP on marine geoengineering activities (only including ocean fertilization so far) undertaken for non-research purposes (not yet entered into force).[272] This moratorium is an application of the precautionary approach to marine geoengineering techniques. According to the examination of precautionary actions in the previous section, the imposition of a moratorium is a strong version of the precautionary approach. However, it is not the strongest action, as it is not a permanent prohibition and does not require a reversal of the burden of proof.

As stated in Chapter 1, most geoengineering techniques, including all of the six selected geoengineering techniques, have adverse impacts on the environment and natural resources, and are still subject to scientific uncertainties in research and deployment. In 2008, a non-binding ban on ocean fertilization was first imposed by Decision IX/16 of the Conference of Parties to the CBD[273] and subsequently by Resolution LC-LP 1 of the Contracting Parties to the LC/LP.[274]

In May 2008, the COP to the CBD recommended a temporary ban on ocean fertilization. Part C of Decision IX/16 of the 9th Meeting of the COP to the Convention on Biological Diversity:

> [R]*equests* parties and *urges* other Governments, in accordance with the precautionary approach, to ensure that ocean fertilization activities do not take place until there is an adequate scientific basis on which to justify such activities, including assessing associated risks, and a global, transparent and effective control and regulatory mechanism is in place for these activities; with the exception of small scale scientific research studies within coastal waters.[275]

In October 2008, the 13th Meeting of the Contracting Parties to the London Convention and the 3rd Meeting of the Contracting Parties to the London Protocol reaffirmed, in a resolution on the regulation of ocean fertilization, the precautionary approach in CBD COP Decision IX/16. In addition, the Contracting Parties to the LC and the LP agreed that the LC and the LP apply to ocean fertilization activities, and that small-scale scientific research of ocean fertilization should be regarded as placement of matter for a purpose other than the mere disposal thereof under the regulation of "dumping" by the LC and the LP.[276]

Two years later, in 2010, Decision X/33 of the CBD COP was adopted covering all geoengineering activities that are bigger than "small scale scientific research studies" and that may affect biodiversity:[277]

> [I]n the absence of science based, global, transparent and effective control and regulatory mechanisms for geo-engineering, and in accordance with the precautionary approach and Article 14 of the Convention, [. . .] no climate-related geo-engineering activities that may affect biodiversity take place, until there is an adequate scientific basis on which to justify such activities and appropriate consideration of the associated risks for the environment and biodiversity and associated social, economic and cultural impacts, with the exception of small scale scientific research studies that would be conducted in a controlled setting in accordance with Article 3 of the Convention, and only if they are justified by the need to gather specific scientific data and are subject to a thorough prior assessment of the potential impacts on the environment.[278]

On 18 October 2013, the Contracting Parties to the LP adopted an amendment to regulate marine geoengineering. This amendment is the first binding document on geoengineering (but has not yet entered into force). The new Annex 4 provides that all ocean fertilization activities other than those referred to in the definition of ocean fertilization (i.e. small-scale, scientific research studies) shall not be permitted.[279] An ocean fertilization activity may only be considered for a permit if it is assessed as constituting legitimate scientific research after taking into account the specific assessment framework developed for an activity.[280] A new Article 6*bis* states that "Contracting Parties shall not allow the placement of matter into the sea from vessels, aircraft, platforms or other man-made structures at sea for marine geoengineering activities listed in Annex 4, unless the listing provides that the activity or the sub-category of an activity may be authorized under a permit".

The moratoriums regulated under the 2013 Amendments to the LP and the CBD Decisions are problematic in their implementation. Without paying due regard to the distinct characteristics of each technique and the scale of activities, the moratorium on geoengineering under the CBD Decision X/33 is a one-size restriction rather than regulating different techniques in accordance with their distinct features. It may lead to disproportionate precautionary actions, in particular, excessive precautionary actions that may impede legitimate geoengineering activities. With regard to the moratorium on ocean fertilization under the 2013 Amendment to the LP, the phrasing "small scale scientific research" is replaced by "legitimate scientific research", which means the scale of scientific research may not be the decisive factor to determine whether such a research activity is "legitimate".[281] Moreover, both documents stress the risks and uncertainties of geoengineering techniques, but downplay the potential of geoengineering as a precautionary action to combat climate change.[282]

Regarding the current application of the precautionary approach – a strong version – to the geoengineering techniques, two questions are worth discussion:

> *Question 1*: How long should a precautionary action be taken with respect to a particular geoengineering technique?

UNEP urged the application of the precautionary approach on the grounds that "waiting for scientific proof regarding the impacts of pollutants discharged into the marine environment may result in irreversible damage to the marine environment and human suffering".[283] Likewise, the precautionary approach in numerous legal instruments and discourses merely articulates the triggers for a precautionary action, but none of them provides clear criteria to determine the timing for terminating a precautionary action. Once the precautionary approach for geoengineering has been used, for how long should a precautionary action stance be maintained? If not, under what circumstances can we terminate a precautionary action? The common formulations of the timing are "when more scientific information becomes available" or "when better understanding of risk becomes available". These formulations are unclear and lack implementability. Timing is an issue that is closely associated with scientific uncertainty. As discussed before, not all scientific uncertainties involved in geoengineering and climate change are conquerable, and decisions are always made with scientific uncertainty. Hence, in many cases, the moment that an adequate scientific basis is available to justify a hazardous activity may never come.[284] Under such an approach, a hazardous activity would likely never be permitted. The lack of the criteria for terminating a precautionary action, in particular terminating a ban, would unreasonably constrain the legitimate use of geoengineering techniques.

In the absence of scientific certainty, the decision of continuing or terminating a precautionary action could be made in the light of a trade-off analysis, which will be addressed in Chapter 5.

> *Question 2:* How can one balance the benefits and the negative effects of geoengineering?

When considering the implementation of the precautionary approach, not only the risks related to geoengineering techniques but also the contribution made by geoengineering to counteract the serious consequences of climate change should be taken into account.

However, the current precautionary action on geoengineering seems to be very conservative. It can be seen from the decisions of the CBD that stress the risks and uncertainties of geoengineering techniques but overlook the potential of geoengineering as a precautionary action to combat climate change.

Actually, precaution does not necessarily mean prohibition,[285] and excessive bans might hinder a legitimate use of geoengineering. In other words, it is necessary to identify criteria in order to exercise precautionary actions in a proportional way. An uncertain risk does not automatically imply the demand for a ban; the question is what kind of action to take, in a world of intricate uncertainties and multiple risks.

2.4.2.5 *The incoherence of the precautionary approach when applying it to geoengineering*

Section 2.4.2.4 has addressed the current application of the precautionary approach – a strong version – to geoengineering techniques, while the present section will discuss the vagueness of the precautionary approach: how to interpret the incoherent application of the precautionary approach in the context of geoengineering? The simplest justification of applying the precautionary approach is that "safe is better than sorry". However, policymakers have often encountered dilemmas in applying the precautionary approach because it is not clear what is "safe" and what is "sorry". Based on the critiques of the precautionary approach as addressed in Section 2.4.2.3, the application of it to geoengineering appears to be unclear as well.

On the one hand, geoengineering activities can be considered hazardous activities that need to be controlled or even (temporarily) prohibited by precautionary actions due to its scientific uncertainty and the potential harm to the environment and human health. On the other hand, geoengineering techniques *per se* could also be seen as precautionary measures to avoid the potentially irreversible harm of climate change. It might not be safe to use geoengineering because the globe will be under the threat of environmental harm resulting from such a planetary intervention. However, facing the threat of climate change, it might not be safer if we refuse to use geoengineering techniques. This dilemma complicates the application of existing provisions regarding the precautionary approach to geoengineering. For instance, Principle 15 of Rio Declaration could be interpreted as constraining the use of geoengineering when lacking scientific certainty: "Where there are threats of serious or irreversible damages, lack of full scientific certainty [in geoengineering] shall not be used as a reason for postponing cost-effective measures to prevent environmental degradation [caused by geoengineering]".[286] It is understandable and reasonable that geoengineering techniques should be properly regulated and very cautiously implemented.

In contrast, the precautionary approach from Article 3.3 of the UNFCCC should not be interpreted as to restrict the utilization of geoengineering by employing "precautionary measures". As shown in Article 3.3, "precautionary measures" refer to the actions to anticipate, prevent or minimize the cause of climate change and mitigate its adverse effects. Geoengineering is evidently not the cause of climate change; on the contrary, it consists of a host of measures aimed at counteracting climate change. Hence, Article 3.3 should not be applied to restrict geoengineering, because the deployment of geoengineering is consistent with the ultimate objective of the UNFCCC.

To this extent, it seems plausible to treat geoengineering as precautionary measures in the context of Article 3.3: "The Parties should take [geoengineering techniques] to anticipate, prevent or minimize the cause of climate change and mitigate its adverse effects. Where there are threats of serious or irreversible damage, lack of full scientific certainty regarding the extent of potential effects [of using geoengineering techniques] to the environment should not be used as a reason for postponing [the use of geoengineering techniques]". However, Article 3.3 cannot be simply read as supporting geoengineering either. The "and" in the first sentence of Article 3.3 implies that the measures should be able to "anticipate, prevent or minimize the cause of climate change" as well as "mitigat[ing] its adverse effects". Such a reading would argue against the use of the precautionary approach to support the implementation of SRM techniques, because SRM techniques are not aimed at dealing with the cause of climate change. With regard to CDR, whether it is appropriate to treat geoengineering techniques as precautionary measures would depend on the environmental risk introduced by a CDR technique and the scientific uncertainty contained.

The precautionary approach has been widely recognized as an effective tool to deal with risks and scientific uncertainties, but the vagueness of the precautionary approach indeed impedes the effective and optimal implementation of the precautionary approach in the context of geoengineering. However, the "vagueness" could be understood as a kind of "flexibility", which could enable the implementation of the precautionary approach to different geoengineering techniques in a flexible manner, taking into account the risks and scientific uncertainties contained in each technique. A proposal of a clear and effective operationalization of the precautionary approach will be introduced in Chapter 5.

2.5 Conclusion

Chapter 2 has sought to elaborate rules and principles applicable to geoengineering techniques under contemporary international law. No current international framework is explicitly applicable to geoengineering in general, but a number of conventions may apply to all of the six geoengineering techniques identified in Chapter 1. First, the climate change regime provides provisions that support CDR techniques, but the role of SRM remains unclear under the climate change regime. The UNFCCC, the KP, the PA and decisions taken by the COP or CMP could be seen as supporting the use of CDR techniques because such techniques contribute to the achievement of the ultimate objective of the UNFCCC and enhancing the implementation of the UNFCCC. On the contrary, the implementation of SRM does not seem consistent with the ultimate objective of the UNFCCC. However, interpretation of the ultimate objective of the UNFCCC, i.e. whether measures do not aim at mitigation carbon emissions could be counted as measures that aim to "prevent dangerous anthropogenic interference with the climate system" would make the conclusion different. The role of the UNFCCC in the governance of geoengineering will be addressed in Chapter 4. Second, a permanent ban under the ENMOD Convention applies to geoengineering techniques only if they are undertaken for military or hostile purposes to change the climate of another state and have long-lasting, widespread and serious effects.

As long as geoengineering techniques are utilized for peaceful purposes, international law does not prohibit such activities. Those activities are not unfettered but rather subject to the prevention principle and the precautionary approach. States should comply with the prevention principle to deal with the harm and known risks. States should adhere to a host of obligations concerning environmental protection and the reasonable use and conservation of natural resources when they conduct research on or deploy a geoengineering technique. These general obligations will be specified in Chapter 3 in relation to each geoengineering technique.

The precautionary approach applies to geoengineering techniques to deal with unknown risks. Currently, the precautionary approach has been implemented in the form of a moratorium on geoengineering, in particular on ocean fertilization. Pursuant to the moratorium, geoengineering activities are not allowed until an adequate scientific basis is available to justify such activities and to abate and eliminate associated risks to the environment. The moratorium is a strong version of the precautionary approach to preempt a hazardous activity, but it may hinder the legitimate development of new technologies. Taking into account the diversity of different geoengineering techniques and the complexity of the impacts caused by geoengineering on the environment and the climate, it is necessary to identify criteria in order to implement precautionary actions in a proportional way.[287]

The key issue in the discussion of geoengineering is how to deal with all risks from both sides. A balancing between the adverse effects resulting from global warming and those from using geoengineering is challenging. How to weigh the risk of climate change against that of biodiversity loss, ocean acidification and land degradation? Facing this challenge, sound risk assessment with due regard to scientific uncertainties is pivotal. Risk assessment should be exercised in order to compare the scenario of climate change with and without geoengineering. At some point, it might be worthwhile to sacrifice certain ecosystems for the climate stability when a geoengineering technique is proved to be effective and efficient and the adverse effects of such a technique on the environment and human health are not likely to be irreversible. The criteria should be cautiously established.[288]

Notes

1 Kyoto Protocol to the United Nations Framework Convention on Climate Change, Kyoto, adopted 10 December 1997, entered into force 16 February 2005, *United Nations Treaty Series* (2005), vol. 2303, no. 30822, p. 162.
2 Convention on the Prevention of Marine Pollution by Dumping of Wastes and Other Matter, London, adopted 29 December 1972, entered into force 30 August 1975, *United Nations Treaty Series* (1984), vol. 1046, no. 15749, p. 120 (hereafter "London Convention" or "LC").

3   United Nations Convention on the Law of the Sea, Montego Bay, adopted 10 December 1982, entered into force16 November 1994, *United Nations Treaty Series* (1998), vol. 1833, no. 31363, p. 3.

4   "All geoengineering techniques" refer to the six techniques selected in Chapter 1; A technique-by technique research correlates with Sections 1.4 and 1.5 concerning environmental risks of each technique.

5   Here and elsewhere, the term "implementation" refers to local-, regional-, continental- or global-scale geoengineering experimental activities and geoengineering activities for the purpose of counteracting global warming, whereas the term "deployment" only refers to regional-, continental- or global-scale activities for the purpose of counteracting global warming.

6   CBD Technical Series No. 66, 127.

7   UNFCCC, Art. 4.1; See Section 1.3.2.

8   UNFCCC, Art. 4.1(c) & 4.1(g).

9   UNFCCC, Art. 4(c), (d), (e), (f), (h) & (j).

10 UNFCCC, Preamble & Art. 4, para. 1 (f).

11 UNFCCC. Art. 3(3).

12 Bodle, R. (2010–2011). Geoengineering and international law: The search for common legal ground. *Tulsa Law Review*, 46(2), 305–322, at 310.

13 The precautionary principle under the UNFCCC will be further addressed in Section 2.4.2.5.

14 UNFCCC, Arts. 3(1) & 4. This principle is also listed in Principle 7 of Rio Declaration.

15 UNFCCC, Arts. 3(1) & 4.

16 UNFCCC, Arts. 3(1) & 4(2)(a).

17 Reynolds, J. (2014). Climate engineering field research: The favorable setting of international environmental law. *Washington and Lee Journal of Energy, Climate, and the Environment*, 5(2), 417–486, at 439. Here the word "might" implies that it is very difficult for developing countries, especially the most vulnerable countries, to obtain the benefit. It depends on the design and operation of the benefit-sharing mechanism.

18 Reynolds, J. (2014), supra note 17, 441.

19 Winter, G. (2011). Climate engineering and international law: Last resort or the end of humanity? *Review of European Community & International Environmental Law*, 20(3), 277–289, at 288.

20 Scott, K. N. (2012–2013). International law in the Anthropocene: Responding to the geoengineering challenge. *Michigan Journal of International Law*, 34, 309–358, at 331.

21 Kyoto Protocol, Art. 3(3).

22 Pursuant to paragraph C of the Doha Amendment to the KP, the second commitment period is from 2013 to 2020, but the KP will not be terminated on the last day of 2020. According to XIII of the Annex to Decision 27/CMP.1, Procedures and Mechanisms relating to Compliance under the Kyoto Protocol, the default would be for activities relating to the second commitment period of the Kyoto Protocol to continue until the completion of the review of the true-up period reports. In light of this, it is better to keep the projection of KP's termination more open-ended.

23 UNFCCC Decision1/CP.13. Bali Action Plan, UN Doc. FCCC/CP/2007/6/Add.1 (14 March 2008), para. 1(b).

24 Cancun Agreements, para. 4.

25 UNFCCC Decision7/CMP.6. Carbon Dioxide Capture and Storage in Geological Formations as Clean Development Mechanism Project Activities, UN Doc. FCCC/KP/CMP/2010/12/Add.2 (15 March 2011); UNFCCC Decision 10/CMP.7. Modalities and Procedures for Carbon Dioxide Capture and

Storage in Geological Formations as Clean Development Mechanism Project Activities, UN Doc. FCCC/KP/CMP/2011/10/Add.2 (15 March 2012).

26 Paris Agreement, Art. 5.1

27 Intended Nationally Determined Contributions (INDCs) refers to the mitigation contributions that parties to the UNFCCC initiate or intensify towards achieving the objective of the UNFCCC prior to joining the PA.

28 Nationally Determined Contributions (NDCs) refers to the mitigation contributions that all parties to the PA initiate or intensify towards achieving the objective of the UNFCCC.

29 Cancun Agreements, para. 4.

30 The Emissions Gap Report 2015, xvii.

31 Synthesis Report on the Aggregate Effect of the Intended Nationally Determined Contributions, UN Doc. FCCC/CP/2015/7, para. 29. Italic added.

32 See e.g. Farber, D. (2015, 14 December). Does the Paris agreement open the door to geoengineering? Retrieved from http://blogs.berkeley.edu/2015/12/14/ does-the-paris-agreement-open-the-door-to- geoengineering/; Shepherd, J. (2016, 17 February). What does the Paris Agreement mean for geoengineering? Retrieved from http://blogs.royalsociety.org/in-verba/2016/02/17/what-does-the-paris-agreement-mean-for- geoengineering/. Regarding negative emission technologies, see McLaren, D. (2011). Negatonnes – an initial assessment of the potential for negative emission techniques to contribute safely and fairly to meeting carbon budgets in the 21st century. *Report for Friends of the Earth, UK.*

33 Ocean fertilization may disturb the marine ecosystem and cause marine pollution.

34 Paris Agreement, Art. 3.

35 Paris Agreement, Art. 3.

36 UNFCCC Decision 1/CP 21, Adoption of the Paris Agreement, UN Doc. FCCC/CP/2015/10/Add.1, para. 31(c).

37 Paris Agreement, Art. 4.13.

38 According to the IPCC AR5 WGI, global surface temperature changes in the end of the 21st century is likely to exceed 1.5 °C relative to 1850 to 1900 for all RCP scenarios except RCP 2.6. ("RCPs" is short for representative concentration pathways, and RCP 2.6 refers to the emission scenario by 2100 with the most ambitious reductions efforts. See more explanation in IPCC AR5 WGI, Glossary, RCPs).

39 Paris Agreement, Art. 4.1. Italic added.

40 As stated in the second paragraph of Section 2.2.1.

41 Convention on the Prohibition of Military or Any Hostile Use of Environmental Modification Techniques, New York, adopted 10 December 1976, entered into force 5 October 1978, *United Nations Treaty Series* (1986), vol. 1108, no. 17119, p. 151. Bodansky, D. (1996). May We Engineer the Climate? Climate Change, 33, 309–321.

42 ENMOD, Annex, Understanding relating to article II.

43 "Understanding relating to article II" states that the examples listed are not exhaustive. Therefore, other geoengineering techniques might also be taken into account if the intervention is great enough to "change the dynamics, composition or structure of the Earth".

44 ENMOD Convention, Arts. I & II.

45 ENMOD Convention, Preamble.

46 ENMOD Convention, Art. III (1) I & Understanding relating to article III.

47 ENMOD Convention, Art. III (2).

48 Winter, G. (2011), supra note 19, 280.

49 E.g. The definition of the global commons is introduced in Section 2.4.1.3(ii); Draft Articles on Prevention of Transboundary Harm from Hazardous Activities,

adopted by the International Law Commission at its fifty-third session, 2001, *Official Records of the General Assembly*, Fifty-sixth Session, Supplement No. 10 (A/56/10), Art. 2(c) (hereafter "2001 Draft Articles on Prevention").

50　E.g. Convention on Long-Range Transboundary Air Pollution, Geneva, adopted 13 November 1979, entered into force 16 March 1983, *United Nations Treaty Series* (1992), vol. 1302, no. 21623, p. 217, Art. 1(b).

51　*Trail Smelter Case (United States v. Canada)*, 16 April 1938 and 11 March 1941, Report of International Arbitral Awards, vol. III, pp. 1905–1982.

52　E.g. International conventions: CBD, Art. 3; UNCLOS, Art. 194. 1992 Convention on the Protection and Use of Transboundary Watercourses and International Lakes, Art. 3. Regional conventions: ASEAN (Association of Southeast Asian Nations) Agreement on the Conservation of Nature and Natural Resources, Kuala Lumpur, adopted 9 July 1985, not yet entered into force, Art. 20. Retrieved from http://environment.asean.org/agreement-on-the-conservation-of-nature-and-natural-resources/; Convention on the Protection of the Rhein, Berne, adopted 12 April 1999, entered into force 1 January 2013, Art.4. Retrieved from http://www.iksr.org/en/international-cooperation/legal-basis/convention/index.html Non-binding legal instruments: UNGA, Development and International Economic Co-operation: Environment, Report of the World Commission on Environment and Development: Our Common Future, UN Doc. A/42/427 (4 August 1987), Annex 1: Summary of Proposed Legal Principles for Environmental Protection and Sustainable Development Adopted by the WCED Experts Group on Environmental Law, para. 10 (hereafter "Our Common Future, Annex 1"); Convention on the Law of the Non-navigational Uses of International Watercourses, adopted 21 May 1997, entered into force 17 August 2014, UN Doc. A/51/49 (vol. III) (UNTS volume number has not yet been determined), Art. 7.

53　*Trail Smelter Case*, pp. 1965.

54　*The Corfu Channel Case (United Kingdom of Great Britain and Northern Ireland v. Albania)*, Judgment of 9 April 1949, ICJ Reports, 1949, p. 4, at p. 22.

55　Ibid.

56　*Lac Lanoux (France/Spain)*, Report of International Arbitral Awards, 16 November 1957, vol. XII, pp. 281–317, p. 27. (Here and below, the page number is based on the translated version of this case (from French to English), which is available on ECOLEX: www.ecolex.org/.)

57　1972 Stockholm Declaration of the United Nations Conference on the Human Environment. See also: Rio Declaration on Environment and Development, Principle 2.

58　Examples of Conventions: Art. 3 of the CBD; Art. 194(2) of the UNCLOS. Examples of academic literatures: Birnie, P., Boyle, A., & Redgwell, C. (2009). *International law & the environment* (3rd ed.). Oxford: Oxford University Press, 143; Lefeber, R. (1996). *Transboundary Environmental Interference and the Origin of State Liability* (1st ed.). The Hague: Kluwer Law International, 23.

59　*Legality of the Threat or Use of Nuclear Weapons*, Advisory Opinion of 8 July 1996, ICJ Reports 1996 (I), pp. 241–242, para. 29.

60　*In the Matter of the Indus Waters Kishenganga Arbitration (The Islamic Republic of Pakistan vs. The Republic of India)*, Partial Award, The Permanent Court of Arbitration,18 February 2013, para. 448–454.

61　*Case Concerning Pulp Mills on the River Uruguay (Argentina v. Uruguay)*, Judgment of 20 April 2010, ICJ Reports 2010, p. 14.

62　In exceptional circumstances "zero transboundary impact" might be appropriate. An example is groundwater. Due to the special vulnerability of groundwater, a "zero tolerance threshold" ought to inform a state's obligation to avoid transboundary effects. Bodansky, D., Brunnée, J., & Hey, E. (Eds.). (2008). *The*

Oxford handbook of international environmental law (1st ed.). Oxford: Oxford University Press, 535.

63 Environment, Justitia et Pace Institut de Droit International, Session of Strasbourg, 1997. Art.9. See also Our Common Future, Annex 1, para. 10; Convention on the Protection and use of Transboundary Watercourses and International Lakes, Art. 1(2); Convention on the Law of the Non-navigational Uses of International Watercourses, Art. 7.

64 *Trail Smelter Case*, pp. 1965. Italic added.

65 *Trail Smelter Case*, pp. 1964.

66 Convention on the Transboundary Effects of Industrial Accidents, Helsinki, adopted 17 March 1992, entered into force 19 April 2000, *United Nations Treaty Series* (2002), vol. 2105, no. 36605, p. 457, Art. 1 (d). Italic added.

67 Draft Articles on Prevention of Transboundary Harm from Hazardous Activities, with commentaries, *Yearbook of the International Law Commission*, 2001, vol. II, Part Two, Article 2, Commentary (4) (hereafter "2001 Draft Articles on Prevention, with commentaries").

68 Knox, J. H. (2002). The myth and reality of transboundary environmental impact assessment. *American Journal of International Law*, 96(2), 291–319, at 294.

69 2001 Draft Articles on Prevention, with Commentaries, Art. 2, Commentary (4).

70 UNEP/GC Decision 6/14. Principles of Conduct for the Guidance of States in the Conservation and Harmonious Exploitation of Natural Resources Shared by Two or More States, 19 May 1978. *UNEP Environmental Law Guidelines and Principles Series, no. 2.*

71 2001 Draft Articles on Prevention, Art. 2.

72 Bodansky, D., Brunnée, J., & Hey, E. (Eds.). (2008), supra note 62, 536.

73 Ibid. For instance, Annex I and II of the 1998 Aarhus Protocol on Persistent Organic Pollutants (POPs), as amended on 18 December 2009, list the substances scheduled for elimination and restricted on use respectively. It could be seen as an example of establishing different technical standards for substances that contain different levels of harm.

74 Commission of the European Communities, Communication from the Commission on the Precautionary Principle, Brussels, 2000, COM (2000)1, 18

75 2001 Draft Articles on Prevention, with commentaries, Art. 2 Commentary (4).

76 Second Report on International Liability for Injurious Consequences Arising out of Acts Not Prohibited by International Law (Prevention of Transboundary Damage from Hazardous Activities) by Pemmaraju Screenivasa Rao, Special Rapporteur, UN Doc. A/CN.4/501 (5 May 1999), para. 18.

77 Convention on the Law of the Non-navigational Use of International Watercourses, Art. 7.

78 *Case Concerning Pulp Mills on the River Uruguay*, para. 178.

79 Ibid., para. 187.

80 Ibid., para. 204. Kiss, A., & Shelton, D. hold the same idea. Kiss, A., & Shelton, D. (2007). *Guide to international environmental law* (1st ed.). Leiden: Martinus Nijhoff Publishers, 92.

81 2001 Draft Articles on Prevention, with commentaries, Art. 3, Commentary (7).

82 Birnie, P., Boyle, A., & Redgwell, C. (2009), supra note 58, 149.

83 *Responsibilities and Obligations of States Sponsoring Persons and Entities With Respect to Activities in the Area*. Advisory Opinion of 1 February 2011, Seabed Dispute Chamber of the International Tribunal for the Law of the Sea (hereafter "ITLOS Advisory Opinion on Activities in the Area"), para. 117.

84 Ibid., para. 220.

85 *Case Concerning Pulp Mills on the River Uruguay*, 220.

86 Convention for the Protection of the Marine Environment of the North-East Atlantic, Paris, adopted 22 September 1992, entered into force 25 March 1998, *United Nations Treaty Series* (2009), vol. 2354, no. 42279, p. 27, Appendix 1 (hereafter "OSPAR Convention", "OS" for Oslo and "PAR" for Paris); UNCLOS, Art. 194(1) "best practical means". See also other examples: Antarctic Treaty, Art. III(1); Convention on the Protection of Marine Environment of the Baltic Sea Area, Helsinki, 1992, entered into force 17 January 2000. Retrieved from www.helcom.fi/about-us/convention/ (hereafter "1992 Helsinki Convention (Baltic Sea Area)"), Annex II, Regulation 2.

87 MVOTMA is an acronym for "Ministerio de Vivienda, Ordenamiento Territorialy MedioAmbiente (Uruguay Ministry of Housing, Land-use Planning and Environmental Affairs)".

88 Lefeber, R. (1996), supra note 58, 65.

89 Lefeber, R. (1996), supra note 58, 68; ILC, Second Report on International Liability for Injurious Consequences Arising Out of Acts Not Prohibited by International Law (Prevention of Transboundary Damage from Hazardous Activities) by Pemmaraju Screenivasa Rao, Special Rapporteur, *Yearbook of the International Law Commission*, vol. II, Part One, 1999, 121.

90 As to the precautionary approach, see Section 2.4.2.

91 ITLOS Advisory Opinion on Activities in the Area, para. 131.

92 *Southern Bluefin Tuna Case (New Zealand v. Japan; Australia v. Japan)*, Request for provisional measures, International Tribunal for the Law of the Sea, Order of 27 August 1999, para. 77.

93 Ibid., para. 79; ITLOS Advisory Opinion on Activities in the Area, para. 132.

94 Lefeber, R. (1996), supra note 58, 30.

95 Ibid., 26.

96 Ibid.

97 *Case Concerning the Gabčikovo-Nagymaros Project (Hungary/Slovakia)*, Judgment of 25 September 1997, ICJ Reports 1997, p. 7, para. 78.

98 *Case Concerning the Gabcikovo-Nagymaros Project*, para. 86.

99 Lefeber, R. (1996), supra note 58, 27; Our Common Future, Annex 1, para. 12; Draft articles on the law of the non-navigational uses of international watercourses and commentaries thereto and resolution on transboundary confined groundwater 1994, *Yearbook of the International Law Commission* 1994, vol. II, Part Two, commentary on Article 7; 1997 Convention on the Law of Non-navigational Uses of International Watercourses, Art. 7.2.

100 E.g. Convention on the Law of Non-navigational Uses of International Watercourses. Art. 7.2.

101 For further discussion, see Section 2.4.1.5(ii)(b) and Chapter 5.

102 Xue, H. (2003). *Transboundary damage in international law* (Vol. 27). New York: Cambridge University Press, 192–193.

103 The atmosphere is a global commons. In the absence of an international regime regulating use of the atmospheric commons, no nation will have an adequate incentive to limit its own use because it will have no assurance that others will do likewise. Stward, R. B., & Wiener, J. B. (1992). The comprehensive approach to global climate policy: Issues of design and practicality. *Arizona Journal of International & Comparative Law, 9*, 83.

104 This statement refers to general cases. However, there is an exception that International Seabed Authority (ISA) may act to represent the deep seabed on behalf of the international community as a whole.

105 Brunnée, J. (2007). International law and collective concerns: Reflections on the responsibility to protect. In Ndiaye, T. M. & Wolfrum, R. (Eds.). (2007). *Law of the sea, environmental law and settlement of disputes: Liber Amicorum Judge Thomas A. Mensah* (pp. 35–52). Leiden: Martinus Nijhoff Publishers, 35.

106 *Case Concerning the Gabčikovo – Nagymaros Project*, Separate opinion of Vice-President Weeramantry, Part C(c).
107 E. g, the UNFCCC, the UNCLOS, the Convention of the High Seas, the LC/LP, the Vienna Convention and its Montreal Protocol, and the CLRTAP.
108 Bodansky, D., Brunnée, J., & Hey, E. (Eds.). (2008), supra note 62, 556.
109 *Nuclear Tests (Australia v. France)*, Joint dissenting opinion of Judges Onyeama, Dillard, Jiménez de Aréchaga and Waldock, para. 118.
110 *Nuclear Tests (Australia v. France)*, Dissenting opinions of Judge de Castro, 390.
111 Draft Articles on Responsibilities of States for Internationally Wrongful Acts, with commentaries, *Yearbook of the International Law Commission*, 2001, vol. II, Part Two, Art. 48.2.
112 Ibid., Art. 54, commentary (6). "Countermeasures" refer to the measures directed against "a State which has committed an internationally wrongful act, and which has not complied with its obligations of cessation and reparation". Art. 49, commentary (4).
113 Ibid.
114 See further discussions in Chapter 5.
115 Draft Principles on the Allocation of Loss in the Case of Transboundary Harm Arising Out of Hazardous Activities, *Yearbook of the International Law Commission*, 2006, vol. II, Part Two, Principle 2.
116 2001 Draft Articles on Prevention, with commentaries, Art. 2, Commentary (2); Kiss, A., & Shelton, D. (2007), supra note 80, 117.
117 2001 Draft Articles on Prevention, with commentaries, Art. 7, Commentary (9).
118 Lefeber, R. (1996), supra note 58, 30.
119 Ibid., 31.
120 *Lac Lanoux (France/Spain)*, 18.
121 Ibid., 26.
122 Ibid., 27.
123 Ibid., 24, para. 13.
124 Ibid., 12 below.
125 *The MOX Plant Case (Ireland/ United Kingdom)*, Request for provisional measures, International Tribunal for the Law of the Sea, Order of 3 December, 2001. Paras, 26, 72 & 89.
126 EIA was first adopted in the US National Environmental Policy Act in 1969, then grew steadily throughout the world. Craik N. (2008). *The international law of environmental impact assessment, process, substance and integration.* Cambridge: Cambridge University Press, 2008, 23; Birnie, P., Boyle, A., & Redgwell, C. (2009), supra note 58, 165.
127 *Case Concerning Pulp Mills on the River Uruguay*, para. 204; ITLOS Advisory Opinion on Activities in the Area, para. 148.
128 *Certain Activities Carried Out by Nicaragua in the Border Area (Costa Rica v. Nicaragua) and Construction of a Road in Costa Rica along the San Juan River (Nicaragua v. Costa Rica)*, Judgment, International Court of Justice, 16 December 2015, pp. 100–105 & 146–162.
129 Ibid., para. 104.
130 For instance, CBD Art 14; ASEAN Agreement, Art. 20 (3) (a); 1992 Helsinki Convention (Baltic Sea Area), Art. 7; Convention for the Protection and Development of the Marine Environment of the Wider Caribbean Region, adopted 24 March 1983, entered into force 11 October 1986, *United Nations Treaty Series* (1997), vol. 1506, no. 25974, p. 157, Art.12; Convention for the Co-operation in the Protection and Development of the Marine and Coastal Environment of the West and Central African Region (Abidjan Convention), Abidjan, adopted in 1981, entered into force 5 August 1984, Art. 13. Retrieved from http://abidjanconvention.org/index.php; The Framework Convention

on the Protection and Sustainable Development of the Carpathians (Carpathian Convention), Kyiv, adopted May 2003, entered into force January 2006, Art. 5. Retrieved from www.carpathianconvention.org/; Convention for the Protection of the Natural Resources and Environment of the South Pacific Region (SPREP Convention), Noumea, adopted 24 November 1986, entered into force 22 August 1990, Art.16. Retrieved from www.sprep.org/legal/the-convention#text

131 Convention on Environmental Impact Assessment in a Transboundary Context (Espoo Convention), Espoo, adopted 25 February 1991, entered into force 10 September 1997, *United Nations Treaty Series* (1997), vol. 1989, no. 34028, p. 309, Article 1(vi). EIA is also defined as "an examination, analysis and assessment" in UNEP Goals and Principles of Environmental Impact Assessment. Retrieved from www.unep.org/regionalseas/publications/reports/RSRS/pdfs/rsrs122.pdf

132 CBD, Art.14.1 (a).

133 CBD Decision VI/7, Identification, monitoring, indicators and assessments, UNEP/CBD/COP/6/20, Annex 1 (b).

134 ITLOS Advisory Opinion on Activities in the Area, para. 148.

135 Resolution LC-LP.2 (2010) on the Assessment Framework for Scientific Research Involving Ocean Fertilization, adopted on 14 October 2010, not yet into force. Retrieved from www.imo.org/en/OurWork/Environment/LCLP/EmergingIssues/geoengineering/Documents/O FassessmentResolution.pdf

136 Vienna Convention for the Protection of the Ozone Layer, Vienna, adopted March 1985, entered into force 22 September 1988, *United Nations Treaty Series* (1997), vol. 1513, no. 26164, p. 293.

137 Referring to, among others, Espoo Convention; Antarctic Environment Protocol; Resolution LC-LP.2 (2010); and new Annex 5 of the LP under Resolution LP.4(8) on the Amendment to the London Protocol to Regulate the Placement of Matter for Ocean Fertilization and Other Marine Geoengineering Activities.

138 UNEP Goals and Principles of Environmental Impact Assessment, January 16 1987, Principle 1.

139 2001 Draft Articles on Prevention, with commentaries, Art. 7, Commentary (9).

140 Protocol on Environmental Protection to the Antarctic Treaty, Madrid, adopted 4 October 1991, entered into force 14 January 1998. (UNTC volume number has not yet been determined), Art. 8 & AnnexII. Retrieved from https://treaties.un.org/doc/Publication/UNTS/No%20Volume/5778/A-5778-0800 00028006ab63.pdf

141 Espoo Convention, Appendix II (h).

142 See Section 2.4.1.5(i)(b) concerning the obligations to notify, exchange information and consult with potentially affected states.

143 CBD Decision VIII/28 on Impact Assessment. Annex: Voluntary Guidelines on Biodiversity-inclusive Impact Assessment, UN Doc. UNEP/CBD/COP/DEC/VIII/28 (15 June 2006), para. 5.

144 Ibid. See Section 2.4.1.5 (ii)(a) concerning the obligation to monitor activities.

145 Abaza, H., Bisset, R., & Sadler, B. (2004). *Environmental impact assessment and strategic environmental assessment: towards an integrated approach.* UNEP/Earthprint, 86. Retrieved from www.unep.ch/etu/publications/text ONUbr.pdf

146 Directive 2001/42/EC on the assessment of the effects of certain plans and programmes on the environment, *Official Journal of the European Communities*, L 197/30 (21 July 2001); Protocol on Strategic Environmental Assessment to the Convention on Environmental Impact Assessment in a Transboundary Context, Kiev, 21 May 2003, *United Nations Treaty Series* (2010), vol. 2685, no. 34028, p. 140.

147 Protocol on Strategic Environmental Assessment to the Convention on Environmental Impact Assessment in a Transboundary Context, Art. 5.

148 Ibid., Art. 6.
149 Abaza, H., Bisset, R., & Sadler, B. (2004), supra note 145, 86.
150 Ibid.
151 Espoo Convention, Art. 3.
152 1992 Helsinki Convention (the Baltic Sea Area), Article 13.
153 *Case Concerning Pulp Mills on the River Uruguay*, paras. 112 & 120. Italic added.
154 See Section 2.4.1.5(ii).
155 2001 Draft Articles on Prevention, Art. 17. See also: Convention on the Law of the Non-navigational Uses of International Watercourses, 1997, Art. 28; CBD Art. 14 (d); UNCLOS, Art.198.
156 *The Corfu Channel Case*, p. 22–23.
157 The scope of the information is interpreted in different ways. Article 13 of the Convention on the Protection and Use of Transboundary Watercourses and International Lakes addresses it as "reasonably available data"; Article 17 of the CBD states "all publicly available sources"; Article 13 of the Convention on the Law of the Non-navigational Uses of International Watercourses provides "readily available data and information"; Article 12 of the 2001 Draft Articles on Prevention expresses the scope as "all available information concerning that activity"; Article 199 of the UNCLOS stipulates "information and data acquired about pollution of the marine environment".
158 CBD, Art.17 (2).
159 International Law Association, The Helsinki Rules on the Uses of the Waters of International Rivers, Helsinki, adopted in August 1966, International Law Association, Report of the fifty-second Conference, 477. Art. XXIX. "[E]ach basin State furnish relevant and reasonable available information. . . "; International Law Association Berlin Conference, Water Resources Law, Fourth Report, 2004, Art. 56.
160 Convention on the Law of the Non-navigational Uses of International Watercourses, Art. 9.
161 Convention on the Protection and Use of Transboundary Watercourses and International Lakes, Helsinki, adopted 17 March 1992, entered into force 6 October 1996, *United Nations Treaty Series* (2001), vol. 1936, no. 33207, p. 209, Arts. 6 &13.
162 The CLRTAP, Art. 8.
163 Ibid., Art.13 (4). Similar obligation can be found in the Antarctic Treaty, Art. III (1): In order to promote international cooperation in scientific investigation in Antarctica . . . to the greatest extent feasible and practicable.
164 Espoo Convention, Art. 5; 2001 Draft Articles on Prevention, Art. 9; Montreal Guidelines for the Protection of the Marine Environment Against Pollution from Land-Based Sources, Decision 13/18/II of the Governing Council of UNEP, 24 May 1985, 15.
165 Espoo Convention, Art. 5; 2001 Draft Articles on Prevention, with commentaries, Art. 9, commentary (1).
166 1992 Convention on the Protection and Use of Transboundary Watercourses and International Lakes, Art. 9; Espoo Convention, Art. 5.
167 *North Sea Continental Shelf (Federal Republic of Germany v. Denmark; Federal Republic of Germany v. Netherlands)*, Judgment of 20 February 1969, ICJ Reports 1969, p. 3, para. 85.
168 *Lac Lanoux (France/Spain)*, 12.
169 2001 Draft Articles on Prevention, Art. 9(2); *Lac Lanoux (France/Spain)*, 22.
170 2001 Draft Articles on Prevention, with commentaries, Art.10 and the commentary.
171 Birnie, P., Boyle, A., & Redgwell, C. (2009), supra note 58, 178.
172 2001 Draft Articles on Prevention, with commentaries, Art. 6, Commentary (1).

173 2001 Draft Articles on Prevention, Art. 7.
174 *The MOX Plant Case*, para. 26.
175 Ibid., para. 89.
176 Directive 2009/31/EC of the European Parliament and of the Council, on the geological storage of carbon dioxide and amending Council Directive 85/337/EEC, European Parliament and Council Directives 2000/60/EC, 2001/80/EC, 2004/35/EC, 2006/12/EC, 2008/1/EC and Regulation (EC) No. 1013/2006, *Official Journal of the European Union*, I.140/114 (5 June 2009), Chapters 2 & 3.
177 Our Common Future, Annex 1, para. 4.
178 Sands, P., Peel, J., & MacKenzie, R. (2012). *Principles of international environmental law* (3rd ed.). Cambridge: Cambridge University Press, 215; Rio Declaration, Principles 3 & 4.
179 *Case Concerning the Gabcikovo-Nagymaros Project*, para. 140; see also *Award in the Arbitration regarding the Iron Rhine ("Ijzeren Rijn") Railway (the Kingdom of Belgium v. the Kingdom of the Netherlands)*, Decision of 24 May 2005, Reports of International Arbitral Awards, volume XXVII, pp. 35–125, para. 59.
180 *Trail Smelter Arbitration*, pp. 1939.
181 See also the *MOX Plant Case*.
182 2001 Draft Articles on Prevention, Art. 9 (2).
183 See also Lefeber, R. (1996), supra note 58, 35: "Relevant factors include the nature of the activity (degree of hazardousness), the nature of potentially affected interests (sensitivity of interests), the nature and the expected value of the potential harm (technical capability and costs of cleaning up), and the cost of prevention and abatement."
184 Espoo Convention, Art. 7.
185 Ibid.
186 Wiener, J. B. (2008). Precaution. In Bodansky, D., Brunnée, J., & Hey, E.(Eds.), *The Oxford handbook of international law* (pp. 597–612). Oxford: Oxford University Press.
187 It is widely agreed that the precautionary principle originated from the German concept of *Vorsorgeprinzip*. Cameron, J., & Abouchar, J. (1991). The precautionary principle: A fundamental rinciple of law and policy for the protection of the global environment. *Boston College International and Comparative Law Review, 14*(1), 1; Wiener, J. B. (2008). supra note 186, 599–600; Hammitt, J. K., Wiener, J. B., Swedlow, B., Kall, D., & Zhou, Z. (2005). Precautionary regulation in Europe and the United States: A quantitative comparison. *Risk Analysis, 25*(5), 1215–1228. doi:10.1111/j.1539–6924.2005.00662.x
188 E.g. UNFCCC, Art. 3; 1992 Helsinki Convention (Baltic Sea area), Art. 3(2); London Protocol, Art. 3(1);1994 Protocol to the 1979 Convention on Long-range Transboundary Air Pollution on Further Reduction of Sulphur Emissions, Preamble; 1998 Protocol to the 1979 Convention on Long-Range Transboundary Air Pollution on Heavy Metals, Preamble; CBD, Art. 3; 2000 Cartagena Protocol on Biosafety, Arts. 1, 10(6) & 11(8).
189 Marchant, G. E., & Mossman, K. L. (2005). *Arbitrary and capricious: The precautionary principle in the European Union Courts* (1st ed.). Washington, DC: The AEI Press, 1.
190 ITLOS Advisory Opinion on Activities in the Area, para. 135; Cameron, J., & Abouchar, J. (1991), supra note 187; Trouwborst, A. (2002). *Evolution and status of the precautionary principle in international law*. The Hague: Kluwer Law International, 34.
191 Wiener, J. B., & Rogers, M. D. (2002). Comparing precaution in the United States and Europe. *Journal of Risk Research, 5*(4), 317–349, at 343.
192 Marchant, G. E., & Mossman, K. L. (2005), supra note 189, 10.
193 Commission of the European Communities, Communication from the Commission on the Precautionary Principle, Brussels, 2000, COM (2000)1, 17.

194   E.g. CBD Preamble; 1990 Bergen Declaration, para. 6; Rio Declaration, Principle 15.
195   E.g. Ministerial Declaration of the Third International Conference on the Protection of the North Sea, The Hague, 8 March 1990, Preamble.
196   E.g., London Protocol, Art. 3.
197   ILA Resolution No. 7/2012, Annex: 2012 Sofia Guiding Statements on the Judicial Elaboration of the 2002 New Delhi Declaration of Principles of International Law Relating to Sustainable Development, para. 7.
198   Bodansky, D. (1995); In paragraph 9 of the *Separate Opinion of Judge Treves* to the Order of the International Tribunal for the Law of the Sea in the *Southern Bluefin Tuna Case*, Judge Treves also opines that "in order to resort to the precautionary approach for assessing the urgency of the measures to be prescribed in the present case, it is not necessary to hold the view that this approach is dictated by a rule of customary international law".
199   For a list of various formulations of the precautionary approach, see Sandin, P. (1999). Dimensions of the precautionary principle. *Human and Ecological Risk Assessment: An International Journal, 5*(5), 889–907, at 902–905. Examples of legal instruments: Principle 15 of the Rio Declaration; ILA New Delhi Declaration of Principles of International Law Relating to Sustainable Development (ILA New Delhi Declaration below), 2 April 2002. Examples of academic publications: Matthee, M., & Vermersch, D. (2000). Are the precautionary principle and the international trade of genetically modified organisms reconcilable? *Journal of Agricultural and Environmental Ethics, 12*(1), 59–70, at 61; Freestone, D., & Hey, E. (Eds.). (1996). *The precautionary principle and international law: The challenge of implementation.* The Hague: Kluwer Law International, 45; Trouwborst, A. (2006). *Precautionary rights and duties of states.* Leiden: Martinus Nijhoff Publishers, 4.
200   Sandin, P. (1999), supra note 199.
201   Cameron, J., & Abouchar, J. (1991), supra note 187, 22.
202   United Nations Agreement for the Implementation of the Provisions of the United Nations Convention on the Law of the Sea of 10 December 1982 Relating to the Conservation and Management of Straddling Fish stocks and Highly Migratory Fish Stocks, entered into force 11 December 2011, UN Doc. A/CONF.164/37 (8 September 1995), Art. 5(c) (hereafter "1995 Agreement on Straddling and Highly Migratory Fish Stocks"). Italic added.
203   Protocol to the 1979 Convention on Long-range Transboundary Air Pollution on Persistent Organic Pollutants, Aarhus, adopted 26 April 1998, entered into force 23 October 2003, *United Nations Treaty Series* (2004), vol. 2230, no. 21623, p. 79. Annex V, Best Available Techniques to Control Emissions of Persistent Organic Pollutants from Major Stationaer Sources, para. 2.
204   See e.g. Trouwborst, A. (2002), supra note 190, 5.
205   Birnie, P., Boyle, A., & Redgwell, C. (2009), supra note 58, 155.
206   Separate Opinion of Judge Laing to the Order of the International Tribunal for the Law of the Sea in the *Southern Bluefin Tuna Case (New Zealand v. Japan; Australia v. Japan)*, Requests for provisional measures, 27 August, 1999, para. 19.
207   Birnie, P., Boyle, A., & Redgwell, C. (2009), supra note 58, 155.
208   See Section 5.5.
209   Communication from the Commission on the Precautionary Principle (2000), supra note 193, 13–14.
210   Cameron, J., & Wade-Gery, W. (1995). Law, policy and the development of the precautionary principle. *Environmental Policy in Search of New Instruments*, 95.
211   ILA New Delhi Declaration of Principles of International Law Relating to Sustainable Development, *Netherlands International Law Review, 49*(2), 211–216.

212 UNECE, Ministerial Declaration on Sustainable Development in the ECE Region, Bergen, May 1990, para. 7.

213 Ministerial Declaration of the Third International Conference on the Protection of the North Sea, The Hague, 8 March 1990, Preamble.

214 Ministerial Declaration of the Second International Conference on the Protection of the North Sea, London, 24–25 November 1987, para. VII.

215 Cameron, J., & Wade-Gery, W (1995). Addressing uncertainty: Law, policy and the development of the precautionary principle. In Dente, B. (Ed). *Environmental Policy in Search of New Instruments* (pp. 95–142). Dordrecht: Springer.

216 Trouwborst, A. (2006), supra note 199, 50.

217 *Concise Oxford Dictionary.* Referring to Trouwborst, A. (2006), supra note 199, 50, footnote 82.

218 Trouwborst, A. (2006), supra note 199, 50.

219 ILC, Draft Articles on the law of the non-navigational uses of international watercourses and commentaries thereto and resolution on transboundary confined groundwater, 1994. Commentary to Art. 3, paras. 13–15.

220 ILC, 2001 Draft Articles on Prevention, with commentaries, Commentary to Article2(a). See Section 2.4.1.1.

221 Trouwborst, A. (2006), supra note 199, 27.

222 The wording "damaging" apparently presents a degree higher than "trivial".

223 The issue of uncertainty will be further examined in Section 2.4.2.2(b).

224 Trouwborst, A. (2006), supra note 199, 62. See Section 5.5.2 relating to the threshold for implementing the precautionary approach to geoengineering.

225 Gündling, L. (1990). Status in international law of the principle of precautionary action, *International Law Journal of Estuarine & Coastal Law*, 5, 23.

226 Gündling, L. (1990), 26.

227 Sandin, P. (1999), supra note 199, 895.

228 These two terms are interchangeable.

229 These two terms are interchangeable.

230 See Section 5.5.2.

231 De Chazournes, L. B. (2007). Precaution in international law: Reflection on its composite nature. In Ndiaye, T. M. & Wolfrum, R. (Eds.). (2007). *Law of the sea, environmental law and settlement of disputes: Liber Amicorum Judge Thomas A. Mensah* (pp. 21–34). Leiden: Martinus Nijhoff Publishers, 22; ILA, Legal Principles Relating to Climate Change, Draft Articles, Art. 7B.

232 Ibid.; Trouwborst, A. (2006), supra note 199, 118.

233 Communication from the Commission on the Precautionary Principle (2000), supra note 193, 9.

234 Sandin, P. (1999), supra note 199, 892.

235 Rio Declaration, Art. 15.

236 E.g. Ministerial Declaration of the Second International Conference on the Protection of the North Sea, London, 1987, para. VII; Ministerial Declaration of the Third International Conference on the Protection of the North Sea, The Hague, 1990, Preamble.

237 Trouwborst, A. (2007). The precautionary principle in general international law: Combating the Babylonian confusion. *Review of European Community & International Environmental Law*, 16(2), 185–195.

238 Trouwborst, A. (2006), supra note 199, 71.

239 Communication from the Commission on the Precautionary Principle, supra note 193, 14.

240 Trouwborst, A. (2006), supra note 199, 72, referring to, *inter alia*, UK Department of the Environment, Transport and the Regions, Guidelines for Environmental Risk Assessment and Management: Revised Department Guidance, 2000, para. 1.6.

241 Trouwborst, A. (2006), supra note 199, 72.
242 Ibid.
243 Trouwborst, A. (2006), supra note 199, 77.
244 Trouwborst, A. (2006), supra note 199, 117.
245 Rio Declaration, Principle 15; 1990 Bergen Declaration, para. 6.
246 OSPAR Convention, Art. 2(2)(a).
247 1995 Agreement on Straddling and Highly Migratory Fish Stock, Art 6 (2).
248 Wiener, J. B., & Rogers, M. D. (2002), supra note 191, 320–321.
249 Under the Rio Declaration and the UNFCCC, "measures" should be "cost-effective".
250 Examples: Ministerial Declaration of Second International Conference on Protection of the North Sea, London, 24–25 November 1987, para. VII; 1992 Helsinki Convention (Baltic Sea area), Art. 3.2; OSPAR Convention, Art.2(2) (a).
251 Protocol to the 1979 Convention on Long-range Transboundary Pollution on Persistent Organic Pollutants, Annex V, para. 2.
252 Wiener, J. B., & Rogers, M. D. (2002), supra note 191, 321.
253 Sunstein, C. R. (2003). Beyond the precautionary principle. *University of Pennsylvania Law Review, 151*(3), 1003–1058.
254 Wingspread conference refers to a conference took place in Wingspread, the U.S. in January 1998 where 32 participants from the U.S., Canada and Europe reached an agreement on the necessity of the precautionary principle in public health and environmental decision-making.
255 The Wingspread Consensus Statement on the Precautionary Principle, Wingspread conference on the precautionary principle, 26 January 1998. Retrieved from www.sehn.org/wing.html
256 Ibid.
257 See also, Trouwborst, A. (2006), supra note 199, 169. (The use of safety margins in the implementation of the precautionary approach with regard to the exploitation of living natural resources.)
258 Stewart, R. B. (2002). Environmental regulatory decision-making under uncertainty. *Research in Law and Economics, 20*, 71–126.
259 International Whaling Commission, International Convention for the Regulation of Whaling, Washington, adopted 2 December 1946, 10 November 1948, as amended by the Commission at the 64 Annual Meeting, Panama City, July 2012, para. 6.
260 Montreal Protocol on Substances that Deplete the Ozone Layer, Montreal, adopted 16 September 1987, entered into force 1 January 1989, *United Nations Treaty Series* (1989), vol. 1522, no. 26369, p. 3, Preamble.
261 Sunstein, C. R. (2003), supra note 253, 1013.
262 The Final Declaration of the First European Seas at Risk Conference, Copenhagen, 1994, Annex I.
263 FAO, Code of Conduct for Responsible Fisheries, Art. 7.5.3. Stockholm Convention on Persistent Organic Pollutants, Stockholm, 22 May 2001, *United Nations Treaty Series* (2006), vol. 2256, no. 40214, p. 119, Part 5, B; Protocol to the 1979 Convention on Long-range Transboundary Air Pollution on Persistent Organic Pollutants, Annex V.
264 FAO, Code of Conduct for Responsible Fisheries, Art.7.5.4. (Cautious conservation and management measures, including, *inter alia*, catch limits and effort limits.)
265 E.g. UNCED, Agenda 21, Rio de Janerio, Brazil, 3 to 14 June 1992, para. 17.21. Retrieved from https://sustainabledevelopment.un.org/content/documents/Agenda21.pdf
266 Sunstein, C. R. (2003), supra note 253, 1016.

267 Examples: 1990 Bergen Declaration, Art. 6; Rio Declaration, Principle 15; Convention on the Protection and Use of Transboundary Watercourses and International Lakes, Helsinki, adopted 17 March 1992, entered into force 6 October 1996, *United Nations Treaty Series* (2001), vol. 1936, no. 33207, p. 269, Preamble; the CBD, Preamble; the UNFCCC, Art. 3(3).

268 Communication from the Commission on the Precautionary Principle (2000), supra note 193, Summary, paras. 3–4.

269 Sunstein, C. R. (2005). *Laws of fear: Beyond the precautionary principle* (1st ed.). New York: Cambridge University Press, 33.

270 Ibid., 27–28.

271 Ellman, L. M., & Sunstein, C. R. (2004). Hormesis, the precautionary principle, and legal regulation. *Human & experimental toxicology*, *23*(12), 601–611, at 603.

272 Resolution LP.4(8), 2013 Amendments to the LP.

273 CBD Decision IX/16, Biodiversity and climate change, UN Doc. UNEP/ CBD/COP/DEC/IX/16 (9 October 2008).

274 Resolution LC-LP. 1 (2008) on the regulation of ocean fertilization, 31 October 2008, Annex 6. Retrieved from www.imo.org/en/OurWork/Environment/ LCLP/EmergingIssues/geoengineering/Pages/default.aspx

275 CBD Decision IX/16, Part C.

276 Resolution LC-LP.1 (2008) on the regulation of ocean fertilization, Annex 6. The meaning of "dumping", see Article III.1(b)(ii) and Article 1.4.2.2 of the London Protocol.

277 CBD Decision X/33, Biodiversity and climate change, UN Doc. UNEP/CBD/ COP/DEC/X/33 (29 October 2010), para. 8(w).

278 CBD Decision X/33, para. 8(w).

279 Resolution LP.4(8), 2013 Amendments to the LP, Annex 4.

280 Resolution LP.4(8), 2013 Amendments to the LP.

281 See further discussion in Section 3.2.3.1.

282 The moratorium on ocean fertilization will be further discussed in Section 3.2.3, and a more flexible operationalization of the precautionary approach in the context of geoengineering will be further discussed in Chapter 5.

283 UNEP, Precautionary approach to marine pollution, including waste-dumping at sea, 12th meeting, 1989.

284 A similar opinion, see Trouwborst, A. (2006), supra note 199, 189.

285 Wiener, J. B., & Rogers, M. D. (2002), supra note 191, 320–321.

286 See also: London Protocol, Art. 3.1; OSPAR Convention, Arts. 2.2 (a) & 2.3 (b).

287 See Chapter 5.

288 See Chapter 5.

3 Contemporary international law and geoengineering – a technique-by-technique approach

3.1 Introduction

Chapter 1 introduced the scientific background of geoengineering, indicating the distinctions between geoengineering methods in terms of the use of materials, location of deployment and scope of impacts. Based on the description of each geoengineering method and its potential adverse transboundary impacts on the environment and the climate in Sections 1.4 and 1.5, six geoengineering techniques were selected for further international legal analysis in this chapter because they raise the most attention in the transboundary context. As international rules and regulations are not identically applicable to every geoengineering technique, there is a need to tailor the analysis to each geoengineering technique via a technique-by-technique approach. Generally, this chapter elaborates on two aspects of each technique: whether the *conduct* of undertaking a technique or the use of a substance in the technique, for the purpose of research or deployment, is lawful under existing international law, and whether the adverse *impacts* caused by a particular technique lead to a prohibition or large restriction of using such a technique under existing international law.

Four marine geoengineering techniques – ocean fertilization, ocean upwelling, ocean alkalinity addition and marine cloud whitening (MCW) – have some crosscutting issues in the application of contemporary international legal rules and principles. One major crosscutting issue concerns the tripartite discussion of the lawfulness of placing pipes or particles into territorial seas, exclusive economic zones or the high seas in accordance with rules under the UNCLOS. Another crosscutting issue comes to the legal implications of similar adverse impacts of different marine geoengineering techniques on the marine environment. In such cases, the same rules under the UNCLOS and the LC/LP apply to different techniques insofar as the adverse impacts are comparable.[1] Taking into account those crosscutting issues, Sections 3.2 to 3.5 address each marine geoengineering technique separately, because such an approach can present the analysis of each technique in a more systematic manner.

It is worth emphasizing at the beginning of this chapter that some of the analysis of the international legal implications on the environmental effects caused by a particular geoengineering technique is made on the basis of computer modelling results rather than clear scientific conclusions. As a result, the legal implications may vary when, for instance, the updated scientific results indicate that a technique may cause a higher or lower degree of harm.

3.2 Ocean fertilization

As introduced in Chapter 1, the effectiveness and the underlying side effects of ocean fertilization are far from fully known. Scientific uncertainties dominate the discussions of both. For instance, the changes in the phytoplankton community and even the marine food web have not yet been fully tested.[2] It is also not known with confidence whether large-scale fertilization would cause increased or decreased production of DMS.[3] Considering the features, limitations, adverse effects and scientific uncertainties, three questions will be addressed in this section: How does international law regulate the placement of ocean fertilizer? How do these legal rules regulate the adverse impacts caused by ocean fertilization? What is the meaning of "small-scale scientific research studies" in the moratorium on ocean fertilization?

3.2.1 Ocean fertilization and the marine environment

A regulatory framework for ocean fertilization requires the application of international law, because ocean fertilization will likely happen in the exclusive economic zone (EEZ) of a coastal state or in the high seas. As introduced in Section 1.5, ocean fertilization may pollute the seawaters by introducing iron or other forms of nutrients and threaten the marine biodiversity by artificially accelerating algae's photosynthesis. As a result, the international rules and regulations on preventing pollution and preserving marine biodiversity are applicable to ocean fertilization. Specific regulations directly governing ocean fertilization are particularly noteworthy. The international regulatory framework for ocean fertilization consists mainly of three treaty regimes: the UNCLOS, the CBD and the LC/LP.

3.2.1.1 The introduction of ocean fertilizer and the obligation to prevent marine pollution

Part XII of the UNCLOS deals with the protection and preservation of the marine environment. Article 192 obliges states to protect and preserve the marine environment. To accomplish this, states are obliged to "take, individually or jointly as appropriate, all measures consistent with this Convention that are necessary to prevent, reduce and control pollution of the marine environment from any source".[4] The UNCLOS also requires states not to transfer, directly or indirectly, damage or hazards from one area to another or transform one type of pollution into another.[5] In addition, states are specifically required to "take all measures necessary to prevent, reduce and control pollution of the marine environment resulting from the use of technologies under their jurisdiction or control, or the intentional or accidental introduction of species, alien or new, to a particular part of the marine environment, which may cause significant and harmful changes thereto".[6] In light of these obligations, the primary question is whether ocean fertilization qualifies as "pollution of the marine environment" and falls within the regulatory ambit of the UNCLOS.[7]

Article 1.1 (4) of the UNCLOS defines the "pollution of the marine environment" as:

> [T]he introduction by man, directly or indirectly, of substances or energy into the marine environment, including estuaries, which results or is likely to result in such deleterious effects as harm to living resources and marine life, hazards to human health, hindrance to marine activities, including fishing and other legitimate uses of the sea, impairment of quality for use of sea water and reduction of amenities.

According to this definition, the use of a substance is prohibited not because of a physical attribute of the substance but because such a substance "results or is likely to result in deleterious effects".[8] The use of a substance may also be prohibited if it contributes to synergetic effects with other substances. Since the placement of iron particles may lead to toxic algae bloom and threaten marine life, Part XII of the UNCLOS clearly applies.

However, the proponents of ocean fertilization argue that ocean fertilization intends to benefit the global climate, and therefore the determination of "deleterious effects" rests with the trade-off between marine pollution and the benefit from preventing irreversible environmental damage caused by climate change.[9] Proponents also emphasize the scientific uncertainty surrounding ocean fertilization and its environmental effects, which makes the definition of "deleterious effects" even more equivocal. To respond to these arguments, it is necessary to invoke the precautionary approach. The UNCLOS does not expressively endorse an application of the precautionary approach to prevent marine pollution.[10] Nevertheless, the precautionary approach is mentioned in the resolutions adopted by the United Nations General Assembly (UNGA) in respect of oceans and the law of the sea.[11] The UNGA encourages states "to enhance their scientific activity to better understand the effects of climate change on the marine environment and marine biodiversity and develop ways and means of adaptation, taking into account, as appropriate, the precautionary approach".[12] Among others, the UNGA recalls that states stressed their concerns on ocean fertilization and are resolved to "continue addressing ocean fertilization with utmost caution, consistent with the precautionary approach".[13]

In contrast to the UNCLOS, which does not expressly refers to the precautionary approach, Article 3 of the London Protocol expressly stipulates the precautionary approach:

> Contracting Parties shall apply precautionary approach to environmental protection from dumping of wastes or other matter whereby appropriate preventative measures are taken when there is reason to believe that wastes or other matter introduced into the marine environment are likely to cause harm even when there is no conclusive evidence to prove a causal relation between inputs and their effects.

Pursuant to Article 3, the precautionary approach applies to ocean fertilization if the addition of fertilizers is considered "dumping wastes or other material". Hence, the next question is whether the addition of iron or other nutrients into the ocean constitutes "dumping".

The UNCLOS, the LC and the LP all define dumping as any deliberate disposal of wastes or other matter from vessels, aircraft, platforms or other man-made structures at sea.[14] Pursuant to Article 1.1(5)(b)(ii) of the UNCLOS, "dumping" does not include the "placement of matter for a purpose other than the mere disposal thereof, provided that such placement is not contrary to the aims of this Convention". Similar provisions can be found in the LC and the LP as well.[15] In order to explore whether ocean fertilization constitutes "dumping" and would therefore be prohibited by the UNCLOS and the LC/LP, two key questions need to be answered: Are iron and other fertilizers "waste" or "other matter", and does ocean fertilization fall under an exemption from the definition of "dumping".

With respect to the first question, iron and other fertilizers, such as nitrogen or phosphate, even if not "wastes", are certainly "other matter".[16] Article IV, paragraph 1, of the LC prohibits the dumping of wastes and other matter listed in Annex I of the LC, while the dumping of substances listed in Annex II requires a prior special permit. All other types of substances may be dumped in accordance with a general permit.[17] Iron, nitrogen and phosphate, substances used for ocean fertilization, are not included in either Annex I or Annex II of the LC. Consequently, they do not belong to the prohibited wastes or other matter in the LC context. However, it is noteworthy that "materials which, though of a non-toxic nature, may become harmful due to the quantities in which they are dumped, or which are liable to seriously reduce amenities", are listed in paragraph D of Annex II, which means that a prior special permit is required for a large-scale ocean fertilization activity. A small-scale ocean fertilization research would require a prior general permit, as the quantity of dumped materials is small.[18]

By contrast, the LP introduces a reverse listing approach to regulate dumping. According to Article 4 of the LP, dumping is generally prohibited. An exception exists for substances listed in Annex 1, which may be dumped subject to a permit. Paragraph 1.5 of Annex 1 allows for the at-sea disposal of "inert, inorganic geological material". Whether iron can be covered by the exception rests on the definition of the term "inert". The LP does not provide such a definition, but it can be found under the Eligibility Criteria for Inert, Inorganic Geological Material in the Guidelines on the Convention on the Prevention of Marine Pollution by Dumping of Waters and Other Matters (LC Dumping Guideline): an inert material and its constituents must be essentially chemically unreactive and the chemical constituents of the material must be unlikely to be released into the marine environment. In addition, an inert material should not result in acute or chronic toxicity.[19] According to the LC, "uncontaminated inert geological materials the chemical constituents of which are unlikely to be released into the marine environment" are excluded from the prohibitive materials".[20] Given that the introduction of iron into the marine environment is deliberately intended to create a reaction – i.e. the simulation of algae bloom – iron is highly unlikely to be considered "inert" in the context of the LC Dumping Guideline.[21] The determination of a material as "inert" in light of the LC Dumping Guideline also satisfies that aspect of the LP, because the geologic material should be "inert" under both LC and LP. Consequently, the dumping of iron cannot be exempted from the LP by referring to Paragraph 1.5 of Annex 1 of the LP.

Paragraph 1.7 of Annex 1 of the LP allows the dumping of a "bulky item primarily comprising iron". There is no consensus on whether this provision is applicable to iron fertilization. Some opine that while iron dust is certainly not "bulky", its chemical composition is similar to the "bulky" forms of iron.[22] In contrast, others hold the view that "bulky items comprising iron" are very unlikely to be considered "iron filings" used in iron fertilization.

It is evident that the LP has a stricter regulatory regime than the LC. The dumping of iron, nitrogen and phosphate is not prohibited by the LC insofar as their placement is subject to a special permit or a general permit, but the dumping of those nutrients is generally prohibited by the LP. Compared to the LC, which contains 87 parties, only 47 states have ratified or accepted the LP and thus are bound by the stricter standard.[23] However, some scholars argue that the rules established by the LP may bind more states than the LP's contracting parties. According to Article 210 of the UNCLOS, states shall adopt laws and regulations to prevent, reduce and control pollution of the marine environment from dumping, and those national laws, regulations and measures shall be no less effective in preventing, reducing and controlling such pollution than the global rules and standards. It might be arguable that the stricter standard set out in the LP is applicable to parties to the UNCLOS, because it could be treated as a global standard.[24] One may argue that the rules and standards agreed by merely 47 states cannot be treated as "global". However, the geographical locations of those states are important. As most of the parties to the LP are coastal states and the total coastline length of those states constitutes a high percentage of that of the world,[25] those states could arguably make considerable influence on establishing global rules and standards relating to the protection and conservation of the marine environment.

Even if the introduction of iron, nitrogen or phosphate is generally prohibited by the LP, the placement of fertilizers would still be excluded from the definition of "dumping". Pursuant to the UNCLOS and the LC/LP, "dumping" does not include the "placement of matter for a purpose other than the mere disposal thereof, provided that such placement is not contrary to the aim of this Convention".[26] To date, neither the LC nor the LP defines the term "disposal". The ordinary meaning of the word is the action or process of getting rid of something.[27] There is no consensus on whether the introduction of nutrients into the ocean is for the purpose of disposal. The parties of the LC/LP have agreed that the primary purpose of ocean fertilization is to stimulate primary productivity in the oceans rather than to merely dispose of them.[28] However, iron, nitrogen or phosphate is poured into the ocean without any intention of recycling. Hence, it might be argued that the introduction of fertilizer can be interpreted as "disposal".[29] Moreover, it might be argued that the ultimate aim of adding fertilizers is to sequester CO_2, which means ocean fertilization constitutes the placement into the ocean, by indirect means, of excess atmospheric CO_2 for the purpose of disposing of that CO_2.[30] This argument may be questioned, because the CO_2 sequestered by algal bloom is deposited in the deep ocean in the form of organic material (dead phytoplankton and zooplankton) instead of dissolved inorganic carbon. According to Paragraph 1.6 of Annex 1 of the LP, organic material of natural origin may be dumped.

Irrespective of the purpose of ocean fertilization, the placement of fertilizers may not be compatible with the objectives of the UNCLOS and the LC/LP.[31] The UNCLOS requires states to protect and preserve rare or fragile ecosystems, as well as the habitat of depleted, threatened or endangered species and other forms of marine life.[32] The LC requires its contracting parties to prevent marine pollution caused by dumping of waste or other matter that is liable to create hazards to human health, or to harm living resources and marine life.[33] If the scientific knowledge confirms that pollution and adverse impacts on living marine resources from ocean fertilization is inevitable when using ocean fertilization technique, ocean fertilization would not be compatible with the aims of the UNCLOS and the LC, and the addition of iron, nitrogen or phosphate would constitute "dumping".

In summary, ocean fertilization is governed by the UNCLOS and the LC/LP to protect the marine environment and prevent marine pollution from dumping. Considering the scientific uncertainty and adverse environmental effects, parties to the LP additionally have to abide by the precautionary approach under Article 3 of the LP.

Since 2007, a series of international documents have been published directly touching upon the issue of ocean fertilization. In 2007, the Scientific Group under the LC and the Scientific Group under the LP jointly released a statement of concern regarding iron fertilization of the ocean to sequester CO_2.[34] The Scientific Group took the view that current knowledge about the effectiveness and potential environmental impacts of ocean iron fertilization was insufficient to justify large-scale operations. They also noted with concern the potential for large-scale ocean iron fertilization to negatively impact the marine environment and human health. Therefore, they recommended that any operations of large-scale ocean iron fertilization should be evaluated carefully to ensure that such operations would not be contrary to the aims of the LC and the LP. In 2008, Resolution LC-LP.1 on the regulation of ocean fertilization stated that ocean fertilization is included within the scope of the LC and the LP. The parties to the LC-LP agreed that legitimate scientific research should be regarded as placement of matter for a purpose other than the mere disposal under Article III.1(b)(iii) of the LC and Article 1.4.2.2 of the LP. The parties also agreed that ocean fertilization for reasons other than legitimate scientific research should not be allowed.[35]

In October 2013, amendments to the London Protocol listed marine geoengineering, including ocean fertilization, as being explicitly regulated by the LP.[36] A new Annex 4 on "Marine Geoengineering" defines "ocean fertilization" as "any activity undertaken by humans with the principal intention of stimulating primary productivity in the oceans.

Ocean fertilization does not include conventional aquaculture, or mariculture, or the creation of artificial reefs".[37] An ocean fertilization activity may only be considered for a permit if it is a legitimate scientific research activity taking into account any specific placement assessment framework.[38] A new Annex 5 adds the Assessment Framework for matter that may be considered for placement under Annex 4. The aforementioned documents show that legitimate scientific research is the only exemption from the temporary ban[39] on ocean fertilization activities. Only ocean fertilization activities for the purpose of scientific research are not contrary to the aim of the LC and the LP, and are currently permitted under the international law. The determination of a legitimate scientific research should be in accordance with the decision of the assessment framework.[40]

3.2.1.2 State jurisdiction over ocean fertilization

State responsibility for preventing marine pollution and conserving the marine environment is allocated based on jurisdictional competencies.[41] Under the UNCLOS, laws and regulations for the prevention, reduction and control of pollution of the marine environment by dumping are to be enforced by coastal states, port states or flag states.

If iron for ocean fertilization is dumped into territorial waters or the EEZ of one state, this coastal state has jurisdiction to enforce its dumping laws and regulations adopted in accordance with the UNCLOS and applicable international rules and standards.[42]

When iron is dumped by a vessel into the high seas, the jurisdiction rests primarily with the flag states. However, flag states might not be a party to relevant treaties or might fail to adopt laws and regulations to enforce international rules. A worse case could be that the proponents of ocean fertilization utilize "flags of convenience"[43] to incorporate their companies and flag their vessels in states that are not parties to the LC or the LP.[44] However, the

UNCLOS does not leave the question of compliance to the flag state alone. When a ship has dumped large quantities of iron into the high seas and is later voluntarily within a port or at an offshore terminal of a state, this port state has the jurisdiction to investigate and prosecute this vessel for violation of international laws.[45] When large quantities of iron have been dumped into a maritime zone within the jurisdiction of another state and then the dumper is voluntarily within a port or at an offshore terminal of a third state, the port state has the same jurisdiction, but it must be based on a request of that coastal state.[46]

The Southern Ocean is of particular interest for ocean fertilization, because modelling studies indicate that adding iron to the waters of that region has the greatest potential to remove atmospheric CO_2.[47] To date, 7 of the 13 existing ocean fertilization studies have taken place in the Southern Ocean.[48] In addition to the UNCLOS, the CBD and the LC/LP, particular treaties with respect to Antarctica and adjacent maritime areas are also applicable to ocean fertilization activities when they are conducted in these maritime areas.[49] Among others, the Antarctic Treaty and its Protocol on Environmental Protection of the Antarctic Treaty, as well as the Convention on the Conservation of Antarctic Marine Living Resources should be taken into account if ocean fertilization projects are carried out in an area within the geographical scope of these Conventions.

3.2.1.3 *The obligation to conserve marine biodiversity*

Ocean fertilization may adversely impact marine biodiversity in several respects. First, the use of fertilizer changes the size of the phytoplankton community and subsequently influences all other species that depend on phytoplankton. Moreover, phytoplankton bloom consumes much more oxygen than in the case without using fertilizer and may even deplete subsurface oxygen. The resulting anoxic water layer may adversely affect marine organisms. In addition, ocean fertilization has the potential to accelerate ocean acidification, which may lead to unforeseen outcomes to ocean ecosystems.

The CBD has near universal participation among states (**196 parties**) and a wide range of mandates. Pursuant to the CBD, all parties are responsible for conserving their biological diversity and for sustainably using their biological resources. Unlike the approach under the UNCLOS, which prevents "deleterious effects as harm to living resources and marine life", the CBD addresses conservation based on a three-layered approach that encompasses diversities within species, between species and of ecosystems.[50] Three parts of the CBD are relevant for the governance of ocean fertilization. The precautionary approach contained in the Preamble of the CBD brings value to the interpretation of the convention but does not function as an operative provision.[51] Article 3 of the CBD addresses the prevention principle, requiring parties to ensure that activities within one state's jurisdiction or control do not cause damage to the environment of other states or of areas beyond the limits of national jurisdiction.[52] Article 7 (c) imposes procedural obligations on parties to "identify" and "monitor" activities that may have significant adverse impacts on the conservation and sustainable use of biodiversity; it does not ban such activities.[53]

The interaction between the CBD and the UNCLOS on the issue of marine biodiversity is reflected in a host of CBD Decisions and UNGA Resolutions. Since 1995, the Conference of Parties to the CBD has adopted a number of decisions on marine and coastal biodiversity.[54] In 2004, the CBD COP 7 adopted Decision VII/5 on Marine and Coastal Biodiversity, which incorporated the work of the UNCLOS. In the same year, UNGA Resolution 58/240 on Oceans and the Law of the Sea welcomed the work of the CBD and invited the CBD, in accordance with its mandate, "to investigate urgently how to better address, on a scientific basis, including the application of precaution, the threats and risks to vulnerable and threatened marine ecosystems and biodiversity in areas beyond national jurisdiction".[55] Also in 2004, the UNGA decided to establish an Ad Hoc Open-ended Informal Working Group (Ad Hoc Working Group) to study issues relating to the conservation and sustainable use of marine biological diversity beyond the areas of national jurisdiction.[56] The most recent outcome from the Ad Hoc Working Group, in 2015, decided to develop an international legally binding instrument under the UNCLOS on the conservation and sustainable use of marine biological diversity of areas beyond national jurisdiction.[57]

In 2008, the CBD COP decided to integrate climate change considerations into each programme of work.[58] A number of decisions directly address ocean fertilization and geoengineering. Part C of Decision IX/16 directly addresses ocean fertilization by suggesting a moratorium on large-scale ocean fertilization.[59] In 2010, Decision X/29 on Marine and Coastal Biodiversity requested the Executive Secretary to include the interaction between oceans and climate change and alternatives to mitigation and adaptation strategies when making a proposal to develop joint activities to the secretariats of the UNFCCC.[60] Decision X/29 also reaffirmed the precautionary approach and requested parties to implement the moratorium in Decision IX/16.[61] Decision X/33 extended the suggested moratorium to geoengineering in general.[62]

3.2.2 *Ocean fertilization and the climate change regime*

As elaborated in Chapter 2, the climate change regime provides enabling rules for CDR techniques. First, the aim of utilizing CDR is compatible with the ultimate objective of the UNFCCC as stated in Article 2.[63] Second, Article 2(1)(a) of the KP encourages land-based CDR methods – i.e. afforestation, reforestation and the development of carbon dioxide sequestration technologies.[64]

A controversial topic relevant to ocean fertilization is whether the carbon credits from iron fertilization can be traded in regulated carbon markets.[65] The regulated carbon markets are established primarily from three mechanisms under the KP: Clean Development Mechanism (CDM), Joint

Implementation (JI) and Emissions Trading Scheme (ETS). CDM is designed to assist Non-Annex I Parties in achieving sustainable development and to assist Annex I Parties in achieving compliance with their quantified emission limitation and reduction commitment under the KP.[66] JI allows Annex I Parties to transfer to, or acquire from, any other such party, emission reduction units in order to achieve their emission reduction or limitation commitment.[67] ETS allows countries that have emission units to spare to sell this excess capacity to countries that are over their targets.[68] The KP also contains strict rules on the use of carbon sinks. According to Article 3.3 of the KP, only "sinks resulting from direct human-induced, land-use change and forestry activities, limited to afforestation, reforestation and deforestation since 1990" are counted as verifiable changes in carbon stock to meet the commitments of Annex I Parties. Article 3.4 further regulates that

> the CMP shall decide how, and which, additional human-induced activities related to changes in greenhouse gas emissions by sources and removals by sinks in the agricultural soils and the land-use change and forestry categories shall be added to [. . .] the assigned amounts for Parties included in Annex I.

To date, iron fertilization has not been mentioned in any decision made by the CMP. Hence, carbon credits generated by iron fertilization projects or any other work conducted in international waters would not be counted as verifiable amounts for meeting the commitments under the KP.

Whether and how to include ocean fertilization in regulated carbon markets requires an economic analysis of the value of ocean fertilization. This economic analysis goes beyond international law. However, should ocean fertilization be recognized as eligible for trading in future carbon markets mechanisms under the KP, it will first of all require an amendment to Article 3.3 of the KP to include carbon credits from iron fertilization projects or more generally the projects conducted in international waters. But such an amendment would not be necessary if using the Paris Agreement (PA) as an alternative to govern ocean fertilization activities. Parties to the PA are free to choose the methods of mitigation to be counted for their NDCs.[69]

3.2.3 The scale and purpose of ocean fertilization activities

3.2.3.1 The restriction of "Small Scale Scientific Research"

No clear definition of the terms "small scale" or "large scale" has ever been given, though it is mentioned in almost each legal instrument concerning ocean fertilization or geoengineering in general. C. S. Law defines "large-scale" as the continuous addition of iron to an area larger than 40,000 km² lasting more than one year.[70] CBD Decision IX/16 requests states not to undertake geoengineering activities except for "small scale scientific research studies". The problem is how to distinguish "small-scale" experiments from "large-scale" deployment. The reason for making this distinction is that in most cases the risks associated with the techniques are highly dependent on the scale at which they are implemented.

Ideally, any experiments should be large enough to generate discernable and statistically significant results, but small enough to avert serious transboundary adverse effects.[71] It seems that "small-scale" implies a strictly controlled condition with adequate scientific data and a thorough prior assessment of the potential impacts. Pursuant to the Statement of the Intergovernmental Oceanographic Commission (IOC) *ad hoc* Consultative Group on Ocean Fertilization, the size of the activity is not the only factor to consider; "large scale" is instead a relative term. This statement illustrates that "[an] ocean fertilization activity might be damaging even if conducted over one square kilometre (for example, over a coral reef) just as another ocean fertilization activity might be benign even though conducted over many thousands of square kilometres".[72] Consequently, in considering the definition of "large scale", attention should be paid not only to the geographical or spatial aspect but also the temporal and environmental aspects of cumulative fertilization on any scale.[73]

As a result, the line between "small scale" and "large scale" should not be drawn by simply setting the number of square kilometres of ocean surface. A set of criteria, encompassing physical size and environmental factors, is required to draw the line in a tailored manner: The scale of an ocean fertilization activity should be large enough for gathering specific scientific data; such an activity should be subject to a thorough prior and posterior assessment of the potential impacts of the research studies on the marine environment; and the activity should not result in significant harm or create a significant risk thereof to the marine environment. To some extent, the availability of scientific knowledge and technologies (methodologies, facilities, etc.) will affect the determination of the boundary of "small scale". In other words, the more scientific knowledge and advanced technologies are available, the clearer the boundary of "small scale" is. This argument can be borne out by the example that sufficient knowledge and advanced technologies could avoid the wrong location for experiments and thus avoid non-spacious but significantly harmful experiments.

SCIENTIFIC RESEARCH[74]

The CBD decisions restrict ocean fertilization activities not only to "small-scale", but also to those with "scientific research studies" as their purpose. Thirteen ocean fertilization experiments have been carried out since 1993, but not all of them were "purely scientific".[75] The CBD decisions do not define the term "scientific research". The case of *Whaling in the Antarctic* contains a discussion of this term.[76][77]This case analysed whether Japan's whaling research program – JARPA II – fell inside Article VIII, paragraph 1, of the International Convention for Regulation of Whaling. Article VIII, paragraph 1, of the convention states:

> Notwithstanding anything contained in this Convention any Contracting Government may grant to any of its nationals a special permit authorizing that national to kill, take and treat whales *for purposes of scientific research* subject to such restrictions as to number and subject to such other conditions as the Contracting Government thinks fit, and the killing, taking, and treating of whales in accordance with the provisions of this Article shall be exempt from the operation of this Convention.

Instead of being persuaded by the characteristics of scientific research asserted by Australia,[78] the court focused on the phrase "for the purpose of". In the court's view, "an objective test of whether a programme is for the purpose of scientific research [. . .] [turns] on whether the design and implementation of a programme are reasonable in relation to achieving the stated research objectives".[79] The court considered that the special permits granted by Japan for the killing, taking and treating of whales in connection with JARPA II were not "for purposes of scientific research", because the lethal sampling was on a greater scale than is otherwise reasonable in relation to achieving the programme's stated objectives.[80] This logic is also applicable to the case of ocean fertilization scientific research. Experiments should not be undertaken at a scale larger than a reasonable scale in relation to achieving the objective of obtaining scientific data.

Ocean fertilization activities for scientific purposes should also follow relevant rules under Part XIII of the UNCLOS regarding marine scientific research. Basically, all states have the freedom to undertake marine scientific research and shall promote and facilitate the development and conduct of it.[81] The rules and principles regarding the protection and preservation of the marine environment (addressed in Section 3.2.1), which are applicable to ocean fertilization activities in general, are applicable to ocean fertilization scientific research activities as well.

3.2.3.2 Large-scale implementation

In the long run, when scientific knowledge about ocean fertilization is sufficient and the risk of adverse environmental impacts is considered to be controllable, ocean fertilization would be further developed for large-scale implementation, including scientific and commercial activities. All of the requirements for small-scale research activities stated under the CBD decisions and the LP resolution[82] would apply to large-scale research activities as well, and large-scale experiments should be subject to a greater degree of scrutiny, oversight and liability.[83] Pursuant to the 2013 Amendments to the LP, the scale of scientific research may not be the decisive factor as long as an activity qualifies for "legitimate scientific research".[84] All of the requirements for legitimate scientific research activities would logically be applicable to research activities at different scales.

As stated in earlier, large-scale ocean fertilization activities for commercial purposes have not yet gained legitimacy under the CBD or the LP. Moreover, ocean fertilization projects for commercial purposes have not been included in any carbon trading mechanisms under the KP.[85] However, as parties to the PA have the freedom to include all mitigation methods in their NDCs, logically including ocean fertilization, large-scale ocean fertilization activities for commercial purposes do not seem to be prohibited by the PA.

3.2.4 Synthetic consideration

Section 3.2 comprehensively analyses the legality of ocean fertilization under international law. Considering the features of ocean fertilization activities, the focus is on the obligation to prevent marine pollution, in particular pollution from "dumping". A full consideration includes but is not limited to, first, small-scale ocean fertilization projects for the purpose of scientific research that are not prohibited by international law. Such projects should be undertaken after comprehensive assessments of environmental impacts, covering the whole process of each project. Second, as scientific uncertainty is one main obstacle in implementing ocean fertilization, the precautionary approach is always important and runs throughout the implementation of ocean fertilization projects. Third, even if the available scientific data prove that an ocean fertilization activity "results in or is likely to result in deleterious effects as harm to living resources and marine life",[86] it is still worth balancing the risk of significant harm to marine ecosystem caused by ocean fertilization against the potential contribution made by ocean fertilization to stabilizing CO_2 concentrations at a secure level. Bear in mind that such a trade-off cannot be achieved only via legal methods; instead, it should be a comprehensive consideration combining economics, politics, ethics, etc. Last but not the least, the LC/LP plays a significant role in governing ocean fertilization. One reason is that the 2013 Amendments provide for a legal regime for ocean fertilization and even more generally for marine geoengineering. The other reason is that the LC/LP is a special convention regarding the protection of the marine environment compared to the UNCLOS as a general one, and the LC/LP would provide for a stricter legal control of ocean fertilization than the UNCLOS. Pursuant to Article 237 of the UNCLOS, provisions of Part XII of the UNCLOS are without prejudice to the obligations under the LC/LP on the protection and preservation of the marine environment.

3.3 Ocean upwelling

This section will address the legal analysis of ocean upwelling in three respects: the legal status of ocean pipes and ocean upwelling activities, rights and duties in ocean upwelling activities, and the regulations regarding the side effects of ocean upwelling on the marine environment.

3.3.1 *The legal status of ocean pipes and ocean upwelling activities*

Part XIII of the UNCLOS regulates marine scientific research, including scientific research installations and equipment (Articles 258 to 262). These five provisions are applicable to artificial ocean upwelling if (a) the placement and use of ocean pipes constitute scientific research and (b) ocean pipes are classified as "installations" or "equipment".

3.3.1.1 *The purpose of placing and using ocean pipes*

"Marine scientific research" is not defined in the UNCLOS, despite a number of proposals that have been made for a definition during the negotiations of the UNCLOS.[87] During the Second Conference on the Law of the Sea, a general definition of marine scientific research was proposed as "any study, whether fundamental or applied, intended to increase knowledge about the marine environment, including all its resources and living organisms, and embraces all related scientific activity".[88] During the Third Conference on the Law of the Sea, the core issue of the negotiations was the distinction between "open basic scientific research", carried out for the benefit of the community, and "industrial research", directed towards the exploration and exploitation of marine resources.[89] "Open basic scientific research" refers to experimental or theoretical work aiming at acquiring new knowledge of the "underlying foundation of phenomena and observable facts"[90] and the yielded data are accessible to all and are public property.[91] Instead, "industrial research" or "applied research" is undertaken primarily for specific practical aims or objectives.[92] Considering some economic purposes, the results of applied research might not be accessible to the public, as it may concern business secrets. Note that the term "industrial research" and "applied research" are not used in any international legal instrument, but they are helpful in shaping the following analysis.

From the negotiations of the UNCLOS, it can be inferred that both types of scientific research are included in the term "marine scientific research" in the UNCLOS. Ocean upwelling, as a technique of CDR, attempts to stimulate the photosynthesis of plankton and sequester more atmospheric CO_2. In other words, the primary goal of the large-scale deployment of the ocean upwelling technique is to combat climate change rather than gain scientific knowledge about the marine environment. However, ocean upwelling experiments in the phase of assessing the preconditions, testing the pipes as well as evaluating the effectivity and efficiency of CO_2 removal could be either "open basic scientific research" (e.g. done by a university team) or "applied research" (e.g. done by a company). Consequently, Articles 258 to 262 of the UNCLOS are applicable to ocean upwelling experiments.

Part XIII of the UNCLOS is not applicable to ocean upwelling pipes that are deployed for the purpose of CO_2 sequestration, because the goal of such activities is not to undertake marine scientific research. The lawfulness of deploying ocean upwelling pipes for geoengineering purposes depends on the location of deployment.[93]

3.3.1.2 Ocean pipes as "Installations" or "Equipment"

Marine scientific research can be undertaken not only on ships but also on installations or equipment deployed in the marine environment.[94] Not being ships, ocean pipes might be regarded as "installations" or "equipment". As neither "installations" nor "equipment" is defined in the UNCLOS, one must resort to the ordinary meaning.[95] The main difference between them is that "installations" are larger types of devices used for scientific research and are fixed to the ocean floor, while "equipment" covers smaller research devices that are not fixed to the seabed, such as floating buoys.[96] Other differences relate to the duration of deployment and the intended functions. "Equipment" remains for a shorter period of time at the proposed sites, being quickly placed, used and then removed, and it is used for a specific purpose or activity. In contrast, "installations" are versatile and would stay in place for a longer time or even permanently.[97]

In terms of size, duration and function, ocean pipes that are used for artificial upwelling meet the criteria of "equipment".[98] The pipes are approximately 200 metres long, 10 metres in diameter and float in the water; they are temporarily used and will be removed after deployment; the single function is to pump nutrient-rich water to the ocean surface. As a result, ocean pipes placed and used for artificial upwelling experiences are to be considered "scientific research equipment".

3.3.2 Rights and duties in the conduct of ocean upwelling

3.3.2.1 The placement and use of ocean pipes

In contrast to a lack of any provision in the UNCLOS on the placement and use of ocean pipes for geoengineering purposes, Part XIII Section 4 of the UNCLOS addresses the requirements for the deployment and use of marine scientific research equipment in the marine environment. Generally, the conditions prescribed in the UNCLOS for the conduct of marine scientific research apply to the placement and use of any type of scientific research equipment (Article 258).[99] The placement and use of scientific research equipment shall not constitute an obstacle to established international shipping routes (Article 261). Article 262 stipulates that scientific research equipment

> shall bear identification markings indicating the [s]tate of registry or the international organization to which they belong and shall have adequate internationally agreed warning signals to ensure safety at sea and safety of air navigation, taking into account rules and standards established by competent international organizations.[100]

As with the flag that shows the nationality of a vessel,[101] the "identification marking" of a scientific research equipment indicates the nationality of ocean pipes. If ocean pipes are placed in the high seas, the state of registry or the international organization has exclusive jurisdiction over those pipes.[102]

Ocean pipes shall also bear warning signals for safety at sea and safety of air navigation. Given that the pipes are underneath the waters, buoys or other floats may be required to make warning signals visible.

Whether a state has the right to conduct ocean upwelling activities depends on the location of the activity: the territorial sea, the EEZ, the continental shelf, or the high seas.[103]

TERRITORIAL SEA

In principle, coastal states have the freedom to place pipes in their territorial sea and conduct artificial ocean upwelling activities. Article 2 of the UNCLOS stipulates that coastal states have sovereignty over their territorial seas. In particular, coastal states have the exclusive right to regulate, authorize and conduct marine scientific research in their territorial sea.[104] Marine scientific research shall be conducted only with the express consent of and under the conditions set forth by the coastal state.[105] The right regarding marine scientific research shall be enjoyed without prejudice to the right of innocent passage through the territorial sea.[106]

A restriction concerns the innocent passage of foreign ships. Article 24 stipulates that the coastal state shall not hamper the innocent passage of foreign ships through the territorial sea. However, the coastal state is still entitled to take measures to prevent foreign ships from damaging underwater pipes during innocent passage. Article 21(1) of the UNCLOS states that

> the coastal state may adopt laws and regulations in conformity with the provisions of this Convention and other rules of international law, relating to innocent passage through the territorial sea, in respect of [. . .] (b) the protection of navigational aids and facilities and other facilities or installations [. . .] (g) marine scientific research.

Although not explicitly mentioning "ocean pipes" in Article 21(1)(b), "other facilities" could be regarded as including ocean pipes. Therefore, the coastal state is entitled to request foreign ships to avoid the areas where ocean pipes are placed during innocent passage by, for instance, giving prior notification.

EEZ

According to Article 56(1)(b)(ii) of the UNCLOS, the coastal state, in its EEZ, has jurisdiction with regard to marine scientific research. In the exercise of their jurisdiction, coastal states have the right to regulate, authorize and conduct marine scientific research in their EEZ and on their continental shelf in accordance with the relevant provisions of the UNCLOS.[107] Marine scientific research in the EEZ and on the continental shelf shall be conducted with the consent of the coastal State.[108] In normal cases, coastal states shall grant their consent for marine scientific research "in order to increase scientific knowledge of the marine environment for the benefit of all mankind", but they may withhold their consent at their discretion.[109] With regard to ocean pipes, the coastal state may withhold its consent if an ocean upwelling project "is of direct significance for the exploration and exploitation of natural resources" or

> contains information communicated pursuant to article 248 regarding the nature and objectives of the project which is inaccurate or if the researching State or competent international organization has outstanding obligations to the coastal State from a prior research project.[110]

Article 248 requires researching states or competent international organizations to provide relevant information to the coastal state prior to the commencement of a scientific research project. One could infer that coastal states might not provide their consent if the objective of using ocean pipes is not to proceed with scientific research.

Regarding ocean pipes deployed in the EEZ for the purpose of geoengineering, all states enjoy the freedom of such deployment, but the freedom is subject to the jurisdiction of the coastal state if the deployment of ocean pipes results or is likely to result in pollution of the marine environment. Generally, all states, "whether coastal or land-locked, enjoy, subject to the relevant provisions of this Convention, the freedoms referred to in [A]rticle 87 of [. . .] the laying of submarine cables and pipelines, and other internationally lawful uses of the sea related to these freedoms".[111] All states, therefore, enjoy the freedom to place ocean pipes for the purpose of removing atmospheric CO_2 in the EEZ, as the placement of ocean pipes can be considered as the lawful use of the sea as referred to in Article 87. However, the deployment of ocean pipes for geoengineering is subject to the jurisdiction of the coastal state in the EEZ if certain conditions are met. According to Article 56(1)(b) of the UNCLOS, the coastal state has the jurisdiction in the EEZ over (i) the establishment and use of artificial islands, installations and structures; ii) marine scientific research; and (iii) the protection and preservation of the marine environment. In the case of ocean upwelling, the coastal state would have the jurisdiction over the deployment of ocean pipes in its EEZ if such deployment results or is likely to result in pollution of the marine environment.

HIGH SEAS

Article 87(1) of the UNCLOS stipulates that the high seas are open to all states and the freedom of scientific research is part of the freedom of the high seas.[112] With regard to the placement and use of ocean pipes in the high seas, all states, in principle, have the freedom to undertake artificial upwelling. Bear in mind that the freedom must be exercised with due regard for the interests of other states in their exercise of the freedom of the high seas.[113]

In addition, Article 257 entitles all states and competent international organizations the right to conduct marine scientific research in the water column beyond the limits of the EEZ. In principle, researching states and competent international organizations enjoy the freedom to place and use ocean pipes as "scientific research equipment" and undertake ocean upwelling research in the high seas. The freedom shall be subject to the exclusive rights of the coastal state when a scientific research project takes place on the continental shelf beyond 200 nautical miles ("outer continental shelf" below). In this case, the coastal state has exclusive rights to undertake such a research project on its outer continental shelf and no one may undertake any research without the express consent of the coastal state.[114] Bear in mind that the rights of the coastal state over the continental shelf do not affect the legal status of the superjacent waters, which belong to the high seas and thus are open to all states. As a result, researching states and competent international organizations have the freedom to carry out ocean pipe upwelling research in seawaters superjacent to the outer continental shelf and on the outer continental shelf outside the specific areas.

3.3.2.2 The removal of pipes

The next issue, after deployment, is the removal of ocean pipes. There are different reasons for removing pipes, such as the decommissioning of ocean pipes after the termination of a scientific research or deployment, or ocean pipes drifting into the area under another state's jurisdiction. A legal analysis of the removal of ocean pipes involves, as a first question, whether the removal of pipes is mandatory under the dumping regime. Abandoning ocean pipes at sea constitutes "dumping" under the LC and the LP. No provision regarding the exemption from "dumping" regulated under the LC is relevant to the abandonment of ocean pipes. The abandonment of ocean pipes requires a prior general permit under the LC because ocean pipes are neither listed in Annex I nor in Annex II of the LC.[115] Article 1(4)(2)(3) of the LP stipulates that "dumping" does not include the abandonment in the sea of matter, such as pipelines and marine research devices, placed for a purpose other than the mere disposal thereof. This provision is not applicable to the abandonment of ocean pipes because the very purpose of leaving them in the sea is to dispose of them. In addition, because ocean pipes are not listed in Annex 1 of the LP as matter that may be considered for dumping, the LP prohibits the abandonment of ocean pipes in the sea.[116]

In contrast, under the OSPAR Convention, "dumping" does not include "the leaving wholly or partly in place of a disused offshore installation[117] or disused offshore pipeline, provided that any such operation takes place in accordance with any relevant provision of the Convention and with other relevant international law".[118] Article 5 of the OSPAR Convention Annex III provides that no disused offshore installation shall be left wholly or partly in place in the maritime area without a permit issued by the competent authority of the relevant contracting party on a case-by-case basis.[119] Because the OSPAR Convention does not differentiate "installation" from "equipment", Article 5 of Annex III could be deemed to be applicable to ocean pipes. However, as most OSPAR Convention parties are also parties to the LP,[120] the less restrictive rules regarding the removal of ocean pipes provided by the OSPAR Convention would not be applicable for the states that are parties to both of the OSPAR Convention and the LP.

The rules regarding the removal of ocean pipes under the UNCLOS are not one size fits all. Instead, it depends on the purpose of using ocean pipes and the location of ocean pipes.

TERRITORIAL SEA

In light of its sovereignty, the coastal state is free to remove or leave the ocean pipes it has placed in its territorial sea and has the jurisdiction to remove the ocean pipes placed by another state or competent organization drifting into its territorial sea and the ocean pipes placed in its territorial sea without its consent.

EEZ

In the case of the EEZ, other states and competent international organizations, when undertaking marine scientific research in the EEZ or on the continental shelf of a coastal state, have the duty to remove the scientific research equipment once the research is completed unless otherwise agreed.[121] States and competent international organizations have the duty to provide the expected dates of first appearance and final departure of the research vessels, or deployment of the equipment and its removal, as appropriate.[122]

If ocean pipes are used for geoengineering, the UNCLOS does not attribute jurisdiction to the coastal state or the researching state. To deal with this problem, one argument is that the deploying state might be responsible for removing the pipes.[123] One legal basis could be Article 210(5) of the UNCLOS. Because disused ocean pipes could be regarded as matter that is not allowed to be dumped at sea, dumping within the EEZ or onto the continental shelf shall not be carried out without the express prior approval of the coastal state.[124] However, such consent must be in conformity with the corresponding rules under the LP, if the consent is given by a coastal state that is a party to it.[125]

With regard to ocean pipes placed by a coastal state in the water of its own EEZ, one may first refer to Article 56.1(b)(1) and Article 60.3 of the UNCLOS. Although not expressly mentioning "equipment", the relevant rules regarding "installations and structures" might be applied analogously. Article 56.1(b)(1) states that the coastal state has jurisdiction with regard to the establishment and use of artificial islands, installations and structures, but it does not mention the jurisdiction of the coastal state regarding the removal of installations and structures. Article 60.3 leaves the discretion to the coastal state to decide whether to remove "installations or structures" it has constructed. Article 60.3 stipulates that

> [a]ny installations or structures which are abandoned or disused shall be removed to ensure safety of navigation, taking into account any generally accepted international standards established in this regard by the competent international organization, and that such removal shall also have due regard to fishing, the protection of the marine environment, and the rights and duties of other states.

In 1989, the International Maritime Organization (IMO) adopted Guidelines and Standards for the removal of offshore installations and structures on the continental shelf and in the EEZ (Removal Guidelines below).[126] The Removal Guidelines can be considered "generally accepted international standards" and provide criteria for determining where non-removal or partial removal could be allowed. Among other things, a case-by-case evaluation is required.[127]

It might be a preliminary conclusion that regarding ocean pipes placed by the coastal state in its EEZ, for the purpose of applied scientific research or CO_2 removal, the coastal state enjoys the discretion to remove them or not, based on a case-by-case assessment. However, the discretion of the coastal state must be in conformity with the LP if the coastal state is a party to it.

HIGH SEAS

Regarding the removal of ocean pipes placed in the high seas, the state of registry or the state acting through a competent international organization that deploys the ocean pipes, has the duty not to pollute the marine environment by dumping matter for the purpose of disposal.[128] Ocean pipes shall not be left in the high seas without the permission of the competent authorities of states.[129] Note that the state of registry is obliged to remove the pipes if it is a party to the LP.

3.3.3 Ocean upwelling and the marine environment

This section will demonstrate the relationship between an ocean upwelling activity and the obligation to protect and preserve the marine environment. Notwithstanding that it is still not fully clear how ocean upwelling could affect the marine environment, it has been found that ocean upwelling has important effects on seawater and ocean life.[130] The UNCLOS and the CBD are applicable to ocean upwelling activities regarding the protection of the aquatic environment and the conservation of marine ecosystems.

Generally, contracting parties to the CBD are obliged to, as far as possible and as appropriate, conserve biological diversity and have the responsibility to ensure that the activities within their jurisdiction or control do not cause damage to the areas beyond the limits of national jurisdiction.[131] In particular, the placement and use of ocean pipes should not impede the conservation of protected marine areas.[132] Article 22 of the CBD stipulates that contracting parties shall implement the CBD with respect to the marine environment consistently with the rights and obligations of states under the law of the sea. Besides, the interaction between the CBD and the UNCLOS with regard to the protection and preservation of the marine environment has been examined in Section 3.2.1.3. The general rules set forth in CBD decisions and UNGA resolutions that are applicable to ocean fertilization are also applicable to ocean upwelling.

As to ocean pipes placed and used for scientific research, Article 240(d) of the UNCLOS states that "marine scientific research shall be conducted in compliance with all relevant regulations adopted in conformity with this Convention including those for the protection and preservation of the marine environment". With respect to ocean pipes placed and used for other purposes, the pipes could be qualified as "other devices" as referred to in Article 194(3)(d) of the UNCLOS. States shall take all measures consistent with the UNCLOS that are necessary to prevent, reduce and control pollution of the marine environment from any source.[133] The measures shall deal with, *inter alia*,

> pollution from other [. . .] devices operating in the marine environment, in particular measures for preventing accidents and dealing with emergencies, ensuring the safety of operations at sea, and regulating the design, construction, equipment, operation and manning of such installations or devices.[134]

3.3.4 Synthetic consideration

As ocean upwelling is a novel technique and has not been explicitly regulated under any legal regime, the legal analysis starts by clarifying the legal status of ocean pipes and the legality of placing pipes in the ocean. Section 3.3.1 has found that the introduction of ocean pipes would be permitted by the UNCLOS if they are used for (applied) scientific research and that ocean pipes could be regarded as "research equipment". The exercise of scientific research activities is not unfettered but restricted depending on the location of an activity. With regard to ocean upwelling activities aiming at geoengineering, ocean pipes could be analogous to pipelines, and the lawfulness of deploying ocean upwelling pipes for geoengineering purposes depends on the location of deployment.

3.4 Ocean alkalinity addition

Considering that ocean alkalinity addition is achieved by introducing chemicals into the ocean, it gives rise to a similar legal discussion as in the case of ocean fertilization. The main issues to be discussed in this section are the legality of the introduction of silicate or carbonate minerals into the ocean and the obligation to protect the marine environment. Ocean alkalinity addition is subject to the UNCLOS and the LC/LP. Other conventions, such as the CBD, may also be applicable if significant transboundary harm occurs.

3.4.1 Alkalinity addition and the obligation to prevent marine pollution

Part XII of the UNCLOS sets forth the obligation to protect and preserve the marine environment. Article 194(1) of the UNCLOS provides that states shall take measures to prevent, reduce and control pollution of the marine environment from any source. The objectives of the LC and the LP are to protect and preserve the marine environment from all sources of pollution and take effective control of marine pollution caused by dumping.[135] The LC, the LP and Part XII of the UNCLOS could be deemed to be applicable to ocean alkalinity addition if the addition constitutes marine pollution. According to Article 1(4) of the UNCLOS, Article 1(10) of the LP and Article 1 of the LC, pollution to the marine environment is defined as the introduction by man, directly or indirectly, of substances into the marine environment that results or likely to result in such deleterious effects as harm to living resources, marine life, human health, hindrance to marine activities and impairment of quality for use of seawater. Unlike ocean fertilization, which attempts to transfer CO_2 from the atmosphere to the ocean, thereby creating a significant risk of disturbing the biological chain of the marine ecosystem and generating toxic pollutants, activities to enhance ocean alkalinity could offset ocean acidification and protect ocean ecosystems, among other things, coral reefs and crustaceans. Despite the unknowns regarding the side effects of ocean alkalinity addition to marine ecosystems and the seawater environment, it would be more plausible to conclude, at least for the moment, that ocean alkalinity addition is not contrary to the objective to protect and preserve the marine environment, provided that the quantity, time and location of alkalinity addition are appropriate.

Should scientists have adequate knowledge to believe that alkaline substances introduced into the marine environment are likely to cause environmental harm, such as negative impacts arising from local and temporal pH spikes or the toxic effects of rock dust and from mineral impurities, the introduction of alkaline substances at sea would breach the obligation to prevent marine pollution. Following this assumption, the precautionary approach would be applicable to the parties to the LP. According to Article 3 of the LP, contracting parties shall apply a precautionary approach to environmental protection from dumping of wastes or other matter. Appropriate precautionary measures are taken where there is reason to believe that alkaline substances introduced into the marine environment are likely to cause harm even when there is no conclusive evidence to prove a causal relation between the input of alkaline substances and their effects. The next issue is whether the introduction of alkaline substance constitutes "dumping of wastes or other matter".

3.4.2 Introduction of alkaline substances and the rules of "dumping"

As for international conventions, it has already been addressed that the UNCLOS and the LC/LP contain provisions regarding dumping. Under the UNCLOS, Article 194(3)(a) stipulates that States Parties shall take all necessary measures to prevent or minimize marine pollution from the release of toxic, harmful or noxious substance by dumping. Article 210 requires states to adopt laws and regulations when it is necessary to take such measures to prevent, reduce and control pollution by marine dumping. The LC and the LP require contracting parties to individually and collectively promote and preserve the marine environment from all sources of pollution, in particular, by taking effective measures to prevent, reduce marine pollution by dumping of wastes and other matter.

Under the OSPAR Convention, contracting parties shall take all possible steps to prevent and eliminate pollution, among other things, from dumping wastes or other matter.[136]

Under the UNCLOS, the LC/LP and the OSPAR Convention, any deliberate disposal into the sea of wastes or other matter from vessels or other man-made structures at sea is defined as dumping.[137] Pursuant to this definition, the introduction of alkaline substances via ships or pipes into the marine environment would constitute "dumping" if the introduction activity is "deliberate disposal" and the substances are deemed to be "wastes or other matter".

The UNCLOS and the LC/LP exempt "the placement of matter for a purpose other than the mere disposal thereof" from dumping, provided that such placement is not contrary to the aims of the conventions.[138] The OSPAR Convention contains a similar provision.[139] It is clear that the addition of alkaline substances into the sea is to increase ocean uptake of atmospheric CO_2 instead of a "deliberate disposal". However, due to the uncertainty relating to the scientific basis, it remains undetermined whether the placement is contrary to the aims of the conventions. If the addition leads to deleterious consequences for the marine environment, one may argue that ocean alkaline addition would not be exempted from "dumping" under those conventions, because such a placement is contrary to the aims of the conventions. In fact, this argument could be used to rule out any exemption of "dumping", because the placement of any type of substance may result in, more or less, some potential negative effects on the marine environment. In other words, a substance that is fully beneficial to the marine environment without any negative effect may not exist.

In the case of ocean alkalinity addition, it might be acceptable to argue that the positive effect of offsetting ocean acidification and protecting living resources could outweigh the likely negative effects. At least, the net benefit could depend on each individual case to what extent an ocean alkaline activity could be exempted from "dumping" rather than categorically ruling out any exemption by the excuse of it being contrary to the objectives of the conventions.[140] However, in cases where the contracting parties to any of the abovementioned conventions agree that ocean alkalinity addition constitutes dumping, the next issue could be the identification of the applicable rules governing the dumping of alkaline substances. The UNCLOS merely contains general obligations without any specific stipulation to allow or prohibit the dumping of alkaline substances.

The LC prohibits the dumping of wastes and other matter listed in Annex I and requires a prior special permit for the dumping of wastes or other matter listed in Annex II. "Wastes and other matter" refers to material and substance of any kind.[141] Since none of the proposed alkaline substances (lime, limestone and silicate minerals) appears to fall under Annex I, the LC does not prohibit the introduction of such alkaline substances at sea. However, according to paragraph D of Annex II, the dumping of large quantities of alkaline substances, though of a non-toxic nature, may become harmful due to, for instance, temporal pH spikes in a local sea area. Consequently, the introduction of alkaline substances at sea may require a prior special permit if a vast volume of rock dust is introduced into the sea. The dumping of alkaline substances at a small scale would only require a prior general permit.[142]

The LP adopts stricter criteria than the LC for the dumping of waste or other matter. Article 4 of the LP stipulates that contracting parties shall prohibit the dumping of any wastes or other matter with the exception of those listed in Annex 1. Lime, limestone and silicate minerals are not covered by the list of exemptions in Annex 1. The exemption of "inert, inorganic geological material" is not applicable to alkaline substances, because they are added for the purpose of chemically reacting with CO_2 and water in the marine environment, and are thus not "inert" substances. However, a new Article 6*bis* under the 2013 Amendments of the LP provides that Article 4 does not apply to activities listed in Annex 4, which provides a new possibility for ocean alkaline addition to be allowed under the LP.[143] According to Article 6*bis*, a marine geoengineering activity listed in Annex 4 shall not be allowed unless the activity is authorized under a permit. A permit shall only be issued after the activity has undergone an assessment that has determined that pollution of the marine environment from the proposed activity is prevented or reduced to a minimum, and the outcome of the assessment is that the activity is not contrary to the aims of the LP. The new Annex 4 currently contains only one listing, namely, ocean fertilization. To apply Article 6*bis* to ocean alkalinity addition, Annex 4 must be amended in the future to contain further listings. Considering that the adverse impacts of ocean alkalinity addition are not to be as serious as that of ocean fertilization, permits might not have to be limited to legitimate scientific research activities.

Regulations regarding the prevention of marine pollution by dumping can also be found in a host of regional sea conventions. For instance, Annex II of the OSPAR Convention prohibits the dumping of all wastes or other matter, except for those wastes or other matter listed in Article 3 of Annex II. As the proposed alkaline substances are not included in the list, the dumping of alkaline substances is not allowed under the OSPAR Convention. The 1992

Helsinki Convention prohibits dumping in the Baltic Sea Area, except for those substances listed in Annex V.[144] Again, lime, limestone or silicate are not included in Annex V, which means the dumping of these substances is not permitted under the 1992 Helsinki Convention. By contrast, the Convention on the Protection of the Black Sea against Pollution does not prohibit the use of alkaline compounds, but rather controls and strictly limits their discharge, taking into the account the fact that "they are less harmful or more readily rendered harmless by natural processes".[145] Other regional sea conventions, though mentioning marine pollution by dumping, do not contain specific lists of prohibited substances.[146]

3.4.3 Potential impacts and relevant conventions

One challenge to ocean alkalinity addition is that the huge amount of alkaline materials placed into the ocean would exceed the ocean's bearing capacity. The CBD would be applicable where ocean alkalinity threatens marine organisms, in particular corals. The relevant provisions of the CBD are the same as in the case of ocean fertilization.[147]

3.4.4 Synthetic consideration

Ocean alkalinity addition shares similarities with ocean fertilization: Both techniques envisage the placement of chemical particles in the sea for the purpose of removing atmospheric CO_2 by means of interacting with certain substances in the marine environment. However, the most significant distinction between the two techniques is that the placement of the ocean alkalinity makes a great contribution to offsetting ocean acidification and preserving coral reefs and shell creatures while ocean fertilization may only have adverse effects on the marine ecosystem. This distinction indicates that it may be reasonable and meaningful to regulate these two similar techniques differently. As concluded in Section 3.2.4, ocean fertilization would qualify as dumping. Even though the purpose of ocean fertilization is to stimulate plankton photosynthesis and remove CO_2 rather than the mere disposal of substances, ocean fertilization should not be exempted from the dumping prohibitions if the potential water pollution and the harm to marine ecosystems cause deleterious effects. In contrast, ocean alkalinity addition might not qualify as dumping, because it aims at CO_2 removal and the placement of alkaline substances in the sea contributes to protecting and preserving the marine environment.

One may still argue that, based on insufficient scientific results, ocean alkalinity addition constitutes dumping and results in deleterious effects to the marine environment. At the moment, there is a lack of rules under the UNCLOS or LC/LP to weigh the positive effects against the negative effects of the placement of a substance. The definition of "deleterious effects" may require a further interpretation for determining the "net" effects after weighing the opposite effects.[148]

Taking into account the scientific uncertainty about the unintended environmental impacts of ocean alkalinity addition, the precautionary approach under Article 3(1) of the LP is applicable. However, the applicability of the precautionary approach does not mean that ocean alkalinity addition research and deployment should be terminated. Instead, a balance between the positive and negative impacts by a case-by-case assessment, based on the location, time and the substance involved, is necessary. The development of the precautionary approach in the context of geoengineering will be discussed in Chapter 5.

In the case that the addition of lime, limestone or silicate minerals into the sea is not exempted from dumping, the respective obligations under the conventions discussed above are different. Currently, no convention explicitly regulates ocean alkalinity addition. The UNCLOS does not contain provisions directly applicable to the dumping of alkaline substances. The LC does not prohibit the dumping of alkaline substances, but a special or general permit in advance is required. The LP currently does not permit the dumping of alkaline substances, but Annex 4 could be amended in the future to incorporate ocean alkalinity addition. Once being listed in Annex 4, placement of alkaline substances may be authorized under a permit. The OSPAR Convention and the 1992 Convention on the Protection of Baltic Sea Area prohibit the dumping of the substances. If the parties would like to allow alkalinity addition, then they should amend the two conventions; if not, the prohibition will remain in place.

3.5 Marine cloud whitening (MCW)

Despite the fact that MCW is a geoengineering technique undertaken at sea, it injects seawater spray into and affects primarily the troposphere. This section will examine the existing international law governing MCW in two respects: the legality of the conduct, i.e. the legality of deploying fleets for spraying seawater droplets into clouds under the coverage of the UNCLOS; and the legal rules relevant to the likely adverse impacts on the atmosphere. So far, the scientific knowledge of MCW has been acquired from computer modelling. The actual impacts on the atmosphere and weather patterns resulting from spraying seawater may differ from the predicted effects. Based on the preliminary prediction that seawater aerosols would adversely affect the atmosphere, the conventions regarding air pollution and ozone layer protection are relevant.

As introduced in Chapter 1, MCW is expected to change weather patterns by, *inter alia*, decreasing precipitation. In this respect, the ENMOD Convention is a relevant legal instrument. The ENMOD Convention has been addressed in Section 2.3.1 on permanently banned geoengineering activities. In this section, the discussion presumes that MCW is utilized for peaceful purposes, notwithstanding the fact that MCW may bring about harm to the atmosphere or the seas.

3.5.1 MCW and the UNCLOS

The UNCLOS applies to MCW involving a fleet of unmanned ships deployed for injecting seawater droplets. The discussion will be divided into three parts based on the location of MCW activities.

3.5.1.1 Territorial sea

The deployment of ships in a coastal state's internal waters or territorial sea requires the coastal state's authorization.[149] The rules concerning innocent passage are not applicable to ships used for MCW in the coastal state's territorial sea. Article 18(2) stipulates that "passage" shall be continuous and expeditious. Stopping and anchoring are allowed only insofar as they are incidental to ordinary navigation or are rendered necessary by *force majeure* or distress or for the purpose of rendering assistance. The deployment of ships for MCW in a foreign state's territorial sea, however, is not merely continuous and expeditious passage. Rather, ships stay at a suitable place for a longer period of time to inject seawater vapour into the atmosphere. Besides, Article 19 demonstrates that passage is innocent so long as it is not prejudicial to the peace, good order or security of the coastal state. Passage of a foreign ship is not innocent if in the territorial sea if it engages in the carrying out of research or survey activities or any other activity not having a direct bearing on passage.[150] Consequently, navigating and stopping in a coastal state's territorial sea for the purpose of cloud whitening would not constitute innocent passage and thus would always require the coastal state's approval, even for the purpose of (applied) scientific research.[151]

3.5.1.2 EEZ

With respect to the EEZ, the legal analysis of MCW is similar to that of ocean upwelling. Pursuant to the UNCLOS, coastal states, in the exercise of their jurisdiction, have the right to regulate, authorize and conduct marine scientific research in their EEZs.[152] Coastal states shall, in normal circumstances, grant their consent for marine scientific research projects by other states or competent international organizations in their EEZs.[153] The rules regarding rights and duties of coastal states in marine scientific research would be applicable to MCW if the ships to be used qualify for marine scientific research. As examined in Section 3.3.1, marine scientific research aims to increase human's knowledge about the marine environment, including all its sources. Distinct from ocean upwelling carried out below the ocean surface, MCW is undertaken above the ocean surface and the seawater is sprayed upward into the atmosphere. Moreover, MCW research regarding assessing cloud whitening conditions and testing spraying facilities aims to increase the knowledge of the troposphere but not the marine environment.[154] For this reason, the research on MCW techniques could be qualified as scientific research but not *marine* scientific research,[155] and is therefore not subject to the jurisdiction of the coastal state. Ambiguously, Article 58 provides the rights of other states in the EEZ by reference to the freedoms stated in Article 87, in which the "freedom of scientific research" is included.[156] It is not clear whether the wording "scientific research" in Article 87(1)(f) refers to "marine scientific research". According to Article 87(1)(f), the freedom of scientific research is subject to Part XIII, which is about "marine scientific research". Furthermore, were "scientific research" in Article 87(1)(f) to mean more than "marine scientific research", states other than the coastal states would enjoy the right to conduct non-marine scientific research in the coastal state's EEZ. Such presumption is obviously not legitimate. Therefore, the provisions relevant to conducting (marine) scientific research in the EEZ are not applicable to MCW.

The question then becomes whether one state enjoys the freedom to use unmanned ships to conduct geoengineering activities in the EEZ of a coastal state. It depends on whether such a right is subject to the freedoms regulated in Article 58. By referring to the freedoms stated in Article 87 about the freedom of the high seas, Article 58 provides that all states enjoy the freedom of navigation and other internationally lawful uses of the sea related to the freedoms of the high seas, such as those associated with the operation of ships.[157] In the case of MCW, large numbers of unmanned ships are directed by human control to arrive at suitable locations for cloud whitening and remain at the same place for a certain period of time. The unmanned ships are utilized for two actions – moving from one place to the destination and floating on the water for spraying operations. To explore the legal status of MCW activities, a legal analysis of mobile offshore drilling units (MODUs) provides an analogy.

MODUs, or deepwater mobile oil rigs, are drilling rigs that float upon the surface of the water when being moved from one drill site to another.[158] MODUs have traditionally been treated as ships because of their physical shapes and their seagoing and navigational abilities.[159] MODUs must fly the flag of the deploying state, and the flag state enjoys the freedom of navigation in the EEZ of another state. It is clear that MODUs navigate on the sea when they move from one drill site to another and thus the deploying state has exclusive jurisdiction during navigation. However, there is no consensus on whether the deploying state has exclusive jurisdiction over the oil rigs when they are engaged in drilling operations. Traditional practices tend to treat the MODUs as ships and the deploying state has the jurisdiction over the MODUs during the drilling phases. However, considering the dangers of potential oil spills that may impact the coastal states' environment and economy (fishing and tourism industries), it is argued that these rigs should not be considered ships once drilling operations begin; these rigs should be treated as an installation during the drilling and production phases of a deepwater oil project.[160] As seabed installations, mobile oilrigs would not have flag states, and the coastal state has the sovereign right to explore and exploit natural resources in the EEZ in the drilling and production phases.[161]

Insofar as unmanned ships cross seawater and arrive at desirable destination to do their work, the action of the planned movement from one place to another could be identified as "navigation".[162] However, when unmanned ships stay at a location for a period of time and inject seawater into the atmosphere, they are no longer ships, but rather "installations" at sea.[163] Pursuant to this differentiation, the coastal state has jurisdiction over unmanned ships in the phase of seawater injection. However, note that there are three significant distinctions between MODUs and ships utilized for MCW: different purposes, different levels of environmental risks and different affected areas. First, MODUs are utilized for the purpose of exploring oil resources, which is one of the coastal state's sovereign rights in its EEZ, whereas MCW aims to decrease the global average temperature. Second, as introduced in Chapter 1 when discussing the adverse impacts of MCW activities on the environment, the harm to marine environment arising from seawater injection seems to be less than that of oil drilling operations. More significantly, the impact that MCW activities would have on the atmosphere and weather patterns and in the affected area is much wider than the space above the coastal state. As a result, ships used for MCW and MODUs might not be subject to comparable rules.

In principle, a coastal state has the freedom to move unmanned ships and uses the ships for injecting seawater in the EEZ, either for scientific research or large-scale deployment, provided that the coastal state has due regard to the rights of other states, in particular, the freedom of navigation of other states.[164] As to states other than the coastal state, they enjoy the freedom to move unmanned ships to a location within the EEZ of a coastal state, provided that the conducting state has due regard to the rights of the coastal state.[165] However, once the ships stay at a location and inject seawater, the freedom of the conducting state is subject to the jurisdiction of the coastal state if the activity of seawater injection causes damage to the marine environment.[166] In fact, if the wind-powered rotor ships were really built and employed for seawater injection, the risk of marine pollution would be very low. The risk of adversely affecting ocean circulation and modifying the local climate require further research.

3.5.1.3 High seas[167]

Article 87 stipulates that the high seas are open to all states. This provision provides the legal basis for conducting MCW activities on the high seas. However, the freedom is not unfettered. Basically, the state that conducts MCW activities must exercise its freedom of the high seas with due regard for the interests of other states in their exercise of the freedom of the high seas, *inter alia*, the freedom of navigation.[168]

3.5.2 MCW and air-related conventions

3.5.2.1 The Vienna Convention for the protection of the ozone layer

The Vienna Convention for the Protection of the Ozone Layer (the Vienna Convention) and its Montreal Protocol on Substances that Deplete the

Ozone Layer have made a great contribution to reducing the production and consumption of ozone depleting substances in order to protect the Earth's fragile ozone layer.[169]

While it seems that seawater aerosol spraying would not reach the ozone layer, it is of importance to take into account the Vienna Convention because water vapour is listed in the convention as a substance thought to have the potential to modify the chemical and physical properties of the ozone layer.[170] Notwithstanding the fact that MCW techniques distribute seawater vapour to the lower atmosphere in order to seed the clouds, a certain amount of water vapour may reach the higher troposphere and even the lower stratosphere. Article 3 requires the parties to conduct research and scientific assessments on, among other things, "[s]ubstances, practices, processes and activities that may affect the ozone layer, and their cumulative effects". Annex I, paragraph 4(e), of the Vienna Convention lists "hydrogen substances" and in particular "water" as a possible sources that may modify the ozone layer. It elaborates that "[w]ater, the source of which is natural, plays a vital role in both troposphere and stratospheric photochemistry. Local sources of water vapour in the stratosphere include the oxidation of methane and, to a lesser extent, hydrogen".[171] It appears from these provisions that the Vienna Convention is applicable to MCW, because pumping seawater vapour into the troposphere would fall within the activities that modify or are likely to modify the ozone layer.[172]

Nevertheless, the difficulty in applying Article 2 remains because geoengineering also aims to "protect human health and the environment against adverse effects". There is a big difference between an activity that emits substances that lead to ozone layer modification and a geoengineering technique that aims to protect the environment against climate change but that leads to deleterious consequences to the ozone layer at the same time.

One may conclude that, pursuant to Article 2 and Annex I, paragraph 4(e), of the Vienna Convention, the use of water vapour in geoengineering for enhancing the cloud albedo would not be lawful because water vapour may modify the ozone layer.[173] However, the Vienna Convention does not provide for concrete actions to control the use of water vapour.

As to the Montreal Protocol, which contains quantified obligations to control the use of substances that deplete the ozone layer, water vapour is not among the substances controlled by it.

3.5.2.2 *Convention on Long-Range Transboundary Air Pollution (CLRTAP)*

The CLRTAP, which obliges its 51 parties in and beyond the UNECE region, was the first international legally binding instrument that endeavours to limit and gradually reduce and prevent air pollution including long-range transboundary air pollution.[174] In contrast to the Vienna Convention, which contains provisions directed at a particular kind of substance used in MCW that may modify the ozone layer, the CLRTAP does not involve any provision that even obliquely touches upon MCW. The CLRTAP has been supplemented by eight protocols, including protocols concerning the control of emissions of nitrogen oxides, sulphur emissions, heavy metals, etc.[175] Regarding MCW, neither water vapour nor sodium chlorine (from sea salt) is listed as an "air pollutant" in any of the protocols to the CLRTAP.

Article 1 of the CLRTAP defines "air pollution" as "the introduction by man [. . .] of substances or energy into the air resulting in deleterious effects [that] endanger human health, harm living resources and ecosystems". Pursuant to this definition, the chemical substances that are proved injurious or harmful, such as sulphur dioxide, are undoubtedly to be regarded as "air pollutants". However, water vapour and sodium chlorine are not inherently harmful. The spraying of seawater and the generation of new cloud nuclei would result in adverse effects on ecosystems and climate patterns only if the anthropogenic seawater vapour is beyond the tolerance level of the environment for these substances. This situation is analogous to CO_2 because CO_2 is also a natural substance on the Earth and it only becomes an environmental problem due to the excessive amount of anthropogenic emissions. As with the international regulation of CO_2, the special feature of seawater vapour may merit a specific regulation to address MCW.

3.5.3 Synthetic consideration

There is no international legal framework explicitly regulating the geoengineering technique of MCW. The unique characteristic of this technique is that it utilizes unmanned ships as a platform on the sea but aims to influence cloud formation in the atmosphere, i.e. the area of deployment is different from the affected area. Pursuant to the UNCLOS, the lawfulness of conducting a MCW activity is subject to the rights and jurisdiction of the conducting state and coastal states, depending on the location of the activity.

Both the Vienna Convention and the CLRTAP do not prohibit or largely restrict the exercise of MCW techniques. Considering the adverse effects that water vapour and sodium chlorine may have on the atmosphere, in particular, the ozone layer, specific rules need to be developed.

3.6 BECCS

As introduced in Chapter 1, BECCS integrates planting and harvesting bioenergy, producing energy, and sequestrating the resulting CO_2. These three steps involve different problems to which different legal norms apply. This section will analyse the legal issues relating to these three steps.

3.6.1 Biomass plantation under the coverage of the biodiversity regime

Regarding the first step of BECCS, biomass supply is constrained by technical limits to biomass yield and due to tension with other types of land use.[176] Large-scale biomass production would adversely impact natural ecosystems because it may compete with the existing agricultural land use as well as forests and other types of natural landscapes. Biodiversity loss would happen if unsustainable agricultural practices are implemented for planting biomass.[177]

Several CBD decisions address the treatment of biomass plantation in the context of biodiversity protection, *inter alia*, agricultural and forest biodiversity. CBD Decision IX/1 integrates biofuel production and use into the programme of work on agricultural biodiversity, in particular by addressing biofuel production, especially when based on feedstock produced through agriculture.[178] In Decision IX/2, the Conference of Parties (COP) agreed that biofuel production and use should be sustainable in relation to biological diversity.[179] The COP also recognized the need to promote the positive and minimize the negative impacts of biofuel production and its use on biodiversity and the livelihoods of indigenous and local communities.[180] In Decision IX/5, the COP invited parties to

> [a]ddress both, direct and indirect, positive and negative impacts that the production and use of biomass for energy, in particular large-scale and/ or industrial production and use, might have on forest biodiversity and on indigenous and local communities, also taking into account the components of the decision IX/2 on biofuels and biodiversity relevant to forest biodiversity, reflecting varying conditions of countries and regions.[181]

The CBD COP 10, in Decision X/37, recalls that Decision IX/2 recognizes the need to improve "policy guidance and decision making to promote the positive and minimize or avoid the negative impacts of biofuels on biodiversity and impacts on biodiversity that affect related socioeconomic conditions".[182] For this purpose, the COP encouraged the parties and other governments to develop and use environmentally sound technologies, and to support the development of research programmes and undertake impact assessments.[183]

3.6.2 *Bioenergy production and air pollution*

With respect to the second step of BECCS, there are high additional energy requirements for bioenergy production when converting biomass to other forms of bioenergy. Biomass power plants would bring about serious air pollution.[184]

Air pollution would occur when extra energy is needed to produce some forms of bioenergy derived from biomass. The burning of cane fields for harvesting and the burning of crop wastes, for instance, can increase local air pollution because such burning produces large amounts of carbon monoxide, nitrogen oxides, and hydrocarbons.[185] Generally, the air pollution caused by bioenergy production is local pollution and thus subject to domestic law or applicable bilateral treaties. If long-range transboundary air pollution caused by bioenergy production occurs, the CLRTAP would be applicable.

3.6.3 International legal regimes relating to CO_2 transportation and sequestration

The third step of BECCS is to transport and sequester CO_2 in underground geological formations in the ocean or on land. The transportation could be onshore or offshore, by pipes, ships, road or rail. The storage includes onshore storage in saline aquifers or depleted oil fields and offshore storage in sub-seabed geological formations.[186] The process of transporting, injecting and storing CO_2 may lead to transboundary environmental harm. The injection and storage of large amounts of CO_2 in deep underground saline formations may contaminate groundwater. More seriously, there is a risk of CO_2 leakage in the process of CO_2 transportation and injection or accidental CO_2 leakage from storage sites. If CO_2 leaks into the soil, it may lead to soil acidification; if CO_2 leaks into the ocean, it will exacerbate ocean acidification; if CO_2 leaks back into the atmosphere, it may result in not only higher CO_2 concentrations in the atmosphere, but, worse, create extremely dangerous situations due to the high density, including the risks of an explosion.

As there is no special legal framework governing BECCS on the previous issues, the existing CCS regulations could be a part of the legal framework for BECCS. An entire CCS project can be broken down into five stages: capture, compression, transport, injection and long-term storage. Except for the LC/LP and the OSPAR Convention, which directly regulate the storage of CO_2 streams in sub-seabed geological formations, many other international legal instruments do not expressly address CCS but may nevertheless be applicable to it. For instance, all states are under the obligation to prevent significant transboundary harm arising from CCS projects in the seabed. Articles 205 and 206 of the UNCLOS provide the obligation for parties to monitor activities and undertake EIA of activities; and Article 4 of the Basel Convention requires the parties to implement environmentally-sound management of hazardous wastes and other wastes to prevent pollution or minimize the consequences of pollution for human health and the environment.[187]

Specifically, several international legal instruments relating to the transboundary movement of CO_2 and CO_2 storage merit a detailed examination as follows.

3.6.3.1 Transboundary movement of CO_2

(I) BASEL CONVENTION

The Basel Convention is designed to establish a global regime to protect human health and the environment against the adverse effects of hazardous wastes.[188] The threshold question for applying the Basel Convention to CO_2 sequestration is whether CO_2 is a "hazardous waste".[189] The categories of "hazardous waste" to be controlled are listed in Annex I of the Basel Convention. *Prima facie*, CO_2 might fall in category Y15 in Annex I: "wastes of an explosive nature not subject to other legislation". CO_2 fluid escaped from a pipeline rupture would rapidly expand and become gas. The expansion would be dangerous if the gas accumulates in trenches or depressions.[190] It is still debated whether CO_2 has an explosive nature.[191] Even if CO_2 does not fall into any category of Annex I, the Basel Convention would still be applicable if CO_2 is defined as, or considered to be, "hazardous wastes by the domestic legislation of the party of export, import or transit".[192]

If CO_2 is characterized as a "hazardous waste" under the Basel Convention, there would be a general requirement for a party not to permit CO_2 to be exported to a non-party or to be imported from a non-party.[193] In addition, parties would also agree not to allow the export of CO_2 for disposal within the area south of 60° south latitude, regardless of whether such wastes are subject to transboundary movement.[194] Besides, parties have the right to refuse the import of CO_2, and after one party's notification of the refusal, other parties shall prohibit or shall not permit the export of hazardous wastes and other wastes to this party.[195] If CO_2 is not prohibited by both import and export parties, the importing party still retains the right not to consent to a specific import of CO_2.[196]

(II) BAMAKO CONVENTION

The Bamako Convention on the Ban of the Import into Africa and the Control of Transboundary Movement and Management of Hazardous Wastes within Africa is a regional agreement that establishes a regime to control the trade in hazardous wastes within Africa.[197] The Bamako Convention goes further than the Basel Convention as the latter does not regulate the trade in hazardous wastes not intended for disposal, while the former prohibits the importation of all hazardous wastes, for any reason, into Africa from non-contracting parties.[198]

CO_2 is not specifically mentioned in any category of hazardous wastes listed in Annex I to the Bamako Convention.[199] However, as in the Basel Convention, CO_2 could still be covered by the Bamako Convention if it possess one of the characteristics, such as explosive, contained in Annex II of Bamako Convention or if CO_2 is defined as, or considered to be, hazardous waste by the domestic legislation of the party of export, import or transit.[200]

Should CO_2 be considered a hazardous waste under the Bamako Convention, it could only be imported from contracting parties to the Bamako Convention. This would effectively prohibit the import of CO_2 from outside Africa.

(III) THE UNCLOS

The UNCLOS does not include explicit language on transboundary movement of hazardous substances. Article 195 states that

> [i]n taking measures to prevent, reduce and control pollution of the marine environment, States shall act so as not to transfer, directly or indirectly, damage or hazards from one area to another or transform one type of pollution into another.

The expression of "from one area to another" is an early reflection of the principle of controlling transboundary movement of hazards and wastes.[201] However, the UNCLOS provides no definition of "hazardous", which makes its applicability to CO_2 open to interpretation.

The UNCLOS regulates CCS in a wider range, as it encompasses not only provisions for marine environmental protection but also a jurisdictional framework for activities at sea.[202] The rights and obligations vary when CO_2 is transported into different zones of the sea. A coastal state has exclusive sovereign rights for the purpose of exploring and exploiting, conserving and managing the natural resources in its EEZ.[203] Since the movement of CO_2 does not belong to any activity associated with natural resources, all states have the freedom to construct pipelines and transport CO_2 by pipelines in a coastal state's EEZ.[204] In exercising this freedom, states shall have due regard to the rights and duties of the coastal state and shall comply with the laws and regulations adopted by the coastal states in accordance with the provisions of this convention and other rules of international law.[205] CO_2 streams may also be transported through pipelines laid in the high seas. Article 87 entitles all states the freedom to lay submarine cables and pipelines. The freedom is subject to Article 79 on the rules of building pipelines on the continental shelf.[206] Although all states enjoy the freedom to lay pipelines on the continental shelf, this freedom is subject to the coastal state's right to take reasonable measures for the exploration of the continental shelf, the exploitation of its natural resources and the prevention, reduction and control of pollution from pipelines. Besides, "[t]he delineation of the course for the laying of such pipelines on the continental shelf is subject to the consent of the coastal State".[207] In addition, states shall have due regard to cables or pipelines already in position when they lay pipelines to transport CO_2 streams.[208] Connecting the rules above to transboundary CCS projects, states enjoy a relatively wide discretion with respect to the laying of pipelines on a coastal state's continental shelf for transporting CO_2 streams.[209]

(IV) THE LC/LP

Section 3.2.1 has elaborated how the LC and the LP regulate the dumping of fertilizers into the ocean. There is still no final conclusion as to whether the placement of iron, nitrogen or phosphate in the ocean for purpose of mitigating CO_2 is lawful under the LC and the LP. With respect to the placement of CO_2 into the sea, the LC contains no explicit prohibition or permission. The LC covers the deliberate disposal into the sea of wastes or other matter from vessels or other man-made structures (e.g. pipes) at sea, but does not include the placement of matter for a purpose other than the mere disposal thereof, provided that such placement is not contrary to the aims of the LC.[210] If CO_2 falls within the definition of "industrial waste" that is referred to in Annex I of the LC, the dumping of CO_2 is definitely prohibited under the LC. If CO_2 does not belong to "industrial waste", the placement of CO_2 for a purpose of sequestrating carbon emissions would not be prohibited by the LC, provided that such placement is not contrary to the aims of the LC.

No consensus has yet been reached by the contracting parties to the LC on CO_2's characteristics.[211]

Since 2008, the contracting parties to the LP have considered conditionally permitting the transboundary movement of CO_2 streams.[212] In 2009, Article 6 of the LP was amended to enable the export of CO_2 for disposal at sea, on the condition that the protection standards of the LP are fully met.[213] Paragraph 2 of Article 6 now stipulates that the export of CO_2 streams for disposal in accordance with Annex 1 is allowed, provided that the countries concerned have entered into an agreement or arrangement that shall include:

> [(a)] confirmation and allocation of permitting responsibilities between the exporting and receiving countries, consistent with the provisions of this Protocol and other applicable international law; and
> [(b)] in the case of export to non-Contracting Parties, provisions at a minimum equivalent to those contained in this Protocol [. . .] to ensure that the agreement or arrangement does not derogate from the obligations of Contracting Parties under this Protocol to protect and preserve the marine environment.[214]

3.6.3.2 CO_2 storage

States have a range of procedural obligations to prevent or minimize the significant risk of CO_2 leakage that may harm the environment or human health. In the process of injection, sealing faults or fissures in an underground reservoir could cause local pressure build-up with potential rock fractures at a weak point.[215] Hence, careful site selection, appropriate monitoring and verification during injection are key to avoiding hazards. Once a storage site is closed, the acting state remains responsible for monitoring the environmental impacts and, if a risk of leakage exists, taking corrective measures. The international rules governing offshore storage are different from those rules governing onshore storage.

(I) OFFSHORE STORAGE

CO_2 streams from CCS processes for sequestration is explicitly addressed by the LP as a matter that can be permitted for dumping into the ocean. Annex 1 of the LP was amended in 2006 to add CO_2 streams from CO_2 capture processes for sequestration to the list of wastes and other matter that may be considered for dumping. The dumping of CO_2 streams must be mindful of the objectives and general obligations set out in Articles 2 and 3 of the LP. Moreover, paragraph 4 of Annex 1 provides that CO_2 streams may only be considered for dumping if they meet three requirements. First, CO_2 streams must be disposed into a sub-seabed geological formation (not into the water column). Second, they must consist predominantly of CO_2. Third, "no wastes or other matter are added for the purpose of disposing of those wastes or other matter".[216]

In June 2007, two decisions were adopted to amend Annexes II and III to the OSPAR Convention to clarify the extent of allowed CCS activities within the geological scope of the OSPAR Convention.[217] Decision 2007/1 expressly prohibits the storage of CO_2 streams in the water column or on the seabed. Decision 2007/2 facilitates the long-term storage of CO_2 streams in sub-soil geological formations.[218] According to Annex II on the Prevention and Elimination of Pollution by Dumping or Incineration and Annex III on the Prevention and Elimination of Pollution from Offshore Sources, CO_2 streams from carbon dioxide capture processes for storage were exempted from the prohibition on dumping waste and other matter.[219] Note that contracting parties should ensure that CO_2 streams are stored permanently in the sub-soil geological formations, and will not lead to significant adverse consequences for the marine environment, human health and other legitimate uses of the maritime area.

If CO_2 streams are injected into the continental shelf of the coastal state, an express consent from the coastal state is required, because the coastal state has the exclusive right to authorize and regulate drilling on the continental shelf for all purposes.[220] Special attention should be paid when storing CO_2 in the Area.[221] According to the UNCLOS, the Area and its resources are the common heritage of mankind and no state shall claim or exercise sovereignty or sovereign rights over any part of the Area or its resources,[222] and activities in the Area shall be carried out exclusively for peaceful purposes and for the benefit of mankind as a whole.[223] As the phrase "activities in the Area" is defined as all activities of exploration for, and exploitation of, the resources[224] of the Area, it does not cover CO_2 storage activities. The rules regarding the International Seabed Authority and organizing and controlling activities in the Area are therefore not applicable to CO_2 storage activities.[225] CO_2 storage in the sub-seabed formations belonging to the Area would follow the general rules on CO_2 sequestration under the LP and the OSPAR Convention as stated in the previous paragraphs of this section.

(II) ONSHORE STORAGE

In addition to marine storage, CO_2 can also be stored in territorial geological formations, among others, saline aquifers. There is no international legal instrument applicable to saline aquifers so far.

3.6.4 Synthetic consideration

BECCS is a promising technology for making a significant contribution to CO_2 mitigation. Similar to afforestation, reforestation and land-use change, the first step of BECCS, namely biomass production, normally does not cause significant transboundary harm as they are carried out under the jurisdiction or control of one state. Nevertheless, the risk of biodiversity loss from land use change may cross borders and thus require bilateral or multilateral collaboration in terms of monitoring, assessment, information sharing, etc.

With regard to the second step of BECCS, extra energy costs and GHG emissions associated with the bioenergy production might counter the benefits of the GHG emissions offset achieved. In addition, the process of producing bioenergy from different forms of biomass impact air quality through the emission of dust and other deleterious compounds. The international legal control on such air pollution should be consistent with the permit or prohibition of the relevant types of gas under international legal instruments.[226]

The third step of BECCS (i.e. carbon capture and sequestration) may create a risk of transboundary environmental harm during the transboundary movement and long-term storage of CO_2. There are various situations that need to be discussed separately. All states have the freedom to lay pipelines in the EEZ or on the continental of another coastal state, as well as in the high seas. This freedom is subject to provisions relevant to the rights of the coastal states for the exploration and exploitation of its natural resources and the duty of the coastal states to prevent or control pollution from pipelines.[227] In particular, the consent of the coastal state is required for the delineation of the course for the laying of the pipelines utilized for transporting CO_2.[228] The deploying state shall also take due regard to the pipelines and cables already in position.[229] With respect to long-term storage of CO_2, the coastal state has the exclusive right to authorize the injection of CO_2 into its continental shelf.[230] In fact, the reality is much more complex than the models summarized above. The rights and obligations may vary with the scenarios of international transportation and storage within the territory of two or more parties (e.g. capture in Party A and storage in Party B; capture in Party A and storage in Party A and B, etc.).

Besides, the characterization of CO_2 should be taken into account in the governance of CO_2 transportation. If CO_2 is regulated as hazardous waste by the domestic law of a state and that state is a party to the Basel Convention or the Bamako Convention, the rules of controlling the import and export of hazardous waste are applicable to CO_2.

3.7 Stratospheric Aerosols Injection (SAI)

SAI, as one of the SRM geoengineering techniques, aims at increasing the albedo of the stratosphere and thereby decreasing incoming solar radiation to the Earth's surface. As mentioned in Chapter 1, a fleet of high-altitude aircraft has been suggested as the easiest and cheapest way to distribute sulphate aerosol into the stratosphere. Other alternatives, such as tethered balloons and artillery, have also been proposed in order to deliver sulphate particles and/or gases into the stratosphere. The first issue to be addressed in this section is the legality of injecting sulphate aerosols (containing sulphuric acid, H_2S or SO_2) by means of aircraft, balloon or artillery into the stratosphere. Second, considering that SAI may bring about far-reaching adverse impacts on the atmosphere, notably the ozone layer, and on the ocean, the ecosystem and the climate, a range of treaties are applicable to SAI in terms of preventing and controlling harm to the environment and humans.

3.7.1 The legality of exercising injection activities in the stratosphere

The delivery of sulphate aerosol takes place in the atmosphere, which consists of two attributes: a spatial dimension above the land surface and fluctuating, dynamic air mass.[231] The legality of injecting sulphate concerns the legality of using aircraft, tethered balloons or artillery in the atmosphere which relates to the attribute of "a spatial dimension", whereas the side effects on air quality concerns the attribute of "air mass", which is the largest single natural resource on the planet.[232]

As one way of introducing sulphate aerosols into the stratosphere is by using aircraft, international rules and principles applying to air travel would be applicable to SAI. The convention on International Civil Aviation, also known as the Chicago Convention, includes almost all member states of the United Nations and established the International Civil Aviation Organization (ICAO), a specialized agency of the United Nations in charge of coordinating and regulating international air travel. Article 3(c) of the Chicago Convention regulates that aircraft used in military, customs and police services are deemed to be state aircraft. The use of aircraft in geoengineering does not pertain to any of the three exceptions and this is therefore deemed to be civil aircraft. Article 1 of the Chicago Convention stipulates that every state has complete and exclusive sovereignty over the airspace above its territory.[233] This provision entitles states to carry out SAI activities in the airspace above its territory. States are therefore generally permitted to deliver aerosols containing sulphuric acid, H_2S or SO_2 by aircraft into the stratosphere over its own territory. However, the lawfulness of conducting such an activity does not necessarily mean an unfettered right; owing to the fluctuating and dynamic property of air mass, the injection activity would be restricted by the obligation to prevent transboundary air pollution.[234]

With regard to overflight and the introduction of sulphate aerosols into the stratosphere over another state's territory, it is subject to the obligation not to violate the sovereignty of another state in accordance with customary international law.[235] In the *Case concerning Military and Paramilitary Activities in and against Nicaragua*, the ICJ found that the United States directly infringed the principle of respect for territorial sovereignty when it carried out unauthorized overflight of Nicaraguan territory by aircraft belonging to or under the control of the United States.[236] Pursuant to this customary international law obligation, the overflight of a state's territory require authorization from that state. However, an exception exists under special circumstances. Article 5 of the Chicago Convention provides that all aircraft of other contracting states, being aircraft engaged in non-scheduled international air services shall have the right, subject to the observance of the terms of this convention, to make flights into or in transit non-stop across one contracting state's territory and to make stops for non-traffic purposes without the necessity of obtaining prior permission. Each state nevertheless reserves the right, for reasons of safety of flight, to require aircraft to follow prescribed routes, or to obtain special permission.[237] Note that no scheduled air service may be operated over or into the territory of a contracting state without the special permission or other authorization of that state.[238] No provision from the Chicago Convention or any other convention can be found to address the release of substances from aircraft over another state's territory. The release of sulphate aerosols into the stratosphere over another state's territory would thus be subject to the authorization from that state.[239] Besides, according to Article 12 of the Chicago Convention, every aircraft flying over one state's territory must carry the nationality mark of the state in which the aircraft is registered and shall comply with the rules and regulations relating to the flight of aircraft in force.

With respect to the introduction of sulphate aerosols into the stratosphere over areas beyond national control, i.e. over the high seas or Antarctica, the UNCLOS and the Antarctic Treaty are applicable. Article 87 of the UNCLOS provides for the freedoms of the high seas, including the freedom of overflight, to all states. However, no provision under the UNCLOS or other conventions specifically regulates the lawfulness of the release of substances from aircraft during the flight over the high seas. The only relevant legal basis is Article 194(3)(a) in conjunction with Article 212 of the UNCLOS. However, these two articles aim to protect the marine environment against the release of harmful substances from the atmosphere. It could be argued that the injection of sulphate aerosols into the stratosphere over the high seas is not prohibited under the UNCLOS as long as it does not cause significant adverse impacts on the marine environment.

The Antarctic Treaty regulates that Antarctica shall be used exclusively for peaceful purposes.[240] SAI activities that are undertaken for the purpose of scientific research are allowed to take place in the atmosphere over the Antarctica.[241] All aircraft at points of discharging in Antarctica, shall be open at all times to inspection by any observers designated by contracting parties.[242] The Antarctic Treaty does not prohibit SAI activities aimed at reflecting sunlight thereby combating climate change, but the activities should be in compliance with the Protocol on Environmental Protection to the Antarctic Treaty. In particular, activities in the Antarctic Treaty area shall be planned and conducted so as to limit adverse impacts on the Antarctic environment and ecosystems and to avoid adverse effects on climate or weather patterns and significant adverse effects on air quality; activities shall also be placed and conducted on the basis of information sufficient to allow prior assessments of their possible impacts on the Antarctic environment.[243]

To date, no specific international rule or regulation mandates or facilitates sulphate aerosols injection by means of tethered balloons or artillery.

3.7.2 The obligations to prevent adverse impacts on the environment

3.7.2.1 Transboundary air pollution

As mentioned previously, a legal analysis of the atmosphere may proceed on the basis of two features – "a spatial dimension" and "fluctuating and dynamic air mass".[244] This section will explore the rules governing the side effects on air quality concerning the feature of "fluctuating and dynamic air mass". To separate the discussion in this section from the next section on the ozone layer, "air pollution" refers to pollution in the lower atmosphere. The CLRTAP sets forth a range of procedural obligations, such as exchange of information, consultation and monitoring,[245] but does not touch upon specific substantive rules for regulating different types of pollutants; instead, it serves as a framework convention for cooperation between contracting parties to develop more specific obligations.

The precondition for applying the CLRTAP to SAI is to find whether the release of additional sulphate aerosols to the lower atmosphere constitutes "long-range air pollution". Pursuant to Article 1(a) of the CLRTAP, the introduction of sulphate aerosols into the air must actually result in "deleterious effects", which means the mere possibility of causing deleterious effects would not be sufficient to prevent the injection of sulphate aerosols. "Deleterious effects" could be understood in a broad way, including harm to human health, living resources and ecosystems.[246] Taking into account the different scales of sulphate aerosol injection, deleterious effects on human health and/or the environment should be assessed before applying the obligation to limit, reduce and prevent air pollution to SAI. Note that the mere possibility of causing deleterious effects is sufficient to invoke procedural obligations. Contracting parties shall adhere to the obligation to exchange information when the discharge of air pollutants *may* have adverse effects.[247]

Even if a SAI activity resulted in deleterious effects, the injection of sulphate aerosols would still be lawful as long as the obligation of due diligence had been fulfilled. Article 2 merely obliges contracting parties to endeavour to "limit and, as far as possible, gradually reduce and prevent air pollution". The wording, "as far as possible" and "gradually", softens the obligation to limit, reduce and prevent air pollution.

Someone may argue that "deleterious effects" should be determined based on the "net" effects after weighing the objective of combating global warming against the consequences of introducing sulphate aerosols into the stratosphere.[248] The balancing of interests is a vital issue in the application of almost every convention relating to preventing or controlling environmental harm to a certain geoengineering technique.[249]

The CLRTAP particularly addresses "long-range transboundary air pollution". "Transboundary air pollution" is defined as "air pollution whose physical origins is situated wholly or in part within the area under the national jurisdiction of one State and which has adverse effects in the area under the jurisdiction of another State". Chapter 1 has explained that additional sulphate particles, in the form of gas, dust or acid rain, might decrease the air quality in the lower atmosphere and pollute water resources. Sulphate aerosols can be injected into the stratosphere within the area under one state's jurisdiction, and the injection might cause air pollution and other adverse effects in the area beyond the jurisdiction of this state. The injection of sulphate aerosols therefore falls within the scope of the CLRTAP when sulphate aerosols are released *wholly* or *in part* from the area under one state party's jurisdiction and the injection causes air pollution in the area under the jurisdiction of another state. In other words, the CLRTAP is not applicable to SAI when sulphate aerosols are injected into the stratosphere above the common atmosphere – i.e. over the high seas. Note that the UNCLOS is not applicable to SAI to prevent atmospheric pollution resulting from sulphate aerosols injected over the high seas either, because it only deals with marine pollution.[250] However, the Protocol on Environmental Protection to the Antarctic Treaty is applicable to a SAI activity if it causes significant atmospheric pollution in Antarctica, because, according to Article 3.2(b)(ii), activities in the Antarctic Treaty area shall be planned and conducted so as to avoid significant adverse effects on air quality.

"Long-range" is defined in Article 1(b) of the CLRTAP as "a distance that it is not generally possible to distinguish the contribution of individual emission sources or groups of sources", which means that it is very difficult to establish the causal link between the source of pollution from one state and the effect of pollution in another.[251] Air pollution caused by SAI activities is very likely to be "long-range" air pollution mainly due to the high-altitude injection and the complexity of wind systems. It would be difficult to establish the causal link if the air pollution caused by SAI cannot be distinguished from air pollution caused by other activities.

The specific provisions of the CLRTAP with respect to the control of sulphur emissions are applicable to SAI. Basically, the CLRTAP calls for international cooperation to control air pollution and its effects, and the development of an extensive programme for the monitoring and evaluation of long-range transport of air pollutants, starting with sulphur dioxide and with the possible extension to other pollutants.[252] Besides, sulphur dioxide and other sulphur compounds are the starting point of cooperated research, data exchange and the monitoring of air pollutants.[253]

The CLRTAP is supplemented by eight protocols, which regulate specific pollutants or pollution. Among the eight protocols, three are relevant to the injection of sulphate aerosols into the stratosphere: the 1985 Helsinki Protocol on the Reduction of Sulphur Emissions or their Transboundary Fluxes by at least 30%, the 1994 Oslo Protocol on Further Reduction of Sulphur Emissions, and the 1999 Gothenburg Protocol to Abate Acidification, Eutrophication and Ground-level Ozone (amended in 2012). The three protocols have 21, 29 and 26 parties respectively. The Helsinki Protocol establishes a quantitative target for parties to reduce their annual sulphur emission or transboundary fluxes by at least 30% by 1993, using 1980 levels as the base year.[254] All of the 21 parties to the Helsinki Protocol have reached the target with the reduction of more than 50% by 1993. The Oslo Protocol adopts an effect-based approach, which aims at not exceeding critical loads by means of setting differentiated sulphur emission ceilings and emission reduction obligations for parties to the Oslo Protocol. It obliges its 29 parties to ensure that the depositions of oxidized sulphur compounds in the long term do not exceed critical loads for sulphur, in accordance with present scientific knowledge.[255] As a first step, the 29 parties shall reduce and maintain their annual sulphur emissions in accordance with the timing and levels specified in Annex

II of the Oslo Protocol.[256] The most recent protocol, the Gothenburg Protocol, sets short-term emission ceilings (2010–2020) and long-term emission reduction commitments (2020 onwards) for the reduction of emissions of four substances, including sulphur dioxide.[257]

As estimated based on volcanic eruptions, up to 15 $MtSO_2$ would be required annually worldwide to effectively increase the stratospheric albedo and decrease the global average temperature.[258] However, according to Annex II of the Gothenburg Protocol, the SO_2 emission ceiling for 2020 and beyond for the European Union is 4.6 Mt per year.[259] Apparently, the need for SO_2 in the deployment of SAI is much greater than the current SO_2 emission ceiling of the EU. Although other states worldwide[260] may participate in the deployment of SAI and share the 15 $MtSO_2$ emissions with the EU member states, the gradually strengthened SO_2 emission trend might still lead to a potential conflict between the need of SO_2 for SAI and the limits on SO_2 emissions.

In sum, the three protocols have established gradually strengthened SO_2 emission ceilings and reduction commitments. The deployment of SAI at a large scale would breach the obligations under the Gothenburg Protocol if a party conducting SAI activities on its territory emits the amount of SO_2 beyond its ceiling or if SAI activities contribute to the failure of this party to achieve its emission reduction commitment.[261]

3.7.2.2 *Ozone layer depletion*

As introduced in Chapter 1, one of the possible effects of SAI on the environment would be that it may contribute to ozone layer depletion because sulphate aerosols could increase chlorine's effectiveness at destroying ozone.[262] The Vienna Convention for the Protection of the Ozone Layer and its Montreal Protocol are thus applicable to SAI.[263]

Article 2(1) of the Vienna Convention stipulates that the parties shall take appropriate measures to protect human health and the environment against adverse effects resulting or likely to result from human activities which modify or are likely to modify the ozone layer. Compared to the CLRTAP, the Vienna Convention is broader in the scope of control (including not only actual impacts but also the likelihood of impacts). Article 2(2) provides for a range of procedural obligations regarding cooperation. Among others, contracting parties have the obligation to adopt appropriate legislative or administrative measures and cooperate in harmonizing appropriate policies to control, limit, reduce or prevent human activities under their jurisdiction or control in so far as these activities have or are likely to have adverse effects as a consequence of modification or likely modification of the ozone layer. The Vienna Convention also mentions in its Preamble that precautionary measures for the protection of the ozone layer have already been taken at the national and international levels.[264]

Annex I, paragraph 4, of the Vienna Convention lists the chemical substances that are thought to have the potential to modify the chemical and physical properties of the ozone layer. The modification would result in a change in the amount of solar ultraviolet radiation having significant deleterious effects on human health or ecosystems, or a change in the temperature structure of the atmosphere and potential consequences for the weather and climate.[265] Sulphur substances are not included in the list. Some scientists predict that the injection of SO_2 or H2S into the stratosphere would contribute to the modification of the ozone layer and lead to strongly increased ozone depletion in the Arctic, and would considerably delay the recovery of the Antarctic ozone hole by several decades.[266] Based on this scenario, SO_2 or H_2S share the same properties with the chemical substances listed in Annex I, paragraph 4. As the list is not exhaustive, it is reasonable to assume that sulphur substances would be covered by the Vienna Convention. However, there is no conclusive opinion on the impacts of SAI on the ozone layer. Some scientists hold a more sanguine view that the impact of SAI on the ozone layer is "likely to be small". In this scenario, SO_2 or H_2S would not be covered by the Vienna Convention for the purpose of prohibiting or largely restricting SAI activities.[267]

The Montreal Protocol contains very specific control measures for the production and consumption of the controlled substances in its Annex A. As with the Vienna Convention, sulphur substances are not included in the controlled substances listed in the annexes of the Montreal Protocol. However, it is noteworthy that the parties to the Montreal Protocol may decide to add substances to any annex to the Protocol, based on an assessment made pursuant to Article 6 of the protocol and in accordance with the procedure set out in Article 9.[268] This flexible mechanism enables the coverage of sulphur substances in the future, if necessary.

3.7.2.3 Marine pollution

Part XII of the UNCLOS formulates a general obligation of environmental protection with respect to all sources of marine pollution. This obligation applies to the release of harmful substances from or through the atmosphere or by dumping.[269] Article 212 provides that states shall adopt laws and regulations to prevent, reduce and control pollution of the marine environment from or through the atmosphere, applicable to the air space under their sovereignty and to aircraft in their registry. Hence, the obligation to prevent marine pollution from the atmosphere applies to the release of sulphate articles by aircraft into the atmosphere that may lead to marine pollution.

The release of sulphate articles may also be understood from the perspective of "dumping". Some of the sulphate aerosols would, in the form of solid particles or acid raindrops, be washed down into the high seas and result in ocean pollution. The dumping regime may be applicable to SAI because the sulphate particles washed down into the sea may constitute "dumping". The definition of "dumping" explicitly includes the deliberate disposal of substances from aircraft.[270] Although the purpose of releasing sulphate aerosols is to increase the stratospheric albedo rather than "the mere disposal", the acid particles might not be exempted from "dumping". The LC and the LP both regulate that the placement of matter for a purpose other than the mere disposal thereof is not considered dumping only if such a placement is not contrary to their aims. SAI activities may be contrary to the objectives of the LC/LP to effective control of all sources of pollution of the marine environment, if such activities significantly worsen ocean acidification.[271] For the same reason, the release of sulphate aerosols may also be considered "dumping" and consequently be regulated under Article 210 of the UNCLOS regarding pollution by dumping. Should scientists find that the introduction of sulphur substances does not result or is not likely to result in "deleterious effects" on the marine environment (because, for instance, the amount of sulphate disposed into the sea is too small), SAI would be exempted from dumping rules and would not be prohibited by Article 210 of the UNCLOS or the LC/LP.[272]

Some argue that the introduction of sulphate aerosols into the stratosphere does not involve *directly* disposing of them *into* the sea.[273] Even though a part of sulphate aerosols injected into the stratosphere is eventually washed down into the sea, they are transformed by chemical actions into other substances. According to this argument, the injection of sulphate aerosols into the stratosphere does not constitute "dumping" and is not prohibited by the UNCLOS or the LC/LP.

3.7.2.4 *Impacts on the ecosystem*

The introduction of sulphur substances into the stratosphere may have adverse effects on species, habitats and ecosystems. One effect could be that the additional SO_2 deposited in the soil might lead to soil acidification and be harmful to crops. The other effect could be that the increased stratospheric albedo reduces the total solar radiation to the Earth's surface. Less solar radiation will decelerate the photosynthesis in plants and thus lessen carbon sinks. However, it should be noted that plants would grow more rapidly under the diffuse sunlight that results from the implementation of SAI. Whether the net effects are hazardous and significant enough to trigger preventive measures depends on specific conditions and requires assessment.

A host of international conventions oblige states to protect species, habitats and ecosystems. The CBD aims at the conservation of biological diversity. It is a framework convention without provisions regarding the protection of any specific species or habitat. The CBD provides for the obligation to prevent transboundary harm.[274] Furthermore, parties to the CBD are required to undertake a series of procedural obligations, among others, the conduct of environmental impact assessments with respect to proposed projects that are likely to have significant adverse effects on biological diversity.[275] Some other conventions provide for rules on the protection and conservation of specific kinds of habitats or species, for instance, the obligation to protect wetlands under the Ramsar Convention and the obligation to conserve migratory species of wild animals under the Convention on the Conservation of Migratory Species of Wild Animals.[276] Also, according to the World Heritage Convention, states have the obligation to take measures to protect natural and cultural heritage. Risk assessments should be prudently made for fear of endangering the heritages.[277]

3.7.2.5 *Climate modification*[278]

Note that the peaceful use of techniques that may modify the weather or climate system is not subject to any binding international legal regime. The ENMOD Convention is thus far the only binding legal authority to regulate techniques that may modify the weather or climate system, but the scope of this Convention is limited to military or hostile uses.[279] However, even if conducted for peaceful purposes, the modifications arising from SAI could also seriously influence the environment and human health in a negative way. A computer simulation of SAI indicates that SAI may modify the climate in two main aspects: the one refers to the possible changes in weather patterns, among other things, the weakening of the India or African monsoons; the other is rapid warming if a SAI project fails or is terminated for any reason.[280]

With regard to the likely modification of the climate arising from SAI activities, there is a need to develop international law to minimize the risk of modifying the weather or climate patterns because of SAI techniques. The UNEP Provisions for Cooperation between States regarding Weather Modification for Peaceful Purposes, though adopted in 1980 and not legally binding, may still shed light on this topic. The Provisions recommend that weather modification should be dedicated to the benefit of mankind and the environment.

States should cooperate by exchanging information with, notifying and consulting the World Meteorological Organization and other states in case of proposed weather modification activities. The activities should be carried out after an assessment of the transboundary environmental consequences and in a manner that is designed to ensure that they do not cause damage to the environment of other states or the global commons.[281] With respect to rapid warming, if a SAI activity terminates artificially, it is not an environmental risk but rather a political one (e.g. due to strong objection raised by some countries or organizations); the rapid warming would be an accident if a SAI activity turns out to be non-effective. Only the latter situation relates to the issue of minimising and control the risk of harm addressed in this chapter. Accidental warming could be avoided by proceeding a prior EIA to identify the risk of accident.

3.7.3 *Synthetic consideration*

SAI brings a new challenge to international law. To date, some rules, though far from enough, can be found to govern sulphate injection by aircraft, but no direct rules are available to regulate the use of tethered balloons and artillery for the injection. With respect to the injection by aircraft, there is no prohibition or large restriction on the use of aircraft for the purpose of

SAI geoengineering. However, owing to the side effects on the ozone layer, the lower atmosphere, the marine environment and the weather and climate systems resulting from SAI, specific rules are required to prevent, reduce or control the side effects.

The CLRTAP generally provides a useful platform for the further regulation of SO_2 injection. The procedural obligations, including information exchange, consultation, monitoring and research, serve as important means to limit, reduce or prevent air pollution from sulphate aerosols injection. The Gothenburg Protocol would restrict the SO_2 used in SAI to the extent that SO_2 emissions are beyond the upper limit under the Protocol. Besides, the limited number of parties to the CLRTAP and its Protocols would also restrict the effective control of sulphur pollution from SAI.

Although the Vienna Convention thus far does not explicitly prohibit or largely restrict the use of sulphur substances, its advantage of universal ratification indicates that it could provide an inclusive forum for the multilateral governance of SAI technique.

Regulatory gaps also remain in, for instance, the peaceful use of techniques that may modify the weather or climate system, and air pollution caused by substances injected into the atmosphere over the high seas.

3.8 Conclusion

This chapter examined the rules and principles under contemporary conventional law (also in conjunction with some non-binding instruments) applicable to six geoengineering techniques. Generally, two main issues are elaborated for each technique. One is the lawfulness of the conduct of undertaking a geoengineering activity or the use of materials in a technique; the other is whether a technique breaches the obligations to protect the environment and to preserve natural resources due to the resulting adverse impacts and, consequently, whether such a technique is allowed or largely restricted.

As set forth in Chapter 2, there is no comprehensive legal framework governing geoengineering under contemporary international law. The existing treaty system is not sufficient to respond to the "greater challenges posed by the Anthropocene".[282] The 2013 Amendments to the LP and a few non-binding CBD decisions are the only legal instruments that explicitly address geoengineering techniques, mainly referring to ocean fertilization. The LP has demonstrated to be a useful model for marine geoengineering techniques. Since four of the techniques discussed in this chapter are marine geoengineering techniques (from Section 3.2 to Section 3.5), the LP could be expected to be the leading and central legal instrument to govern the other three marine geoengineering techniques in addition to ocean fertilization. SAI is the most disputable geoengineering technique because of the risk of various adverse effects on environmental media. The Vienna Convention and the CLRTAP might be the proper instruments to regulate the use of SAI techniques, but both of them have their limitedness. The choice of suitable legal institutions for governing geoengineering will be discussed further in Chapter 4.

One problem in the legal examination in this chapter is the determination of "deleterious effects", which is a vital concept in many conventions.[283] Contemporary international law is confronted with an unprecedented challenge to interpret the meaning of "deleterious effects" in the context of geoengineering.[284] Whether the environmental effects are "deleterious" is still undetermined, mainly because of scientific uncertainties and the difficulty in risk trade-offs. Scientific uncertainties make the adverse effects of geoengineering techniques far from fully known; the risk trade-off is difficult due to the lack of criteria for weighing the positive results against the negative impacts of geoengineering. Therefore, customary international law needs to be operationalized in order to assess and evaluate the competing risks. Chapters 5 will address a normative analysis of the balancing of risks and interests in geoengineering governance through the conduct of EIAs as well as the implementation of the precautionary approach.

A science-based global, transparent and effective control of geoengineering is required. Bearing in mind that there is no sharp line between lawful and unlawful geoengineering activities (except for military or hostile use of geoengineering that have long-lasting, widespread and serious effects, which is clearly unlawful), the lawfulness of a geoengineering activity depends on the characteristics of a particular activity. Therefore, the international legal framework of geoengineering techniques may incorporate not only binding rules but also soft norms to leave more flexibility in governance. Further discussion regarding the form of the legal framework will be addressed in Chapter 4.

Notes

1   See, for instance, Section 3.2.1.3 and Section 3.4.3 concerning the obligation to conserve marine biodiversity.
2   Fisheries and Oceans Canada. (2010). *Ocean fertilization: Mitigating environmental impacts of future scientific research.* (Canadian Science Advisory Secretariat Science Advisory Report No. 2010/012, 7). Retrieved from www.dfo-mpo. gc.ca/csas-sccs/publications/sar-as/2010/2010_012_e.pdf
3   Fisheries and Oceans Canada. (2010), supra note 2, 8.
4   UNCLOS, Arts. 192 & 194.1.
5   UNCLOS, Art. 195.
6   UNCLOS, Art. 196.
7   Dean, J. (2009). Iron fertilization: A scientific review with international policy recommendations. *Environs: Environmental Law and Policy Journal, 32*(2), 321–344, at 334.
8   Rayfuse, R., Lawrence, M. G., & Gjerde, K. M. (2008). Ocean fertilization and climate change: The need to regulate emerging high seas uses. *The International Journal of Marine and Coastal Law, 23*, 297–326, at 308; Freestone, D., & Rayfuse, R. (2008). Ocean iron fertilization and international law. *Marine Ecology Progress Series, 364*, 227–233, at 229.
9   Abate, R. S., & Greenlee, A. B. (2009–2010). Sowing seeds uncertain: Ocean iron fertilization, climate change, and the international environmental law. *Pace International Law Review, 27*, 555–598, at 575.
10 Scott, K. N. (2005–2006). The day after tomorrow: CO_2 sequestration and the future of climate change. *The Georgetown International Environmental Law Review, 18*, 57–108, at 69.

11 UNGA Resolution 68/70. Oceans and the law of the sea, UN Doc. A/RES/68/70 (27 February 2014), paras. 182–185; UNGA Resolution 69/245. Oceans and the law of the sea, UN Doc. A/RES/69/245 (24 February 2015), paras. 198–199.

12 UNGA Resolution 68/70, para. 157; UNGA Resolution 69/245, para. 171.

13 UNGA Resolution 68/70, para. 183; UNGA Resolution 69/245, para. 199.

14 UNCLOS, Art. 1(5)(a); London Convention, Art. III (1)(a)(i); London Protocol, Art. 1.4.1.1.

15 London Convention, Art. III.1(b)(ii); London Protocol, Art. 1.4.2.2.

16 Scott, K. N. (2013). Regulating ocean fertilization under international law: The risks. *Carbon Climate Law Review*, 2013(2), 108–116, 112; Rayfuse, R., Lawrence, M. G., & Gjerde, K. M. (2008), supra note 8, 312.

17 London Convention, Art. IV.1.

18 London Convention, Art. IV.1(c).

19 IMO. (2006). Guidelines on the Convention on the Prevention of Marine Pollution by Dumping of Waters and Other Matter, 1972, IMO Publication, Sales number 1531 E, Appendix: Eligibility Criteria for Inert, Inorganic Geological Material, paras. 13–14.

20 London Convention, Annex 1, para. 11(c).

21 Scott, K. N. (2013), supra note 16, 113.

22 Dean, J. (2009), supra note 7, 336.

23 The number of parties to the LP is based on the status as of March 2016. Retrieved from www.imo.org/en/OurWork/Environment/LCLP/Pages/default.aspx

24 See e.g. Scott, K. N. (2013), supra note 16, 113; Birnie, P., Boyle, A., & Redgwell, C. (2009). *International law & the environment* (3rd ed.). Oxford: Oxford University Press, 389.

25 12 of the top 15 countries in terms of the coastline lengths for the countries of the world are parties to the LP. World by Map. (2015). The Length of the Coast for the Countries of the World. Retrieved December 9, 2015, http://world.bymap.org/Coastlines.html

26 UNCLOS, Art. 1.1(5)(b)(ii); London Convention, Art.III.1(b)(ii); London Protocol, Art. 1.4.2.2.

27 Oxford Dictionaries. Retrieved from www.oxforddictionaries.com/definition/english/disposal

28 Resolution LC-LP.1(2008) on the regulation of ocean fertilization. Annex 6, para. 2.

29 Similar arguments can be found in: Rayfuse, R., Lawrence, M. G., & Gjerde, K. M. (2008), supra note 8, 314; Scott, K. N. (2013), supra note 16, 112.

30 Rayfuse, R., Lawrence, M. G., & Gjerde, K. M. (2008), supra note 8, 314.

31 Scott, K. N. (2013), supra note 16, 112.

32 UNCLOS, Arts. 192 & 194.5.

33 London Convention, Art. I.

34 IMO (2007). Statement of concern regarding iron fertilization of the oceans to sequester CO_2, IMO DOCS LC-LP.1/Circ.14 (13 July 2007).

35 Resolution LC-LP.1 (2008) on the Regulation of Ocean Fertilization.

36 IMO. (2013). Marine geoengineering including ocean fertilization to be regulated under amendments to international treaty. Retrieved April 22, 2014, from www.imo.org/MediaCentre/PressBriefings/Pages/45-marine-geoengieneering.aspx

37 Resolution LP.4(8), 2013 Amendments to the LP, Annex 4.

38 Ibid.

39 Emphasizing again, that 2013 Amendments to the LP has not yet entered into force.

40 This will be further discussed in Section 3.2.3 concerning the scale of ocean fertilization.

41 Freestone, D., & Rayfuse, R. (2008), supra note 8, 230.

42 UNCLOS, Art. 216.

43 "Flag of convenience" refers to the phenomenon that ships are registered not where they are owned but in another state, where the owners or operators pay less tax, employ cheaper crew and regulations may be less stringent or less efficiently applied than it would be under more established flag states. Birnie, P., Boyle, A., & Redgwell, C. (2009), supra note 24, 398.

44 Birnie, P., Boyle, A., & Redgwell, C. (2009), supra note 24, 398; Rayfuse, R., Lawrence, M. G., & Gjerde, K. M.(2008), supra note 16, 319.

45 UNCLOS Art. 218(1).

46 UNCLOS Art. 218(2).

47 Boyd, P. W., Watson, A. J., Law, C. S., Abraham, E. R., Trull, T., Murdoch, R., . . . Charette, M. (2000). A mesoscale phytoplankton bloom in the polar Southern Ocean stimulated by iron fertilization. *Nature, 407*(6805), 695–702.

48 Williamson, P., Wallace, D. W., Law, C. S., Boyd, P. W., Collos, Y., Croot, P., . . . Vivian, C. (2012). Ocean fertilization for geoengineering: A review of effectiveness, environmental impacts and emerging governance. *Process Safety and Environmental Protection*, 90(6), 475–488, at 478, Figure 1.

49 The Antarctic Treaty, Washington, adopted 1 December 1959, entered into force 3 June 1962, *United Nations Treaty Series* (1961), vol. 402, no. 5778, p. 71; Protocol on Environmental Protection to the Antarctic Treaty; Convention on the Conservation of Antarctic Marine Living Resources, Canberra, adopted 20 May 1980, entered into force 7 April 1982, *United Nations Treaty Series* (1994), vol. 1329, no. 22301, p. 47.

50 CBD, Art. 2.

51 CBD, Preamble, para. 10.

52 CBD, Art. 3.

53 Dean, J. (2009), supra note 7, 337.

54 CBD Decision II/10, Conservation and Sustainable Use of Marine and Coastal Biological Diversity, 1995. Retrieved from www.cbd.int/decision/cop/default.shtml?id=7083; CBD Decision IV/5 (this decision has partly retired); CBD Decision V/3, 2000 (this decision has retired); CBD Decision VI/3 on Marine and Coastal Biodiversity, 2002; CBD Decision VII/5, Maine and Coastal Biodiversity, UN Doc. UNEP/CBD/COP/DEC/VII/5, 13 April 2004.

55 UNGA Resolution 58/240. Oceans and the Law of the Sea, UN Doc. A/RES/58/240 (5 March 2004), para. 52.

56 UNGA Resolution 59/24, Oceans and the Law of the Sea, UN Doc. A/RES/59/24 (4 February 2005), para. 73.

57 UNGA, Letter dated 13 February 2015 from the Co-Chair of the Ad Hoc Open-ended Informal Working Group to the President of the General Assembly, Annex, Recommendations, para. 1(e). UN Doc. A/69/780 (13 February 2015).

58 CBD Decision IX/16, Part A.

59 A detailed analysis, see Section 2.4.2.4.

60 CBD Decision X/29, Marine and coastal biodiversity, UN Doc. UNEP/CBD/COP/DEC/X/29 (29 October 2010), para. 9.

61 CBD Decision X/29, paras. 58–59.

62 CBD Decision X/33, para. 8 (w). A detailed analysis, see Section 2.4.2.4.

63 UNFCCC, Art. 2 "[. . .] stabilization of greenhouse gas concentration in the atmosphere at a level that would prevent dangerous anthropogenic interference with the climate system."

64 Kyoto Protocol, Art. 2(1)(a)(ii): "Protection and enhancement of sinks and reservoirs of greenhouse gases [. . .] promotion of sustainable forest management practices, afforestation and reforestation." Art. 2(1)(a)(iv): "Research on, and

promotion, development and increased use of, new and renewable forms of energy, of carbon dioxide sequestration technologies and of advanced and innovative environmentally sound technologies[.]"

65 Powell, H. (2008). Dumping Iron and Trading Carbon – Profits, pollution and politics all will play roles in ocean iron fertilization, Oceanus Magazine *Oceanus Magazine, 46*(1), 22–25; Leinen, M. (2008) Building relationship between scientists and business in ocean iron fertilization. *Marine Ecology Progress Series, 364,* 251–256.
66 Kyoto Protocol, Art. 12.2.
67 Kyoto Protocol, Art. 6.
68 Kyoto Protocol, Art. 17.
69 See Section 2.2.4; Paris Agreement, Art. 6.
70 Law, C. S. (2008). Predicting and monitoring the effects of large-scale ocean iron fertilization on marine trace gas emission. *Marine Ecology Progress Series, 364,* 283–288.
71 Davis, W. D. (2009), 945; Caldeira, K., & Keith, D. W. (2010). The need for climate engineering research. *Issues in Science and Technology, 27*(1), 57–62, at 62.
72 IOC. (2008). Statement of the IOC ad hoc consultative group on ocean fertilization. Paris, 14 June, 2008. Retrieved from www.climos.com/ext/ioc/ IOC%20Group%20Submission_June14.pdf
73 Rayfuse, R., Lawrence, M. G., & Gjerde, K. M. (2008), supra note 16, 321.
74 Genzky, H. (2010). Ocean fertilization as climate change mitigation measure – consideration under international law. *Journal for European Environmental and Planning Law, 7*(1), 57–78, at 76; Fisheries and Oceans Canada. (2010), supra note 2, 10; Resolution LC-LP.2 (2010), Assessment Framework for Scientific Research Involving Ocean Fertilization. Preston, C. J. (2013). Ethics and geoengineering: Reviewing the moral issues raised by solar radiation management and carbon dioxide removal. *WIREs Climate Change, 4,* 23–37, at 27.
75 Preston, C. J. (2013), supra note 74, 27.
76 *Whaling in the Antarctic (Australia v. Japan: New Zealand Intervening)*, Judgment of 31 March 2014, ICJ Reports 2014, p. 226.
77 International Convention for the Regulation of Whaling, adopted in Washington, USA, 2 December 1946. Italic added.
78 *Whaling in the Antarctic*, para. 74. Australia refers to the characteristics of scientific research proposed by a scientific expert that under the context of the Convention, four essential characteristics of scientific research are: (1) defined and achievable objectives (questions or hypotheses) that aim to contribute to knowledge important to the conservation and management of stocks; (2) appropriate methods, including the use of lethal methods only where the objectives of the research cannot be achieved by any other means;(3) peer review; and (4) the avoidance of adverse effects on stock.
79 *Whaling in the Antarctic*, para. 97.
80 *Whaling in the Antarctic*, para. 94.
81 UNCLOS, Arts. 238–239.
82 See Section 2.4.2.4.
83 Abate, R. S., & Greenlee, A. B. (2009–2010), supra note 9, 595.
84 See Section 2.4.2.4.
85 See Section 3.2.2.
86 UNCLOS Art. 1.1(4).
87 United Nations Division for Ocean affair and the Law of the Sea Office of Legal Affairs. (2010). Marine scientific research: *A revised guide to the implementation of the relevant provisions of the United Nations Convention on the Law of the Sea,* United Nations publication, Sales No. E.10.V.12 (hereafter "Revised guide 2010"), paras. 7–10.

88   Revised guide 2010, para. 8, referring to *Official Records of the General Assembly, Twenty-seventh Session, Supplement No.21*, (A/8721), documents annexed to Part IV, document A/AC.138/SC. III/L.18 (Canada), Preamble, para. 2, and principle 2.

89   Revised guide 2010, para. 10, referring to *Official Records of the Third United Nations Conference on the Law of the Sea*, vol. III (United Nations publication, Sales No.E.75.V.5), Trinidad and Tobago: draft arts. On marine scientific research, Art. 1, paras. (a) and (b), p. 252.

90   OECD. (1994). *The measurement of scientific and technical activities* Organisation for Economic Co-operation and Development, 13. doi:10.1787/9789264063525-en

91   Revised guide 2010, para. 10.

92   OECD. (1994), supra note 90, 13.

93   It will be examined in Section 3.3.2.

94   Revised guide 2010, para. 62; Part XIII Section 4 of the UNCLOS.

95   Weglein, A. H. (2005). *Marine scientific research: The separation and status of research vessels and other platforms in international law.* The Hague: Martinus Nijhoff, 137.

96   Tanaka, Y. (2012). *The international law of the sea* (1st ed.). New York: Cambridge University Press, 343; See also Bork, K., Karstensen, J., Visbeck, M., & Zimmermann, A. (2008). The Legal Regulation of Floats and Gliders – In Quest of a New Regime? *Ocean Development & International Law, 39*(3), 298–328, at 309. Weglein holds a different view that "installation" could be free floating or fixed. An example of free-floating installation is the General Positioning Systems. Weglein, A. H. (2005), supra note 95, 138. The OSPAR Convention only contains "installation" which includes "any man-made structure, plant or vessel or parts thereof, whether floating or fixed to the seabed".

97   Proelss, A., & Hong, C. (2012). Ocean upwelling and international law. *Ocean Development & International Law, 43*(4), 371–385, (2012), 374, referring to Weglein, A. H. (2005), supra note 95, 138.

98   Proelss, A., & Hong, C. (2012), supra note 97, 374.

99   See also Art. 240 of the UNCLOS about the general principles for the conduct of marine scientific research.

100 UNCLOS, 262. According to the Revised guide 2010, para. 18, although the term "competent international organizations" is not defined in the UNCLOS, it may be considered to generally include intergovernmental organizations which are empowered by their constituting instruments or other rules to undertake, coordinate, or promote and facilitate the development and conduct of marine scientific research. An indicative list of such organization is provided in Annex VIII to the UNCLOS, Art. 2.

101 UNCLOS, Art. 91.

102 Ibid.

103 Note that the rules stated in the UNCLOS regarding states' rights and duties relating to conducting scientific research in different locations in the sea are also applicable to ocean fertilization and ocean alkalinity addition.

104 UNCLOS, Art. 245.

105 Ibid.

106 UNCLOS, Art. 17.

107 UNCLOS, Art. 246(1).

108 UNCLOS, Art. 246(2).

109 UNCLOS, Art. 246 (3) & (5).

110 UNCLOS, Art. 246 (5).

111 UNCLOS, Art. 58(1).

112 UNCLOS, Art. 87(1)(f).

113 UNCLOS, Art. 87(2).
114 UNCLOS, Art. 77(1) & (2).
115 London Convention, Art. IV(1)(c).
116 London Protocol, Art. 4(1)(1).
117 "Offshore installation" means any man-made structure, plant or vessel or parts thereof, whether floating or fixed to the seabed, placed within the maritime area for the purpose of offshore activities. The OSPAR Convention, Art. 1(l).
118 OSPAR Convention, Art. 1(g)(iii).
119 OSPAR Convention, Annex III, On the Prevention and Elimination of Pollution from Offshore Sources.
120 Except for Portugal, according to the status as of December 2015.
121 UNCLOS, Art. 249 (1)(g).
122 UNCLOS, Art. 248 (d).
123 Proelss, A., & Hong, C. (2012), supra note 97, 381.
124 UNCLOS, Art. 210(5).
125 See the first paragraph of this section.
126 IMO Resolution A.672(16). Guidelines and Standards for the Removal of Offshore Installations and Structures on the Continental Shelf and in the Exclusive Economic Zone, adopted on 19 October 1989.
127 Ibid., para. 2.1.
128 UNCLOS, Art. 210(2).
129 UNCLOS, Art. 210(3).
130 Sea Web. (2014). Ocean issue briefs – large scale ocean circulation. Retrieved from www.seaweb.org/resources/briefings/circulation.php
131 CBD, Arts. 1, 3& 4.2.
132 CBD, Art. 8.
133 UNCLOS, Art. 194(1).
134 UNCLOS, Art. 193(3)(d).
135 London Convention, Art. 1; London Protocol, Art. 2.
136 OSPAR Convention, Arts. 2 & 4 and Annex II.
137 UNCLOS, Art. 1(1)(5)(a); London Convention, Art. III(1)(a)(i); London Protocol, Art. 1(4)(1)(1); OSPAR Convention, Annex II, Art. 1.
138 UNCLOS, Art. 1(1)(5)(b)(ii); London Convention, Art. 1(b)(ii); London Protocol, Art. 1(4)(2)(2); OSPAR Convention, Art. 1(f)(i).
139 Dumping does not include "placement of matter for a purpose other than the mere disposal thereof, provided that, if the placement is for a purpose other than that for which the matter was originally designed or constructed, it is in accordance with the relevant provisions of the Convention". OSPAR Convention, Art. 1(g)(ii).
140 Bodle, R., Oberthür, S., et al. (2013). *Options and proposals for the international governance of geoengineering* (No. (UBA-FB) 001886/E). Dessau-Roßlau: Umweltbundesamt, 96. Retrieved from www.umweltbundesamt.de/sites/default/files/medien/376/publikationen/climate_chang e_14_2014_komplett_korr.pdf
141 London Protocol, Art. 1(8).
142 London Convention, Art. IV(1)(c).
143 Resolution LP.4(8), 2013 Amendments to the LP.
144 1992 Helsinki Convention (Baltic Sea Area), Art. 11.
145 Convention on the Protection of the Black Sea Against Pollution, Bucharest, adopted 21 April 1992, entered into force 15 January 1994, *United Nations Treaty Series* (2000), vo. 1764, no. 30674, p. 3. Annex II Noxious Substances and Matter.
146 E.g. Convention for the Protection of the Marine Environment and the Coastal Region of the Mediterranean, Barcelona, 1995; Amended Nairobi Convention

148

for the Protection, Management and Development of the Marine and Coastal Environment of the Western Indian Ocean, Nairobi, 2010; Convention for the Protection and Development of the Marine Environment of the Wider Caribbean Region, Cartagena de Indias, 1983.

147   See Section 3.2.1.3.

148   Bodle, R., & Oberthür, S., et al. (2013), supra note 140, 97.

149   UNCLOS, Art. 2.

150   UNCLOS, Art. 19(1), (2)(j) & (l).

151   Proelss, A. (2012). International legal challenges concerning marine scientific research in the era of climate change. *2012 LOSI-KIOST Conference on Securing the Ocean for the Next Generation*, Seoul, Korea. Retrieved from www.law.berkeley.edu/files/Proelss-final.pdf

152   UNCLOS, Arts. 56(1)(b)(ii) & 246(1).

153   UNCLOS, Art. 246(2) & (3).

154   The UNCLOS does not provide the definition of the term "marine environment", but Article 2 provides a definition of the "pollution of the marine environment" as "the introduction by man, directly or indirectly, of substances or energy into the marine environment, including estuaries, which results or is likely to result in such deleterious effects as harm to living resources and marine life, hazards to human health, hindrance to marine activities, including fishing and other legitimate uses of the sea, impairment of quality for use of sea water and reduction of amenities". Since no pollution relating to the atmosphere is mentioned, it is reasonable to infer that the atmosphere is not included as a part of marine environment.

155   Proelss, A. (2012), supra note 151, 14; Bodle, R., & Oberthür, S., et al. (2013), supra note 140, 76.

156   UNCLOS, Art. 87(1)(f).

157   UNCLOS, Art. 58(1).

158   The definition of mobile offshore drilling unit, Oil & gas field technical terms glossary, www.oilgasglossary.com/mobile_offshore_drilling_unit.html (retrieved on 17 April 2015). Note that there are two basic types of mobile offshore drilling units – bottom-supported rigs and floating drilling rigs. Only floating drilling rigs are used in this analogy.

159   Richards, R. K. (2011). Deepwater mobile oil rigs in the exclusive economic zone and the uncertainty of coastal state jurisdiction. J. *Journal of International Business & Law*, 10, 387; Park, P. (2013). *International law for energy and the environment* (2nd ed.). the U. S.: CRC Press, 83.

160   Richards, R. K. (2011), supra note 159, 410.

161   UNCLOS, Art. 56(1)(b)(i).

162   Mandaraka-Sheppard, A. (2013). Modern maritime law (vol. 1). *Jurisdiction and risks*, the U. S.: CRC Press, 21.

163   The definition of "installation", see Section 3.3.1.2.

164   UNCLOS, Art. 56(2).

165   UNCLOS, Art. 58(1) & 58(3).

166   UNCLOS, Art. 56(1)(b)(iii).

167   Were it not effective to apply MCW on the high seas, the discussion here may not be necessary. (According to some scientific research results, MCW seems to be feasible only close to the continents. See e.g. Aswathy, V. N., Boucher, O., Quaas, M., Niemeier, U., Muri, H., & Quaas, J. (2014). Climate extremes in multi-model simulations of stratospheric aerosol and marine cloud brightening climate engineering. *Atmospheric Chemistry and Physics Discussions*, 14(23), 32393–32425.)

168   UNCLOS, Arts. 87 & 90.

169   Montreal Protocol on Substances that Deplete the Ozone Layer, Montreal, 16 September 1987, *United Nations Treaty Series* (1989), vol. 1522, no. 26369, p. 3.

170   Ozone Layer Convention, Annex I, para. 4(e).

171 Ozone Layer Convention, Annex I, para. 4(e)(ii).

172 Bear in mind that the amount of water vapour that reaches the stratosphere is probably insignificant.

173 Zedalis, R. J. (2010). Climate change and the national academy of sciences' idea of geoengineering: One American academic's perspective on first considering the text of existing international agreements. *European Energy and Environmental Law Review, 19(1)*, 18–32, at 23.

174 The Convention on Long-range Transboundary Air Pollution, Art. 2. The number of 51 parties reflects the status as of April 2016.

175 Protocol to the 1979 Convention on Long-Range Transboundary Air Pollution on the Reduction of Sulphur Emissions or their Transboundary Fluxes by at Least 30 Per Cent, Helsinki, adopted in 1985 (the goal of this convention has been achieved in 1993); Protocol to the 1979 Convention on Long-Range Transboundary Air Pollution Concerning the Control of Emissions of Nitrogen Oxides or their Transboundary Fluxes, 1988; Protocol to the 1979 Convention on Long-Range Transboundary Air Pollution on Heavy Metals, Aarhus, adopted 24 June 1998, entered into force 29 December 2003, *United Nations Treaty Series* (2005), vol. 2237, no. 21623, p. 4.

176 Rhodes, J., & Keith, D. W. (2007). Biomass with capture: Negative emissions within social and environmental constraints: An editorial comment. *Climate Chang 87*(3–4), 321–328. doi: 10.1007/s10584-007-9387-4

177 E.g. overuse of chemical inputs that may lead to eutrophication and water pollution, tillage that can result in soil erosion or compaction. CBD. (2007). Biofuel electronic forum – impacts. Retrieved from www.cbd.int/forums/biofuel/impacts.shtml

178 CBD Decision IX/1. In-depth review of the programme of work on agricultural biodiversity, UN Doc. UNEP/CBD/COP/DEC/IX/1, 9 October 2008, para. 31.

179 CBD Decision IX/2, Agricultural biodiversity: biofuels and biodiversity, UN Doc. UNEP/CBD/COP/DEC/IX/2, 9 October 2008, para. 1.

180 CBD Decision IX/2, para. 2.

181 CBD Decision IX/5, Forest biodiversity, UN Doc. UNEP/CBD/COP/DEC/IX/5, 9 October 2008, para. 2(b).

182 CBD Decision X/37, Biofuels and biodiversity, UN Doc. UNEP/CBD/COP/DEC/X/37, 29 October 2010.

183 CBD Decision X/37, para. 10.

184 For instance, Seneca Sawmill's biomass power plant in Eugene, Oregon, the U.S. releases 500 tonnes of pollution per year. Mortensen, C. (2012). Biomass vs. environmental justice issues. Retrieved from www.eugeneweekly.com/2009/08/20/news.html#2

185 UNEP. Water, soil and air. Retrieved from www.unep.org/climatechange/mitigation/Bioenergy/Issues/WaterSoilAir/tabid/29468/Default. aspx

186 IPCC. (2006). 2006 IPCC guidelines for national greenhouse gas inventories – energy, vol. 2, Chapter 5. Retrieved from www.ipcc-nggip.iges.or.jp/public/2006gl/

187 Basel Convention on the Control of Transboundary Movements of Hazardous Wastes and their Disposal, Basel, adopted 22 March 1989, entered into force 5 May 1992, *United Nations Treaty Series* (1999), vol. 1673, no. 28911, p. 57, Art. 4 (b) & (c).

188 It entered into force in 1992. A list of the contracting parties to the Basel Convention is available at: www.basel.int/Countries/StatusofRatifications/partiesSignatories/tabid/1290/.

189 Raine, A. (2008). Transboundary transportation of CO_2 associated with carbon capture and storage – an analysis of issues under international law. *Carbon and Climate Law Review, 4*, 353–365, at 358.

190   UK Health and Safety Executive. General hazards of carbon dioxide. Retrieved from www.hse.gov.uk/carboncapture/carbondioxide.htm

191   For the view that CO_2 is not explosive, see e.g. Damen, K., Faaij, A., & Turkenburg, W. (2006). Health, safety and environmental risks of underground CO_2 storage – overview of mechanisms and current knowledge. *Climatic Change*, 74(1–3), 289–318.

192   Basel Convention, Art.1.1 (b). For instance, CO_2 is classed as a "substance hazardous to health" under the UK Health and Safety Executive, Control of Substances Hazardous to Health Regulations 2002 (COSHH). Retrieved from www.hse.gov.uk/coshh/

193   Basel Convention, Art. 4(5). As to the scope of "parties", the Ban Amendment provides for the prohibition by each party in the proposed new Annex VII (Parties and other States which are members of the OECD, EC, Liechtenstein) of all transboundary movements to States not included in Annex VII of hazardous wastes covered by the Convention that are intended for final disposal, and of all transboundary movements to States not included in Annex VII of hazardous wastes covered by paragraph 1 (a) of Article 1 of the Convention that are destined for reuse, recycling or recovery operations. Decision III/1 Amendment to the Basel Convention, UNEP/CHW.3/35, 28 November 199. Not yet entered into force.

194   Basel Convention, Art. 4(6).

195   Basel Convention, Art. 4(1)(a) & (b).

196   Basel Convention, Art. 4(1)(c).

197   Bamako Convention on the Ban of the Import into Africa and the Control of Transboundary Movement and Management of Hazardous Wastes within Africa, Bamako, adopted 30 January 1991, entered into force 22 April 1998, *United Nations Treaty Series* (2002), vol. 2101, no. 36508, p. 177.

198   Bamako Convention, Art. 4(1).

199   Bamako Convention, Annex I: Categories of Wastes which are Hazardous Waste.

200   Bamako Convention, Art. 2(1).

201   Raine, A. (2008), supra note 189, 360.

202   Redgwell, C. (2008). International legal responses to the challenges of a lower-carbon future: Climate change, carbon capture and storage, and biofuels. In Zillman, D., Redgwell, C., Omorogbe, Y., & Barrera-Hernandez, L. K. (Eds). *Beyond the Carbon Economy: Energy Law in Transition* (1st ed., pp. 85–108). Oxford: Oxford University Press, at 104.

203   UNCLOS, Art. 56.

204   UNCLOS, Arts. 58 & 87(1)(c).

205   UNCLOS, Art. 58(3).

206   UNCLOS, Art. 87(1)(c).

207   UNCLOS, Art. 79(1) & (3).

208   UNCLOS, Art. 79(5).

209   UNFCCC, Transboundary carbon capture and storage project activities. Technical paper, UN Doc. FCCC/TP/2012/9 (1 November 2012), para. 42–45.

210   London Convention, Art. 3(1)(b).

211   UNFCCC, Transboundary carbon capture and storage project activities, supra note 209, para. 18.

212   IMO. Report of the thirtieth consultative meeting and the third meeting of Contracting Parties, IMO DOCS LC 30/16 (9 December 2008), para. 5.1–5.34.

213   Resolution LP.3(4) on the Amendment to Article 6 of the London Protocol, adopted on 30 October 2009, not yet entered into force, IMO DOCS LC-LP.1/Circ.36 (17 June 2010).

214 Resolution LP.3(4) on the Amendment to Article 6 of the London Protocol, adopted on 30 October 2009, Annex. "Annex 2" refers to the "Assessment of wastes or other matter that may be considered for dumping".

215 U.S. Government Accountability Office (2011). Technology assessment: Climate engineering technical status, future directions, and potential responses. (No. GAO-11–71), 23.

216 London Protocol, Annex 1, para. 4.

217 OSPAR Decision 2007/1 to Prohibit the Storage of Carbon Dioxide Streams in the Water Column or on the Sea-bed and OSPAR Decision 2007/2 on the Storage of Carbon Dioxide Streams in Geological Formations. Both of the decisions entered into force in January 2008.

218 For an overview of the two decisions to the OSPAR Convention, see Redgwell, C. (2008), supra note 202.

219 OSPAR Annex II, Art. 3(2)(f) and Annex III, Arts. 3(3) & 3(4).

220 UNCLOS, Art. 81.

221 "Area" means the seabed and ocean floor and subsoil thereof, beyond the limits of national jurisdiction. UNCLOS, Art. 1.1(1).

222 UNCLOS, Arts. 136 & 137.

223 UNCLOS, Arts. 140 & 141.

224 "Resources" refers to all solid, liquid or gaseous mineral resources *in situ* in the Area at or beneath the seabed. UNCLOS, Art. 133.

225 UNCLOS, Part XI, Section 4 & Annex III.

226 UNFCCC, Transboundary carbon capture and storage project activities, supra note 209, paras. 82–148.

227 UNCLOS, Arts. 58, 79 & 112–114.

228 UNCLOS, Art. 79(3).

229 UNCLOS, Art. 74(5).

230 UNCLOS, Art. 81.

231 Birnie, P., Boyle, A., & Redgwell, C. (2009), supra note 24, 337.

232 See Section 3.7.2.1.

233 Convention on International Civil Aviation, Chicago, adopted 7 December 1944, entered into force 4 April 1947, *United Nations Treaty Series* (1948), vol. 5, no. 102, p. 295 (hereafter "Chicago Convention").

234 See Section 3.7.2.1.

235 The basic formulation of state sovereignty in customary international law can be found in Art. 2(1) of the UN Charter: "The Organization is based on the principle of the sovereign equality of all its Members."

236 *Case concerning Military and Paramilitary Activities in and against Nicaragua (Nicaragua v. United States of America)*, Merits, Judgment of 27 June 1986, ICJ Reports 1986, p. 14, para. 251.

237 Chicago Convention, Art. 5.

238 Chicago Convention, Art. 6.

239 Bodle, R., & Oberthür, S. et al. (2013), supra note 140, 70.

240 The Antarctic Treaty, Art. I.

241 The Antarctic Treaty, Art. II.

242 The Antarctic Treaty, Art. VII.3.

243 Protocol on Environmental Protection to the Antarctic Treaty, Art. 3.2(a), 3.2(b) & 3.(c).

244 UNGA. ILC First Report on the Protection of the Atmosphere, Sixty-six Session Sixty-six Session by Shinya Murase, Special Repporteur, UN Doc. A/CN.4/667 (14 February 2014), 53.

245 The CLRTAP, Arts. 3–9.

246 The CLRTAP, Art. 1(a).

247 The CLRTAP, Art. 4.

248 Bodle, R., & Oberthür, S. et al. (2013), supra note 140, 63.

249 The determination of "net effects" has also been addressed in Section 3.4.4.
250 See PART XII of the UNCLOS and Annex IV to the Protocol on Environmental Protection to the Antarctic Treaty, Prevention of Marine Pollution.
251 Bodle, R., & Oberthür, S. et al. (2013), supra note 140, 61.
252 The CLRTAP, Preface.
253 The CLRTAP, Arts. 7, 8(a) & 9(a).
254 Protocol to the 1979 Convention on Long-range Transboundary Air Pollution on the Reduction of Sulphur Emissions or Their Transboundary Fluxes by at least 30 per cent, Art. 2.
255 Protocol to the 1979 Convention on Long-range Transboundary Air Pollution on Further Reduction of Sulphur Emissions, Oslo, adopted 14 June 1994, entered into force 5 August 1998, *United Nations Treaty Series* (2001), vol. 2030, no. 21623, p. 122, Art. 2.
256 Ibid.
257 Protocol to Abate Acidification, Eutrophication and Ground-level Ozone to the Convention on Long-range Transboundary Air Pollution, Gothenburg, adopted 30 November 1999, entered into force 17 May 2005, *United Nations Treaty Series* (2005), vol. 2319, no. 21623, p. 80. Note that The United States and Canada, as parties to the Gothenburg Protocol, have not provided its commitment to the SO_2 emission ceiling in Annex II.
258 See Chapter 1, Section 1.4.2.2.
259 According to Table 2 of Annex II, EU's emission level of SO_2 in 2005 is 78 Mt, and it target of reduction from 2005 level is 59%.
260 "Worldwide" means both parties and non-parties to the Gothenburg Protocol are included.
261 Same opinion can be found in Bodle, R., & Oberthür, S. et al. (2013), supra note 140, 66, and Rickels, W., Klepper, G., et al. (2011). *Large-scale intentional interventions into the climate system? Assessing the climate engineering debate.* Scoping report conducted on behalf of the German Federal Ministry of Education and Research (BMBF), Kiel: Kiel Earth Institute, 90.
262 See Section 1.5.4.
263 Vienna Convention for the Protection of the Ozone Layer and its Montreal Protocol, Vienna, 22 March 1985, *United Nations Treaty Series* (1997), vol. 1513, no. 26164, p. 293.
264 Vienna Convention, Preamble.
265 Vienna Convention, Annex I, para. 1.
266 Tilmes, S., Müller, R., & Salawitch, R. (2008). The sensitivity of polar ozone depletion to proposed geoengineering schemes. *Science, 320*(5880), 1201–1204.
267 Wigley, T. (2006). A combined mitigation/ geoengineering approach to climate stabilization. *Science, 314*, 452–454.
268 Montreal Protocol, Art. 2(10)(a).
269 UNCLOS, Art. 194(3)(a).
270 UNCLOS, Art. 1.1(5)(a); London Convention Art. III (1)(a); London Protocol, Art. 1(4)(1)(1).
271 London Convention, Art. III(b)(ii); London Protocol, Art. 1(4).
272 UNCLOS, Art. 1.1(4); London Protocol, Art. 2.
273 Bodle, R., & Oberthür, S. et al. (2013), supra note 140, 71–72.
274 CBD, Art. 3.
275 CBD, Art. 14.
276 Convention on the Conservation of Migratory Species of Wild Animals, Bonn, 23 June 1979, *United Nations Treaty Series* (1998), vol. 1651, no. 28395, p. 333.

277 More about these conventions concerning the preservation of naturel resources, see Section 2.4.1.

278 Relevant rules in this section also apply to MCW.

279 See Section 2.3 for the discussion of the ENMOD.

280 See Chapter 1, Section 1.5.5.

281 UNEP/GC Decision 8/7, Earthwatch: assessment of outer limits, A: Provisions for co-operation between States in Weather Modification, 29 April 1980, paras. 1(a), (b), (e) & (f). Retrieved from www.unep.org/Documents.multilingual/Default.asp?DocumentID=62&ArticleID=549&l=en

282 Scott, K. N. (2012–2013) International law in the Anthropocene: Responding to the geoengineering challenge. *Michigan Journal of International Law, 34,* 309–358.

283 See e.g. the CLRTAP, Art. 1(a); Vienna Convention, Art. 1(2); UNCLOS, Art. 1.1(4).

284 See e.g. Section 3.2.1.1 & Section 3.4.1.

Part III
Towards better governance

4 Main scenarios of the future of geoengineering governance

4.1 Introduction

Chapters 2 and 3 addressed the contemporary international legal rules and principles that are applicable to geoengineering in general as well as to individual techniques. The conclusion is that regulatory gaps exist and the existing international institutions cannot govern geoengineering in a sufficient manner. This chapter and Chapter 5 attempt to close the regulatory gaps and to provide suggestions to govern geoengineering in a proper, sufficient and proportionate manner.

The term "governance" in Chapters 4 and 5 relates to the complex of actors, mechanisms and processes, in the context of international law, for making and applying rules for the use of geoengineering technology. The actors could be states, international institutions or a group of geoengineering experts. It is important to realize that various governance models for geoengineering reflect the values of different countries and are designed for different governing purposes. The primary purposes of geoengineering governance could be to develop new technologies to combat climate change, to prevent damage to the environment and human health, to avoid political tensions, to avoid moral hazards, etc. The purposes of governing geoengineering vary in accordance with the rights and interests that states and private actors wish to gain from the future implementation[1] of geoengineering. This book also has its primary concerns in the design of the governance model, and is not able to cover all of the important issues.

This book, from the perspective of international environmental law, places the emphasis on controlling the risk of significant harm to the environment and human health, taking into account that different geoengineering techniques and different scales of activities should be assessed separately in order to avoid indiscriminate inhibition or restriction of the development of new technologies that could contribute to the avoidance of serious or irreversible climate change. Note that both under- and over-regulation of geoengineering should be avoided, but controlling the risk of significant harm to the environment and human health should be prioritized in decision-making. The legal analysis in Chapters 4 and 5 thus surrounds two aspects of the international legal implications of geoengineering: a) to control the risk of such harm arising from research activities and the deployment of geoengineering; and b) to cautiously develop geoengineering by paying due regard to the degree of risks and scientific uncertainties in particular techniques. These two aspects are also two core elements for moving toward a legitimate and effective governance of geoengineering in the future.

This chapter reviews the main scenarios of the governance for geoengineering in the future and then provides some suggestions on the international legal framework that can best address the two aspects above. From Section 4.2 to Section 4.5, four different approaches, viz. unilateralism, minilateralism, multilateralism and non-state governance, are addressed respectively. Section 4.4 examines the multilateral approach by comparing the proposals of different governance models in two respects: the choice of appropriate institutions and the form of rules and principles (as soft or hard law). Section 4.6 reflects on the design of the multilateral framework and the improvement of the multilateral approach.

It should also be noted that the governance framework proposed in this chapter would not be much relevant to BECCS. Distinct from the other five geoengineering techniques, BECCS is unlikely to give rise to governance problems at the global level, and almost all problems arising from BECCS activities could be solved through existing mechanisms (negotiations, etc.) between states.

4.2 Unilateralism

4.2.1 A brief introduction to unilateralism

Unilateralism refers to any action that one state takes independently, with minimal consultation and involvement of other states.[2] In principle, states are entitled to act unilaterally because it is the essence of sovereignty.[3] However, the sovereign right of one state may be at odds with the sovereignty of another state when one state's action directly impacts another state. Hence, unilateral action is less desirable than multilateral action when a unilateral action may cause international consequences, because unilateral action does not favour negotiations and mutual understanding between countries. Moreover, unilateral action may bring benefits to the acting state while causing harm to other states, and it may consequently create international tensions and conflicts.[4]

It is without doubt that one state should not arbitrarily impose its will on other states or make decisions that harm the international community. However, unilateral action aimed at developing international standards and advancing shared objectives, rather than merely pursuing self-interest, could play a critical role in promoting the development of relevant international law.[5] A typical example is the development of the international regime to prevent oil pollution. In the 1970s, the United States' unilateral decision to establish a double-hull standard for oil drilling equipment entering its port catalysed the inclusion of this standard by the MARPOL Convention.[6] Another example is the development of the exclusive economic zone under the UNCLOS in response to Canada's unilateral initiative[7] and other coastal states' follow-ups. Apart from that, unilateral action by one state may provide precedents and experiences for other states coping with similar threats.[8]

More importantly, although multilateralism is and will be the mainstream approach to address international issues, unilateralism still has its advantages in solving environmental problems. Typically, when international cooperation and multilateral action are unachievable or ineffective to deal with urgent environment threats, unilateral action may be the only means for promoting and enforcing shared values.[9]

In summary, unilateralism can be compared to a double-edged sword: if used in a proper way, unilateral action could solve international problems more effectively when multilateral negotiations enter a deadlock. It could also have far-reaching impacts on the international community in terms of developing new solutions that could be generalized for other states to solve similar problems. However, if it is used improperly, it would give rise to instability in the international system.

4.2.2 Unilateralism and geoengineering

The debate about unilateral decision-making and implementation of geoengineering focuses on SRM techniques.[10] Unilateral implementation of SRM would make the international governance of SRM more complex and sensitive. On the one hand, it is technically and financially feasible for one state to implement SRM techniques alone; on the other hand, the result of the unilateral decision-making would very likely influence populations excluded from the decision-making process, and the adverse impacts of SRM activities would be regional or global and would be uneven in different regions. Should a developed country deploy SRM techniques for preserving a "public good", developing countries might not want to believe such a motive if they were the main victims of serious side effects. Hence, the unilateral implementation of large-scale geoengineering activities is very unlikely to proceed without protests from potentially affected states. In view of this, it would not be surprising to see considerable objections to any proposal for unilateral geoengineering action, even a field research activity.

In addition, considering the latest success in the Paris Climate Change Conference in December 2015, one could optimistically envisage that the approach of international cooperation and multilateral action is still effective and that the collective goals based on consensus are not unachievable. Hence, the focus of SRM governance should be on enhancing cooperation among states in rule-making, decision-making and implementation.[11]

4.3 Minilateral governance

4.3.1 The emergence of minilateralism

The idea of minilateralism has been frequently proposed over the last decade as an alternative to intergovernmental efforts. Minilateralism, also formulated as an "exclusive club"[12] or "exclusive coalition",[13] distinct from multilateralism, attempts to achieve largely inclusive agreements. Instead of waiting for the consensus of nearly 200 states, minilateralism suggests a more responsive pattern of governance, bringing to the table a small number of participants who have contributed most to creating certain international problems and may have the largest impact on solving those problems.[14] Minilateralism is described as "the magic number to get real international action".[15]

Exclusive minilateralism has become an important development in the process of international climate change governance.[16] It has been observed that fewer than twenty states account for more than 80% of the world's GHG emissions, and thus these states should make greater contributions to emission reductions.[17] In addition, only a few states are capable of pioneering technological innovations relevant to climate change.[18] The rest of more than 150 states actually contribute very little in causing and/or resolving the climate change problem. In view of this, commentators proposed a minilateral model of governance that excludes non-key players from the decision-making process. As Victor argued, "in the area of international cooperation the solutions lie in efforts to create a club of a small number of important countries and craft the elements of serious cooperation".[19]

4.3.2 *The legitimacy and feasibility of minilateralism*

The issue of legitimacy addressed in this section consists of two aspects: input legitimacy and output legitimacy. The former relates to the functioning of an institution, such as the way in which the members of an institution are selected and the procedures by which decisions are made, while the latter relates to the public assessment of the relevance and the quality of the institution's performance.[20]

The legitimacy of minilateralism first concerns effectiveness, which relates to the output legitimacy. Two schools of thoughts in international relations, neoliberalism and realism, criticize the reliance on multilateral cooperation in the international governance of climate change. The neoliberals attempt to find more desirable collective outcomes through interaction and collaboration.[21] They contend that any advantage of inclusive multilateralism would pale when the cumbersome system designed for the purpose of approaching consensus proves to be ineffective.[22] In other words, legitimacy does not solely mean broad participation and inclusion in international issues; legitimacy depends partly on effectiveness.[23] Realists criticize that great powers are more willing to pursue their interests in bilateral bargaining instead of being restricted by multilateral mechanisms.

In practice, it is common to see that the more states are involved in negotiations, the fewer shared interests are likely to be found. For instance, high-latitude states may welcome a certain degree of global warming, as their agriculture would benefit from the longer growing time. Likewise, developing states prefer to invest their available resources today in development rather than make short-term sacrifices at present for uncertain long-term benefits.[24] Hence, due to the highly diverse interests among states, efforts to attain universal collaboration to control climate change often fail. In contrast, with an "exclusive club", countries will choose to join the club in accordance with their own interests and undertake high levels of mitigation because of the penalties for non-participation.[25]

The legitimacy of minilateralism also concerns the constitution of an exclusive club, which relates to the input legitimacy. The constitution of an exclusive club consists of two aspects: which and how many states should be included. As mentioned in Section 4.3.1, the majority opinion is that the "exclusive club" should include the states that account for the majority of GHG emissions and that are most capable of contributing to solving the problem of global warming. Regarding the size of the "exclusive club", the number of states varies per issue. Naím submitted that a "magic number" is about twenty because the number of major countries involved in various international problems is always around twenty: no more than twenty states account for approximately 80% of GHG emissions; and the Group of Twenty (G20) accounts for 85% of the world's economy.[26] Victor suggested that the number of ten to a dozen would be the most effective and efficient group for climate change collaboration.[27] Wright proposed that "a small number of very important states", even as small as two or three, could take rapid coordinated actions.[28]

However, regardless of how the "exclusive club" is composed, minilateralism still bears the legitimacy deficits of unequal participation of states and exclusion of non-participants. In addition, minilateralism is interest-driven and represents the interests of a small group of states, whereas the implementation of geoengineering would impact a great number of states unevenly. The criteria for determining whether to implement geoengineering, in particular SRM techniques, can hardly be established on the basis of "common good" for all by applying minilateralism.

In addition to the questioned legitimacy, the feasibility of minilateralism is in doubt as well. Opponents of minilateralism argue that many of the obstacles to inclusive collaboration do not result from inefficiency of large number participants but rather lie with the great powers.[29] The Major Economies Forum on Energy and Climate (MEF) is a good example for showing that minilateralism cannot better cope with the problem of climate change compared to a multilateral approach via the UNFCCC. MEF, launched in March 2009 by US then-President Obama, primarily intended to facilitate a candid dialogue among major developed and developing economies, and help generate the political leadership necessary to achieve a successful outcome at the annual UN climate negotiations.[30] In the negotiations of the post-2012 mitigation target, the G8 countries,[31] as large emitters and most capable countries to contribute to resolving the climate change problem, proposed a long-term mitigation target, but were unwilling to commit to an interim target for 2020. China and India, as major developing country emitters, refused to agree on the long-term reduction target because industrial countries refused to commit to mid-term goals and to provide developing countries financial and technical assistance.[32] The MEF in July 2009 failed to agree on a specific mitigation target. This example shows that, in climate change negotiations, minilateralism might not be a more effective means to achieve collaboration, because major emitters, albeit a small number, still have diverse interests.

In response to the criticism, one may argue that the MEF at least brings together the United States, Russia, Australia and Canada, the countries that did not join the KP or withdrew from the KP. Minilateral actions could serve as a "confidence-building measure"[33] as well as a precursor to attract broader involvement instead of enabling great powers to evade their responsibilities. Ultimately, minilateralism, as a strong and flexible model of cooperation, is expected to exert its leverage to achieve multilateral collaboration.

4.3.3 Minilateralism and geoengineering

Minilateralism seems to be a legitimate and feasible approach in some situations to resolve climate change problems in a more flexible and responsive manner, as shown in the examples of the WTO and G20.[34] However, the desirability of applying minilateralism to international trade and economic cooperation does not necessarily mean that minilateral geoengineering governance is also legitimate, because minilateral governance by a small group of states should be a net gain[35] for all states and should have no detrimental impact upon the interests of other states.[36] A small group of states should not decide whether to undertake potentially harmful geoengineering activities that might lead to harm occurring in other states' territorial areas or in the global commons. This characteristic is the decisive factor that marine geoengineering techniques and SRI should not be governed by a small group of states.

However, in the event that a multilateral agreement is (temporarily) unachievable, actions initiated by a small group of states might catalyse broader participation in mitigation and innovative activities counteracting global warming.

4.4 Multilateral governance

Compared to unilateralism and minilateralism, multilateralism will enjoy more legitimacy, as it represents an inclusive approach for equitable participation of states. More importantly, multilateral governance could provide international oversight over geoengineering activities. In particular, once a SAI project has begun, the incentive to sustain international cooperation in such a project is much stronger than in conventional emission control, because failure to sustain it could lead to rapid and dangerous climate change.[37]

Note that the resort to a multilateral approach does not equate the pursuit of a global consensus among all states; this approach underlines the inclusion of potentially affected states, in particular most vulnerable states, through an appropriate international institution or a group of international institutions. Hence, the discussion of inclusiveness in this section is based on the number of parties and the functioning of various international institutions rather than the assumption of an absolutely global consensus. This method provides a more practical entry point for discussion.

4.4.1 Geoengineering and equity concerns

The deployment of geoengineering techniques at the global level would bring broad and far-reaching moral implications, mainly surrounding the topic of equity. The deployment of SRM techniques would result in uneven impacts in different countries or regions, and there could be a delay of adverse impacts on the environment, up to decades, in comparison with the rapid decrease of the global average temperature. If the removal of atmospheric CO_2 by CDR methods is merely temporary, it also brings the concern of intergenerational equity to our attention. Against this background, the equity between states and generations is a significant issue that needs to be taken into account in the governance of geoengineering.

Instead of answering the abovementioned questions from an ethical perspective, the present section will address equity issues insofar as the application of equity-related principles under contemporary international law to geoengineering techniques.

In the domain of international law, it is still controversial whether the general concept of equity has been translated into a general principle under contemporary international law.[38] Nevertheless, concrete interpretations of equity in a legal context can be, for instance, an equitable balancing of interests between states.[39] To narrow down the discussion to the subject of geoengineering, equity concerns refer to the equity between countries and the equity between generations.

Regarding the equity between countries, the vital issue is how to protect the most vulnerable populations that are unable to enjoy the benefit from deploying a geoengineering technique, or that are likely to be first exposed to the risk of adverse impacts caused by the deployment of a geoengineering technique. The principle of common but differentiated responsibilities and respective capabilities (CBDR) is the core. The principle of CBDR can be clearly traced in the climate change regime. Article 3(1) of the UNFCCC articulates that "[t]he Parties should protect the climate system [. . .] on the basis of equity and in accordance with their common but differentiated responsibilities and respective capabilities". Under the principle of CBDR, "the developed country Parties should take the lead in combating climate change and the adverse effects thereof", and "[t]he specific needs and special circumstances of developing country Parties, especially those that are particularly vulnerable to the adverse effects of climate change [. . .] should be given full consideration".[40] Article 2.2 of the Paris Agreement stipulates that "the Agreement will be implemented to reflect equity and the principle of common but differentiated responsibilities and respective capabilities, in the light of different national circumstances". Under the climate change regime, developed countries should bear higher responsibilities on the ground that they have contributed most to causing the problem of climate change historically and that they have greater capacity to tackle the problem.

The application of the principle of CBDR to geoengineering is twofold. On the one hand, regarding some expensive negative emissions techniques the effectiveness of which in removing excessive CO_2 has been acknowledged, developed countries should bear higher responsibilities of developing and deploying such techniques and should provide technological and financial assistance for developing countries to develop and deploy such techniques. On the other hand, developed countries should not take their advantages to deploy SRM techniques without involving developing countries into the decision-making process. Against the background that the effectiveness and adverse impacts of SRM techniques are not yet sufficiently clear, the involvement of developing countries in SRM-related decision-making processes could prevent any unequal action that results in damages to developing countries, in particular to the most vulnerable populations.[41]

Regarding intergenerational equity, the basic concept is that each generation has the responsibility to pass on the planet in no worse condition than received and have equitable access to its resources.[42] The connotation of intergenerational equity has been proposed as the conservation of the diversity of the natural and cultural resources base, the conservation of the quality of the planet, and the conservation of equitable access to the use and benefit of the legacy. Intergenerational equity has been recognized by a number of treaties and other international legal instruments, either explicitly or implicitly. Principle 3 of Rio Declaration articulates that the right to development "must be fulfilled so as to equitably meet developmental and environmental needs of present and future generations". Article 3.1 of the UNFCCC addresses intergenerational equity as one of the principles that guide the parties: "The Parties should protect the climate system for the benefit of present and future generations of humankind, on the basis of equity". Under the CBD, however, maintaining the biological diversity to "meet the needs and aspirations" of present and future generations is formulated as the goal of pursuing "sustainable development".[43] In addition, implicit recognition of intergenerational equity can be found in the International Convention for the Regulation of Whaling, which recognized the conservation of whale stocks for "future generations".[44]

What remains unclear is the translation of the theory of intergenerational equity into specific rights of future generations, in particular, justiciable rights in international law.[45] Core issues include, for instance, the valid representation of future generations, and the design of operational mechanisms, which enable international institutions to accommodate the protection of the interest of future generations in actual practices.

Setting aside the difficulty of operationalizing the principle of intergenerational equity, such a principle could nevertheless bring added value to the multilateral governance of geoengineering, First, it justifies from the intergenerational perspective that states have the obligation to prevent irreversible harm to the environment for the sake of passing a no-worse planet to future generations. Second, it stresses that the impacts on future generations is a valid concern for the present generation to take into account in decision-making. Seen in this way, competent authorities in a multilateral governance structure might need to rethink about their decisions, when they take due regard to the delay of adverse impacts on the environment for up to decades from a SRM activity, and the temporary storage of CO_2 via CDR methods.

4.4.2 International institutions

4.4.2.1 A new binding instrument

It is generally agreed that creating a new overarching treaty to deal with all geoengineering techniques in a comprehensive manner is neither necessary nor likely.[46] First, although regulatory gaps remain, the existing institutions appear to be equipped to deal with geoengineering issues.[47] In particular, the recent development of specific rules and principles regulating marine geoengineering techniques proves the effectiveness of governing geoengineering through existing instruments. Second, because the risks and the benefits arising from geoengineering activities will likely be unevenly distributed over different areas, states would have polarized opinions and thus are very unlikely to agree on the form and content of a new treaty.

4.4.2.2 Through existing international institutions

(I) AN OVERARCHING APPROACH

Under the UNFCCC Some scholars suggest governing geoengineering under the UNFCCC, as the UNFCCC is the most legitimate, inclusive and experienced body to address the danger of climate change, and the purpose of deploying geoengineering techniques is consistent with the objective of the UNFCCC. One proposal is that the UNFCCC could govern the research and deployment of geoengineering through a new protocol that would have an adaptive management mechanism, with a default presumption against the implementation of any geoengineering project.[48] Such an adaptive management mechanism would operate through an incremental decision-making process that is responsive and adaptive to the changing environment.[49] This proposal appears to be unrealistic, taking into account the herculean efforts required in the negotiation process to adopt a document with binding effect.

The opponents of this proposal argue that the involvement of SRM geoengineering might negatively interfere with the already delicate negotiations under the UNFCCC, as it might send the wrong message by diverting attention away from mitigation and adaptation efforts.[50] Notably, this argument is based on the belief that moral hazards exist and geoengineering is merely a backup to mitigation efforts. Furthermore, the characteristics of universal participation and consensus-based decision-making process indicate that the UNFCCC might not be able to deal with geoengineering issues in a responsive and efficient manner. In addition, considering that the benefits and the adverse environmental impacts of geoengineering are both far from fully identified, it seems premature to include geoengineering in the portfolio of strategies counteracting climate change under the UNFCCC, on the one hand, and unwise to ban it now, on the other hand.[51]

Under the CBD   Some scholars have suggested governing geoengineering under the CBD, because it has a broad mandate to prevent environmental damages to species and ecosystems, and it has completed preliminary work on the topic of geoengineering governance.[52] The CBD COP Decisions could provide a basis for further work on regulating geoengineering in a more precise and consistent way.

However, it is not self-evident that it is best to regulate geoengineering under the CBD, as the objectives of the CBD are different from those of the UNFCCC. This difference could eventually lead to regime conflicts if a link between the mandate of the CBD and that of the UNFCCC is not formalized.[53] More importantly, the CBD COP only treats geoengineering as a potential threat to biodiversity and neglects the contribution that geoengineering can make to avert the dangers of climate change on biodiversity.[54] This argument is supported by the two CBD COP Decisions on the governance on geoengineering,[55] which show that the CBD did not acknowledge the potential of geoengineering in avoiding dangerous climate change, but rather suggested a general prohibition on all geoengineering techniques with exceptions under well-defined circumstances. Were the CBD to play the leading role in governing geoengineering techniques, the room for the development of such techniques would be very limited. In view of this, the CBD might not be the preferred choice to perform overarching functions in relation to geoengineering governance, mainly because a proper governance model should take into account both the benefits and risks instead of being guided by a negative attitude from the outset.

Under the UNEP   The UNEP has been proposed as a potential forum to govern geoengineering in a comprehensive manner.[56] Since 1972, the UNEP has served as a permanent institution within the UN for the protection and improvement of the environment. The UNEP has the functions and responsibilities, among others, to promote international cooperation in the field of the environment and to provide general policy guidance for the direction and coordination of environmental programmes within the UN.[57] As climate change is one of UNEP's six thematic priorities, it could be appropriate and practicable to negotiate and regulate geoengineering issues under the UNEP. Furthermore, the UNEP has rich experience in catalysing multilateral environmental negotiations and developing soft-law instruments. As to its potential contribution to the governance of geoengineering, the UNEP is capable of identifying environmental challenges at an early stage, bringing both scientific and policy inputs and developing guidelines and principles that could influence the final outcomes of negotiations.[58] More specifically, the examples of the UNEP's work are widely referred to throughout Chapters 1 to 3 of this book, ranging from shared natural resources,[59] EIA,[60] and protection of the marine environment[61] to the cooperation between states in weather modification.[62] These examples indicate that the UNEP's work has already covered some issues relevant to the governance of geoengineering.

The main restraints are the UNEP's limited governing power and the potential conflicts with other UN bodies. A recent development is that a reform aiming at strengthening and upgrading the UNEP was proposed in the outcome document of the Rio+20 Summit in 2012.[63] The result was the establishment of a new governing body, United Nations Environmental Assembly (UNEA), which enjoys the universal involvement of 193 states, major groups and stakeholders. This institutional reform might enhance the governance ability of the UNEP, but potential conflicts with, for instance the CBD, may arise. UNEP would be more likely to serve as a facilitator in terms of shepherding the governance of geoengineering, without serving as the actual governing body.

(II) A SECTORAL APPROACH

In contrast to an overarching approach that attempts to govern geoengineering in a comprehensive manner, a sectoral approach has been suggested to address specific geoengineering techniques separately by various sectoral regimes that already exist. The 2013 Amendments to the LP on marine geoengineering typically demonstrate such a sectoral approach. In addition, as examined in Chapter 3, the 1985 Vienna Convention and its 1987 Montreal Protocol could be options to address SAI and arguably MCW. The CLRTAP would be a less desirable option due to its limited number of parties.[64]

The main restraint of the sectoral approach concerns the different objectives of specific regimes. On the one hand, as every geoengineering technique may create more than one type of risk, the direct application of an existing regime to a particular geoengineering technique would be insufficient to cope with all risks, whereas the development of new rules with respect to a particular geoengineering technique under an existing regime might inappropriately stretch its mandate too far. On the other hand, if one geoengineering technique were addressed by more than one specific regime, it might lead to fragmentation and incoherence between specific regimes. Bearing these caveats in mind, it is suggested to apply the sectoral approach in a manner that enhances the cooperation and interaction between regimes, for instance, through joint liaison groups.[65]

4.4.3 The proper form

This section aims to identify the preferable form of the legal framework to govern geoengineering techniques. International law and international relations scholars have distinct understandings on the distinction between hard law and soft law. Legal scholars tend to focus on the binding force of law. Legal positivists make a binary division between hard law and soft law. In this view, the fundamental distinction between hard law and soft law is the distinction between binding and non-binding obligations.[66] In comparison, political scientists have largely adopted a three-dimensional definition made by institutionalists, who contend that soft law differs from hard law in terms of obligation, precision of rules and delegation to a third-party decision-maker or a dispute settlement body.[67] Hard law is understood as legally binding obligations that are precise, and that delegate authority to interpret and apply the law, whereas the realm of soft law begins once one or more of the three dimensions are weakened in a legal arrangement.[68]

This section will address the proper form for a legal framework for geoengineering techniques by assessing the dimensions of obligation and precision. The dimension of delegation actually relates to the issue of institutional arrangement, which is addressed in the discussion of a proper institution to govern geoengineering in Section 4.4.2.

With respect to the dimension of obligation, it refers to the binding force of legal rules. Treaties, as one of the main forms of binding law, impose obligations on and attribute rights to contracting parties, and some of them stipulate substantive and procedural mechanisms for the interpretation and application of obligations and the consequences of non-compliance. Binding law thus makes state commitments more credible because it increases the cost of reneging, either because of legal sanctions or because of the reputational cost of non-compliance.[69] However, this does not mean that non-binding norms and principles are not able to contribute to effective law making and enforcement. Those norms and principles still embrace an element of good faith commitment, and in many cases, "a desire to influence state practice and an element of law-making".[70] Moreover, non-binding instruments enable states to be more ambitious and engage in deeper cooperation because the consequences of non-compliance are limited.[71] In addition, the procedural costs of binding law, such as the time for its entering into force and the complexity of adopting amendments, make binding law much less responsive to emergent needs of regulation. Compared to binding law, non-binding law decreases the costs of negotiation and achieving an agreement as well as of non-compliance.

So, in which situation is it better to use binding instruments to govern geoengineering, and in which situations is it better to use non-binding instruments? According to the features of binding and non-binding law stated previously, one may preliminarily conclude that non-binding norms and principles are more desirable when ambitious cooperation is required on an emergent issue and the consequences of non-compliance are not serious; binding-rules are more desirable when the consequences of non-compliance are serious. Hence, regarding the legal framework for geoengineering, the hardness of rules varies with the substance. A framework agreement which contains fundamental obligations and general principles should be formulated in a binding form. For instance, the obligation to prevent significant transboundary harm to the environment and human health and to act with precaution should have a binding character, as they are of fundamental importance in the governance of geoengineering. By contrast, more specific regulations on how to make decisions on and to undertake a particular geoengineering activity are better if non-binding, as states could achieve agreement more quickly and ambitiously, and take collective actions more responsively.

Non-binding norms are more desirable not only when ambitious cooperation is required but also when an issue is complex and contains uncertainties. When scientific features and underlying impacts of a technique are far from fully identified or understood, a binding instrument with specific regulations or technical standards is not desirable, because the specific regulations could be so often modified and thus a binding form could make the cost of future amendment much higher. For instance, regarding the issues of the specific requirements and procedures of an environmental impact assessment, a non-binding form allows states to adapt to new knowledge and to avoid being locked into unfavourable commitments.[72]

The dimension of precision is closely related to the dimension of obligation in dealing with uncertainties. First, uncertainty makes the formulation of precise rules under binding instruments not attainable; the reduction of precision of treaty provisions could be an alternative to non-binding norms to deal with uncertainties. Formulating less precise content and wording of a binding instrument provides a rational adaptation to uncertainty.[73] In this case, treaties do not impose specific obligations, because the provisions are general, undetermined or vague. The UNFCCC provides a typical example. Article 3 of the UNFCCC is generally recognized as a significant article that provides for the fundamental principles that guide states' behaviour, but the principles are open-textured in the sense that the specific content is uncertain and those principles leave much room for interpretation and elaboration.[74] Another example is the 2013 Amendments to the LP on marine geoengineering that are binding in form (not into force) but imprecise in substance. The new Annex 4 leaves the scope of marine geoengineering techniques undetermined in order to take into account the development of new technologies. Second, uncertainty also makes precision less desirable.[75] Here, the difference between risks and uncertainties matters. If risk is the dominant concern, precise norms could provide a way to manage and optimize risk-sharing. In contrast, when confronting significant *uncertainties*, such as future potential political changes, states are likely to be more willing to engage in cooperation through less precise commitments.[76]

In summary, a legally binding agreement for geoengineering could contain merely fundamental obligations, together with some general principles to shape the framework agreement. But specific matters, at least in the near term, favour the formulation of non-binding norms and principles. To deal with uncertainty, legal instruments should be dynamic, adaptive and future-proof.[77] Norms could be later formulated more precisely in non-binding instruments (such as decisions, resolutions and guidelines adopted by international institutions), or be formulated in binding instruments with undetermined or general wording (such as Article 3 of the UNFCCC).

4.5 A non-state governance approach

A non-state governance approach concentrates on the conduct of scientists and private actors instead of states. Considering the divergent interests among states in geopolitics and the difficulty of developing modalities for the assessment and regulation of geoengineering techniques in a formal, multilateral and integrated manner at the present stage, some scientists are concerned that any immature multilateral regulation would inhibit the development of technologies. They, hence, propose a decentralized approach to build up norms from the bottom up, concentrating on "laying the groundwork for future negotiations over norms rather than attempting to codify immature norms now".[78] This approach starts by stimulating scientists and private actors to conduct research and assessment, to gain knowledge and experience, and to build up preliminary norms and voluntary guidelines. Then the cooperation between research teams, entrepreneurs and NGOs would be gradually expanded and the relationship between the governance and the emerging scientific research could be developed.[79]

Non-state governance could be effective and practicable at the stage of laboratory research and local field experiments; the loosely coordinated relationship among scientists and private actors is not stable enough and reliable to govern large-scale experiments or actual deployment. A risk of non-state governance is that research and field experiments of geoengineering might set the world on a "slippery slope" to ultimate development, as the interests of scientists and private actors on the fundamental work lie in future outputs.[80] Private actors might have strong interests in investing in geoengineering research because of the financial gain (carbon credits and patents on geoengineering technologies). This might create the risk of technological lock-in in geoengineering research and lead to inevitable deployment.

4.6 Some reflections on the international governance of geoengineering

The overview of different approaches in the previous Sections 4.2 to 4.5 delivers two vital messages. First, in a normative sense, multilateralism seems to be the most desirable option to achieve the best practices of SRM techniques compared to the other three approaches. The main consideration is that multilateral negotiations and decision-making would enjoy the greatest level of legitimacy and would less likely lead to political collisions. Second, in practice, each governance approach may have its advantages in governing certain types of techniques at certain phases (early research, experiment or deployment). Notably, the main advantage that is enjoyed by unilateralism and minilateralism, effectiveness, is also the weakness of multilateralism. In order to propose some practical suggestions on the international governance of geoengineering, the discussion could be divided into three parts: short-term, mid-term and long-term scenarios.

4.6.1 *Short-term scenario*

The short-term scenario describes the governance of geoengineering in the coming years. As addressed in Section 4.4.2.2 (i) regarding the UNFCCC, it is too soon to put geoengineering, in particular SRM techniques, in the portfolio of methods to combat global warming at the moment, as it would deliver the wrong message to the already intricate international negotiations. However, scientific exploration of new possibilities to cope with the problem of global warming could still proceed.

In the short term, the first focal point is that the governance of geoengineering will concentrate on enhancing the synergies of scientific institutions, experts and relevant international organizations to actively engage in the inclusive discussion and deepen the understanding of geoengineering technology. In particular, the IPCC interfaces scientific aspects of geoengineering with political ones, as it has actively participated in assessing the feasibility, effectiveness and risks associated with various geoengineering techniques and has provided advice on governance as well as the science. In addition, the World Meteorological Organization (WMO), as a specialized agency of the UN with the authority to speak "on the state and behaviour of the Earth's atmosphere, its interaction with the oceans, the climate it produces and the resulting distribution of water resources",[81] has identified geoengineering as an area of research priority and is attempting to find WMO's role in current international deliberations.[82] The Congress of the WMO also requested its Commission on Atmospheric Sciences (CAS) to coordinate its contribution to a comprehensive assessment of the state of knowledge, science capacity and understanding of information gaps in close cooperation with the IMO, Intergovernmental Oceanographic Commission of the United Nations Educational, Science and Cultural Organization (UNESCO), IPCC and other international, science and academic bodies.[83] The WMO seems to be an appropriate international body in terms of facilitating information exchange and guiding research to coordinate SAI, MCW and new geoengineering techniques that deliberately intervene in the atmosphere and may impact the marine environment. However, its limited political weight and the lack of regulatory experience indicate that the WMO cannot function more than an informal coordinator and is not suitable to perform overarching governance.

Second, as the risks and the state of knowledge vary from technique to technique, not all geoengineering techniques need to be developed simultaneously; low-risk and scientifically valuable research could proceed and less controversial geoengineering techniques could be developed as a first step.[84] Compared to SRM, CDR techniques directly address CO_2 emissions and are subject to less scientific uncertainties. Scientists have projected that achieving mitigation will strongly rely on the availability and wide deployment of negative emission techniques, including BECCS.[85] Also, policymakers have realized the significance of involving negative emission techniques into the mitigation portfolio.[86] BECCS is expected to be widely deployed in the coming years.

Third, although many scholars have submitted that research in geoengineering and the deployment of geoengineering face different regulatory challenges,[87] there is no need to differentiate the legal implications of research and deployment of geoengineering because the purpose is not the decisive factor that makes a difference relating to risks and adverse impacts. An international governance arrangement should encompass both research experiments and deployment. Separated governance for research and the deployment, however, makes sense when certain emerging techniques are relatively inexpensive and individual states, corporations or even wealthy individuals want to undertake experiments. Under these circumstances, the lack of norms for at least preliminarily and temporarily governing such techniques would not only impede the legitimate development of those techniques but also lead to undesired and uncontrolled consequences for the environment.

4.6.2 Mid-term scenario

The mid-term scenario describes the governance of geoengineering after one decade, and perhaps two or more. At that time, it will be clear whether most parties to the UNFCCC will have reached global peaking of GHG emissions as they project today. In addition, by then, it will become more clear whether and when the goal of keeping the global temperature increase below 2° C and even 1.5° C above pre-industrial levels, under the PA, can be achieved.[88] In addition, geoengineering techniques will be more mature at that time, and thus it will be a suitable time to discuss the further step of governing such techniques in a systematic manner.

4.6.2.1 Applying the multilateral approach and finding a leading institution

This book inclines to suggest that a multilateral approach is preferred over unilateralism or minilateralism. More specifically, the multilateral mechanism could consist of a central institution as a first point of contact[89] in conjunction with several specialized regimes to govern specific techniques. The leading institution could serve as a forum for legitimate and effective negotiations. No existing institution is ready to play the leading role in governing geoengineering, but a host of institutions, as listed in Section 4.4.2.2, have the potential to play such a role, notwithstanding some institutional shortcomings they have in doing so. Although taking into account the caveats of employing the UNFCCC to govern geoengineering, this book still suggests that the UNFCCC (and perhaps together with the PA) could play a leading role in governing geoengineering in the future. Given the fundamentally distinct objectives, attributes and likely consequences, it is necessary to treat SRM and CDR under the UNFCCC distinctly. It will not be surprising if the UNFCCC becomes the main institution to govern CDR, as it is not difficult to incorporate CDR techniques into mitigation mechanisms. However, it would be very challenging to govern SRM under the UNFCCC if SRM has to be framed as a separate modality in addition to mitigation and adaptation.

There are two main advantages of employing the UNFCCC as the leading legal instrument to govern CDR geoengineering. First, the implementation of CDR techniques is consistent with the objective of the UNFCCC to stabilize greenhouse gas concentrations in order to prevent dangerous climate change. Such a common objective enables the UNFCCC to be the most suitable forum to discuss issues regarding the use of novel technologies to counteract global warming. Compared to the UNFCCC, other relevant treaties intersect with CDR techniques only insofar as certain types of environmental harm that CDR techniques may cause are under their mandates.

Second, the existing mechanisms under the UNFCCC could be useful for the governance of CDR, and making use of the existing mechanisms could considerably decrease political costs compared to establishing new mechanisms. For instance, the technology mechanism could be applied to CDR techniques which are technically mature for implementation, as it supports country efforts to accelerate and enhance action on climate change by promoting, facilitating and financing environmentally-sound technologies.[90] In particular, the technology mechanism helps countries to undertake assessments of country-specific technology needs, thereby facilitating the development of appropriate CDR techniques as appropriate to country-specific circumstances, and building up the pathway to successfully transfer those techniques to, in particular, developing countries.[91] The development of appropriate CDR would contribute to enhanced actions taken by countries on mitigation.

Making use of the existing mechanisms could considerably decrease the political costs compared to establishing another regime of similar complexity as the UNFCCC. In addition, two subsidiary bodies of the UNFCCC, the Subsidiary Body for Implementation (SBI) and the Subsidiary Body for Scientific and Technological Advices (SBSTA), further address the development of technological and technical research as well as the impact of various response strategies under their corresponding agenda items.[92] The SBI and the SBSTA work on the impact of the implementation of response measures by encouraging parties to exchange information on both the positive and the negative consequences of response measures and by developing a work programme to facilitate assessment and analysis and to recommend specific actions.[93] In addition, the SBSTA works closely with IPCC, the WMO and UN-Oceans for facilitating and promoting scientific research.[94] In particular, the SBSTA "encouraged the scientific community to address information and research gaps identified during the research dialogue, including scenarios that limit warming in 2100 to below 1.5 °C relative to pre-industrial levels, and the range of impacts at the regional and local levels associated with these scenarios".[95] The existing mechanisms and bodies enable the UNFCCC to have the potential to properly govern CDR, because they have already been working on facilitating research and assessing the feasibility of implementing a CDR technique as appropriate to country-specific circumstances.

In addition to the UNFCCC, the PA should not be ignored. The main difference between the UNFCCC and the PA regarding the negotiation forum would be the broadness of participation by states.[96] Needless to say, a larger number of parties means more inclusive negotiations. It is particularly significant when the issue in question would unevenly impact a wide range of countries. Although the PA does not enjoy as inclusive participation as the UNFCCC initially,[97] the PA will enjoy broader participation in implementing the commitments once it is ratified, accepted, approved or accessed by all parties to the UNFCCC. The reason is that, while under the UNFCCC most commitments are defined in terms of developed country party commitments and developing country party commitments, under the PA the common commitments are defined for all parties, with the operative provisions indicating that some flexibility would be allowed for developing country parties and least developed country parties. This makes the PA a potentially more fertile ground for the governance of CDR techniques.

Regarding the relationship between the UNFCCC (together with the PA) and SRM techniques, it is not realistic to expect the inclusion of SRM under the umbrella of the UNFCCC in view of the mandates of and the existing mechanisms under the UNFCCC as well as the difficulty of achieving consensus through inclusive and transparent negotiations. It has been argued that the discussion on SRM techniques may divert attention from mitigation and adaptation efforts, which are the clear priorities under the terms of the UNFCCC and the PA.[98] In addition, emphasizing SRM may also divert limited financial resources from mitigation and adaptation actions. The question of whether the implementation of SRM techniques is consistent with the ultimate objective of the UNFCCC would depend on how that objective is read. In other words, the question is whether the objective of preventing dangerous anthropogenic interference with the climate system could be read independently of the stabilization of greenhouse gas concentrations. After all, when the UNFCCC was adopted in 1992, no state was able to predict the development of novel technologies to combat global warming in two decades. It is a question whether and to what extent old treaties could be updated to catch up with the pace of technological development.[99] If SRM were accepted as a supplement to mitigation and adaptation under the UNFCCC, the future of SRM would then depend on the sufficiency of mitigation efforts to limit the temperature increase to 1.5 °C above pre-industrial levels. The IPCC has been invited by the COP of the UNFCCC to provide a Special Report in 2018 on the impacts of global warming of 1.5 °C above pre-industrial levels and related GHG emission pathways.[100] Also in 2018, the COP will convene a facilitative dialogue among parties to take stock of the collective efforts of parties in relation to progress towards the long-term temperature goal and to inform the preparation of NDCs.[101] In 2023, the CMA will undertake its first global stocktaking to assess the collective progress towards achieving the purpose of the PA and its long-term goals.[102] It would not be clear to project the future of SRM being governed under the UNFCCC until 2023 at the earliest.

4.6.2.2 *Complementary regimes and institutions*

Note that the UNFCCC, as an international institution with established legitimacy and authority in international environmental matters, provides a forum for inclusive,[103] equitable and transparent negotiations and decision-making. As a result, several sectoral regimes that aim to control the risk of environmental harm could be complementary to the UNFCCC. Regarding SRM, the question of whether to permit the implementation of SRM is different from the question of whether to govern it under the climate change regime. If SRM techniques were proved in the next decade to be environmentally and socially sound for large-scale implementation, there would be other possibilities to govern such techniques, which will be discussed in this section.

As addressed in Section 4.4.2.2 (ii), the main risk of using a sectoral approach is the likely fragmentation, incoherence, and even conflicts between different sectoral regimes. One way to avoid this problem and to enhance the synergies among multilateral regimes is to connect some relevant regimes in a more coordinated and interactive manner.[104] Two successful precedents illustrate this approach. The one is the Joint Liaison Group between the UNFCCC, the CBD and the Convention to Combat Desertification which facilitates cooperation at the national and international level on the issues of, *inter alia*, adaptation, capacity building and technology transfer. An example of a stronger collaboration is the synergy process among three chemical agreements, viz. the Basel Convention,[105] the Rotterdam Convention[106] and the Stockholm Convention.[107] Catalysed by the UNEP's initiatives to build capacities of governments for the management of hazardous chemicals and wastes, the Conference of Parties of the three conventions decided to strengthen cooperation and alignment of the three conventions by establishing an ad hoc joint working group and by taking a series of measures covering the issues of decision-making, information exchange, etc.[108]

With respect to the coordination of sectoral regimes that are applicable to geoengineering, the regimes for marine geoengineering techniques and for atmospheric and territorial geoengineering techniques should be separated, given the distinct attributes that different techniques have. First, the regimes to govern marine geoengineering techniques could be developed in the framework of the LP, as it already provides a specific example of regulating and managing ocean fertilization activities in terms of, in particular, the impact assessment framework. Nevertheless, the limited participation of states in the LP should not be neglected.[109] Considering that the UNCLOS has not directly addressed geoengineering and the provisions are less up to date than the LP, the UNCLOS might arguably be complementary to the LP in terms of the issues that are relevant to the governance of marine geoengineering but are not addressed under the LP. The OSPAR Convention and several other regional marine conventions[110] could play a complementary role as well, because they provide a much less inclusive forum than the LP. Second, with respect to SAI, the CLRTAP, the Vienna Convention and its Montreal Protocol could address SAI together, because none of them is able, within their current mandates, to regulate all types of risks created by SAI activities. However, one should not neglect the limited participation of parties to the CLRTAP, and the fact that the Vienna Convention and the Montreal Protocol are not able to address SRM techniques if they do not significantly impact the environment in a negative manner. Third, as examined in Chapter 3, the regimes for BECCS and MCW relate to more than one legal sector, and both marine and atmospheric regimes could be relevant. In this regard, the place where a BECCS activity takes place is vital in determining which group of regimes is applicable; it might be more reasonable to categorize MCW as an atmospheric geoengineering technique because MCW is designed to produce changes in the atmosphere. Fourth, notably, the CBD is special, as it may be relevant to every geoengineering technique, as long as a technique poses a risk to biodiversity.

It should be born in mind that governance-related risks are associated with increased cooperation and linkages between legal regimes and institutions.[111] For instance, different legal regimes and institutions may overreach their regulatory mandates, or a cooperative management might be dominated by one institution or by a small group of institutions.[112] In order to cooperate in a really effective manner, many elements of a regime or institution, such as the mandate, working modalities, leadership and oversight, need to be taken into account.[113]

It should be ensured that all relevant regimes together will be able to deal with all types of risks posed by different geoengineering techniques and different scales of activities. The enhancement of synergies among sectoral environmental regimes demands coordinative work carried out by scientific experts and relevant international bodies.

4.6.2.3 Dealing with the deficits in multilateralism

Having regard to the deficits of effectiveness and efficiency in multilateralism, a minilateral mechanism could be employed at the early stage of negotiations in order to respond to the emerging challenges more promptly. Responsive and effective negotiations might begin with a few states that have an interest in moving forward with the governance of geoengineering.[114] For instance, a group of like-minded states, based on mutual understanding, has made great contributions in responding to the delaying and blocking of constructive discussions on developing regulations on ocean fertilization.[115] In the negotiations during the preparation of the 2013 Amendments to the LP, a common ground for the like-minded states gradually emerged: the requirement of binding regulations; the regulations should potentially apply to other marine geoengineering techniques rather than merely ocean fertilization; and marine geoengineering activities should be treated as "placement" activities instead of "dumping".[116] Such a kind of small group could compensate for the deficits of multilateralism, at least building some soft-law norms that can deal with the stage of research and experiments for the short term. The common ground might be gradually expanded and shared by more states, and a more inclusive agreement could eventually be attained.

From a normative perspective, a constructive approach could improve the effectiveness and efficiency of multilateralism in the long term. In contrast to the traditional theory of international agreements that are based on the pursuit of states' interest and contractual arrangement, the theory of interactional law contends that building shared understandings among states is crucial for accelerating the pace of achieving an agreement. Taking the development of the climate change regime as an example, Brunneé and Toope argue that shared understandings of the meaning of the regime objective and of the core principle of CBDR have been the lynchpins for regime development.[117] During the climate change negotiations of the past two decades, shared understandings have emerged among states, notwithstanding their divergent interests: since 2010, states have achieved consensus to hold the increase in global average temperature below 2 °C;[118] major developing countries with large emissions have voluntarily begun to share the burden of mitigation.[119]

In particular, the negotiations revealed concerted efforts by industrialized and developing counties as well as other participants to shift the meaning of the CBDR principle in various respects, and the CBDR principle has provided the foundation for the gradual emergence of shared understandings concerning emission reduction commitments.[120] The problem in applying the CBDR principle is that developing countries emphasized the historical responsibilities of industrial countries, whereas industrial countries insisted on the unfairness of not imposing commitments on major developing emitters. Shared understandings have emerged between industrialized and developing countries, when industrialized countries maintained some North-South differentiation and major developing emitters acknowledged the differentiation between developing countries and showed willingness to take actions on mitigation.[121]

This constructive approach illustrates how states could try to find shared understandings in negotiations on geoengineering. This approach might be helpful to break the deadlock between the proponents and opponents of geoengineering. Most importantly, negotiations should not merely concentrate on restricting geoengineering activities and preventing environmental damages arising from such activities; a balanced approach that makes a trade-off between the benefits for the climate stability and the risks of environmental damages could be employed.

4.6.3 Long-term scenario

It is difficult to project the long-term scenario because it contains too many uncertainties. Many commentators would say the best long-term scenario would be no deployment of SRM geoengineering.[122] Whether to deploy SRM geoengineering in the long run would depend on the mitigation efforts made by each and every country in the post-Paris era, and also on adaptation efforts, on climate sensitivity and on the vulnerability of societies and ecosystems to climate change. Where the deployment of SRM techniques is inevitable, it would be necessary to develop mechanisms regarding the distribution of risks arising from SRM activities and the compensation for damages.

4.7 Conclusion

This chapter first compared four scenarios of the future of geoengineering governance, *viz.* unilateralism, minilateralism multilateralism and non-state governance, with a preliminary finding that the approaches of making rules for implementing geoengineering by a single state, a small group of states and non-state actors could be employed in limited cases, depending on the attributes of different geoengineering techniques and the stage of implementing geoengineering activities. Unilateralism features rapid decision-making and effective implementation, which are particularly valuable at the crucial moment of controlling catastrophic climate change. However, these advantages are outweighed by the potential hazards arising from unilateral action, as it might encompass a higher possibility of jeopardizing legitimacy and might bring about instability in the international community.[123] Minilateralism has a similar problem of lacking a legitimate basis to justify exclusive decision-making. Nevertheless, if developed properly, minilateralism might be more flexible and responsive to emerging problems and might catalyse a broader participation in innovative activities counteracting global warming.

In comparison, the multilateral approach enjoys higher legitimacy in terms of more inclusive participation and appears to be more likely to gain wider support.[124] The discussion of the future governance of geoengineering via the multilateral approach was divided into three scenarios: the short-term, mid-term and long-term scenarios. In the short term, the focus of geoengineering would be on enhancing the synergies of scientific institutions, experts and relevant international organizations to actively engage in the inclusive discussion, and to deepen the understanding of geoengineering technology. In the mid-term, the discussion surrounds the choice of appropriate institutions to govern geoengineering techniques and the proper form of rules. This chapter first suggested that the UNFCCC together with the PA are likely to be the most appropriate forum to negotiate CDR issues and to regulate CDR in an overarching manner. Whether the UNFCCC and the PA would be the leading instruments to govern SRM depends on how the ultimate objective of the UNFCCC will be interpreted. The UNFCCC and the PA are unlikely to govern SRM if non-mitigation methods cannot be used to contribute to achieving the ultimate objective of the UNFCCC.

Second, a host of sectoral regimes could play complementary roles to control the risk of harm to environmental media and human health created by specific geoengineering techniques. It is important to note that sectoral regimes should be connected with each other in a more interactive and cohesive manner to avoid the potential conflict between regimes and to enhance synergies between them. In the long term, it is difficult to anticipate how geoengineering will be governed due to various uncertainties.

Regarding the form of rules and principles, the preliminary finding is that a framework agreement containing fundamental obligations and general principles should be formulated in a binding form. However, specific rules on, for instance, the procedures for an environmental impact assessment, favour a non-binding form, as states could achieve a non-binding agreement more quickly and ambitiously, and a non-binding form allows for a certain degree of flexibility to adapt to technological developments in the future.

This chapter also briefly touched upon the issue of how to deal with the deficits of effectiveness in multilateralism. A constructive approach, which stresses the significance of finding shared understandings among countries, could contribute to finding focal points of negotiations and attaining consensus.

Echoing the two aspects of analysis addressed in Section 4.1, the regulatory framework for geoengineering should satisfy two basic criteria: a) it has jurisdiction (through synergies between different regimes and institutions) over all types of physical risks rather than one or a few of them; b) instead of creating a taboo against geoengineering research activities from the outset,[125] it should provide a framework to balance the risk of dangerous global warming and the potential adverse impacts arising from geoengineering on the environment and human health. This chapter has addressed the institutions and relevant legal regimes that satisfy the two criteria from a general perspective. Chapter 5 will go further into developing specific rules that satisfy those two criteria for the purpose of the balancing of risks.

Notes

1 The implementation of geoengineering, in this book, includes geoengineering experiments and deployment. See also supra note 5 in Chapter 2.
2 Bilder, R. (1981). The Role of Unilateral Action in Preventing International Environmental Injury. *Vanderbilt Journal of Transnational Law*, *14*(1), 51–95, at 53; Bodansky, D. (2000). What's so bad about unilateral action to protect the environment? *European Journal of International Law*, 11(2), 339–348, at 340; Hartmann, J. (2015). Unilateralism in International Law: Implications of the Inclusion of Emissions from Aviation in the EU ETS. *Questions of International Law, Zoom In*, *11*, 19–32, at 20.
3 Bodansky, D. (2000), supra note 2, 340.
4 Ibid.
5 Ibid., 345.
6 Ibid., 344.
7 Bilder, R. B. (1970). The Canadian Arctic Waters Pollution Prevention Act: New Stresses on the Law of the Sea. *Michigan Law Review*, *69*(1), 1–54.
8 Bilder, R. (1981), supra note 2, 80.
9 Bodansky, D. (2000), supra note 2, 346; Bilder. R (1981), supra note 2, 91.
10 Virgoe, J. (2009). International governance of a possible geoengineering intervention to combat climate change. *Climatic Change*, *95*(1–2), 103–119, at 115; Keith, D. (2000). Geoengineering the climate: History and prospect. *Annual Reviews of Energy Environment*, *25*(1), 245–284, 275; Tanimura, E. (2013). Geoengineering Research Governance: Foundation, Form, and Forum. *Environs: Environmental Law & Policy Journal*, *37*, 167–195, at 177; Abelkop, A. D. K., & Carlson, J. C. (2013). Reining in Phaethon's Chariot: Principles for the Governance of Geoengineering, *Transnational Law & Contemporary Problems*, *21*, 771.
11 The similar argument can be found in: Parson. E. A. and Ernst. L. N (2013). International Governance of Climate Engineering. *Theoretical Inquiries in Law*, *14*, 307.

12 Nordhaus, W. (2015). Climate clubs: Overcoming free-riding in international climate policy. *American Economic Review, 105*(4), 1339–70.

13 Hale, T. (2011). A climate coalition of the willing. *The Washington Quarterly, 34*(1), 89–101.

14 Naím, M. (2009). Minilateralism. *Foreign Policy, 173,* 136.

15 Ibid.

16 McGee, J. (2011). Exclusive minilateralism: An emerging discourse within international climate change governance? *PORTAL Journal of Multidisciplinary International Studies, 8*(3), 1–9.

17 Rayner, S., & Prins, G. (2007). The Wrong Trousers: Radically Rethinking Climate Policy. Retrieved from http://eureka.sbs.ox.ac.uk/66/, 27.

18 Giddens, A. (2009). *The politics of climate change.* Polity Press, Cambridge, UK, 220.

19 Victor, D. G. (2006). Toward effective international cooperation on climate change: Numbers, interests and institutions. *Global Environmental Politics, 6*(3), 90–103, at 101.

20 Concerning the topic of two kinds of legitimacy, see, e.g. Kelso, A. (2006). Reforming the House of Lords: navigating representation, democracy and legitimacy at Westminster. *Parliamentary Affairs, 59*(4), 563–581, at 566.

21 Collins, J. (2012). Assessing International Cooperation on Climate Change: A Neoliberal Analysis of the Effectiveness of Formal International Environmental Institutions. *Mapping Politics, 4.*

22 Kahler, M. (1992). Multilateralism with small and large numbers. *International Organization, 46*(03), 681–708, at 682.

23 Keohane, R., & Nye Jr, J. S. (2001). Between centralization and fragmentation: the club model of multilateral cooperation and problems of democratic legitimacy, KSG Working Paper No. 01–004, 26. Retrieved from SSRN: http://ssrn.com/abstract=262175

24 Collins, J. (2012), supra note 21; Victor, D. G. (2006), supra note 19, 94.

25 The penalties for non-participation mean that countries that do not participate in the club and reduce their emissions will be penalized in the form of, for instance, uniform percentage tariffs on the imports of nonparticipants into the club region. See Nordhaus, W. (2015), supra note 12, 1341.

26 Naím, M. (2009), supra note 14, 137.

27 Victor, D. G. (2006), supra note 19, 95.

28 Wright, T. (2009). Toward effective multilateralism: why bigger may not be better. *The Washington Quarterly, 32*(3), 163–180, at 168.

29 Eckersley, R. (2012). Moving forward in the climate negotiations: Multilateralism or minilateralism? *Global environmental politics, 12*(2), 24–42, at 33; Kahler, M. (1992), 707.

30 Major Economies Forum on Climate and Energy. (2015). About. Retrieved from www.majoreconomiesforum.org/

31 The Group of Right (G8) refers to the group of eight highly industrialized nations – France, Germany, Italy, the United Kingdom, Japan, the United States, Canada, and Russia.

32 Backer, P. (2009, 8 July). Poorer nations reject a target on emission cut. *The New York Times.* Retrieved from www.nytimes.com/2009/07/09/world/europe/09prexy.html?_r=0; Brunnée, J., & Toope, S. J. (2010). *Legitimacy and legality in international law: an interactional account* (Vol. 67). Cambridge: Cambridge University Press, 141.

33 Wright, T. (2009), supra note 28, 169.

34 The Group of Twenty is an international forum for the governments and central bank governors. G20 comprises twenty states, which are the world's largest advanced and emerging economies.

35 Net gain, or absolute gain, is a term interrelated with a non-zero-sum game in economics, referring to the total effects of a decision on both parties. In a non-zero-sum game, states favour cooperation and they believe that cooperation can

expand wealth. The opposite term is relative gain, which is interrelated with a zero-sum game, referring to the stronger party's wealth that is taken from the weaker party.

36 Wright, T. (2009), supra note 28, 168.
37 Victor, D. G. (2008). On the regulation of geoengineering. *Oxford Review of Economic Policy*, 24, 322–336.
38 Birnie, P., Boyle, A., & Redgwell, C. (2009). *International law & the environment* (3rd ed.). Oxford: Oxford University Press, 202.
39 See Section 2.4.1.5(ii)(b).
40 See also the Kyoto Protocol, Art. 10.
41 The potential of applying the principle of CBDR in the multilateral governance of geoengineering will be further addressed in Section 4.6.2.3.
42 Brown Weiss, E. (2007). Climate change, intergenerational equity, and international law. *Vermont Journal of Environmental Law*, 9, 615–627, at 623. (Originally from Brown Weiss, E. (1989). In fairness to future generations: international law, common patrimony, and intergenerational equity, 345–51.)
43 CBD, Preamble & Art. 2.
44 Preamble, para. 2.
45 Birnie, P., Boyle, A., & Redgwell, C. (2009), supra note 38, 121.
46 Kuokkanen, T., & Yamineva, Y. (2013). Regulating Geoengineering in International Environmental Law. *Carbon and Climate Law Review*, 7(3), 161–167; Scott, K. N. (2012). Transboundary environmental governance and emerging environmental threats: Geo-engineering in the marine environment. In Warner, R., & Marsden, S. (Eds.). *Transboundary Environmental Governance: Inland, Coastal and Marine Perspectives*. Surrey, England: Ashgate Publishing, Ltd., Chapter 9.
47 Regarding the sufficiency of the existing legal institutions, see Section 4.4.2.2.
48 Lin, A. (2009). Geoengineering Governance. *Issues in Legal Scholarship*, 8(3), Article 2, 22–23.
49 Ibid. The opposite approach is a single binary choice to be made once and for all.
50 Kuokkanen, T., & Yamineva, Y. (2013), supra note 46; Virgoe, J. (2009), supra note 10, 113; Reynolds, J. (2015). Why the UNFCCC and CBD Should Refrain from Regulating Solar Climate Engineering. Opinion Article, Geoengineering Our Climate Working Paper and Opinion Article Series. Retrieved from SSRN: http://ssrn.com/abstract=2559643
51 Reynolds, J. (2015), supra note 50, 3.
52 Bodle, R. (2010–2011), Geoengineering and international law: The search for common legal ground. *Tulsa Law Review*, 46(305), 322, 320.
53 Bodle, R., & Oberthür, S. et al. (2013). Options and proposals for the international governance of geoengineering (No. (UBA-FB) 001886/E). Dessau-Roßlau: Umweltbundesamt, 159.
54 Honegger, M., Sugathapala, K., & Michaelowa, A. (2013). Tackling climate change: Where can the generic framework be located. *Carbon & Climate Law Review*, 7(2), 125–135, at 129.
55 CBD COP Decision IX/16 and Decision X/33.
56 Bodle, R., & Oberthür, S. et al. (2013), supra note 53, 161–163.
57 UNGA Resolution 2997 (XVII). Institutional and financial arrangements for international environmental cooperation, UN Doc. A/RES/27/2997 (15 December 1972), Preamble and para. 2(a) & (b).
58 Bodle, R., & Oberthür, S. et al. (2013), supra note 53, 163.
59 UNEP/GC, Decision 6/14. Principles of Conduct for the Guidance of States in the Conservation and Harmonious Exploitation of Natural Resources Shared by Two or More States, 19 May 1978. *UNEP Environmental Law Guidelines and Principles series, no. 2.*
60 UNEP/GC, Decision 14/25. Goals and Principles of Environmental Impact Assessment, 17 June 1987. *UNEP Environmental Law Guidelines and Principles series, no. 9.*

61   UNEP/GC, Decision 13/18/II. 1985 Montreal Guidelines for the Protection of the Marine Environment Against Pollution from Land-Based Sources, 24 May 1985. *UNEP Environmental Law Guidelines and Principles series, no. 7.*

62   UNEP/GC, Decision 8/7/A.1980 Provisions for Co-operation between States in Weather Modification, 29 April 1980. *UNEP Environmental Law Guidelines and Principles series, no. 3.*

63   UNGA, Resolution 66/288. The Future We Want, UN Doc. A/RES/66/288 (11 September 2012), para. 88.

64   The CLRTAP has 51 parties as of May 2016.

65   Kuokkanen, T., & Yamineva, Y. (2013), supra note 46, at 165.

66   Shaffer, G., & Pollack, M. A. Hard and Soft Law, in, Dunoff, J. L., & Pollack, M. A. (Eds.). (2013). *Interdisciplinary perspectives on international law and international relations: The state of the art* (1st ed.). New York: Cambridge University Press.

67   Ibid.

68   Abbott, K. W., & Snidal, D. (2000). Hard and soft law in international governance. *International organization, 54*(03), 421–456, at 421 & 423.

69   Ibid., 431.

70   Boyle, A. E. (1999). Some reflections on the relationship of treaties and soft law. *International and Comparative Law Quarterly, 48*(04), 901–913, at 902.

71   Ibid., 903.

72   Abbott, K. W., & Snidal, D. (2000), supra note 68, 442.

73   Ibid., 443.

74   Boyle, A. E. (1999), supra note 70, 908.

75   Abbott, K. W., & Snidal, D. (2000), supra note 68, 442.

76   Ibid.

77   Armen, C., & Redgwell, C. (2015). *International legal and regulatory issues of climate geoengineering governance: Rethinking the approach.* (Climate Geoengineering Governance Working Paper Series No. 021), 20. Retrieved from http://geoengineering-governance-research.org/perch/resources/working-paper21armeniredgwellthe internationalcontextrevise-.pdf

78   Victor, D. G. (2008), supra note 37, 332.

79   Keith, D. W., Parson, E., & Morgan, M. G. (2010). Research on global sun block needed now. *Nature, 463*(7280), 426–427.

80   Hamilton, C. (2013). *Earth masters: the dawn of the age of climate engineering.* New Haven, CT: Yale University Press, 147.

81   Bodle, R., & Oberthür, S. et al. (2013), supra note 53, 166.

82   WMO. (2015). Abridged final report with resolutions. 17th World Meteorological Congress, Geneva, 25 May-12 June 2015, para. 2.1.15. Retrieved from http://www.wmo.int/aemp/sites/default/files/wmo_1157_en.pdf

83   WMO. (2015). WMO greenhouse gas bulletin: The state of greenhouse gases in the atmosphere based on global observations through 2014. (No. 11), para. 4.3.101. Retrieved from http://scifun.chem.wisc.edu/news/ghg-bulletin_2015.pdf?id=8495

84   Parson, E. A., & Keith, D. W. (2013). End the deadlock on governance of geoengineering research. *Science, 339*(6125), 1278–1279.

85   IPCC AR5 WGIII, 12, 21 & 52.

86   See e.g. Neslen, A. (2015, 14 December). EU says 1.5° C global warming target depends on 'negative emissions' technology. *The Guardian.* Retrieved from www.theguardian.com/environment/2015/dec/14/eu-says-15c-global-warming-target-depen ds-on-negative-emissions-technology

87   E.g. Cicerone, R. J. (2006). Geoengineering: Encouraging research and over-
     seeing implementation. *Climate Change*, *77*, 221–226; Reynolds, J. (2011).
     The regulation of climate engineering. *Law, Innovation and Technology*, *3*(1),
     113–136.
88   Paris Agreement, Arts. 2.1(a) & 4.1.
89   Bodle, R., & Oberthür, S. et al. (2013), supra note 53, 143.
90   E.g. UNFCCC, Decision 7/CP.2, Development and transfer of technolo-
     gies, UN Doc. FCCC/CP/1996/15/Add.1 (29 October 1996), preamble;
     UNCED, Agenda 21, para. 34.
91   UNFCCC, Art. 4.5; UNFCCC, Decision 4/CP.7, Development and transfer
     of technologies, Annex: Framework for meaningful and effective actions to
     enhance the implementation of Article 4, paragraph 5, of the Convention,
     UN Doc. FCCC/CP/2001/13/Add.1 (21 January 2012); UNDP. (2010).
     Handbook for conducting technology needs assessment for climate change.
     Retrieved from http://unfccc.int/ttclear/misc_/StaticFiles/gnwoerk_static/
     TNA_HAB_infobox_1/3a34f12bf10d4b7ba e791d0d7ad572eb/c29096556
     b034760b94273b0124039ac.pdf
92   For instance, the development and transfer of technologies and implementa-
     tion of the technology mechanism is a standing agenda item in the sessions of
     SBI; research and systematic observation is a standing agenda item in the ses-
     sions of SBSTA.
93   UNFCCC, Decision 11/CP.21, Forum and work programme on the impact of
     the implementation of response measures, UN Doc. FCCC/CP/2015/10/
     Add.2 (29 January 2016), Preamble & para. 1.
94   E.g. UNFCCC, Research and system systematic observation, Draft conclusions
     proposed by the Chair, UN Doc. FCCC/SBSTA/2015/L.4 (9 June 2015).
95   Ibid., para. 5.
96   The features of the PA relating to the substantive rules can be found in
     Section 2.2.4.
97   The Paris Agreement entered into force on 4 November 2016. As of
     March 2017, 133 parties have ratified the Paris Agreement.
98   Kuokkanen, T., & Yamineva, Y. (2013), supra note 46, 161; Virgoe, J. (2009),
     supra note 10, 113; Reynolds, J. (2015), supra note 50.
99   A good example of the development of treaties to catch up with the devel-
     opment of science and technology is the adoption of the London Protocol
     (LP) to the London Convention (LC) on the Prevention of Marine Pollu-
     tion by Dumping of the Wastes and other Matters. Distinct from the LC
     which adopted the approach of listing the substances that are prohibited from
     dumping and the substances that require special permits for dumping, the LP
     adopted a reversing approach to prohibit the dumping of all substances with
     the exceptions listed in Annex I. (See Art. IV of the LC and Art. 4 of the LP.)
     In addition, the LP has been amended several times. For instance, in 2006, the
     LP was amended to permit the dumping of carbon dioxide streams from car-
     bon dioxide capture processes for sequestration under certain circumstances.
     See, Annex 1, para. 1.8 of the LP.
100 UNFCCC, Decision 1/CP 21, Adoption of the Paris Agreement, UN Doc.
     FCCC/CP/2015/10/Add.1 (29 January 2016), para. 21.
101 Decision 1/CP 21, Adoption of the Paris Agreement, para. 20.
102 Paris Agreement, Art. 14.1.
103 The UNFCCC has been ratified by 197 parties (196 states plus the European
     Union) as of March 2016.
104 Kuokkanen, T., & Yamineva, Y. (2013), supra note 46, 165; Tanimura, E.
     (2013), 191.

105 Basel Convention on the Control of Transboundary Movements of Hazardous Wastes and their Disposal.

106 Rotterdam Convention on the Prior Consent Procedure for Certain Hazardous Chemicals and Pesticides in international Trade, Rotterdam, adopted 10 September 1998, entered into force 24 February 2004, *United Nations Treaty Series* (2005), vol. 2244, no. 39973, p. 337.

107 Convention on Persistent Organic Pollutants, Stockholm, 22 May 2001, *United Nations Treaty Series* (2006), vol. 2256, no. 40214, p. 119.

108 Basel Convention, Decision IX/10 (2012), Cooperation and coordination among the Basel, Rotterdam and Stockholm conventions. Retrieved from http://basel.int/TheConvention/ConferenceoftheParties/Reportsand Decisions/tabid/3303/Default.aspx

109 The number of parties to the LP is based on the status as of March 2016. Retrieved from www.imo.org/en/OurWork/Environment/LCLP/Pages/default.aspx

110 See e.g. a host of conventions listed in the last paragraph of Section 3.4.2.

111 Scott, K. N. (2012), supra note 46.

112 Ibid.

113 Kuokkanen, T., & Yamineva, Y. (2013), supra note 46, 165.

114 Leal-Arcas, R., & Filis-Yelaghotis. (2012). Geoengineering a future for humankind: Some technical and ethical considerations. *Carbon and Climate Law Review*, 6(2), 128–148, at 136.

115 Ginzky, H., & Frost, R. (2014). Marine Geo-Engineering: Legally Binding Regulation under the London Protocol. *Carbon & Climate Law Review*, 8(2), 82–96.

116 Ibid., 96.

117 Brunnée, J., & Toope, S. J. (2010), supra note 32, 142.

118 Cancun Agreements, para 4.

119 UNFCCC Decision 2/CP 15. Copenhagen Accord, UN Doc. FCCC/CP/2009/11/Add.1 (30 March 2010), paras. 4–5.

120 Brunnée, J., & Toope, S. J. (2010), supra note 32, 166.

121 Ibid., 164–166; see also Rajamani, L. (2006). *Differential treatment in international environmental law* (Vol. 175). Oxford: Oxford University Press, 250. Some developing should take on more stringent mitigation commitments than other developing countries.

122 E.g. Farber, D. (14 December, 2015). Does the Paris agreement open the door to geoengineering? Retrieved from http://legal-planet.org/2015/12/14/does-the-paris-agreement-open-the-door-to-geoengineering/

123 Carlin, A. (2007). Implementation & Utilization of Geoengineering for Global Climate Change Control. *Sustainable Development Law & Policy*, 7(2), 22, at 58; Lin, A. (2009). Balancing the risks: Managing technology and dangerous climate change. *Issues in Legal Scholarship*, 8(3), Article 2; Davies, G. (2010). Framing the social, political, and environmental risks and benefits of geoengineering: Balancing the hard-to-imagine against the hard-to-measure. *Tulsa Law Review*, 46(2), 261–282.

124 Carlin, A. (2007), supra note 123, 58; Parson, E., & Ernst, L. (2013). International governance of climate engineering. *Theoretical Inquiries in Law*, 14, 307–336, at 327.

125 Victor, D. G. (2008), supra note 37, 332.

5 Balancing the risk of climate change against geoengineering – controlling environmental risk and coping with scientific uncertainty

5.1 Introduction

As introduced in Chapter 1, geoengineering may be a promising tool to deal with the serious and irreversible harm arising from anthropogenic climate change; meanwhile, it may harm the biosphere, pollute the ocean, soil and air, and disturb the climate system. Chapters 2 and 3 both point out that the existing international environmental rules and principles cannot effectively respond to the balancing of the risk of climate change against the risk created by the implementation of geoengineering techniques. In response to such a regulatory gap, Chapter 4 addresses the appropriate institutional design and applicable regulatory mechanisms; this chapter attempts to propose a framework for the balancing of risks.

In Chapter 5, Section 5.2 proposes a framework for the balancing of risks. Section 5.3 examines the main factors that should be taken into account in the balancing of risks. Section 5.4 proposes an assessment framework for geoengineering activities. Section 5.5 proposes to implement the precautionary approach in a tailored manner for each geoengineering project. Section 5.6 evaluates the criteria for balancing the positive and negative dimensions of geoengineering.

5.2 Designing a framework for balancing the risk of climate change against geoengineering

Based on the investigation of the prevention principle and the precautionary approach in Chapter 2, the present section attempts to propose a framework for the balancing of risks arising from geoengineering against that of global warming and its effects. This framework is aimed to ensure not only that any geoengineering activities are carried out in a way that assess adverse environmental impacts, but also that the interests of states, in particular the most vulnerable ones, as well as the interests of future generations are respected.

The proposed framework departs from investigating four main factors related to the balancing of risks, which are target and countervailing risks, different types of scientific uncertainties, a variety of interests and categories of geoengineering activities. In particular, due regard to various interests reflects the respect for the equity among states as well as generations, which is a significant issue in the discourse of the deployment of geoengineering techniques. A redefinition of the term "small scale" and a separation of small-scale geoengineering activities from large-scale activities will provide a more logical basis for the balancing process (see Section 5.3).

After identifying all relevant factors, the next step is to proceed the balancing by combining the procedural obligations under the prevention principle with the precautionary approach based on the survey of them in Chapter 2. With respect to the former, the procedural obligations addressed in Section 2.4.1 provides the basis for the assessment framework proposed to deal with risk-based challenges associated with geoengineering activities. The obligation to proceed an EIA process is the most significant obligation of states to assess all risks related to geoengineering activities. In addition to an EIA process, procedural obligations of consultation, monitoring and the exchange of information are also core components of the proposed assessment framework (see Section 5.4).

With respect to uncertainty-based challenges, a tailored operationalization of the precautionary approach is proposed in Section 5.5. Section 2.4.2 addressed the concept, legal status and elements of the precautionary approach, pointing out the challenges in applying it to geoengineering techniques.[1] The precautionary approach has been widely recognized useful in protecting human health and the environment by taking early action in response to the risk of significant or irreversible harm, even when scientific evidences of the nature, severity or likelihood of that risk are not conclusive. The central discussion in Section 5.5 surrounds therefore not the applicability of the precautionary approach to geoengineering techniques, "but rather its operationalization".[2] The proposed tailored operationalization of the precautionary approach is aimed to deal with the problem of indiscriminate restriction of geoengineering techniques as shown in the current application as well as the critiques associated with incoherent applications of the precautionary approach.

After addressing the assessment framework and operationalization of the precautionary approach, seeking a balance is a complex issue which needs to take into consideration not only scientific risks and uncertainties, but also interests across national boundaries and beyond the current generation. The discourse on "climate emergency" is an example that complicates the decision-making about whether a geoengineering technique could proceed (see Section 5.6).

5.3 Main factors relating to the balancing of risks

5.3.1 *Target risk vs. countervailing risk*

As stated in the previous chapters, while geoengineering can offset some risks of dangerous climate change, it creates a variety of new risks for environmental media. The change in the portfolio of risks is called a risk-risk trade-off, which occurs when a "countervailing risk" is generated by the intervention to reduce a "target risk".[3] Geoengineering is designed to reduce the target risk – the risk of serious damages from anthropogenic global warming – by removing atmospheric CO_2 and reducing radiative forcing. Regarding the "countervailing risk", the main factor is the risk of causing significant harm to the environment and human health arising from geoengineering activities.

The efforts to reduce a "target risk" may knowingly or unintentionally foster an increase in a "countervailing risk" which is equal to or even more problematic than the original risk.[4] Decision makers need to weigh the competing risks in light of the severity and likelihood of the risks and make decisions as to the optimal option. As per a common way of thinking, the cure should not lead to a worse consequence than the disease itself. In reality, the weighing of different risks is not simple but rather complex, especially when taking scientific uncertainties into account, as the estimates of risks are uncertain and unreliable. For instance, what if the use of marine geoengineering techniques results in mitigating climate change at the price of marine pollution? How does one evaluate different environmental risks in order to make a decision between the environmental benefits of marine environment maintenance and climate stability? Iron fertilization could reduce one environmental risk by creating another, and it is, at least to date, unknown which type of risk is less significant to the environment and human beings.

5.3.2 Scientific uncertainty

In the case of geoengineering, uncertainties merit particular concern, as the fear of unknowns has become one of the main reasons for resistance of the undertaking of geoengineering activities.[5] A vital feature of the governance problem with respect to some chemical and biological geoengineering techniques, e.g. enhanced weathering or MCW, is that "the state of knowledge regarding geoengineering techniques is in its early stages of development".[6] There are three layers of scientific uncertainties relating to geoengineering: the uncertainties of geoengineering techniques, the uncertainties of the adverse impacts on the environment, and the uncertainties of the science of climate systems.

First, scientific uncertainties relate to the contribution that a geoengineering technique can make to mitigate CO_2 emissions or to modify solar radiation. The scientific uncertainties of CDR techniques make it difficult to quantify to what extent CO_2 emissions could be offset by CDR techniques. Take ocean fertilization as an example. As introduced in Chapter 1, the effectiveness of direct ocean fertilization in the process of phytoplankton photosynthesis depends on the respiration of zooplankton and other organic materials. It is uncertain how much organic carbon will actually sink to deeper waters. According to the 2009 Royal Society Report, iron fertilization may only play "a modest role in carbon sequestration", because merely a fraction of dissolved CO_2 can sink deep enough to be sequestered for centuries.[7] How much carbon is actually sequestered will likely be unclear because the effectiveness varies in different areas and under different conditions. In addition, outcomes of the small-scale experiments thus far do not necessarily predict the effectiveness of large-scale iron fertilization until the technology is mature. With regard to SRM, scientific uncertainties are associated with the total radiative forcing by anthropogenic aerosols. For instance, the properties of sea-spray aerosols, including the production, size and chemical composition of sea-spray aerosols, largely depend on seawater chemistry and will influence the effectiveness of MCW. The seawater chemistry is controlled by physical, chemical and biological processes in the ocean. At the moment, the results from laboratorial modelling of MCW are still not sufficient to clarify the relationship between marine movement and the properties of sea-spray aerosols.[8] Such uncertainty hinders the understanding of the contribution of seawater aerosols to reflecting solar radiation.

Second, uncertainties of the adverse impacts on the environment make the utilization of geoengineering techniques more complicated. For instance, the oxygen minima in subsurface waters and the corresponding "dead zone" in deeper waters are poorly known.[9] It is also not yet clear how large-scale iron ocean fertilization might affect zooplankton, fish and seafloor biota. Likewise, scientists are still researching how chemical CDR techniques, and the corresponding ocean alkalinity enhancement, will affect marine biological diversity; it is to date indeterminable how alkaline rocks change the soil quality and affect territorial biological diversity. More uncertainties of adverse effects concern MCW and SAI. As introduced in Chapter 1, it is far from fully known how MCW activities would impact the climate system in the long term and whether such activities will cause significant adverse impacts on the marine environment. The long-term effects of SAI on the atmosphere, among others, how SAI would change regional precipitation, are still in the stage of simulation studies.

Third, uncertainties of the science of global climate systems cannot be ignored. On the one hand, human activities have been identified as "extremely likely" to be the dominant cause of unprecedented global warming since 1950.[10] According to the IPCC AR5 WGI, it is *virtually certain* that human influence has warmed global climate systems, including the surface of the Earth, the atmosphere and the ocean. On the other hand, uncertainties remain in the understanding of the climate system and the ability to project changes in response to anthropogenic influences.[11]

According to the theory of various uncertainties introduced in Section 2.4.2.2(ii), uncertainties in the functioning and effectiveness of geoengineering techniques due to the lack of data and research results can be decreased with the development of research tools and skills; uncertainties relating to adverse impacts on the environment and the science of climate systems, however, are more difficult to be decreased due to the complexity and variability of nature. This categorization is helpful to find rational methods to deal with distinct uncertainties relating to geoengineering techniques.

5.3.3 *Various interests*

In principle, the good governance of geoengineering techniques need to pay due regard not only to the risks and scientific uncertainties but also to other relevant factors. In a broad sense, such factors refer to various interests that need to be taken into consideration for an equitable balance of interests in geoengineering activities. With regard to transboundary activities, there is a balancing between states concerned, paying due regard to their different geographical, economic, and political characteristics. A full-view picture of an equitable balance of interests can be found in the 2001 Draft Articles on Prevention. Article 10 of the 2001 Draft Articles on Prevention incorporates risk analysis into an equitable balance of interests. A host of factors are to be taken into account to balance interests. Among others, Paragraph (b) of Article 10 indicates the factor of "the importance of the activity, taking into account its overall advantages of a social, economic and technical character for the State of origin in relation to the potential harm for the State likely to be affected". In addition, the degree of risk of significant transboundary harm is balanced with the availability of means of minimizing the risk or repairing the harm; the risk of significant harm to the environment is balanced with the availability of means of minimizing the risk or restoring the environment following the materialization of the risk, taking into account the resilience of the environment. Other factors include the willingness of the state of origin and states likely to be affected to contribute to the costs of prevention; the economic viability of the activity in relation to the costs of prevention; and the standards of prevention applied to the same or comparable activities.[12]

There should also be a balancing of interests between generations for some geoengineering techniques. With respect to BECCS, the long-term storage of CO_2 and the risk of leakage touch upon the issue of intergenerational equity. Long-term impacts of SAI on the climate systems and the atmosphere also attract considerable attention to the interests of future generations. Continuous ocean iron fertilization activities may also harm the marine ecosystem for a long term.

To deal with the two types of balancing described here, scientific knowledge of geoengineering techniques as well as the climate system is crucial for decision-making. In addition, the choice between the different strategies to deal with SRM geoengineering,[13] which are highly associated with political interests and values, is also a decisive factor that influences the balancing of risks.

5.3.4 *Categories*

The division of geoengineering activities into small-scale scientific research and large-scale deployment has been addressed in Section 3.2.3, and a preliminary finding is that it is difficult to draw the line between "small scale" and "large scale". The main reason is that "small scale" cannot be defined by simply setting the number of square metres: a "small-scale" ocean fertilization activity may still create a significant risk to the marine ecosystem, if such an activity is carried out in an unsuitable area, such as a high-yield fishing zone. Hence, for the sake of a clear, accessible and reasonable governance of geoengineering activities and an effective control of the risk of environmental harm, it is more appropriate to categorize geoengineering activities by colligating temporal, spatial, and quantitative factors. This section makes a bipartite categorization of "small-scale field experiments" and "large-scale experiments and deployment", which will be the basis of Section 5.4.1 regarding the EIA process of a geoengineering activity. This categorization does not separate large-scale scientific research studies from deployment because the purpose of an activity is not the decisive factor that creates different degrees of the risk of harm. Note that laboratory research studies will not be discussed in this section because no substance is placed into the environment outside of the laboratory and thus the conduct of a contained laboratory environment does not bring about harm to the environment outside of the laboratory unless there is an accidental release.

The three-dimensional coordinate system in Figure 5.1 demonstrates the categories of geoengineering activities. The horizontal axis shows the spatial range for conducting a geoengineering activity, and the origin indicates the national boundary in the transboundary context or the line between small and large areas in the global commons.[14] The left side of the origin represents

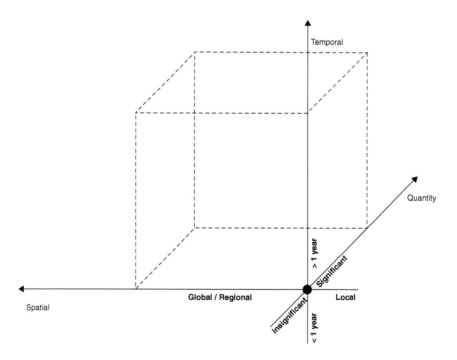

Figure 5.1 Categories of geoengineering activities

regional or global areas. The vertical axis shows the temporal duration of geoengineering activities, and the origin indicates that the activity has lasted at this point for one year (tentatively). The upper side of the origin represents long-lasting activities. The oblique axis shows the quantity of substance released (or the pipes placed, in the case of ocean upwelling) into environmental media by geoengineering activities. The origin indicates the threshold of the "significant amount" of substance, and the axis after the origin (direction of the arrow) indicates that the amount of substance is more than significant. The threshold of "significant amount" varies from technique to technique.

The spatial scale, temporal duration and the amount of substance can be categorized by the key words of regional/global or local, long lasting or transitory, and significant or insignificant respectively. Based on the bipartite categorization of the three factors, geoengineering activities can be categorized into eight groups as shown in Table 5.1.

Table 5.1 Categories of geoengineering activities

(1) Regional/global, long lasting and significant	(4) Regional/global, transitory and significant	(7) Local, transitory and significant
(2) Regional/global, long lasting and insignificant	(5) Local, long lasting and significant	(8) Local, transitory and insignificant
(3) Regional/global, transitory and insignificant	(6) Local, long lasting and insignificant	

5.3.4.1 Small-scale field experiments

Only category (8) represents small-scale field experiment. As a small-scale field experiment, the quantity of substances placed into the environment should be small and the spatial scale should not be larger than one state's territorial area. With respect to a marine geoengineering activity, the term "local" might not relate to a national boundary; "local" means in this context a small area in the area beyond the limits of national jurisdiction. As to the temporal duration, a tentative suggestion is one year, but it may be changed along with the increase of scientific knowledge. Categories (5) to (7) do not fall within the scope of small-scale experiments because, although undertaken at a local scale, these categories of activities are undertaken either for long time or with a significant amount of substance.

Normally, the environmental impact of small-scale field experiments is insignificant or negligible. However, the risk of causing significant environmental harm still exists. The risk might arise from temporal, spatial and delivery dimensions.[15] A spatial restraint could be that the ocean zone identified for an ocean fertilization project is a zone of high seas fish stocks; a temporal restraint could be that the planned time of deployment is an important biological timing for species of concern.[16] Delivery restraint refers to the substance selected and the amount delivered in the ocean or into the atmosphere. One example is the choice between iron, nitrogen and phosphorous as well as the amount of substance placed in ocean fertilization activity. Other factors that might pose a risk include, for instance, the movement of ocean currents and the seasonal changes of seawater, as well as the cumulative effects of multiple experiments taken place simultaneously in the same region.

Taking into account these risks, a preliminary environmental assessment would be required to determine whether a small-scale experiment activity of local scale, transitory duration and insignificant amount of substance can be carried out.[17]

5.3.4.2 *Large-scale experiments and deployment*

As shown in Table 5.1, categories (1) to (7) represent large-scale experiments and deployment of geoengineering. Large-scale experiments and deployment, although distinct in terms of purposes, could both lead to significant impacts on the environment and climate systems on a transboundary scale. For the sake of managing and minimizing significant risks, the governance of these two categories can be discussed together.

Nevertheless, given that the deployment of geoengineering aims at effectively alleviating the impacts of global change, the duration of effects is likely to be much longer than regional or global field experiments and, during that time, a larger quantity of substances would be delivered.

5.4 The assessment framework for geoengineering

The factors identified in Section 5.2 answer the question of what factors should be taken into account in the balancing of risks. Since the real world is much more complicated than abstract models, it is hardly possible to identify "safe activities" without knowledge of all relevant factors. However, people feel less uncomfortable with a risk if procedures have been established to control and minimize such a risk, and to maximally ensure their safety and health. Risk assessment can provide pathways to achieve the optimal balancing of risks, while also increasing perceived legitimacy as well as preventing conflicts.[18] This section attempts to propose a general assessment framework for geoengineering activities. Such a framework would consist of not only an obligation to conduct an EIA process but also of other procedural obligations. Although specific elements in an assessment vary from technique to technique, such a general assessment framework could provide a preliminary structure for the techniques for which (e.g. SAI) an assessment framework is not yet available, and could also supplement techniques (e.g. ocean fertilization) in situations where the existing assessment framework has room for improvement.

The first reason for proposing such a framework is that the existing legal instruments containing an assessment framework for geoengineering techniques are limited to marine geoengineering and BECCS, and no assessment framework exists for MCW and SAI. Moreover, the assessment framework for marine geoengineering is only applicable to ocean fertilization scientific research activities so far. In addition, the assessment framework for BECCS is only available under an EU Directive rather than an international treaty, and is only designed for assessing another state and thus cannot bring added value to the assessment framework for geoengineering activities that may cause harm to the global commons.

In addition, the Espoo Convention is not applicable to geoengineering activities, because geoengineering techniques are not listed in Appendix I of the Espoo Convention.[1920] Even if marine or atmospheric geoengineering activities were to be added to Appendix I in the future, or concerned parties determine that the proposed activities not listed in Appendix I are likely to cause a significant adverse transboundary impact and thus should be treated as if they were so listed, the Espoo Convention would not be applicable to those activities proposed to be undertaken in the global commons, because the Espoo Convention aims to cope with transboundary environmental impact between UNECE states.[21]

Nevertheless, the existing assessment frameworks still provide structures as well as elements that are valuable for designing the assessment framework for geoengineering activities. Resolution LC-LP.2 on the Assessment Framework for Scientific Research Involving Ocean Fertilization and the new Annex 5 of the LP on the Assessment Framework for Matter that May Be Considered for Placement under Annex 4[22] are the two legal instruments that are directly applicable to marine geoengineering. Although Resolution LC-LP.2 is not binding and the 2013 Amendments to the LP that contain the new Annex 5 have not yet entered into force, these two instruments are the basis of the assessment framework for marine geoengineering in general, leaving room for the future assessment framework for marine geoengineering techniques in addition to ocean fertilization.[23] With respect to BECCS, relevant provisions of the Directive 2009/31/EC on CO_2 storage provide useful elements for the EIA for BECCS.[24] With regard to SAI, general rules of assessment would not vary from the ones for marine geoengineering, but the objects (chemical substances and the location of impacts on the environment) of specific assessments of SAI activities differ. Regarding MCW, it is a technique that may impact the marine environment, the atmosphere and the climate, and thus the assessment framework for MCW may cover a broad range of issues which relate to marine biodiversity, protection of the atmosphere and the weather system.

This book proposes an assessment framework to be applicable to all of the six geoengineering techniques, while functioning in different ways. First, with regard to SAI, for which no assessment framework currently exists, the proposed framework would provide a model for the future. Second, with respect to ocean fertilization, the proposed assessment framework would supplement Resolution LC-LP.2 and the new Annex 5 of the LP for assessments of all ocean fertilization activities regardless of the scale and purposes (provided that, in the future, large-scale and non-scientific ocean fertilization activities could be permitted under the LP on the basis of the result of an assessment). Third, regarding marine geoengineering methods other than ocean fertilization, the proposed assessment framework would supplement the new Annex 5 of the LP when more marine geoengineering methods (ocean upwelling, ocean alkalinity addition, MCW, and any new geoengineering technique emerging in the future) are listed in Annex 4 of the LP. Fourth, the proposed assessment framework would be applicable to BECCS activities, taking into account the existing rules under Directive 2009/31/ EC relating to the impact assessment for CO_2 sequestration.

5.4.1 Environmental Impact Assessment (EIA) and geoengineering

Section 2.4.1.5(i)(a) examines the sources of international EIA obligations, concluding that EIA, as a component of the prevention principle under customary law, shall be imposed on all geoengineering activities that may create a risk of significant harm. Distinct from Chapter 2 which examined the procedural obligation to conduct an EIA as *de lege lata*,[25] this section addresses *de lege ferenda*[26] relating to a normative analysis of applying such an obligation to geoengineering techniques.

EIA could play a very important rule in the governance of geoengineering. First, it is a procedural obligation under customary law and that applies to all geoengineering activities that may create a risk of significant transboundary harm. Different treaties impose the obligation of conducting an EIA on particular geoengineering activities falling within their scope of application.[27] Second, EIA, as a process to assess the adverse impacts of a geoengineering activity, could contribute to satisfying the duty of due diligence.[28] Third, the results of an EIA could contribute to the legitimacy of an activity through the transparent and participatory process of an assessment.

To implement the obligation to assess environmental impact for geoengineering activities, one important issue is that the assessment of environmental impacts on another state needs to be separated from an EIA assessing environmental impacts in areas beyond the limits of national jurisdiction or control, as the legal consequences would be different in the two situations.[29] The dichotomous analysis approach will be used in the discussion of the EIA framework for geoengineering below. Basically, a transboundary EIA assesses the environmental risks of an activity undertaken in the territorial area of the state of origin or in areas shared by two or more states of origin, and it focuses on the state(s) of origin making a transboundary environmental impacts assessment of the potential impacts on the environment of the potentially affected state(s). On the contrary, an EIA in the global commons assesses environmental risks of an activity undertaken in the areas beyond the limits of national jurisdiction or control, or an activity undertaken in the territorial area of the state(s) of origin but with environmental impacts that extend beyond the limits of national jurisdiction or control. Notably, the term "potentially affected state" does not apply to the latter situation.

A further consequence of such a situation could be the lack of a clear institution for implementing the obligation of consultation.[30]

5.4.1.1 *EIA process for geoengineering projects*

This book proposes an EIA process for geoengineering activities, which is adapted from the three-level EIA framework under Annex I to the Protocol on Environmental Protection to the Antarctic Treaty (hereafter, the Antarctic Environment Protocol). The Antarctic Environment Protocol distinguishes among three levels of assessment: the preliminary stage, the initial environmental evaluation and the comprehensive environmental evaluation.[31] As a minimum requirement, a preliminary assessment shall be applied to every activity under the protocol to determine whether the proposed activity has less than a minor or transitory impact; an initial environmental evaluation shall be undertaken if the likely impacts of the proposed activity are minor or transitory, but no more than that. A comprehensive environmental evaluation shall be prepared if an activity is likely to have more than a minor or transitory impact.[32]

The main reason for proposing an EIA process adapting from the structure of the EIA framework under the Antarctic Environment Protocol is that the categorized approach is suitable for geoengineering activities. It would be more effective and efficient to assess geoengineering projects via a categorized approach, namely separating the assessment of small-scale field experiment and large-scale experiments and deployment. Although via a similar approach, distinctions still exist. The Antarctic Environment Protocol provides for the threshold of "minor or transitory impact" to conduct an environmental assessment, which is lower than the commonly used threshold of "significant" impact. The lower threshold under the Antarctic Environmental Protocol is reasonable, considering the intrinsic value of Antarctica and the fragile Antarctic environment, but such a threshold is not suitable for geoengineering activities unless a geoengineering activity is undertaken in Antarctica. The threshold of "significant" impact would be applied to geoengineering activities undertaken in places other than Antarctica.

The proposed EIA process consists of: (a) an initial assessment for each and every project to identify the scale of the proposed activity and to determine whether the proposed activity merely has a risk of non-transboundary harm or a risk of insignificant harm; (b) preliminary environmental assessment (PEA) for a small-scale experiment that has a risk of more than insignificant transboundary harm or harm in the global commons; and (c) comprehensive EIA (CEIA) for a large-scale experiment or deployment that has a risk of more than insignificant transboundary harm or harm in the global commons. In terms of specific rules in the proposed EIA process, the rules under Resolution LC-LP.2, the new Annex 5 of the LP and Directive 2009/31 EC will still be applicable to corresponding techniques.

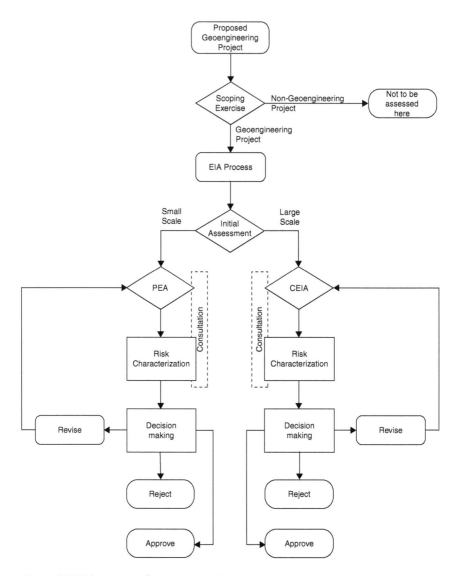

Figure 5.2 EIA process of a geoengineering project

Figure 5.2 illustrates the general process of EIA for geoengineering activities (for the six techniques). Depending on the attributes of each technique, some specific procedures and substances required in the three levels may vary from technique to technique. It is important to bear in mind that the EIA framework for geoengineering is designed based on the available knowledge relating to the proposed geoengineering techniques and their impacts on the environment. Such a framework might not fit new geoengineering techniques, and it would need to be modified based on new information. In view of this, for some parts of this framework it may suffice to provide a general structure thereby enabling such a framework to be as future-proof and adaptive as possible.

Prior to conducting an EIA, there should be a scoping exercise to determine whether a proposed activity falls within the definition of one of the six geoengineering techniques (or the definition of any new geoengineering techniques proposed in the future).

(I) INITIAL ASSESSMENT

This initial assessment is to identify the scale (temporal duration, spatial scale and quantity) of the proposed geoengineering project and to determine whether the proposed activity merely has a risk of non-transboundary harm or insignificant harm. If yes, such a project can proceed immediately. If the proposed project has a risk of causing significant transboundary harm or significant harm to the global commons, then the proposed activity will proceed through either a PEA (for a small-scale project) or a CEIA (for a large-scale project).

(II) PRELIMINARY ENVIRONMENTAL ASSESSMENT (PEA)

The main purpose of introducing the PEA in the EIA process for geoengineering activity is to simplify the assessment process for small-scale geoengineering experiments to avoid excessive restriction on the proper development of geoengineering technologies. If a PEA indicates that a proposed activity is likely to have no more than insignificant adverse impact, the activity may be approved;[33] if a PEA indicates that the proposed activity is likely to have more than insignificant impacts, this activity should be revised or rejected.[34]

(III) COMPREHENSIVE ENVIRONMENTAL ASSESSMENT (CEIA)

Categories (1) to (7) as shown in Table 5.1 represent large-scale geoengineering experiments or the deployment. A CEIA is required if the proposed project has a risk of causing significant transboundary harm or significant harm to the global commons. As indicated in Section 2.4.1.5(i)(a), no geoengineering technique is explicitly listed in Appendix I of the Espoo Convention. Appendix III suggests general criteria to assist in the determination of the environmental significance of activities not listed in Appendix I. General criteria are: (a) size; (b) location (whether located close to an area of special environmental sensitivity or importance and whether in locations where the characteristics of proposed development would likely to have significant effects on the population); and (c) effects (serious effects on humans or on valued species or organisms, and threats to the sustainable development of the environment).[35]

Although the required information in the EIA framework for each geoengineering technique differs, common stages of EIA can be generalized by making reference to, e.g., the EIA frameworks for ocean fertilization,[36]

CCS,[37] hazardous activities listed in Annex I of the Espoo Convention, and activities subject to the Antarctic Environment Protocol. General steps of a CEIA are (i) describing the activity; (ii) site selection; (iii) exposure assessment; and (iv) effects assessment.[38] The general process of an EIA may need to be modified to adapt to the development of new geoengineering techniques.

5.4.1.2 Risk characterization

Risk characterization shall provide an estimate of the magnitude and likelihood of adverse impacts on the environment and human health. An estimate of the magnitude of adverse impacts takes into account the temporal and spatial scales of the impacts as well as the number of different types of adverse impacts. Basically, the magnitude of adverse impacts has a positive correlation with the temporal and spatial scales as well as the number of impacts.[39] More specifically, the larger the scale and the longer the time an activity is carried out and the more types of harmful impacts it has on environmental media and human health, the greater the magnitude of adverse impacts this activity would result in. The likelihood of adverse impacts is associated with a given magnitude and is predicted based on evidence regarding the strength of relevant cause-and-effect relationships.[40]

It has been noted that the characterization of risks is getting harder due to the prominence of new and less visible hazards, among others, the hazards arising from new technologies.[41] In this sense, it is very difficult to characterize risks because the uncertainties associated with the magnitude and likelihood of adverse impacts block the comprehensive understanding of risks. To clarify the constraints of risk characterization, a description of the uncertainties and reasonable assumptions should also be included in the risk characterization.[42]

The biggest challenge in conducting an EIA is that many unintended consequences will remain unknown until regional or global pilot experiments are carried out. In other words, the conclusion of an EIA may not be conclusive if it is simply based on the outcomes projected by computer modelling. When regulatory decisions can only be made based on limited data and considerable uncertainties, the application of the precautionary approach is required. The risk characterization, together with other factors including various types of interests,[43] is taken into account in the balancing of risks. Considering the different degrees of risk and uncertainty involved in each technique and even in each individual activity, the choice of strategy to balance the risks inclining to be more conservative or more progressive, is essentially the choice of precautionary measures.

Another concern is not the main focus of this section but merits a brief mention. Traditionally, social impacts fall outside of the bounds of the obligation to conduct an EIA, or are considered only insofar as they are directly caused by physical impacts.[44] But a special concern could be a hybrid of risks, in which "social risks" would cause physical risks – e.g. the termination of SRM due to political reasons. Some geoengineering techniques pose far more than direct physical impacts to a society, and the social impacts, such as the implementation of SRM by one state or private actors, unjust distribution of harms and benefits, moral hazards and technological lock-in, are vexing concerns that challenge decision-makers. The concerns about the social impacts of geoengineering also explain why some small-scale experiments that are anticipated to have non-significant environmental impacts may still encounter strong resistance from potentially affected states. This suggests that risk characterization and evaluation of geoengineering activities may need to take social impacts into account in decision-making. However, the methods of assessing various social impacts is beyond the scope of this book.

5.4.1.3 Consultation

Consultation is a procedure during the carrying-out of an EIA as well as a procedural obligation under the obligation to prevent and abate transboundary harm.[45] As a constituent element of an EIA, consultation should be included in an EIA throughout and after the process.

As for a proposed activity undertaken in one state that may create a risk of significant transboundary harm, the state of origin shall ensure that the operator consults with the authorities of that state when preparing the description and selecting the site for the activity. After the completion of the description and site selection of the proposed activity, the state of origin shall consult with potentially affected states on the potential transboundary impacts of the proposed activity and on measures to reduce or eliminate its impacts.[46] As part of the consultation process, the state of origin should also share information with potential affected states and notify them about the potential risks. As for the result of consultations, consent is generally not required when a proposed activity creates a risk of causing transboundary harm to the environment or human health. However, according to the assessment framework for marine geoengineering under the LP, the consent should be obtained from all countries with jurisdiction or with interests in the region of potential impact without prejudice to international law.[47] The main reason for requiring consent could be to avoid or minimize the pollution of the marine environment from marine geoengineering activities, taking into account the unprecedented methods used in marine geoengineering and its unexpected impacts on the marine environment.

As for a proposed activity undertaken in the global commons, the state of origin could consult with bodies of the competent international or regional conventions. Pursuant to the UNCLOS, states are required to cooperate with "competent international organizations" in terms of consultation, notification, exchanging information, etc.[48] One competent international organization could be the IMO. The new Annex 5 of the LP provides that states shall consult with "regional intergovernmental agreements and arrangements".[49]

As no international body is available to consult on the admissibility of atmospheric activity, one may consider the role of all states as members of the international community as a whole. Unlike the term "air space" which refers to the spatial dimension where states exercise their jurisdiction or control, it has been asserted that the atmosphere should be recognized as an international resource and the protection of the atmosphere has been considered as a common concern of humankind.[50] Special Rapporteur Shinya Murase of the International Law Commission has submitted that the protection of the atmosphere relating to global issues such as ozone depletion and climate change could be characterized as an obligation *erga omnes*.[51] Accordingly, it could be argued that all other states have a legal interest in the protection of the atmosphere and thus are entitled to be consulted by the acting state. However, to date, state practice does not support the existence of obligations *erga omnes* in this regard.[52] Hence, one could preliminarily conclude that, at least to date, only potentially affected states are entitled to be involved in the consultation process.

5.4.1.4 Making a decision

Before making a decision of approving, revising or rejecting a geoengineering project, the result of an EIA process serves as the basis for decision-making, and a consultation process should take place. With respect to a geoengineering activity that is proposed to be undertaken across national boundaries, the national authority of the state of origin, or an authority that is established or designated by states concerned, would permit or reject such an activity.[53] With regard to a geoengineering activity that may create a risk of significant harm to global commons, consent should be sought from all states. The forum for negotiations between the relevant states could be provided by the legal instrument that is applicable to major issues of a particular geoengineering technique. For instance, the LP could provide such a forum for all relevant states in which to decide whether a proposed ocean fertilization project qualifies as a legitimate scientific research.

5.4.2 Monitoring geoengineering projects

Section 2.4.1.5(ii)(b) has introduced the obligation of authorizing and monitoring an activity by a state within its jurisdiction or control as a procedural obligation encompassed by the obligation to prevent and abate transboundary harm. This section addresses monitoring as a procedural norm to improve future assessments and to modify or revoke the authorization of a project provided by the competent authority in the decision-making process for a geoengineering project.

The main rules related to monitoring can be generated from the LP assessment framework for marine geoengineering and Directive 2009/31 EC. Pursuant to the former, monitoring shall be based on a monitoring plan designed by the operator of the proposed activity. A monitoring plan should assess both short- and long-term impacts to verify that permit conditions are met – compliance monitoring – and that the assumptions made during the risk characterization are sufficient to protect human health and the environment –

impact monitoring.[54] In addition, monitoring is also used to determine the area of impact and to ascertain that changes to the environment are within the range of those predicted.[55] Annex II of Directive 2009/31/EC provides criteria in detail for establishing and updating monitoring plans in CCS projects.[56] It is important that a monitoring plan is updated pursuant to the requirements laid down in the plan and that it takes account of changes to the assessed risks to the environment and human health, new scientific knowledge and improvements in best available technology. Furthermore, monitoring shall be continued in the post-operation phase of a geoengineering project (see Section 2.4.1.5 (iii)).

5.4.3 Strategic Environmental Assessment (SEA)

As addressed in Section 2.4.1.5(i)(a), SEA could bring added value to the future assessment framework for geoengineering, mainly because, first, SEA allows problems to be addressed at the earliest possible stage of decision-making, when a wider range of alternatives are available and there is a greater scope than at the project level to integrate environmental considerations into development goals and objectives; second, SEA can provide early warning to large-scale and cumulative effects resulting from a number of small-scale projects. As the implementation of geoengineering techniques in the future might play a significant role in states' commitments to counteract anthropogenic global warming under the climate change regime, it would be necessary to apply SEA when a range of geoengineering activities in a wide area over a long time span need to be systematically planned.

Nevertheless, the scope of applications of SEA remains incomplete, and no practice of SEA so far includes any of the six geoengineering techniques. For instance, pursuant to the SEA Protocol to the Espoo Convention, a SEA shall be carried out for plans and programmes that are prepared for a range of major sectors of a country, such as energy, forestry and industry, that are known to have significant environmental implications on the environment.[57] It remains open how to apply SEA to geoengineering in the future. One likely scenario is the inclusion of a certain geoengineering technique into the list of activities that are subject to SEA under an international agreement. Another scenario is that SEA would be applied voluntarily by the state of origin, and the state of origin would arrange dialogues with potentially affected states as well as relevant experts, organizations and authorities. Under both scenarios, it is suggested by this book that the individual EIA of any geoengineering project that belongs to a systematic plan or programme should be preceded by an SEA for the plan or programme as a whole. In addition, considering the distinct attributes of various geoengineering techniques, it would be more reasonable to apply SEA to geoengineering based on a specific technique rather than based on a category of geoengineering (CDR or SRM) or geoengineering in general.

5.5 Implementing the precautionary approach for geoengineering

As stated previously, scientific uncertainties and reasonable assumptions should also be addressed in risk characterization. In this regard, the decision on the admissibility of an activity following the conduct on an EIA is not made based on comprehensive understanding. Under this circumstance, how to choose the most appropriate measure to minimize the risks and maximize the benefits? How to treat scientific uncertainties when there is an urgency to make a decision?

Given the scientific uncertainties surrounding geoengineering and climate change, the precautionary approach is *prima facie* applicable. As concluded in Section 2.4.2.4, the existing moratorium on geoengineering, as a strict version of the precautionary approach, fails to clarify the terminating condition of the moratorium and to balance the benefits to the global climate brought by geoengineering and the risks to the environment and human health caused by geoengineering. In other words, the existing application of the precautionary approach to geoengineering does not involve a symmetric weighing of "target risks" and "countervailing risks".[58] Unlike the common application of the precautionary approach, which applies precaution to target risks, the existing restriction on the use of geoengineering applies asymmetric precaution to countervailing risks.

The remaining question is how to deal with the paradox where the implementation of the precautionary approach in the form of stringent regulation would reduce the risk of environmental harm but deprive the society of the potential benefit of reducing the risk of dangerous climate change. In addition, for the sake of operationalizing the precautionary approach in a more flexible manner for different geoengineering techniques, another question is whether various soft precautionary measures can provide clear guidance for policymakers in regulating distinct geoengineering techniques.

There is no one-size-fits-all measure to decide whether a geoengineering activity may proceed. First, in response to a risk that is likely to cause catastrophe, it would be necessary to apply the strong versions of the precautionary approach to prevent any irreversible harm to the environment and human health. Second, in the cases other than catastrophe, the precautionary approach does not need to provide precise rules for decision; instead, it functions as soft norms that provide guidance, recommendations, deliberative processes and opportunities for decision-makers to pay attention to the full screen of risks and the cost and benefit of precautionary measures. Third, competent authorities could conduct periodical evaluations to find whether the current precautionary measure is no more proportionate or necessary, and modification or termination of a precautionary measure is thus needed.

Sections 5.5.1–5.5.4 propose a flexible implementation of the precautionary approach, which encompasses four main aspects: a clear scope of application, flexible triggering criteria, proportionate actions and a fair distribution of the burden of proof.

5.5.1 *Clarifying the scope of application*

To clarify the scope of implementing the precautionary approach for geo-engineering activities, this discussion is divided into three parts: whether the precautionary approach should be used in small-scale field experiments, in large-scale experiments and in deployment. Without doubt, the precautionary approach should apply to the deployment of geoengineering; it still merits further debate whether the precautionary approach should apply to research, in particular local field experiments. According to the existing non-binding legal instruments regulating geoengineering,[59] "small scale scientific research" is the only exception to the moratorium on geoengineering. Such an exception to the moratorium means that small-scale field experiments should not be subject to the strict version of the precautionary approach.

An alternative approach is not to separate small-scale research from large-scale research but rather to discuss them together as scientific research, which is differentiated from deployment in terms of the aim.[60] The 2013 Amendment to the LP uses the phrase "legitimate scientific research", which may not necessarily exclude the moratorium on small-scale field experiments if they are not "legitimate", on the one hand, and may exclude the moratorium on large-scale scientific experiments as long as they are "legitimate", on the other hand. The term "legitimate" refers to "a legitimate use of the sea" – i.e. "not contrary to the aims of the London Protocol".[61] In this regard, an activity can be treated as a legitimate scientific research when the result of the EIA indicates so. "Legitimate scientific research" activities should not be subject to the strong version of the precautionary approach. A controllable level of harm may be considered a necessary sacrifice for scientific improvement and technological innovation.

Some commentators view that the strong version (a restrictive limit or a ban)[62] of the precautionary approach should not apply to geoengineering research in terms of limiting or prohibiting research activities, because such highly restrictive measures or even a ban would impede the improvement of knowledge achieved by scientific research. For instance, the UK House of Commons, Science and Technology Committee recommends that the precautionary principle (referring to a moratorium) should not be one of the five key principles to guide geoengineering research,[63] because it may halt all kinds of geoengineering research, including local tests by applying an indiscriminate ban on geoengineering without a sufficient basis.[64] In the long term, the premature rejection of geoengineering research based on inadequate knowledge is likely to stifle not only scientific development and technological innovation, but also humanity's endeavours to avoid disasters.[65]

For the sake of scientific development and technological innovation, this book suggests that the strong version of the precautionary approach should generally not be applicable to small-scale experiments of geoengineering techniques. At the same time, for the purpose of minimizing the risk of significant harm, the strong version could apply to regional or global geoengineering activities, irrespective of their purpose, being scientific studies, or deployment. In contrast, milder versions of the precautionary approach in the form of non-binding instruments regarding cautious and prudent action could apply to all categories of activities.[66]

5.5.2 Flexible thresholds of triggering the precautionary approach

Section 5.5.1 clarified the scope of application of different versions of the precautionary approach to different categories of geoengineering activities. However, not all versions of the precautionary approach can be invoked in every geoengineering activity. This section will further discuss how the precautionary approach may be applied in accordance with the attributes of each geoengineering technique and the scale of the activity. Basically, flexible thresholds for triggering the precautionary approach are required: local field experiments should be differentiated from regional or global field experiments and deployment.

Table 5.2 illustrates the different thresholds of risk of harm that trigger different precautionary measures. As addressed in Section 5.5.1, small-scale experiments of the six geoengineering techniques would not pose a risk of significant harm to the environment or human health at a transboundary level, and thus a strong version of the precautionary approach should not apply to those activities; mild precautionary measures in the form of soft instruments may be applied. Whether to trigger a precautionary action and to trigger a specific type of precautionary action is determined on the basis of a case-by-case analysis, taking into account the location, scale, duration and other factors[67] of the proposed activity. With respect to regional or global geoengineering activities, the thresholds of triggering the precautionary approach are the same for field experiments and deployment. The choice of mild or strong precautionary measures depends on the severity of harm.[68] A significant risk of harm may trigger either strong or mild precautionary measures. Whether to trigger a precautionary action and to trigger a specific type of precautionary action is determined on the basis of a case-by-case analysis, taking into account the location, scale, duration and other factors of the activity. Considering that the serious or irreversible harm caused by regional or global geoengineering activities may be catastrophic, it should trigger strong precautionary measures to restrict or even (temporarily) prohibit the

Table 5.2 Flexible thresholds of triggering the precautionary approach

Small-scale field experiments	Large-scale experiments & deployment
Should not trigger a restriction or a ban, but *may* trigger the mild precautionary approach (depending on the location, scale, duration, etc.).	A risk of *significant* harm *may* trigger either the strong or mild precautionary approach (depending on the location, scale, duration, etc.); a risk of *serious or irreversible* harm *should* trigger measures to restrict or (temporarily) prohibit the proposed activity.

proposed activity (and may also trigger other milder precautionary measures at the same time).

In addition to the thresholds stated here, a special threshold of triggering the precautionary approach could be established for geoengineering activities that are proposed to take place in special areas, such as areas with vulnerable ecosystems: if an activity proposed to take place in such a special area poses a probable risk[69] of harm – maybe lower than significant harm – any precautionary measure *may* be triggered.

Another dimension of the flexible threshold of triggering the precautionary approach relates to the degree of uncertainty. On the one hand, the degree of uncertainty is one component of the trigger for the application of the precautionary approach; on the other hand, it functions in the opposite direction to clarify the threshold condition under which the precautionary approach should be applied, for fear that indiscriminately restrictive actions are taken as a substitute for risk assessment on the basis of inadequate knowledge.[70] Regarding the threshold of uncertainty to trigger the precautionary approach with respect to geoengineering activities, "reasonable grounds for concern" could be considered a maximal level of tolerable uncertainty, which could also be the burden of proof by the party who claims that precautionary action should be taken.[71] The term "reasonable grounds of concern" could be understood as more than a pure hypothetical threat but less than a conclusively proven threat. Reasonable grounds of concern, as a maximum level of uncertainty, would avoid the unworkable situation where every hypothetical risk would require a precautionary response.[72]

In the situation of an uncertain risk of serious or irreversible harm, a "worst case scenario"[73] may be taken into consideration in special cases. Such a scenario follows the "maximum principle": choosing the policy that avoid the worst-case scenario. Given that regional or global implementation of SAI would pose indirect serious impacts on the climate system, among others, the effects of termination or the change of weather patterns, it might be sufficient to stop a SAI activity from taking place due to even a low degree of doubt as to the safety of that activity.

5.5.3 Proportionate actions

The discussion of proportionate actions is associated with the balancing of interests. Although the precautionary approach advises decision-makers to take action on an indeterminate risk, it does not aim at achieving "zero risk".[74] Society may be prepared to live with a risk because of the benefits it is expected to bring.[75] As stressed in Sections 2.4.2.4 and 2.4.2.5, proportionate actions are intended to prevent indiscriminate restrictions on or a blanket prohibition of geoengineering activities. The precautionary approach can be viewed as a soft norm rather than providing a precise rule of decision. The following examples are some less restrictive alternatives that could also contribute to an effective, sufficient and proportionate governance of geoengineering in the light of the existence of scientific uncertainty.

Deliberative process: The implementation of the precautionary approach can be reflected as deliberative processes rather than any specific regulatory result.[76] Viewed in this way, the precautionary approach suggests as much information as possible to be collected for decision-makers and the public prior to a decision. The collected information could alert decision-makers as well as the public particularly to the potential risks that may lead to catastrophic effects in the future. Through the information gathering and dissemination process, the public could also overcome cognitive and other biases in favour of one risk over another. Specifically, monitoring, gathering and disseminating information and measures related to facilitating transparency are included in the deliberative process. Monitoring, for instance, could be seen as a precautionary measure that enables the early identification of adverse effects over time.[77]

Local field experiments: Notwithstanding a general consensus that the large-scale deployment of geoengineering should not be allowed, because the techniques are *per se* risky and may pose new or further threats to the environment,[78] some scholars consider that the precautionary approach favours local field experiments, because such experiments could decrease the uncertainty regarding the implementation of specific geoengineering techniques, which have the potential to effectively reduce the risk of climate change.[79] Meanwhile, it is possible to monitor local field experiments and effectively control the risks. Even so, the implementation of local field experiments should also adhere to the precautionary approach.

A code of conduct: At the present stage, soft-law instruments, such as public or private initiatives in the form of a code of conduct or principles of conduct, may have a precautionary function in terms of guiding the research of geoengineering and finding a possible way for further development.[80] Soft-law instruments may also guide the behaviour of stakeholders, scientists and social researchers in exploring the science, applying the techniques, and framing the governance. As suggested by some commentators, precautionary measures should be tailored to each technique and each particular activity, taking into account the dynamic conditions of scientific uncertainties and many other factors, such as the location, scale and duration of an activity.[81] The determination of undertaking precautionary action should be based on the result of an EIA as elaborated in Section 5.3.1 and should be made by comparing the results with the scenario of anthropogenic climate change without geoengineering.

Notably, depending on the progress of scientific research and the development of technologies, the assessment of the thresholds and the selection of a precautionary measure could be an iterative process, which means that periodical reviews could be undertaken. An example can be found from the EU General Food Law, which articulates that the precautionary measures "shall be proportionate" and "shall be reviewed within a reasonable period of time, depending on the nature of the risk to life or health identified and the type of scientific information needed to clarify the scientific uncertainty".[82] Regarding the bodies which are responsible for taking the periodical review, the institutions, such as the IMO and the WMO, would be eligible for conducting the iterative evaluations for marine and atmospheric geoengineering techniques respectively. The modification or termination of a precautionary measure would be required if the current one is no more proportionate or necessary.

5.5.4 *The burden of proof*

As addressed in Section 2.4.2.2, the triggers for invoking the precautionary approach are the risk of significant or serious harm and the lack of scientific certainty. Once these two triggers are met, the precautionary approach should be applied. The strong version of the precautionary approach requires a substantive rule regarding the burden of proof.[83] This comprises two aspects: who bears the burden of proof and what is the standard of proof.[84] There is so far no consensus on the answers to these questions. The common known rule of evidence, *actori incumbit onus probandi*,[85] requires the party who alleges something to bear the burden of proof. Neither international legal instruments nor international courts show that the reversal of the burden of proof is a corollary of the application of the precautionary approach. In the *Pulp Mills* case, the ICJ considered that the precautionary approach does not imply a reversal of the burden of proof and thus Argentina had the duty to provide "clear",[86] "convincing"[87] and "conclusive"[88] evidence to prove that the Orion (Botina) mill would not cause significant damage to the environment.

However, some commentators opine that the proponent of a hazardous activity bears the burden of proof to demonstrate that such an activity would not result in harm. Judge Wolfrum views that it is generally agreed that the burden of proof regarding the possible impact of an activity should be placed on the proponents.[89] Judge Laing is also of the opinion that the "thrust" of the precautionary approach is the reversal of the burden of proof to "the state in control of the territory from which the harm might emanate".[90] There are two main reasons to relocate the burden of proof in the implementation of the precautionary approach for geoengineering. First, the impacts of the proposed activity are still under exploration and far from fully clear. The lack of clarity regarding the techniques as well as the consequences of applying them requires the proponent to bear the burden of proof, because the proponent of the proposed activity, as the implementer of the techniques or the state to which those implementers belong, is in possession of the relevant knowledge. Second, reversing or lowering the burden of proof would lead to a more effective enforcement of precautionary measures.[91] Obliging the proponent to bear the burden of proof would prevent it from non-compliance with the precautionary approach.

Nevertheless, the reversal of the burden of proof in the implementation of the precautionary approach is not common in state practice. The reversal of the burden of proof is rarely applied in cases where the proposed activities would cause serious or irreversible harm.[92] Typical examples include the moratorium on commercial whaling, the ban on industrial waste dumping at sea and the phase-out of CFCs. The application of the precautionary approach in those cases is to require states to "submit proposed activities affecting the global commons to international scrutiny and demonstrate that they will not cause harm".[93]

The standard of proof may vary along with the nature of the activity and the vulnerability of the environmental interests in question.[94] The state that alleges a risk of significant harm is not required to provide "clear", "convincing" and "conclusive" evidence to prove that the deployment of a new technology is absolutely dangerous; instead, the standard of proof is lowered to "a reasonable ground of concern on the basis of the best available information".[95] In the *Southern Bluefin Tuna* case, the plaintiffs, Australia and New Zealand, provided evidence of serious environmental harm. Both the plaintiffs and the defendant (Japan) agreed that the "stock of southern Bluefin tuna is severely depleted and is at its historically lowest levels and that this is a cause for serious biological concern".[96] In addition, Australia and New Zealand maintained that "the scientific evidence available shows that the amount of southern Bluefin tuna taken under the experimental fishing programme could endanger the existence of the stock".[97] Considering the risk of "deterioration of the southern Bluefin tuna stock", the tribunal granted provisional measures in a situation of urgency to protect the rights of the plaintiffs despite the scientific uncertainty.[98] By contrast, in the *MOX Plant* case, Ireland argued, relying on the precautionary approach, that the UK should bear the burden of proof while the UK argued that the harm is "infinitesimally small".[99] Since Ireland failed to provide evidence of the risk of serious harm, at least *prima facie*, the tribunal ruled that there was insufficient urgency in this case and did not prescribe provisional measures.[100]

Given the discussion here, whether to reverse the burden of proof and what the standard of proof is may vary with the particular situation of the matter at stake, including the degree of risks and uncertainties, the scale of the activity as well as the location of the activity. The situations are particularly complex as to the implementation of the precautionary approach due to the attributes of different geoengineering techniques. Nevertheless, establishing some basic rules relating to the reversal of the burden of proof or at least lowering the standard of proof would be very helpful for potentially affected states, in particular the most vulnerable ones, to avoid irreversible damage. It could be argued that a geoengineering activity that causes risk of serious or irreversible harm should not be permitted (by the competent authority) unless the acting state proves that it is unlikely to cause serious or irreversible harm.

Regarding lowering the standard of proof for potentially affected states, they may be able to establish a significant risk *prima facie* rather than provide clear and convincing evidence. Some precedents might shed light on *prima facie* evidence in the case of geoengineering. With respect to the substance of the evidence, the findings from the *MOX Plant* case, the *Gabčíkovo-Nagymaros*

Project case and the *Bluefin Tuna* case indicate that "the state of urgency" or "necessity"[101] of taking precautionary measures to protect essential interests threatened by a grave and imminent risk must be established "*prima facie*". The Final Declaration of the First European Seas at Risk Conference states that it is important to provide "evidence of effect", but proof of a causal link is not necessary; where no clear evidence is available the environment must be given "the benefit of doubt".[102] Regarding the standard of proof, the evidence could be merely reasonable assumptions in consideration of highly scientific uncertainty. It means that the state that may be adversely affected by a geoengineering activity should provide minimum evidence to show that it is necessary to take a precautionary measure, as the environment or human health is threatened by a significant and imminent risk arising from such a geoengineering activity. The standard of proof is a minimum level, merely providing a reasonable assumption or preliminary evidence as to the likely effects.

Commentators have pointed out that the establishment of the causal relationship between the conduct of a hazardous activity and the damage in question is a very challenging issue.[103] The uncertainties involved in geoengineering techniques indicate a great challenge in proving the factual basis of the causal relationship in the application of the precautionary approach. In the implementation of SAI, for instance, the place that suffers harm arising from the modification of weather patterns, particularly precipitation, may deviate from the spot of spraying sulphate aerosols. In addition, there is a time lag between the termination of a SAI activity and the occurrence of impacts, which makes the causal relationship more intricate. Hence, it is challenging to prove the causal relationship between the activity and its adverse impacts.

5.6 Seeking a balance

The target risk of dangerous climate change could be transformed into, for instance, the countervailing risk of marine biodiversity degradation by implementing ocean fertilization. Whether and to what extent the target risk could be transformed by the countervailing risk depends not only on the severity and likelihood of risk, but also on a comprehensive consideration of diverse interests. The balancing of interests seeks to minimize the risks and maximize the benefits. Sections 5.4 and 5.5 provided two important tools – the risk assessment framework for geoengineering and the tailored implementation of the precautionary approach to facilitate the balancing of risks, taking into account scientific uncertainty and various interests. This section further addresses the complexity of seeking a balance.

Generally, the balancing of interests involves a comparison of the identified risks and benefits and determining whether the activity in question brings net benefit. From a legal point of view, the balancing of interests serves to achieve justice for all parties.[104] In practice, however, the balancing is seldom a pure legal matter; political considerations as well as legal rules together determine the outcome of the balancing. The debate on the benefit and risk of SRM is a typical example. Even if the result of an EIA indicates that a proposed SRM activity may lead to significant adverse consequences, such an activity might still be justified to take place, if the climate were to approach "tipping points" and such a circumstance were to constitute a "climate emergency".[105] An opposite scenario could be that, even if the outcome of an EIA indicates that a proposed SRM activity would not result in significant adverse consequence, such an activity might still not take place due to other fears, for instance, the "moral hazard". Compared to CDR techniques, SRM techniques give rise to more debates due to their rapid effectiveness, one the one hand, and the widely dispersed and uneven side effects and high degree of uncertainties, on the other hand.

The topic of "climate emergency" merits some further discussion in the context of the balancing of interests. It is an emerging idea that the transgression of "tipping points" of climate change may lead to abrupt, drastic and dangerous climate impacts, *inter alia*, extreme climate events. It is argued that, in the situation of a "climate emergency", severe consequences are expected to occur too rapidly to be effectively averted by mitigation methods. SRM is proposed as a promising option in response to a climate emergency, because it can be effective at a large scale within a short period of time. In addition, the implementation of SRM could also "win time" for long-term mitigation.

However, the necessity and feasibility of declaring a "climate emergency" are both doubted. With regard to the former, it has been argued that one state may take unilateral SRM geoengineering action if it felt an urgent need to do so and the possibility of achieving multilateral agreement on taking such an action were very low.[106] This argument could justify the exercise of a geoengineering activity on a large scale, even if a balance between the interests of the acting state and the interests of the potentially affected state were not attained. A state must prove that the action fulfils certain criteria in order to invoke a state of emergency. Such criteria are also referred to as circumstances precluding wrongfulness in the context of the responsibility of states for internationally wrongful acts: first, the action aims to safeguard an "essential interest" of the state; second, the interest must have been threatened by "grave and imminent danger"; third, the action is the only means of safeguarding the danger; fourth, the action does not impair the essential interests of another state or the international community as a whole; and last but not the least, the acting state has not contributed to the state of emergency.[107] The first two requirements would be met when global warming reaches the "tipping point" and the impacts would be serious or irreversible. However, as to the third requirement, it is hard to say that SRM is the only means of safeguarding the danger of global warming. Taking into account the great success of the Paris Agreement, one could be optimistic on the future of ambitious mitigation efforts to combat global warming. The fourth requirement would not be met where the SRM activity leads to serious damage to other states or to the global commons. The last requirement would not be met because, if global warming reached the "tipping point", it would be hard for a state to argue that it has not contributed to the state of dangerous global warming. Consequently, it does not seem convincing to invoke a climate emergency as an exemption to the need to balance the interests when determining whether the implementation of a geoengineering proposal is justified.

With regard to doubts concerning the feasibility, first, it is difficult to define a "tipping point", because serious climate impacts will normally result from numerous individual events during a long period, and thus there is hardly an obvious trigger for an "emergent" response. Second, SRM may not be effective in response to regional climate extremes at a precise location. Third, even if SRM were an effective response, it would be very difficult to attribute an extreme weather event to anthropogenic climate change and to justify declaring a climate emergency.[108] Additional issues include identifying who might have the authority to declare a climate emergency. If a climate emergency would be a threat to international peace and security, the UN Security Council would have the authority under the UN Charter.[109] Considering the complicated geopolitics in climate debates, one could doubt that the international community would agree to temporarily implement SRM, let alone any unilateral or minilateral implementation.

5.7 Conclusion

This chapter proposes a framework for the balancing of the risk of implementing geoengineering techniques versus the contribution that geoengineering can make to counteracting dangerous climate change and its impacts. Many commentators have submitted that there is no one-size-fits-all criterion to evaluate the risks and benefits of geoengineering activities, and the balance of interests should be tailored in accordance with the individual situation of each geoengineering activity. However, a detailed tailored analysis is not available in literature. For this reason, this chapter analyses the balancing of risks via a categorized approach, scrutinizing the six geoengineering techniques in two categories of geoengineering activities, namely small-scale field experiment and large-scale experiment and deployment.

As suggested in Section 5.3, a number of factors should be taken into account in the balancing of risks, including but not limited to: assessment regarding risks and scientific uncertainties of geoengineering techniques; the spatial and temporal scale and the quantity of substance; the geographical, social, economic and technical characters of the states that may suffer potential harm; the concern of intergenerational equity; the economic viability of a proposed geoengineering activity or alternative mitigation activities.

Finding a balance is not only a legal discussion, but also involves scientific, economic and ethical aspects. The purpose of this chapter was therefore not to achieve a balanced outcome, but rather to identify the essential legal issues that should be taken into account in the balancing process.

This chapter concludes that the obligation to conduct an EIA and the precautionary approach play important roles in the governance framework for geoengineering. More specifically, three aspects are addressed in this chapter. First, one should find all relevant factors that should be taken into consideration (see Section 5.3). Second, the proposed activity should proceed through the framework of an EIA, and the state conducting the activity or allowing it to be conducted should comply with the procedural obligations of notification, exchange of information, consultation and monitoring. Depending on the scale of the proposed activity, the proper assessment processes, i.e. PEA or CEIA, would be applied. The proposed assessment framework could, among others, supplement the new Annex 5 of the LP in order to assess the impacts and risks of various marine geoengineering techniques and provide a model for the assessment of SAI in the future (see Section 5.4). Third, based on the risks and uncertainties identified in EIA process, the precautionary approach may be triggered, and proportionate precautionary measures may or should be applied, paying due regard to both the potential contribution made by the proposed geoengineering activity and the severity of harm it may give rise to (see Section 5.5).

As stressed several times in this chapter, the balancing of risks in practice is a multidisciplinary task and in particular, to some extent, a political game rather than a legal analysis. Notably, in some circumstances, the result of the balancing of risks might not follow the result of an EIA and the proposed choice of a precautionary measure. As discussed in Section 5.6, the balancing might include the strategy of declaring a "climate emergency". The choice of evaluation criteria is beyond this legal discussion.

In addition, this chapter can, from the legal perspective, provide a response to the problems associated with the implementation of the precautionary approach. Due to a lack of information or the variability and complexity of climate change and its impacts, not all uncertainties are identifiable. There is no simple rule to establish under what circumstances it is better to wait for identifying more information versus immediately triggering an action to restrict or prohibit such techniques. However, the flexible thresholds of triggering the precautionary approach and the categorized application of proportionate measures could provide general standards for evaluating the risk of harm and scientific uncertainties regarding geoengineering techniques and activities. In addition, the possible reversal of the burden of proof to the state that carries out a geoengineering activity and a lower standard of proof for the states that are potentially affected by the activity could be helpful for the potentially effected states, in particular the most vulnerable ones, to avoid irreversible damage. Regarding the "unknown unknowns" that cannot be predicted prior to the deployment, the focus on minimizing uncertainties could be shifted to increasing resilience against the unforeseen harm and to developing mechanisms for the fair distribution of the benefit and burden sharing. Such purposes imply that one may try to learn how to co-exist with uncertainty and try to weigh how much uncertainty is worth to accept in return for some given benefits.[110] The precautionary approach is vital in enhancing resilience and the balancing of the price of under-protection and the costs of over-protection. With respect to the question regarding the balancing of risks and benefits created by a geoengineering activity, a flexibly triggered precautionary approach could make up for the shortcomings of the existing moratorium on geoengineering.

Notes

1 Section 2.4.2.
2 Rayfuse, R. (2017). Precaution and Climate Change: What Role for the Precautionary Principle in Addressing Global Warming? In Hebeler, T., Hofmann, E., Proelss, A., & Reiff, P. (Eds.). *Protecting the environment for future generations – principles and actors in international environmental law* (1st ed.). Berlin: Erich Schmidt Verlag.
3 Graham, J. D., & Wiener, J. B. (Eds.). (1995). *Risk versus risk: Tradeoffs in protection health and the environment* (1st ed.). Cambridge, Massachusetts: Harvard University Press, 23.
4 Ibid., 2.
5 Davies, G. (2010). Framing the Social, Political, and Environmental Risks and Benefits of Geoengineering: Balancing the Hard-to-Imagine against the Hard-to-Measure, *Tulsa Law Review (46)*, 282.
6 Abelkop, A. D. K., & Carlson, J. C. (2013). Reining in Phaethon's Chariot: Principles for the governance of geoengineering, *Transnational Law & Contemporary Problems, 21*, 787.
7 Shepherd, J., et al. (2009), *Geoengineering the climate: science, governance and uncertainty.* London, UK: Royal Society, 17.
8 Prather, K. A., Bertram, T. H., Grassian, V. H., Deane, G. B., Stokes, M. D., Demott, P. J., . . . Zhao, D. (2013). Bringing the ocean into the laboratory to probe the chemical complexity of sea spray aerosol. *Proceedings of the National Academy of Sciences of the United States of America, 110*(19), 7550–7555. doi:10.1073/pnas.1300262110
9 Watson, A. J., et al. (2008). Designing the next generation of ocean iron fertilization experiments, Theme Section 'Implications of large-scale iron fertilization of the oceans'. *Marine Ecology Progress Series, 364*, 303–309, at 304.
10 IPCC AR5 WGI, 17.
11 Ibid., 114–115.
12 2001 Draft Articles on Prevention, Art. 10.
13 Main strategies include "long-time tool", "climate emergency" and "most economically efficient measure". The term "long-time tool" refers to the strategy that treats SRM geoengineering as a means to gain some time for greater emission reductions with cheaper technologies. SRM would be supplementary to mitigation and adaptation. The term "most economically efficient measure" refers to the strategy that treats SRM as an alternative to mitigation, as SRM can deal with the problem of global warming with a much lower price and much less requirement of international collaboration. As for "climate emergency", see Section 5.6. As for the categorization, see Hamilton, C. (2013). *Earth masters: the dawn of the age of climate engineering.* New Haven, CT: Yale University Press, 154.
14 The number of square metres to define the term "small area" remains to be determined.
15 Resolution LC-LP.2 (2010) on the Assessment Framework for Scientific Research Involving Ocean Fertilization, Section 3.6.4; Resolution LP.4 (8), Annex: Amendments to Article 1 and New Articles 6 and New Annex 4 and 5, Annex 5: Assessment Framework for Matter that May Be Considered for Placement under Annex 4, para. 21.
16 Resolution LC-LP.2 (2010), Section. 3.2.4.3.6.1 (concerning "areas of special concern and value, and traditional use of the sea").

17 See Section 5.2.4.
18 Through the consultation during and after an EIA process.
19 See Section 2.4.1.5(i)(a).
20 Espoo Convention, Art. 2.5 & Appendix III.
21 Espoo Convention, Art. 1(viii).
22 Resolution LP.4(8), 2013 Amendments to the LP, Annex 5: Assessment Framework for Matter that May Be Considered for Placement under Annex 4. Regarding the relation between Resolution LC-LP.2 and the 2013 Amendments to the LP, the former continues "to apply for all Contracting Parties, pending the entry into force of the amendments to the London Protocol set out in the annex to this resolution for those Contracting Parties that accept them". Resolution LP.4(8), Preamble, para. 2.
23 According to the new Annex 5 of the LP, "[t]he purpose of this Framework is to assess placement activities listed in annex 4". To date only ocean fertilization is listed in Annex 4.
24 Directive 2009/31/EC on the Geological Storage of Carbon Dioxide and amending Council Directive 85/337/EEC, European Parliament and Council Directives 2000/60/EC, 2001/80/EC, 2004/35/EC, 2006/12/EC, 2008/1/EC and Regulation (EC) No 1013/2006. Annex I, Criteria for the Characterisation and Assessment of the Potential Storage Complex and Surrounding Area Referred to in Article 4(3).
25 The law as it exists.
26 The law as it ought to be made.
27 See examples in Section 2.4.1.5 (i)(a).
28 *Case Concerning Pulp Mills on the River Uruguay (Argentina v. Uruguay)*, para. 204.
29 See also Section 2.4.1.3 regarding the dichotomous analysis of significant transboundary harm between states and significant harm in the global commons.
30 See further discussion in Section 5.4.1.3.
31 As to the analysis of the three-level EIA framework under the Antarctic Environmental Protocol, see Bastmeijer, C. J., Bastmeijer, K., & Koivurova, T. (2008). *Theory and practice of transboundary environmental impact assessment* (Vol. 1). Leiden: Martinus Nijhoff Publishers.
32 Protocol on Environmental Protection to the Antarctic Treaty, Madrid, 1991, Art. 8; Annex I to the Protocol on Environmental Protection to the Antarctic Treaty: Environmental Impact Assessment, Arts. 1–3; ATCM XXVIII – CEP VIII Resolution 2 (2005). Guidelines for Environmental Impact Assessment in Antarctica, Stockholm, 2005, para. 1. Retrieved from www.ats.aq/devAS/info_measures_listitem.aspx?lang=e&id=347
33 The discussion regarding the authority to render an approval is addressed in Section 5.4.1.4.
34 UK House of Commons, Science and Technology Committee. (2010). *The regulation of geoengineering – fifth report of session 2009–10*. (No. HC221). London: The Stationary Office. Retrieved from www.publications.parliament.uk/pa/cm200910/cmselect/cmsctech/221/221.pdf. On p. 38, "the development and small tests of SRM geoengineering should be allowed provided they [. . .] b) have negligible or predictable environmental impact; and c) have no transboundary effects". Retrieved from www.publications.parliament.uk/pa/cm200910/cmselect/cmsctech/221/221.pdf
35 Espoo Convention, Appendix III.
36 Resolution LC-LP.2 (2010); Resolution LP.4(8), new Annex 5 of the LP.
37 Directive 2009/31/EC, Annex I.
38 See, for instance, Resolution LC-LP.2 (2010).
39 Resolution LC-LP.2 (2010), Section 3.5.9.
40 Resolution LC-LP.2 (2010), Section 3.5.11.4.
41 McQuaid, J., & Le Guen, J. (1998). The use of risk assessment in government. *Issues in Environmental Science and Technology, 9*, 21–36.

42 Resolution LC-LP.2 (2010), Section 3.5.13.
43 See Section 5.3.3.
44 Espoo Convention, Art. 1(vii) regarding cultural heritages; Craik, N. (2015). International EIA law and geoengineering: Do emerging technologies require special rules? *Climate Law*, 5(2–4), 111–141, at 119.
45 See Section 2.4.1.5(i).
46 Espoo Convention, Art. 5; Resolution LP.4(8), new Annex 5, paras. 10–12.
47 Resolution LP.4(8), new Annex 5, para. 11.
48 UNCLOS, Arts. 197–201.
49 Craik, N. (2015), supra note 44, 136.
50 ILC First Report on the Protection of the Atmosphere, sixty-six Session, by Shinya Murase, Special Repporteur, UN Doc. A/CN.4/667 (14 February 2014), 53.
51 ILC Second Report on the Protection of the Atmosphere, sixty-seven Session, by Shinya Murase, Special Rapporteur, UN Doc. A/CN.4/681 (2 March 2015), 31.
52 To date, obligation relating to fundamental values of the international community, such as the prohibition of genocide, acts of aggression and self-determination, have been widely recognized as obligations *erga omnes*. See Institute of International Law. (2005). Resolution: Obligations *erga omnes* in international law, fifth commission, Rapporteur Giorgio Gaja, Preamble. As to a summary of the case law relating to obligations *erga omnes*, see ILC Second Report on the Protection of the Atmosphere, 25–30.
53 Regarding the definition of "competent authority", see Espoo Convention, Art. 1(ix).
54 Resolution LC-LP.2 (2010), Section 3.6.6.
55 Resolution LP.4(8), new Annex 5, para. 25. Regarding the regulation of impact monitoring, see also Art. 12 of the Protocol on Strategic Environmental Assessment to the Convention on Environmental Impact Assessment in a Transboundary Context.
56 Directive 2009/31/EC, Annex II: Criteria for Establishing and Updating the Monitoring Plan Referred to in Article 13(2) and for Post-closure Monitoring.
57 UNECE Protocol on Strategic Environmental Assessment to the Convention on Environmental Impact Assessment in a Transboundary Context, Art. 4.2, Annexes I & II.
58 Similar opinion can be found in Graham, J. D., & Wiener, J. B. (2008). The precautionary principle and risk – risk tradeoffs: a comment. *Journal of Risk Research*, 11(4), 465–474.
59 Resolution LC-LP.1 (2008), Annex 6; CBD COP Decision IX/16, Part C; CBD COP Decision X/33, para. 8 (w).
60 Long, J., & Winickoff, D. (2010). Governing geoengineering research: Principles and process. *Governing*, 1(5), 60–62.
61 Resolution LP.4(8), Preamble.
62 Regarding different versions of the precautionary approach, see Section 2.4.2.3.
63 The five key principles, so called "the Oxford Principles", refer to: Principle 1: Geoengineering to be regulated as a public good; Principle 2: Public participation in geoengineering decision-making; Principle 3: Disclosure of geoengineering research and open publication of results; Principle 4: Independent assessment of impacts; and Principle 5: Governance before deployment.
64 UK House of Commons, Science and Technology Committee (2010), supra note 34.
65 Bodansky, D. (2013). The who, what, and wherefore of geoengineering governance. *Climatic Change*, 121(3), 539–551.
66 Regarding different versions of the precautionary approach, See Section 2.4.2.3.
67 See Section 5.3.3.
68 Trouwborst submitted that the precautionary approach is applicable when the adverse effects of an activity are significant, but it is a *right* for a state to take such measures; it is a *duty* for a state to take precautionary measures if an activity

poses a risk of serious or irreversible harm. Trouwborst, A. (2006). *Precautionary rights and duties of states*. Leiden: Martinus Nijhoff Publishers, 62.

69 See Section 2.4.2.2.

70 Hubert, A., & Reichwein, D. (2015). An exploration of a code of conduct for responsible scientific research involving geoengineering. Potsdam: IASS working paper. Potsdam: Institute for Advanced Sustainability Studies (IASS),45. Retrieved from www.insis.ox.ac.uk/fileadmin/images/misc/An_Exploration_of_a_Code_of_Conduct.pdf; UK House of Commons, Science and Technology Committee. (2006). *Scientific advice, risk and evidence based policy making.* (No. HC900-I). London: The Stationary Office. Retrieved from www.publications.parliament.uk/science

71 Regarding the burden of proof, see Section 5.5.4.

72 Trouwborst, A. (2006), supra note 68, 118; De Chazournes, L. B. (2007), supra note 68, 22.

73 The Final Declaration of the First European Seas at Risk Conference, Copenhagen, 1994, Annex I; Sunstein, C. R. (2009). *Worst-case scenarios.* (1st ed.). Cambridge, Massachusetts, USA: Harvard University Press.

74 Commission of the European Communities, Communication from the Commission on the Precautionary Principle, Brussels, 2000, COM (2000)1, 18.

75 UK Department of the Environment, Transport and the Regions, Guidelines for Environmental Risk Assessment and Management: Revised Department Guidance, 2000, 13.

76 Mandel, G. N., & Gathii, J. T. (2006). Cost-Benefit Analysis Versus the Precautionary Principle: Beyond Class Sunstein's Laws of Fear. *University of Illinois Law Review, 2006*, 1037–1079, at 1072.

77 Schomberg, R. von. (2006). The precautionary principle and its normative challenges. In Fisher, E., Jones, J. and Schomberg, R. von. (Eds). *In Implementing the Precautionary Principle: Perspectives and Prospects.* Cheltenham, UK and Northampton, MA, US: Edward Elgar.

78 Hartzell-Nichols, L. (2012). Precaution and solar radiation management. *Ethics, Policy & Environment, 15*(2), 158–171, at 166.

79 Climate engineering field research: The favorable setting of international environmental law. *Washington and Lee Journal of Energy, Climate, and the Environment, 5*(2), 417–486; Rickels, W., Klepper, G., et al. (2011). *Large-scale intentional interventions into the climate system? Assessing the climate engineering debate.* Scoping report conducted on behalf of the German Federal Ministry of Education and Research (BMBF), Kiel: Kiel Earth Institute, 102; Tedsen, E., & Homann, G. (2013). Implementing the precautionary principle for climate engineering. *Carbon & Climate Law Review, 7*(2), 90–100, at 99.

80 See examples: The Oxford Principles; Asilomar Recommendations; Hubert, A., & Reichwein, D. (2015). An exploration of a code of conduct for responsible scientific research involving geoengineering.

81 Tedsen, E., & Homann, G. (2013), supra note 79, 98; Hartzell-Nichols, L. (2012), supra note 78, 161.

82 Regulation (EC) No 178/2002 of the European Parliament and of the Council of 28 January2002 laying down the general principles and requirements of food law, establishing the European Food Safety Authority and laying down procedures in matters of food safety, Official Journal of the European Communities L 31/1, 1.2.2002.

83 See Section 2.4.2.3.

84 Wiener, J. B. (2008). Precaution. In Bodansky, D., Brunnée, J., & Hey, E.(Eds.), *The Oxford handbook of international law* (pp. 597–612). Oxford: Oxford University Press, 606; Trouwborst, A. (2006), supra note 68, 222.

85 The (burden of) proving weighs on the plaintiff. Fellmeth, A., & Horwitz, M. (2009). *Guide to Latin in International Law.* Oxford University Press. Retrieved from www.oxfordreference.com/view/10.1093/acref/9780195369 380.001.0001/acref-9780195369 380-e-77

86 *Case concerning Pulp Mills on the River Uruguay*, paras. 225 & 257.

87 Ibid., paras. 189 & 228.

88 Ibid., para. 265.

89 *The MOX Plant Case*, Provisional Measures, Separate Opinion of Judge Wolfrum, 3.

90 *Southern Bluefin Tuna Case*, Provisional Measures, Separate Opinion of Judge Laing, para. 14.

91 Ambrus, M. (2012). The precautionary principle and a fair allocation of the burden of proof in international environmental law. *Review of European Community & International Environmental Law*, 21(3), 259–270, at 266.

92 See Section 2.4.2.3.

93 Birnie, P., Boyle, A., & Redgwell, C. (2009). *International law & the environment* (3rd ed.). Oxford: Oxford University Press, 159.

94 Trouwborst, A. (2006), supra note 68, 226; Wiener, J. B. (2008), supra note 84, 606; Birnie, P., Boyle, A., & Redgwell, C. (2009), supra note 93, 158; Kazhdan, D. (2011). Precautionary pulp: Pulp mills and the evolving dispute between international tribunals over the reach of the precautionary principle. *Ecology Law Quarterly*, 38, 527, at 534.

95 Trouwborst, A. (2006), supra note 68, 224. Examples of "best available techniques" regulated under legal instruments: the 1995 Fish Stocks Agreement, Art. 6; Best available Techniques to Control Emissions of Persistent Organic Pollutions from Major Stationaer Sources, Annex.

96 *Southern Bluefin Tuna Case*, Provisional Measures, para. 71.

97 Ibid., para. 74.

98 Ibid., para. 80.

99 *The MOX Plant Case*, Provisional Measures, paras. 71–72.

100 *The MOX Plant Case*, Provisional Measures, para. 81; see also the Separate Opinion of Judge Treves.

101 *Case Concerning the Gabčikovo-Nagymaros Project*, paras. 49–54.

102 The Final Declaration of the First European Seas at Risk Conference, Copenhagen, 1994, Annex I.

103 Saxler, B., Siegfried, J., & Proelss, A. (2015). International liability for transboundary damage arising from stratospheric aerosol injections. *Law, Innovation and Technology*, 7(1), 112–147, at 146.

104 Xue, H. (2003), *Transboundary damage in international law* (Vol. 27). New York: Cambridge University Press, 144.

105 Blackstock, J. J., Battisti, D. S., Caldeira, K., Eardley, D. M., Katz, J. I., Keith, D. W., . . . Koonin, S. E. (2009). Climate engineering responses to climate emergencies. Retrieved from http://arxiv.org/pdf/0907.5140

106 Virgoe, J. (2009). International governance of a possible geoengineering intervention to combat climate change. *Climatic Change*, 95(1–2), 103–119.

107 *Case concerning the Gabčikovo-Nagymaros Project*, paras. 50–52. The ICJ followed the definition of "necessity" stated in Article 25 of the Draft Articles on Responsibility of States for Internationally Wrongful Acts. See also Winter, G. (2011). Climate engineering and international law: Last resort or the end of humanity? *Review of European Community & International Environmental Law*, 20(3), 277–289, 284.

108 Sillmann, J., Lenton, T. M., Levermann, A., Ott, K., Hulme, M., Benduhn, F., & Horton, J. B. (2015). Climate emergencies do not justify engineering the climate. *Nature Climate Change*, 5(4), 290–292.

109 UNSC has addressed the security implication of climate change in 2007. See UNSC press release on 17 April 2007: Security Council holds first-ever debate on impact of climate change on peace, security, hearing over 50 speakers. Retrieved from www.un.org/press/en/2007/sc9000.doc.htm

110 Renn, O. (2008). *Risk governance: Coping with uncertainty in a complex world*. London: Earthscan publishers Ltd, 193 &196–197.

Conclusion

This book addressed the international legal framework for geoengineering techniques. Instead of covering all types of techniques, this book merely embraces the techniques that are designed to be deployed in the areas beyond national jurisdiction, or the techniques that may cause interference to the environment of another state or the areas beyond national jurisdiction. Hence, the objects of legal analysis in this book are: ocean fertilization, ocean upwelling, ocean alkalinity addition, BECCS, SAI and MCW.

Chapters 2 and 3 addressed positive analyses, explored contemporary international rules and principles applicable to geoengineering technology in general and each specific technique respectively. Although regulatory gaps remain in specific issues, contemporary international law is generally adequate for the governance of geoengineering. A new treaty to specially govern geoengineering is not required.

Chapter 2 sought to elaborate rules and principles applicable to all geoengineering techniques in general under contemporary international law. The climate change regime, among others, the UNFCCC and the Paris Agreement, is applicable to CDR, mainly because the deployment of CDR can contribute to the achievement of the ultimate objective of the UNFCCC. However, it is unclear whether the climate change regime is applicable to SRM techniques. The ENMOD Convention provides for a permanent ban on geoengineering activities that are undertaken for non-peaceful purposes and have widespread, long-lasting or severe effects. Third, geoengineering activities are subject to the prevention principle and the precautionary approach. The prevention principle applies to geoengineering activities in order to prevent or abate significant harm or to control the risk of significant harm to another state or in the global commons. In contrast, the precautionary approach applies to geoengineering to deal with future risks. The moratorium on marine geoengineering under the 2013 Amendment to the LP (not yet entered into force), as an application of the precautionary approach, may effectively control the risk of significant or irreversible harm rising from geoengineering before scientific knowledge is fully available, but it underplays the potential of geoengineering in combating anthropogenic climate change, which would also result in serious or irreversible harm to the planet.

Chapter 3 concluded that the lawfulness of a geoengineering activity depends, among others, on the location of implementation. The UNCLOS is applicable to geoengineering activities carried out at sea (marine geoengineering techniques or the transport and storage of CO_2 streams as procedures of BECCS) in terms of determining the lawfulness of an activity undertaken in the territorial sea, the EEZ or the high seas. With regard to SAI, the lawfulness of injecting sulphate concerns the legality of using aircraft in the atmosphere. In this case, the Chicago Convention applies to the injection of sulphate by aircraft over one state's own territory; the UNCLOS and the Antarctic Treaty are applicable when the injection of sulphate by aircraft is undertaken beyond national jurisdiction; in regard to overflight and the introduction of sulphate aerosols into the stratosphere over another state's territory, such actions should be subject to the obligation not to violate the sovereignty of another state in accordance with the Chicago Convention and customary international law. Chapter 3 also concluded that the implementation of geoengineering techniques is subject to various conventions. For instance, the CBD is applicable to all types of the geoengineering techniques as long as they might adversely affect biodiversity. UNCLOS is applicable to geoengineering activities for the purpose of protecting and conserving the marine environment, but the parties to the LP must comply with the stricter rules under the LP relating to the prevention of marine pollution from dumping. Because SAI may adversely affect the lower atmosphere, the ozone layer, the marine environment and the ecosystems, the CLRTAP, the Vienna Convention and its Montreal Protocol, the UNCLOS and the CBD are applicable. Chapter 3 also concluded that regulatory gaps remain in, for instance, the peaceful use of techniques that may modify the weather or climate system, and the air pollution caused by substances injected into the atmosphere over the high seas. Also, no specific international rule or regulation mandates or facilitates sulphate aerosols injection by means of tethered balloons or artillery.

Chapters 4 and 5 addressed normative analyses, attempting to provide suggestions for improved governance of geoengineering. The positive analyses in Chapters 2 and 3 show that the existing rules and principles are not sufficient to weigh the scenario of adverse effects brought by geoengineering activity against the scenario of the impacts of anthropogenic climate change without implementing geoengineering. In response to this, Chapters 4 explored legitimacy and institutional issues with respect to the governance of geoengineering, and Chapter 5 proposed a framework for balancing the risk of climate change against geoengineering.

Chapter 4 concluded that, due to the lack of legitimacy, it would not be surprising to see considerable objections against any proposal of regulating geoengineering by a single state or a group of states. On the contrary, multilateral governance would be the most likely scenario, as it provides an inclusive forum for equitable participation of states and can provide international oversight over geoengineering activities. The UNFCCC together with the PA are likely to be the most appropriate forum to negotiate CDR issues and to regulate CDR in an overarching manner. The UNFCCC and the PA are unlikely to govern SRM if non-mitigation methods cannot be used to contribute to achieving the ultimate objective of the UNFCCC. In addition, a host of sectoral regimes could play complementary roles to control the risk of harm to environmental media and human health created by specific geoengineering techniques. Sectoral regimes should be connected with each other in a more interactive and cohesive manner in order to avoid a potential conflict between regimes and to enhance synergies between them. With regard to the form of law, the preliminary finding is that fundamental obligations and general principles should be formulated in a binding form. In contrast, specific rules on, for instance, an environmental impact assessment, favour a non-binding form in order to leave flexibility for adaptation.

Chapters 4 emphasized that, first, as the risks and the state of knowledge vary from technique to technique, not all geoengineering techniques need to be developed simultaneously; low-risk and scientifically valuable research could proceed and less controversial geoengineering techniques could be developed as a first step. Second, to deal with uncertainty, legal instruments should be dynamic, adaptive and future-proof. Hence, the legal implications may vary when the updated scientific results indicate that a technique may cause a higher or lower degree of harm. Third, in the coming years (less than one decade), the governance of geoengineering will focus on enhancing the synergies of scientific institutions, experts and relevant international organizations to actively engage in an inclusive discussion and deepen the understanding of geoengineering technology. At the moment, it is neither feasible nor desirable to develop an international framework for geoengineering in a systematic manner.

Chapter 5 proposed a framework for the balancing of the risk of implementing geoengineering techniques versus the contribution that geoengineering can make to counteracting dangerous climate change and its impacts. The balancing of risks could be undertaken in three steps. First, set up the criteria in order to find out all relevant factors that need to be taken into consideration in the balancing of risks. Second, the proposed activity proceeds through an assessment process, which includes an EIA and the procedural obligations of consulting, notifying and exchanging information with all relevant parties and monitoring the proposed activity and its impacts. The proposed assessment process could, among others, supplement the new Annex 5 of the LP in order to assess the impacts and risks of various marine geoengineering techniques (when more marine geoengineering techniques are listed in the new Annex 4 of the LP) and provide a model to assess the impacts and risks of SAI projects in the future. Third, depending on the risks and uncertainties identified in the EIA process, the precautionary approach may be triggered and proportionate precautionary measures are to be applied to the proposed activity. The burden of proof might be lowered or shifted, depending on the particular situation of the matter at stake. Chapter 5 also points out that the balancing of risks is not a purely legal matter but rather a multi-disciplinary task and in particular, to some extent, a political one. Notably, in some circumstances, the result of the balancing of risks might not follow the result of an EIA and the implementation of precautionary measure.

In the end, this book turns back to the context of Anthropocene, trying to answer the question proposed in the Introduction – could we and should we save the planet by manipulating it – from a legal perspective. It is self-evident that the discussion of the legal framework of geoengineering should never be separated from the context of protecting and preserving the environment. It would be ironic if the legal framework that facilitates the development of geoengineering ultimately results in widespread and irreversible damage to the planet. Therefore, the rules and principles that aim at controlling the risk of significant harm to the environment and human health should be developed first.

Meanwhile, the potential of geoengineering techniques in combating serious or irreversible climate change and its impacts should not be downplayed. Facing large numbers of unknowns contained in various geoengineering techniques, the comprehensive risk assessment and the flexible implementation of the precautionary approach could serve as two vital tools to facilitate the appropriate development of a certain geoengineering technique. In the foreseeable future, CDR techniques are likely to play a significant role in complementing conventional mitigation methods to achieve the temperature goal under the Paris Agreement.

Some final remarks are given to the future of SRM technologies. From a historical point of view, would large implementation of SRM technologies be a sensible decision even if they proved to be effective and the adverse impacts were acceptable? From the study of the past climates, palaeoclimatologists found that the global average temperatures in the past two decades were not the highest, neither was the concentration of CO_2. Against this background, it is not convincing to use a "doomsday scenario" as the pretext to implement SRM. Then, if the unprecedented climate and environmental challenge today does not derive from the (relatively) high global average temperature or the (relatively) high concentration of CO_2, why should we still worry about the climate instability and its impacts today? In the author's opinion, the main reason is that global warming and other environmental problems are not isolated but rather interrelated. A simple example could be that the excessive use of fossil fuels causes not only greenhouse gases emissions but also the exhaustion of non-living resources. In fact, the unprecedented challenges at present are the exhaustion of living and non-living resources, the degradation of ecosystems and the pollution of water, the atmosphere and soil. Such degradation and damage are the very reasons that are unprecedentedly challenging our "Mother Earth". Unfortunately, SRM technologies fail to address such challenges in a holistic manner.

Then, how to address climate and environmental problems in a holistic manner? The vital meaning of counteracting anthropogenic climate change is to call for the change of every consumer's behaviour and to spare no effort on creating and maintaining the environmental-friendly and sustainable development of a society. The protection of the environment, the conservation of natural resources, the improvement of energy efficiency and the increasing use of renewable energy are in line with a holistic approach.

Humans should not manipulate the Earth by the excuse of "saving" it; we are not the lifesaver for the Earth but rather for ourselves. Tracing back the process of evolution on the Earth, early and modern humans constitute merely a small part of species over hundreds of millions of years. Humans would violate the rule of nature at their own peril – ending up with extinction due to the no more inhabitable environment and the exhaustion of resources. The process of evolution tells us to stand in awe of nature.

Appendix

An overview of the main geoengineering experiments over the world

The status of research and practice on different geoengineering techniques varies hugely. The techniques of direct air capture and enhanced weathering are at the stage of laboratorial research and field trial. Several small-scale ocean fertilization projects have been undertaken in northern and southern oceanic regions since 1993. BECCS projects or biomass/fossil-fuel (combined) CCS projects have been increasingly operated at small and big scales. Afforestation, reforestation and land-use change have been carried out extensively for a long time and are treated more as traditional tools to increase carbon sinks than geoengineering techniques. Biochar and biomass burial are traditional tools to improve soil quality. SAI technique is still at the stage of computer-modelling and laboratorial experiment.[1] The research on the MCW technique is at the stage of computer modelling and preparations for field trial. This Appendix is a supplement to Chapter 1, providing an overview of main experiments of ocean fertilization, BECCS, SAI and MCW.

1. Ocean fertilization experiments

There have been 13 ocean fertilization experiments in different ocean regions since 1993 with the primary aim of investigating the effect of iron as a nutrient to stimulate plankton bloom in oceans. This section introduces three experiments called SOFeX, EIFEX and LOHAFEX in the Southern Ocean as well as one experiment in the Northern Pacific Ocean. Most experiments happen in the Southern Ocean because it is one of the largest sinks of anthropogenic CO_2. Theoretically, surface seawater starts to freeze in autumn around Antarctica. The water below the sea ice becomes salty and dense and therefore sinks to the deep ocean. Inversely, the water high in nutrients moves from the deep ocean to the surface. When the sea ice melts in spring, plankton breeds in the nutrient-rich water.[2]

From 5 January to 26 February 2002, the Southern Ocean Iron Experiment (SOFeX) was undertaken in the Southern Ocean.[3] Three research vessels were involved in this experiment. Two of them were the largest ships in the UNOLS[4] fleet, the *Revelle*[5] and the *Melville*. The third ship is the icebreaker *Polar Star* (US Coast Guard). The three ships sailed at different times to trace the iron-fertilized patches. The *Revelle* added iron to both the North and the South patches and mapped the size characteristics of the South patch. The *Melville* sailed several weeks later when the patches were formed and made detailed measurements of phytoplankton physiology and rate processes. Finally, the *Polar Star* arrived to assess how much carbon was removed from the iron-fertilized patches.

In February 2004, 167 square kilometres of the Southern Ocean was fertilized with several tonnes of iron sulphate in the European Iron Fertilization Experiment (EIFEX).[6] The research team on the German research vessel *Polarstern* monitored the bloom and demise of algae in the fertilized area. Samples from the experimental area showed that each atom of added iron grasped at least 13,000 atoms of carbon out of the atmosphere by enhancing photosynthesis and at least half of the carbon deposited in the ocean deeper than 100 meters; samples collected outside the fertilized area showed substantially less carbon being deposited in the deep ocean. The EIFEX results vindicated the hypothesis that iron insufficiency limits algae productivity, thus backing up the finding that iron fertilization contributes to capturing more atmospheric CO_2.[7]

On 7 January 2009, in the project LOHAFEX co-funded by the German Ministry of Environment and the Indian government, the research vessel *Polarstern* set sail from Cape Town to arrange an iron-fertilization experiment.[8] This project involved dumping six tonnes of iron sulphate to fertilise approximately 300 km² of ocean surface between 200 and 500 nautical miles north to northwest of South Georgia Island to trap CO_2 from the atmosphere by encouraging the growth of algae. Two aims of this experiment were examining the role of iron in the ocean and the actual sedimentation of the produced algae bloom. The LOHAFEX went one step further than previous field experiments because it also aimed at examining the impacts of ocean fertilization on biodiversity and the reproductivity of krill.[9]

There are experiments of iron fertilization in northern oceans as well. In July 2012, an American company, Haida Salmon Restoration Corporation (HSRC), attempted to fertilize an important fishing region off the west coast of Canada, which is near a small fishing village named Old Massett. The goals of this experiment were to boost salmon population as well as to sequestrate carbon. Around 100 tonnes of iron sulphate were dumped in the Pacific Ocean off the west coast of Canada. The Canadian company thought to commercialize iron fertilization by selling carbon credits to those companies seeking to buy the credits to offset their carbon emissions. The adverse effect on the indigenous villagers and the local environment worried scientists and enraged opponents to ocean fertilization.

2. Experiments of Bioenergy Carbon Capture and Sequestration (BECCS)

The United States

The primary goal of many BECCS projects in the United States is not to mitigate carbon emissions but to augment production from depleted oil fields. CO_2 storage, to some extent, is taken as "serendipity" or an "enlightened accident".[10][11] The first BECCS project was operated from 2003 to 2005 in Russel County, located in the central part of Kansas in the United States. This project was managed by the University of Kansas and supported by a fossil fuel research institute of the U.S. Department of Energy. In this project, CO_2 was sourced from an ethanol plant in Russel, compressed and liquefied at the plant, then transported by truck, and injected into old and depleted oil wells. Even though the primary goal of the project was not to utilize CO_2 from a biogenic source for climate change mitigation, but to explore the feasibility of Enhanced Oil Recovery (EOR), the project increased the production of oil by approximately 27,900 barrels and injected 7,700 tonnes of CO_2.[12] In Texas, a similar but larger-scale EOR project has been under operation since 2009, which can pipeline 105,000 tonnes CO_2 from a Kansas ethanol plant to the oil fields in Texas.[13] The U.S. oil and gas producer Chaparral Company operates this project as a commercial venture instead of a research project.

In the State of Illinois, a large demonstration of utilizing CO_2 from ethanol production for geological storage started to operate in 2011. This project is led by the Illinois State Geological Survey at the University of Illinois and advised by the partners from the Midwest Geological Sequestration Consortium. In this project, CO_2 is captured, compressed and liquefied, then delivered through pipelines, and injected into the saline aquifer Mount Simon Sandstone at a depth of 2,000 meters.[14] The capacity of CO_2 storage is 3.6 million in total during the operation time between 2011 and 2015.

The Netherlands

The Rotterdam Climate Initiative is making an effort to cut 50% of Rotterdam's carbon emissions by 2025. To achieve this goal, a wide range of mitigation activities have been and will be started. RCI is planning to build an extensive CCS network among industries and electricity plants.[15] Some projects integrate traditional CCS (fossil fuel sourced) and BECCS since biomass is used as a source of energy. For example, in the project ROAD (*Rotterdam Opslag en Afvang Demonstratieproject*), biomass provides 20% of the energy for the pilot power plant. The captured CO_2 is transferred through a pipeline and stored in depleted gas fields. From 2017 onwards, the ROAD project is expected to capture approximately 1.1 million tonnes of CO_2 annually.[16]

Another type of BECCS is the OCAP (Organic CO_2 for Assimilation by Plants), which delivers CO_2 from a bio-ethanol plant to greenhouses in order to augment plant growth.[17] In addition, the OCAP has the ambition to expand the pipeline to transport the remaining CO_2 for permanent storage.

3. Experiments of Sulphate Aerosols Injection (SAI)

The SPICE (Stratospheric Particle Injection for Climate Engineering) project is a 3.5-year collaboration between the Universities of Bristol, Cambridge, Oxford and Edinburgh, which began in 2010.[18] The SPICE project aimed at investigating the effectiveness of SAI and planned to undertake experiments to simulate the cooling effect of volcanoes. However, an experiment was cancelled in 2012 due to various reasons, including the concern over a perceived conflict of intellectual property interests with some scientists involved in this project.[19] This experiment would have injected 150 litres of fine water spray into the atmosphere from a weather balloon via a one-kilometre pipe tethered to a ship in order to collect data on the motion of balloon and pipe in various wind conditions.[20]

In 2014, a group of scientists from Harvard University proposed a small-scale SAI experiment called stratospheric controlled perturbation experiment, or SCoPEx. The SCoPEx project aims to improve understanding of the risks of solar geoengineering by quantifying the risk of ozone depletion caused by stratospheric sulphate injection. This experiment is designed to inject sulphate aerosols to 20-kilometre altitude via a balloon with a propeller.[21] To date, the ScoPEx project is at the most advanced stage of planning of all SAI proposed experiments.

4. Marine cloud whiting (MCW)

As of early 2016, the research on MCW is at the stage of preparing for field trial. In March 2016, scientists and unmanned aircraft systems engineers from Nevada, in the United States, have successfully tested the first autonomous MCW aircraft platform.[22] This test flight verified that unmanned aircraft systems are capable of carrying active MCW payloads and could be considered as a milestone towards the stage of field trials of MCW technique.

Notes

1 Noting that the SPICE experiment was cancelled in 2012. See Section 3 below.
2 Iron Fertilization Develops a New Wrinkle. Retrieved from http://news.discovery.com/earth/oceans/iron-fertilization-develops-a-new-wrinkle-130617.htm
3 SOFeX Cruise, History & Purpose, Monterey Bay Aquarium Research Institute. Retrieved from www.mbari.org/expeditions/SOFeX2002/history&purpose.htm#DetailsofthemissionaboardtheUSCGCPolarStar
4 University-National Oceanographic Laboratory System. Retrieved from www.unols.org/
5 Information on Ship Revelle, see http://shipsked.ucsd.edu/Ships/Roger_Revelle/; information about Ship Melville, see http://shipsked.ucsd.edu/Ships/Melville/.

6   Schiermeier, O. (2012, 18 July). Dumping iron at sea does sink carbon. Retrieved from www.nature.com/news/dumping-iron-at-sea-does-sink-carbon-1.11028

7   This hypothesis was proposed by John Martin in 1988. See: John H. Martin & Steve E. Fitzwater. (1988). Iron deficiency limits phytoplankton growth in the north-east Pacific subarctic, *Nature*, *331*, 341–343.

8   AWI, Background information on the project of LOHAFEX as of 22 January 2009.

9   Ibid.

10 Global CCS Institute, & Biorecro. (2011). Global status of BECCS projects 2010, 28.

11 Ibid., 27.

12 Ibid., 27.

13 Ibid., 28.

14 BECCS projects. Retrieved from http://biorecro.com/?page=beccs_projects; ibid., 30.

15 Rotterdam Climate Initiative, Three pillars. Other two are energy efficiency and sustainable energy. Retrieved from www.rotterdamclimateinitiative.nl/en/english-2011-design/three-pillars-50procent

16 Rotterdam Climate Initiative. (2016). CO_2 capture, transport and storage. Retrieved from www.rotterdamclimateinitiative.nl/uk/projects/co2-capture,-transport-and-storage?portfolio_i d=282

17 Berkum, E. van. (2012, August). CO_2 in horticultural greenhouses. Retrieved from http://blog.maripositas.org/horticulture/ocap-organic-carbon-dioxide-for-assimilation-of-plants; OCAP: www.ocap.nl

18 SPICE. (2012). The SPICE project. Retrieved from www.spice.ac.uk/about-us/aims-and-background/

19 Hale, E. (2012, 16 May). Geoengineering experiment cancelled due to perceived conflict of interest. *The Guardian*. Retrieved from www.theguardian.com/environment/2012/may/16/geoengineering-experiment-cancelled

20 Kuo, K. (2012, 18 June). Geoengineering trial cancelled: More regulation needed. Retrieved from https://theconversation.com/geoengineering-trial-cancelled-more-regulation-needed-7297

21 Dykema, J. A., Keith, D. W., Anderson, J. G., & Weisenstein, D. (2014). Stratospheric controlled perturbation experiment: a small-scale experiment to improve understanding of the risks of solar geoengineering. *Philosophical Transactions of the Royal Society of London A: Mathematical, Physical and Engineering Sciences*, *372*(2031), 20140059. doi: 10.1098/rsta.2014.005

22 Desert Research Institute (DRI). (2016, 25 March). Autonomous cloud seeding aircraft successfully tested in Nevada. *Science Daily*. Retrieved from www.sciencedaily.com/releases/2016/03/160325093945.htm

References

A. Treaties and European regulations and directives

The Antarctic Treaty, Washington, adopted 1 December 1959, entered into force 3 June 1962, *United Nations Treaty Series* (1961), vol. 402, no. 5778, p. 71.

ASEAN Agreement on the Conservation of Nature and Natural Resources, Kuala Lumpur, adopted 9 July 1985, not yet entered into force. Retrieved from http://environment.asean.org/agreement-on-the-conservation-of-nature-and-natural-resource/

Bamako Convention on the Ban of the Import Into Africa and the Control of Transboundary Movement and Management of Hazardous Wastes Within Africa, Bamako, adopted 30 January 1991, entered into force 22 April 1998, *United Nations Treaty Series* (2002), vol. 2101, no. 36508, p. 177.

Basel Convention on the Control of Transboundary Movements of Hazardous Wastes and Their Disposal, Basel, adopted 22 March 1989, entered into force 5 May 1992, *United Nations Treaty Series* (1999), vol. 1673, no. 28911, p. 57.

Convention for the Co-Operation in the Protection and Development of the Marine and Coastal Environment of the West and Central African Region, Abidjan, adopted in 1981, entered into force 5 August 1984. Retrieved from http://abidjanconvention.org/index.php

Convention for the Protection and Development of the Marine Environment of the Wider Caribbean Region, Cartagena de Indias, adopted 24 March 1983, entered into force 11 October 1986, *United Nations Treaty Series* (1997), vol. 1506, no. 25974, p. 157.

Convention for the Protection of the Marine Environment of the North-East Atlantic, Paris, adopted 22 September 1992, entered into force 25 March 1998, *United Nations Treaty Series* (2009), vol. 2354, no. 42279, p. 27.

Convention for the Protection of the Natural Resources and Environment of the South Pacific Region, Noumea, adopted 24 November 1986, entered into force 22 August 1990. Retrieved from www.sprep.org/legal/the-convention#text

Convention on Biological Diversity, Rio de Janeiro, adopted 5 June 1992, entered into force 29 December 1993, *United Nations Treaty Series* (2001), vol. 1760, no. 30619, p. 79.

Convention on Environmental Impact Assessment in a Transboundary Context (Espoo Convention), Espoo, adopted 25 February 1991, entered into force 10 September 1997, *United Nations Treaty Series* (1997), vol. 1989, no. 34028, p. 309.

Convention on International Civil Aviation, Chicago, adopted 7 December 1944, entered into force 4 April 1947, *United Nations Treaty Series* (1948), vol. 5, no. 102, p. 295.

Convention on Long-Range Transboundary Air Pollution, Geneva, adopted 13 November 1979, entered into force 16 March 1983, *United Nations Treaty Series* (1992), vol. 1302, no. 21623, p. 217.

Convention on the Conservation of Antarctic Marine Living Resources, Canberra, adopted 20 May 1980, entered into force 7 April 1982, *United Nations Treaty Series* (1994), vol. 1329, no. 22301, p. 47.

Convention on the Law of the Non-Navigational Uses of International Watercourses, adopted 21 May 1997, entered into force 17 August 2014, UN Doc. A/51/49 (vol. III) (UNTS volume number has yet been determined).

Convention on the Prevention of Marine Pollution by Dumping of Wastes and Other Matter, London, adopted 29 December 1972, entered into force 30 August 1975, *United Nations Treaty Series* (1984), vol. 1046, no. 15749, p. 120.

Convention on the Protection of the Black Sea Against Pollution, Bucharest, adopted 21 April 1992, entered into force 15 January 1994, *United Nations Treaty Series* (2000), vol. 1764, no. 30674, p. 3.

Convention on the Prohibition of Military or Any Hostile Use of Environmental Modification Techniques, New York, adopted 10 December 1976, entered into force 5 October 1978, *United Nations Treaty Series* (1986), vol. 1108, no. 17119, p. 151.

Convention on the Protection and Use of Transboundary Watercourses and International Lakes, Helsinki, adopted 17 March 1992, entered into force 6 October 1996, *United Nations Treaty Series* (2001), vol. 1936, no. 33207, p. 269.

Convention on the Protection of Marine Environment of the Baltic Sea Area, Helsinki, adopted in 1992, entered into force 17 January 2000. Retrieved from www.helcom.fi/about-us/convention/

Convention on the Protection of the Rhein, Berne, adopted 12 April 1999, entered into force 1 January 2013. Retrieved from www.iksr.org/en/international-cooperation/legal-basis/convention/index.html

Convention on the Transboundary Effects of Industrial Accidents, Helsinki, adopted 17 March 1992, entered into force19 April 2000, *United Nations Treaty Series* (2002), vol. 2105, no. 36605, p. 457.

Convention on the Transboundary Effects of Industrial Accidents, Helsinki, adopted 17 March 1992, entered into force 19 April 2000, *United Nations Treaty Series* (2005), vol. 2105, no. 33605, p. 457.

Directive 2001/42/EC on the Assessment of the Effects of Certain Plans and Programmes on the Environment, *Official Journal of the European Communities*, L 197/30 (21 July 2001).

Directive 2009/31/EC on the Geological Storage of Carbon Dioxide and amending Council Directive 85/337/EEC, European Parliament and Council Directives 2000/60/EC, 2001/80/EC, 2004/35/EC, 2006/12/EC, 2008/1/EC and Regulation (EC) No 1013/2006, *Official Journal of the European Communities*, L 140/114 (5 June 2009).

The Framework Convention on the Protection and Sustainable Development of the Carpathians, Kyiv, adopted May 2003, entered into force January 2006. Retrieved from www.carpathianconvention.org/

International Convention for the Regulation of Whaling, Washington, adopted 2 December 1946, entered into force 10 November 1948, as amended by the Commission at the 64 Annual Meeting, Panama City, July 2012. Retrieved from https://iwc.int/convention

Kyoto Protocol to the United Nations Framework Convention on Climate Change, Kyoto, adopted 10 December 1997, entered into force 16 February 2005, *United Nations Treaty Series* (2005), vol. 2303, no. 30822, p. 162.

Montreal Protocol on Substances That Deplete the Ozone Layer, Montreal, adopted 16 September 1987, entered into force 1 January 1989, *United Nations Treaty Series* (1989), vol. 1522, no. 26369, p. 3.

Paris Agreement, adopted 12 December 2015, entered into force 4 November 2016, (UNTS volume number not available). Retrieved from https://treaties.un.org/Pages/showDetails.aspx?objid=0800000280458f37

Protocol on Environmental Protection to the Antarctic Treaty, Madrid, adopted 4 October 1991, entered into force 14 January 1998, (UNTS volume number not available). Retrieved from https://treaties.un.org/doc/Publication/UNTS/No%20Volume/5778/A-5778-080000028006ab63.pdf

Protocol on Strategic Environmental Assessment to the Convention on Environmental Impact Assessment in a Transboundary Context, Kiev, 21 May 2003, *United Nations Treaty Series* (2010), vol. 2685, no. 34028, p. 140.

Protocol to Abate Acidification, Eutrophication and Ground-Level Ozone to the Convention on Long-Range Transboundary Air Pollution, Gothenburg, adopted 30 November 1999, entered into force 17 May 2005, *United Nations Treaty Series* (2005), vol. 2319, no. 21623, p. 80.

Protocol to the 1979 Convention on Long-Range Transboundary Air Pollution on Further Reduction of Sulphur Emissions, Oslo, adopted 14 June 1994, entered into force 5 August 1998, *United Nations Treaty Series* (2001), vol. 2030, no. 21623, p. 122.

Protocol to the 1979 Convention on Long-Range Transboundary Air Pollution on Heavy Metals, Aarhus, adopted 24 June 1998, entered into force 29 December 2003, *United Nations Treaty Series* (2005), vol. 2237, no. 21623, p. 4.

Protocol to the 1979 Convention on Long-Range Transboundary Air Pollution on Persistent Organic Pollutants, Aarhus, adopted 26 April 1998, entered into force 23 October 2003, *United Nations Treaty Series* (2004), vol. 2230, no. 21623, p. 79.

Regulation (EC) No 178/2002 of the European Parliament and of the Council of 28 January2002 laying down the general principles and requirements of food law, establishing the European Food Safety Authority and laying down procedures in matters of food safety, *Official Journal of the European Communities*, L 31/1, 1.2.2002, p. 1–24.

Rotterdam Convention on the Prior Consent Procedure for Certain Hazardous Chemicals and Pesticides in International Trade, Rotterdam, adopted 10 September 1998, entered into force 24 February 2004, *United Nations Treaty Series* (2005), vol. 2244, no. 39973, p. 337.

Stockholm Convention on Persistent Organic Pollutants, Stockholm, 22 May 2001, *United Nations Treaty Series* (2006), vol. 2256, no. 40214, p. 119.

United Nations Convention on the Law of the Sea, Montego Bay, adopted 10 December 1982, entered into force 16 November 1994, *United Nations Treaty Series* (1998), vol. 1833, no. 31363, p. 3.

United Nations Framework Convention on Climate Change, New York, adopted 9 May 1992, entered into force 31 March 1994, *United Nations Treaty Series* (2000), vol. 1771, no. 30822, p. 107.

Vienna Convention for the Protection of the Ozone Layer and Its Montreal Protocol, Vienna, adopted March 1985, entered into force 22 September 1988, *United Nations Treaty Series* (1997), vol. 1513, no. 26164, p. 293.

B. International cases and decisions

ICJ cases

Case Concerning Gabčikovo-Nagymaros Project (Hungary v. Slovakia), Judgment of 25 September 1997, ICJ Reports 1997, p. 7.

Case Concerning Military and Paramilitary Activities in and Against Nicaragua (Nicaragua v. United States of America), Merits, Judgment of 27 June 1986, ICJ Reports 1986, p. 14.

Case Concerning Pulp Mills on the River Uruguay (Argentina v. Uruguay), Judgment of 20 April 2010, ICJ Reports 2010, p. 14.

Certain Activities Carried Out by Nicaragua in the Border Area (Costa Rica v. Nicaragua) and Construction of a Road in Costa Rica along the San Juan River (Nicaragua v. Costa Rica), Judgment of 16 December 2015.

The Corfu Channel Case (United Kingdom v. Albania), Judgment of 9 April 1949, ICJ Reports 1949, p. 4.

Legality of the Threat or Use of Nuclear Weapons, Advisory Opinion of 8 July 1996, ICJ Reports 1996 (I).

North Sea Continental Shelf (Federal Republic of Germany v. Denmark; Federal Republic of Germany v. Netherlands), Judgment of 20 February 1969, ICJ Reports 1969, p. 3.

Whaling in the Antarctic (Australia v. Japan: New Zealand Intervening), Judgment of 31 March 2014, ICJ Reports 2014, p. 226.

Other sources of international decisions

Award in the Arbitration regarding the Iron Rhine ("Ijzeren Rijn") Railway (the Kingdom of Belgium v. the Kingdom of the Netherlands), Decision of 24 May 2005, Reports of International Arbitral Awards, volume XXVII, pp. 35–125.

In the Matter of the Indus Waters Kishenganga Arbitration (The Islamic Republic of Pakistan vs. The Republic of India), Partial Award, The Permanent Court of Arbitration, 18 February 2013.

Lac Lanoux (France/Spain), Reports of International Arbitral Tribunal Awards, 16 November 1957, volume XII, pp. 281–317.

The MOX Plant Case (Ireland/ United Kingdom), Request for provisional measures, International Tribunal for the Law of the Sea, Order of 3 December 2001.

Responsibilities and Obligations of States Sponsoring Persons and Entities With Respect to Activities in the Area, Seabed Disputes Chamber of the International Tribunal for the Law of the Sea, Advisory Opinion of 1 February 2011.

Southern Bluefin Tuna Case (Australia and New Zealand v. Japan), Request for provisional measures, International Tribunal for the Law of the Sea, Order of 27 August 1999.

Trail Smelter Case (United States v. Canada), 16 April 1938 and 11 March 1941, Report of International Arbitral Awards, volume III, pp. 1905–1982.

C. United Nations and other intergovernmental documents

ATCM XXVIII – CEP VIII Resolution 2, Guidelines for Environmental Impact Assessment in Antarctica, Stockholm, 2005, para. 1. Retrieved from www.ats.aq/devAS/info_measures_listitem.aspx?lang=e&id=347

BC Decision IX/10, Cooperation and Coordination Among the Basel, Rotterdam and Stockholm Conventions. Retrieved from http://basel.int/TheConvention/ConferenceoftheParties/ReportsandDecisions/tabid/3303/Defaul t.aspx

CBD Decision II/10, Conservation and Sustainable Use of Marine and Coastal Biological Diversity, 1995. Retrieved from www.cbd.int/decision/cop/default.shtml?id=7083

CBD Decision VI/3 on Marine and Coastal Biodiversity, 2002. Retrieved from www.cbd.int/decision/cop/default.shtml?id=7177

CBD Decision VI/7, Identification, Monitoring, Indicators and Assessments, UNEP/CBD/COP/6/20 (19 April 2002).

CBD Decision VII/5, Maine and Coastal Biodiversity, UNEP/CBD/COP/DEC/VII/5 (13 April 2004).

CBD Decision VIII/28 on Impact Assessment, UNEP/CBD/COP/DEC/VIII/28 (15 June 2006).

CBD Decision IX/1, In-Depth Review of the Programme of Work on Agricultural Biodiversity, UNEP/CBD/COP/DEC/IX/1 (9 October 2008).

CBD Decision IX/2, Agricultural Biodiversity: Biofuels and Biodiversity, UNEP/CBD/COP/DEC/IX/2 (9 October 2008).

CBD Decision IX/5, Forest Biodiversity, UNEP/CBD/COP/DEC/IX/5 (9 October 2008).

CBD Decision IX/16, Biodiversity and Climate Change, UNEP/CBD/COP/DEC/IX/16 (19–30 May 2008).

CBD Decision X/33, Biodiversity and Climate Change, UNEP/CBD/COP/DEC/X/33 (29 October 2010).

CBD Decision X/37, Biofuels and Biodiversity, UNEP/CBD/COP/DEC/X/37 (29 October 2010).

CBD. (2009). Scientific Synthesis of the Impact of Ocean Fertilization on Marine Biodiversity. Montreal, Technical Series No. 45. Retrieved from www.cbd.int/doc/publications/cbd-ts-45-en.pdf

CBD. (2012). Biofuels and Biodiversity, CBD Technical Series No. 65. Retrieved from www.cbd.int/doc/publications/cbd-ts-65-en.pdf

CBD. (2012). Geoengineering in Relation to the Convention on Biological Diversity: Technical and Regulatory Matters, Technical Series No. 66. Retrieved from www.cbd.int/doc/publications/cbd-ts-66-en.pdf

Commission of the European Communities, Communication from the Commission on Precautionary Principle, Brussels, 2000, COM (2000)1.

Declaration of the United Nations Conference on the Human Environment, *Report of the United Nations Conference on the Human Environment*, United Nations Publication, Sales No. E.73.II.A.l4.

Development and International Economic Co-Operation: Environment Report of the World Commission on Environment and Development Note by the Secretary-General, Annex: Our Common Future, UN Doc. A/42/427 (4 August 1987).

Directive 2009/31/EC of the European Parliament and of the Council, on the geological storage of carbon dioxide and amending Council Directive 85/337/EEC, European Parliament and Council Directives 2000/60/EC, 2001/80/EC, 2004/35/EC, 2006/12/EC, 2008/1/EC and Regulation (EC) No. 1013/2006, *Official Journal of the European Union*, I.140/114 (5 June 2009).

Draft Articles on Prevention of Transboundary Harm From Hazardous Activities, *Yearbook of the International Law Commission*, 2001, volume II, Part Two.

Draft Articles on the Law of the Non-Navigational Uses of International Watercourses, Report of the International Law Commission on the Work of Its Forty-Sixth session, *Yearbook of the International Law Commission*, 1994, volume II, Part Two.

Draft Principles on the Allocation of Loss in the Case of Transboundary Harm Arising Out of Hazardous Activities, Report of the International Law Commission on the Work of Its Fifty-Eighth Session, *Yearbook of the International Law Commission*, 2006, volume II, Part Two.

First Report on the Protection of the Atmosphere, by Shinya Murase, Special Rapporteur, International Law Commission Sixty-six Session, UN Doc. A/CN.4/667 (14 February 2014).

ILA New Delhi Declaration of Principles of International Law Relating to Sustainable Development, *Netherlands International Law Review*, 49(2), 211–216.

ILA The Helsinki Rules on the Uses of the Waters of International Rivers, Helsinki, adopted in August 1966, International Law Association Report of the Fifty-Second Conference.

IMO Resolution A.672(16). Guidelines and Standards for the Removal of Offshore Installations and Structures on the Continental Shelf and in the Exclusive Economic Zone, adopted 19 October 1989.

IMO. (2006). Guidelines on the Convention on the Prevention of Marine Pollution by Dumping of Waters and Other Matter, 1972. IMO Publication, Sales number 1531 E.

IMO. (2007). Statement of Concern Regarding Iron Fertilization of the Oceans to Sequester CO_2, IMO DOCS LC-LP.1/Circ.14 (13 July 2007).

IMO. (2008). Report of the Thirtieth Consultative Meeting and the Third Meeting of Contracting Parties, IMO DOCS LC 30/16 (28 August 2008).

IMO. (2008). Report of the Thirtieth Consultative Meeting and the Third Meeting of Contracting Parties, IMO DOCS LC 30/16 (9 December 2008).

IMO. (2013). Marine Geoengineering Including Ocean Fertilization to Be Regulated Under Amendments to International Treaty. Retrieved from www.imo.org/Media Centre/PressBriefings/Pages/45-marine-geoengieneering.aspx

IMO. (2016). IMO and the Environment. Retrieved from www.imo.org/en/Our Work/Environment/LCLP/Pages/default.aspx

IOC. (2008). Statement of the IOC Ad Hoc Consultative Group on Ocean Fertilization. Paris, 14 June 2008. Retrieved from www.climos.com/ext/ioc/IOC%20 Group%20Submission_June14.pdf

IPCC. (1995). Climate Change 1995: Impacts, Adaptations and Mitigation of Climate Change: Scientific-Technical Analyses, Contribution of Working Group II to the Second Assessment Report of the Intergovernmental Panel on Climate Change. Retrieved from www.ipcc.ch/pdf/climate-changes-1995/ipcc-2nd-assessment/2nd-assessment-en.pdf

IPCC. (2001). Climate Change 2001: Working Group III: Mitigation. Retrieved from www.grida.no/publications/other/ipcc_tar/?src=/climate/ipcc_tar/

IPCC. (2006). 2006 IPCC Guidelines for National Greenhouse Gas Inventories – Energy, volume 2, chapter 5. Retrieved from www.ipcc-nggip.iges.or.jp/public/2006gl/

IPCC. (2007). Climate Change 2007: Contribution of Working Group III to the Fourth Assessment Report of the Intergovernmental Panel on Climate Change, Metz, B., Davidson O. R., Bosch, P. R., Dave, R. and Meyer, L. A. (eds.), Cambridge, United Kingdom and New York, NY: Cambridge University Press.

IPCC. (2013). Climate Change 2013: The Physical Science Basis. Contribution of Working Group I to the Fifth Assessment Report of the Intergovernmental Panel on Climate Change, Stocker, T. F., Qin, D., Plattner, G.-K., Tignor, M., Allen, S. K., Boschung, J., Nauels, A., Xia, Y., Bex V., and Midgley P. M. (eds.), Cambridge, United Kingdom and New York, NY: Cambridge University Press.

IPCC. (2013). Summary for Policymakers. In: Climate Change 2013: The Physical Science Basis. Contribution of Working Group I to the Fifth Assessment Report of the Intergovernmental Panel on Climate Change, Stocker, T. F., Qin, D., Plattner, G.-K., Tignor, M., Allen, S. K., Boschung, J., Nauels, A., Xia, Y., Bex V., and Midgley, P. M. (eds.), Cambridge, United Kingdom and New York, NY: Cambridge University Press.

IPCC. (2014). 2013 Supplement to the 2006 IPCC Guidelines for National Greenhouse Gas Inventories: Wetlands. Switzerland: IPCC. Retrieved from www.ipcc-nggip.iges.or.jp/public/wetlands/

IPCC. (2014). Climate Change 2014: Mitigation of Climate Change. Contribution of Working Group III to the Fifth Assessment Report of the Intergovernmental Panel on Climate Change, Edenhofer, O., Pichs-Madruga, R., Sokona, Y., Farahani, E., et al. (eds.), Cambridge, United Kingdom and New York, NY: Cambridge University Press.

Ministerial Declaration of the Second International Conference on the Protection of the North Sea, London, 24–25 November 1987.

Ministerial Declaration of the Third International Conference on the Protection of the North Sea, The Hague, 8 March 1990.

OSPAR Decision 2007/1 to Prohibit the Storage of Carbon Dioxide Streams in the Water Column or on the Sea-Bed. Retrieved from www.ospar.org/convention/agreements

OSPAR Decision 2007/2 on the Storage of Carbon Dioxide Streams in Geological Formations. Retrieved from www.ospar.org/convention/agreements

Resolution LC-LP.1 (2008) on the Regulation of Ocean Fertilization, 31 October 2008. Retrieved from www.imo.org/en/OurWork/Environment/LCLP/EmergingIssues/geoengineering/Pages/def

Resolution LC-LP.2 (2010) on the Assessment Framework for Scientific Research Involving Ocean Fertilization, 14 October 2010. Retrieved from www.imo.org/en/OurWork/Environment/LCLP/EmergingIssues/geoengineering/Documents/OFassessmentResolution.pdf

Resolution LP.3(4) on the Amendment to Article 6 of the London Protocol, adopted 30 October 2009, IMO DOCS LC-LP.1/Circ.36 (17 June 2010).

Resolution LP.4(8) on the Amendment to the London Protocol to Regulate the Placement of Matter for Ocean Fertilization and other Maine Geoengineering Activities, IMO Report of the Thirty-Fifth Consultative Meeting and the Eighth Meeting of Contracting Parties, IMO DOCS LC 35/15 (21 October 2013).

Second Report on International Liability for Injurious Consequences Arising Out of Acts Not Prohibited by International Law (Prevention of Transboundary Damage

From Hazardous Activities) by Pemmaraju Screenivasa Rao, Special Rapporteur, International Law Commission Fifty-First Session, UN Doc. A/CN.4/501 (5 May 1999).

Second Report on the Protection of the Atmosphere, by Shinya Murase, Special Rapporteur, International Law Commission Sixty-Seven Session, UN Doc. A/CN.4/681(2 March 2015).

UNCED, Agenda 21, Rio de Janerio, Brazil, 3 to 14 June 1992. Retrieved from https://sustainabledevelopment.un.org/content/documents/Agenda21.pdf

UNCED, Rio Declaration on Environment and Development, Report of the United Nations Conference on Environment and Development, UN Doc. A/CONF.151/26 (Vol. I) (12 August 1992).

UNDP. (2010). Handbook for Conducting Technology Needs Assessment for Climate Change. Retrieved from http://unfccc.int/ttclear/misc_/StaticFiles/gnwoerk_static/TNA_HAB_infobox_1/3a34f12bf10d4b7bae791d0d7ad572eb/c29096556b034760b94273b0124039ac.pdf

UNECE, Ministerial Declaration on Sustainable Development in the ECE Region, Bergen, May 1990.

UNEP, The Emissions Gap Report 2015. Retrieved from http://uneplive.unep.org/media/docs/theme/13/EGR_2015_301115_lores.pdf

UNEP, The Emissions Gap Report 2016. Retrieved from http://web.unep.org/emissionsgap/

UNFCCC Decision1/CP.13, Bali Action Plan, UN Doc. FCCC/CP/2007/6/Add.1 (14 March 2008).

UNFCCC Decision 1/CP.16, The Cancun Agreements: Outcome of the work of the Ad Hoc Working Group on Long-term Cooperative Action Under the Convention, Report of the Conference of the Parties on Its Sixteenth Session, Held in Cancun From 29 November to 10 December 2010. UN Doc.FCCC/CP/2010/7/Add.1.

UNFCCC Decision 1/CP 21, Adoption of the Paris Agreement, FCCC/CP/2015/10/Add.1.

UNFCCC Decision 1/CP 21, Adoption of the Paris Agreement, UN Doc. FCCC/CP/2015/10/Add.1 (29 January 2016).

UNFCCC Decision 4/CP.7, Development and transfer of technologies, Annex: Framework for Meaningful and Effective Actions to Enhance the Implementation of Article 4, paragraph 5, of the Convention, UN. Doc FCCC/CP/2001/13/Add.1 (21 January 2012).

UNEP/GC Decision 6/14, Principles of Conduct for the Guidance of States in the Conservation and Harmonious Exploitation of Natural Resources Shared by Two or More States, 19 May 1978. *UNEP Environmental Law Guidelines and Principles series, no. 2.*

UNFCCC Decision7/CMP.6, Carbon Dioxide Capture and Storage in Geological Formations as Clean Development Mechanism Project Activities, UN Doc. FCCC/KP/CMP/2010/12/Add.2 (15 March 2011).

UNFCCC Decision 7/CP.2, Development and Transfer of Technologies, UN Doc. FCCC/CP/1996/15/Add.1 (29 October 1996).

UNEP/GC Decision 8/7/A, 1980 Provisions for Co-operation between States in Weather Modification, 29 April 1980. *UNEP Environmental Law Guidelines and Principles series, no. 3.*

UNFCCC Decision 10/CMP.7, Modalities and Procedures for Carbon Dioxide Capture and Storage in Geological Formations as Clean Development Mechanism Project Activities, UN Doc. FCCC/KP/CMP/2011/10/Add.2 (15 March 2012).

UNFCCC Decision 11/CP.21, Forum and Work Programme on the Impact of the Implementation of UNFCCC Decision 2/CP 15, Copenhagen Accord, UN Doc. FCCC/CP/2009/11/Add.1 (30 March 2010).

UNEP/GC Decision 13/18/II. 1985 Montreal Guidelines for the Protection of the Marine Environment Against Pollution From Land-Based Sources, 24 May 1985. *UNEP Environmental Law Guidelines and Principles series, no. 7.*

UNEP/GC Decision 14/25, Goals and Principles of Environmental Impact Assessment, 17 June 1987.

UNFCCC, Research and System Systematic Observation, Draft Conclusions Proposed by the Chair, UN Doc. FCCC/SBSTA/2015/L.4 (9 June 2015).

UNFCCC, Synthesis Report on the Aggregate Effect of the Intended Nationally Determined Contributions, UN Doc. FCCC/CP/2015/7 (27 October 2015).

UNFCCC, Transboundary Carbon Capture and Storage Project Activities. Technical paper, UN Doc.FCCC/TP/2012/9 (1 November 2012).

UNGA Resolution 2997 (XVII). Institutional and Financial Arrangements for International Environmental Cooperation, A/RES/27/2997 (15 December 1972).

UNGA Resolution 58/240, Oceans and the Law of the Sea, UN Doc. A/RES/58/240 (5 March 2004).

UNGA Resolution 59/24, Oceans and the Law of the Sea, UN Doc. A/RES/59/24 (4 February 2005).

UNGA Resolution 66/288, The Future We Want, UN Doc. A/RES/66/288 (11 September 2012).

UNGA Resolution 68/70, Oceans and the Law of the Sea, UN Doc. UN Doc. A/RES/69/245 (24 February 2015).

UNGA Resolution 70/1, Transforming Our World: The 2030 Agenda for Sustainable Development, UN Doc. A/RES/70/1(21 October 2015).

UNGA, Letter dated 13 February 2015 From the Co-Chair of the Ad Hoc Open-Ended Informal Working Group to the President of the General Assembly, UN Doc. A/69/780 (13 February 2015).

United Nations Agreement for the Implementation of the Provisions of the United Nations Convention on the Law of the Sea of 10 December 1982 Relating to the Conservation and Management of Straddling Fish Stocks and Highly Migratory Fish Stocks, entered into force 11 December 2011.

United Nations Division for Ocean Affair and the Law of the Sea Office of Legal Affairs. (2010). *A Revised Guide to the Implementation of the Relevant Provisions of the United Nations Convention on the Law of the Sea.* New York: United Nations Publication, Sales No. E.10.V.12.

WMO. (2015). WMO Greenhouse Gas Bulletin: The State of Greenhouse Gases in the Atmosphere Based on Global Observations Through 2014. (No. 11). Retrieved from http://scifun.chem.wisc.edu/news/ghg-bulletin_2015.pdf?id=8495

D. Books and chapters

Bastmeijer, C. J., Bastmeijer, K., & Koivurova, T. (2008). *Theory and practice of transboundary environmental impact assessment* (Vol. 1). Leiden: Martinus Nijhoff Publishers.

Birnie, P., Boyle, A., & Redgwell, C. (2009). *International law & the environment* (3rd ed.). Oxford: Oxford University Press.

Bodansky, D., Brunnée, J., & Hey, E. (Eds.). (2008). *The Oxford handbook of international environmental law* (1st ed.). Oxford: Oxford University Press.

Brunnée, J. (2007). International law and collective concerns: Reflections on the responsibility to protect. In Ndiaye, T. M. & Wolfrum, R. (Eds.), *Law of the sea, environmental law and settlement of disputes: Liber Amicorum Judge Thomas A. Mensah* (pp. 35–52). Leiden: Martinus Nijhoff Publishers.

Burns, W. C., & Strauss, A. L. (Eds.). (2013). *Climate change geoengineering: Philosophical perspectives, legal issues, and governance frameworks.* New York: Cambridge University Press.

Cameron, J., & Wade-Gery, W. (1995). Addressing uncertainty. Law, policy and the development of the precautionary principle. In Dente, B. (Ed). *Environmental Policy in Search of New Instruments* (pp. 95–142). Dordrecht: Springer.

De Chazournes, L. B. (2007). Precaution in international law: Reflection on its composite nature. In Ndiaye, T. M. & Wolfrum, R. (Eds.), *Law of the sea, environmental law and settlement of disputes: Liber Amicorum Judge Thomas A. Mensah* (pp. 21–34). Leiden: Martinus Nijhoff Publishers.

Dunoff, J. L., & Pollack, M. A. (Eds.). (2013). *Interdisciplinary perspectives on international law and international relations: The state of the art* (1st ed.). New York: Cambridge University Press.

Freestone, D., & Hey, E. (Eds.). (1996). *The precautionary principle and international law: The challenge of implementation.* The Hague: Kluwer Law International.

Garrison, T. S. (2005). *Oceanography: An invitation to marine science* (8th ed.). Cole Belmont: Thompson Brooks.

Giddens, A. (2009). *The politics of climate change* (1st ed.). Cambridge, UK: Polity Press.

Goodell, J. (2010). *How to cool the planet: Geoengineering and the audacious quest to fix earth's climate* (1st ed.). New York: Houghton Mifflin Harcourt Publishing Company.

Graham, J. D., & Wiener, J. B. (Eds.). (1995). *Risk versus risk: Tradeoffs in protection health and the environment* (1st ed.). Cambridge, MA: Harvard University Press.

Hamilton, C. (2013). *Earthmasters: The dawn of the age of climate engineering.* New Haven, CT: Yale University Press.

Kiss, A., & Shelton, D. (1997). *Manual of European environmental law* (2nd ed.). Cambridge: Cambridge University Press.

Lefeber, R. (1996). *Transboundary environmental interference and the origin of state liability* (1st ed.). The Hague: Kluwer Law International.

Lehmann, J., & Joseph, S. (2009). Biochar for environmental management: An introduction. In Lehmann, J. & Joseph, S. (Eds.), *Biochar for environmental management: Science and technology and implementation* (2nd ed., pp. 1–13). London: Earthscan Publishers Ltd.

Mandaraka-Sheppard, A. (2013). *Modern maritime law (vol. 1): Jurisdiction and risks.* Boca Raton, FL: CRC Press.

Marchant, G. E., & Mossman, K. L. (2005). *Arbitrary and capricious: The precautionary principle in the European Union Courts* (1st ed.). Washington, DC: The AEI Press.

Metz, B., Davidson, O., De Coninck, H. C., Loos, M., & Meyer, L. A. (2005). IPCC special report on carbon dioxide capture and storage. Prepared by Working Group III of the Intergovernmental Panel on Climate Change. IPCC, Cambridge, United Kingdom and New York, NY: Cambridge University Press.

Morrow, D. R., Kopp, R. E., & Oppenheimer, M. (2013). Political legitimacy in decisions about experiments in solar radiation management. In Burns W. C., & Strauss A. L., (Eds.), *Climate change geoengineering: Philosophical perspectives, legal issues, and governance frameworks* (1st ed.). Cambridge, United Kingdom and New York, NY: Cambridge University Press.

Park, P. (2013). *International law for energy and the environment* (2nd ed.). Boca Raton, FL: CRC Press.

Rajamani, L. (2006). *Differential treatment in international environmental law* (Vol. 175). Oxford: Oxford University Press.

Rayfuse, R. (2017). Precaution and climate change: What role for the precautionary principle in addressing global warming? In Hebeler, T., Hofmann, E., Proelss, A., & Reiff, P. (Eds.). (2017). *Protecting the environment for future generations – principles and actors in international environmental law* (1st ed.). Berlin: Erich Schmidt Verlag.

Redgwell, C. (2008). International legal responses to the challenges of a lower-carbon future: Climate change, carbon capture and storage, and biofuels. In Zillman, D., Redgwell, C., Omorogbe, Y., & Barrera-Hernandez, L. K. (Eds.), *Beyond the carbon economy: Energy law in transition* (1st ed., pp. 85–108). Oxford: Oxford University Press.

Renn, O. (2008). *Risk governance: Coping with uncertainty in a complex world*. London: Earthscan Publishers Ltd.

Ryngaert, C. (2015). *Jurisdiction in international law*. Oxford: Oxford University Press.

Sands, P., Peel, J., & MacKenzie, R. (2012). *Principles of international environmental law* (3rd ed.). Cambridge: Cambridge University Press.

Schomberg, R. von. (2006). The precautionary principle and its normative challenges. In Fisher, E., Jones, J. & Schomberg, R. von. (Eds.), *In implementing the precautionary principle: Perspectives and prospects*. Cheltenham, UK and Northampton, MA: Edward Elgar.

Scott, K. N. (2012). Transboundary environmental governance and emerging environmental threats: Geo-engineering in the marine environment. In Warner, R. & Marsden, S. (Eds.) *Transboundary environmental governance: Inland, Coastal and Marine perspectives*. London: Ashgate Publishing, Ltd.

Self, S., Zhao, J., Holasek, R. E., Torres, R. C., & King, A. J. (1996). The atmospheric impact of the 1991 Mount Pinatubo eruption. In Newhall, C. G. & Punongbayan, R. S. (Eds.), *Fire and mud: Eruptions and Lahars of Mount Pinatubo, Philippines*. Seattle and London: University of Washington Press.

Shepherd, J. G., et al. (2009). *Geoengineering the climate: Science, governance and uncertainty*. London, GB: Royal Society.

Soons, A. A. H. (1982). *Marine scientific research and the law of the sea* (1st ed.). The Hague: Kluwer Law and Taxation Publishers.

Stocker, T. F., Qin, D., Plattner, G.-K., Tignor, M., Allen, S. K., Boschung, J., Nauels, A., Xia, Y., Bex, V., & Midgley, P. M. (Ed.). (2013). *Summary for policymakers. In: Climate change 2013: The physical science basis. contribution of working group I to the fifth assessment report of the intergovernmental panel on climate change*. Cambridge, United Kingdom and New York, NY: Cambridge University Press.

Sunstein, C. R. (2005). *Laws of fear: Beyond the precautionary principle* (1st ed.). New York: Cambridge University Press.

Sunstein, C. R. (2009). *Worst-case scenarios* (1st ed.). Cambridge, MA: Harvard University Press.

Tanaka, Y. (2012). *The international law of the sea* (1st ed.). New York: Cambridge University Press.

Trouwborst, A. (2002). *Evolution and status of the precautionary principle in international law*. The Hague: Kluwer Law International.

Wiener, J. B. (2008). Precaution. In Bodansky, D., Brunnée, J., & Hey E. (Eds.), *The Oxford handbook of international law* (pp. 597–612). Oxford: Oxford University Press.

Xue, H. (2003). *Transboundary damage in international law*. Cambridge: Cambridge University Press.

E. Journal articles

Abate, R. S. (2011). A tale of two carbon sinks: Can forest carbon management serve as a framework to implement ocean iron fertilization as a climate change treaty compliance mechanism? *Seattle Journal of Environmental Law, 1*(1), 1–18.

Abate, R. S., & Greenlee, A. B. (2009–2010). Sowing seeds uncertain: Ocean iron fertilization, climate change, and the international environmental law framework. *Pace International Law Review, 27*, 555–598.

Abbott, K. W., & Snidal, D. (2000). Hard and soft law in international governance. *International Organization, 54*(3), 421–456.

Albrecht, B. A. (1989). Aerosols, cloud microphysics, and fractional cloudiness. *Science (New York, N.Y.), 245*(4923), 1227–1230.

Ambrus, M. (2012). The precautionary principle and a fair allocation of the burden of proof in international environmental law. *Review of European Community & International Environmental Law, 21*(3), 259–270.

Azar, C., et al. (2006). Carbon capture and storage from fossil fuels and biomass – costs and potential role in stabilizing the atmosphere. *Climate Change, 74*, 47–79.

Baker, T. (1996). On the genealogy of moral hazard. *Texas Law Review, 75*(2), 237–292.

Barrett, S. (2008). The incredible economics of geoengineering. *Environmental Resource Economy, 39*, 45–54.

Bilder, R. B. (1970). The Canadian arctic waters pollution prevention act: New stresses on the law of the sea. *Michigan Law Review 69*(1), 1–54.

Bilder, R. B. (1981). The role of unilateral action in preventing international environmental injury. *Vanderbilt Journal of Transnational Law, 14*(1), 51–95.

Bodansky, D. (1995). Customary (and not so customary) international environmental law. *Indiana Journal of Global Legal Studies, 3*, 105–119.

Bodansky, D. (1996). May we engineer the climate? *Climate Change, 33*, 309–321.

Bodansky, D. (2000). What's so bad about unilateral action to protect the environment? *European Journal of International Law, 11*(2), 339–348.

Bodansky, D. (2013). The who, what, and wherefore of geoengineering governance. *Climatic Change, 121*(3), 539–551.

Bodle, R. (2010–2011). Geoengineering and international law: The search for common legal ground. *Tulsa Law Review, 46*(2), 305–322.

Bork, K., Karstensen, J., Visbeck, M., & Zimmermann, A. (2008). The legal regulation of floats and Gliders – in quest of a new regime? *Ocean Development & International Law, 39*(3), 298–328.

Boyd, P. W., et al. (2008). Introduction and synthesis, theme section implications of large-scale iron fertilization of the oceans. *Marine Ecology Progress Series, 364*, 213–218.

Boyd, P. W., Watson, A. J., Law, C. S., Abraham, E. R., Trull, T., Murdoch, R., . . . Chang, H. (2000). A mesoscale phytoplankton bloom in the polar Southern Ocean stimulated by iron fertilization. *Nature, 407*(6805), 695–702.

Boyle, A. E. (1999). Some reflections on the relationship of treaties and soft law. *International and Comparative Law Quarterly*, *48*(4), 901–913.

Brasseur, G. P., & Granier, C. (2013). Mitigation, adaptation or climate geoengineering. *Theoretical Inquiries in Law*, *14*, 1–20.

Brown, D. (1998). Environmental risk assessment and management of chemicals. *Issues in Environmental Science and Technology*, *9*, 91–112.

Brown Weiss, E. (2007). Climate change, intergenerational equity, and international law. *Vermont Journal of Environmental Law*, *9*, 615–627.

Burton, I., et al. (2002). From impacts assessment to adaptation priorities: The shaping of adaptation policy. *Climate Policy*, *2*, 145–159.

Caldeira, K., & Keith, D. W. (2010). The need for climate engineering research. *Issues in Science and Technology*, *27*(1), 57–62.

Cameron, J., & Abouchar, J. (1991). The precautionary principle: A fundamental principle of law and policy for the protection of the global environment. *Boston College International and Comparative Law Review*, *14*(1), 1.

Canadell, J. G., & Raupach, M. R. (2008). Managing forests for climate change mitigation. *Science*, *320*, 1456–1457.

Canadell, J. G., et al. (2007). Contributions to accelerating atmospheric CO_2 growth from economic activity, carbon intensity, and efficiency of natural sinks. *Proceedings of the National Academy of Sciences*, *104*, 18866–18870.

Carlin, A. (2007). Implementation & utilization of geoengineering for global climate change control. *Sustainable Development Law & Policy*, *7*(2), 22.

Cicerone, R. J. (2006). Geoengineering: Encouraging research and overseeing implementation. *Climate Change*, *77*, 221–226.

Collins, J. (2012). Assessing international cooperation on climate change: A neoliberal analysis of the effectiveness of formal international environmental institutions. *Mapping Politics*, *4*.

Corner, A., & Pidgeon, N. (2010). Geoengineering the climate: The social and ethical implications. *Environment: Science and Policy for Sustainable Development*, *52*(1), 24–37.

Craik, N. (2015). International EIA law and geoengineering: Do emerging technologies require special rules? *Climate Law*, *5*(2–4), 111–141.

Crutzen, P. (2006). Albedo enhancement by stratospheric sulfur injections: A contribution to resolve a policy dilemma? *Climate Change*, *77*, 211–219.

Damen, K., Faaij, A., & Turkenburg, W. (2006). Health, safety and environmental risks of underground CO_2 storage – overview of mechanisms and current knowledge. *Climatic Change*, *74*(1–3), 289–318.

Davies, G. (2009). Law and policy issues of unilateral geoengineering: Moving to a managed world. *Available at SSRN 1334625*.

Davies, G. (2010). Framing the social, political, and environmental risks and benefits of geoengineering: Balancing the hard-to-imagine against the hard-to-measure. *Tulsa Law Review*, *46*(2), 261–282.

Davis, W. D. (2009). What does "green" mean: Anthropogenic climate change, geoengineering, and international environmental law. *Georgia Law Review*, *43*, 901–951.

Dean, J. (2009). Iron fertilization: A scientific review with international policy recommendations. *Environs Environmental Law and Policy Journal*, *32*(2), 321–344.

De Baar, H. J. W., et al. (2005). Synthesis of iron fertilization experiments: From the iron age in the age of enlightenment. *Journal of Geophysical Research*, 110, 1–24.

Downie, A., et al. (2012). Biochar as a geoengineering climate solution: Hazard identification and risk management. *Critical Reviews in Environmental Science and Technology, 42*(3), 225–250.

Dupuy, P. (2000). The place and role of unilateralism in contemporary international law. *European Journal of International Law, 11*(1), 19–29.

Eckersley, R. (2012). Moving forward in the climate negotiations: Multilateralism or minilateralism? *Global Environmental Politics, 12*(2), 24–42.

Eick, M. (2010). A navigational system for uncharted waters: The London Convention and London Protocol's assessment framework on ocean iron fertilization. *Tulsa Law Review, 46*(2), 351–378.

Ellman, L. M., & Sunstein, C. R. (2004). Hormesis, the precautionary principle, and legal regulation. *Human & experimental toxicology, 23*(12), 601–611.

Farber, D. A. (2010–2011). Uncertainty. *Georgetown Law Journal, 99,* 901–960.

Fleming, J. R. (2007). The climate engineers. *The Wilson Quarterly (1976), 31*(2), 46–60.

Franklin, B. (1784). Meteorological imaginations and conjectures. *Manchester Literary and Philosophical Society Memoirs and Proceedings, 2*(122), 1784.

Freestone, D., & Rayfuse, R. (2008). Ocean iron fertilization and international law. *Marine Ecology Progress Series, 364,* 227–233.

Gardiner, S. M. (2013). The desperation argument for geoengineering. *Political Science & Politics, 46*(1), 28–33.

Genzky, H. (2010). Ocean fertilization as climate change mitigation measure – consideration under international law. *Journal for European Environmental and Planning Law, 7*(1), 57–78.

Gerrard, S., & Petts, J. (1998). Isolation or integration? The relationship between risk assessment and risk management. *Issues in Environmental Science and Technology, 9,* 1–20.

Ginzky, H., & Frost, R. (2014). Marine geo-engineering: Legally binding regulation under the London protocol. *Carbon & Climate Law Review, 8*(2), 82–96.

Gomes, M. S. d. P., & de Araújo, M. S. M. (2011). Artificial cooling of the atmosphere – a discussion on the environmental effects. *Renewable and Sustainable Energy Reviews, 15*(1), 780–786.

Graham, J. D., & Wiener, J. B. (2008). The precautionary principle and risk – risk tradeoffs: A comment. *Journal of Risk Research, 11*(4), 465–474.

Gundling, L. (1990). The status in international law of the principle of precautionary action. *International Journal of Estuarine & Coastal Law, 5,* 23.

Güssow, K., et al. (2010). Ocean iron fertilization: Why further research is needed. *Marine Policy, 34,* 911–918.

Hale, B., & Dilling, L. (2011). Geoengineering, ocean fertilization, and the problem of permissible pollution. *Science, Technology & Human Values, 36*(2), 190–212.

Hale, T. (2011). A climate coalition of the willing. *The Washington Quarterly, 34*(1), 89–101.

Hansen, J., Lacis, A., Ruedy, R., & Sato, M. (1992). Potential climate impact of Mount Pinatubo eruption. *Geophysical Research Letters, 19*(2), 215–218.

Hansen, S. F., Krauss, M. K. von, & Tickner, J. A. (2008). The precautionary principle and risk-risk tradeoffs. *Journal of Risk Research, 11*(4), 423–464.

Hartmann, J. (2015). Unilateralism in international law: Implications of the inclusion of emissions from aviation in the EU ETS. *Questions of International Law, Zoom In, 11,* 19–32.

Hartzell-Nichols, L. (2012). Precaution and solar radiation management. *Ethics, Policy & Environment, 15*(2), 158–171.

Harvard Law Review Association, Harvard Law Review & United States of America. (1991). Developments in the law: International environmental law. *Harvard Law Review, 104*(7), 1484–1639.

Herzog, H., Caldeira, K., & Reilly, J. (2003). An issue of permanence: Assessing the effectiveness of temporary carbon storage. *Climatic Change, 59*, 293–310.

Heyward, C. (2013). Situating and abandoning geoengineering: A typology of five responses to dangerous climate change. *PS: Political Science & Politics, 46*(1), 23–27.

Honegger, M., Sugathapala, K., & Michaelowa, A. (2013). Tackling climate change: Where can the generic framework be located. *Carbon & Climate Law Review, 7*(2), 125–135.

Hudson, H. (1991). A space parasol as a countermeasure against the greenhouse effect. *Journal of the British Interplanetary Society, 44*, 139.

Jiao, N., Herndl, G. J., et al. (2010). Microbial production of recalcitrant dissolved organic matter: Long-term carbon storage in the global ocean. *Nature Reviews, 8*, 593–599.

Kahler, M. (1992). Multilateralism with small and large numbers. *International Organization, 46*(3), 681–708.

Kazhdan, D. (2011). Precautionary pulp: Pulp mills and the evolving dispute between international tribunals over the reach of the precautionary principle. *Ecology Law Quarterly, 38*, 527.

Keith, D. W. (2000). Geoengineering the climate: History and prospect. *Annual Review of Energy and the Environment, 25*(1), 245–284.

Keith, D. W., Parson, E., & Morgan, M. G. (2010). Research on global sun block needed now. *Nature, 463*(7280), 426–427.

Kelso, A. (2006). Reforming the House of Lords: Navigating representation, democracy and legitimacy at Westminster. *Parliamentary Affairs, 59*(4), 563–581.

Knox, J. H. (2002). The myth and reality of transboundary environmental impact assessment. *American Journal of International Law, 96*(2), 291–319.

Kuokkanen, T., & Yamineva, Y. (2013). Regulating geoengineering in international environmental law. *Carbon and Climate Law Review, 7*(3), 161–167.

Latham, J. (1990). Control of global warming? *Nature, 347*, 339–340.

Law, C. S. (2008). Predicting and monitoring the effects of large-scale ocean iron fertilization on marine trace gas emission. *Marine Ecology Progress Series, 364*, 283–288.

Leal-Arcas, R., & Filis-Yelaghotis, A. (2012). Geoengineering a future for humankind: Some technical and ethical considerations. *Carbon and Climate Law Review, 6*(2), 128–148.

Leinen, M. (2008). Building relationships between scientists and business in ocean iron. *Marine Ecology Progress Series, 364*, 251–256.

Lin, A. (2013). Does geoengineering present a moral hazard? *Ecology Law Quarterly, 40*, 673–712.

Lin, A. (2009). Geoengineering governance. *Issues in Legal Scholarship, 8*(3), Article 2.

Long, J., & Winickoff, D. (2010). Governing geoengineering research: Principles and process. *Governing, 1*(5), 60–62.

Mandel, G. N., & Gathii, J. T. (2006). Cost-benefit analysis versus the precautionary principle: Beyond class Sunstein's laws of fear. *University of Illinois Law Review, 2006*, 1037–1079.

Marchetti, C. (1977). On the geoengineering and the CO_2 problem. *Climate Change, 1*, 59–68.

Markus, T., & Ginzky, H. (2011). Regulating climate engineering: Paradigmatic aspects of the regulation of ocean fertilization. *Carbon and Climate Law Review, 5*(4), 477–490.

Martin, J. H. (1990). Glacial-interglacial CO_2 change: The iron hypothesis. *Paleoceanography, 5*(1), 1–13.

Martin, J. H., & Fitzwater, S. E. (1988). Iron deficiency limits phytoplankton growth in the north-east pacific subarctic. *Nature, 331*, 341–343.

Martin, J. H., Gordon, R. M., & Fitzswater, S. E. (1991). Iron limitation? *Limnology and Oceanography, 36*(8), 1793–1802.

Matthee, M., & Vermersch, D. (2000). Are the precautionary principle and the international trade of genetically modified organisms reconcilable? *Journal of Agricultural and Environmental Ethics, 12*(1), 59–70.

Matthews, H. D., & Caldeira, K. (2007). Transient climate-carbon simulations of planetary geoengineering. *Proceedings of the National Academy of Science of the United States of America, 104*, 9949–9954.

McGee, J. (2011). Exclusive minilateralism: An emerging discourse within international climate change governance? *PORTAL Journal of Multidisciplinary International Studies, 8*(3), 1–9.

McInnes, C. R. (2002). Minimum mass solar shield for terrestrial climate control. *Journal of the British Interplanetary Society, 55*, 307–311.

McQuaid, J., & Le Guen, J. (1998). The use of risk assessment in government. *Issues in Environmental Science and Technology, 9*, 21–36.

Michaelson, J. (2010). Geoengineering and climate management: From marginality to inevitability. *Tulsa Law Review, 46*, 221–260.

Naím, M. (2009). Minilateralism. *Foreign Policy, 173*, 136.

Nash, J. R. (2008). Standing and the precautionary principle. *Columbia Law Review, 108*, 494–527.

Nordhaus, W. (2015). Climate clubs: Overcoming free-riding in international climate policy. *American Economic Review, 105*(4), 1339–1370.

Olson, R. L. (2012). Soft geoengineering: A gentler approach to addressing climate change. *Environment: Science and Policy for Sustainable Development, 54*(5), 29–39.

Parson, E., & Ernst, L. (2013). International governance of climate engineering. *Theoretical Inquiries in Law, 14*, 307–336.

Parson, E. A. (2006). Reflections on air capture: The political economy of active intervention in the global environment. *Climate Change, 74*, 5–15.

Pearson, J., Oldson, J., & Levin, E. (2006). Earth rings for planetary environment control. *Acta Astronautica, 58*(1), 44–57.

Pimentel, D., Lal, R., & Singmaster, J. (2010). Carbon capture by biomass and soil are sound: CO_2 burial wastes energy. *Environment, Development and Sustainability, 12*(4), 447–448.

Pongratz, J., Lobell, D. B., Cao, L., & Caldeira, K. (2012). Crop yields in a geoengineered climate. *Nature Climate Change, 2*(2), 101–105.

Powell, H. (2008). Fertilizing the ocean with iron. *Oceanus Magazine, 46*(1), 4–9.

Powell, H. (2008). What are the possible side effects? The uncertainties and unintended consequences of manipulating ecosystems. *Oceanus Magazine, 46*(1), 14–17.

Preston, C. J. (2013). Ethics and geoengineering: Reviewing the moral issues raised by solar radiation management and carbon dioxide removal. *WIREs Climate Change, 4*, 23–37.

Proelss, A., & Hong, C. (2012). Ocean upwelling and international law. *Ocean Development & International Law, 43*(4), 371–385.

Raine, A. (2008). Transboundary transportation of CO_2 associated with carbon capture and storage – an analysis of issues under international law. *Carbon and Climate Law Review, 4*, 353–365.

Rasch, P. J., Latham, J., & Chen, C. J. (2009). Geoengineering by cloud seeding: Influence on sea ice and climate system. *Environmental Research Letters, 4*(4), 045112.

Rayfuse, R., Lawrence, M. G., & Gjerde, K. M. (2008). Ocean fertilization and climate change: The need to regulate emerging high seas uses. *The International Journal of Marine and Coastal Law, 23*, 297–326.

Read, P., & Lermit, J. (2005). Bio-energy with carbon storage (BECS): A sequential decision approach to the threat of abrupt climate change. *Energy, 30*, 2654–2671.

Reynolds, J. (2011). The regulation of climate engineering. *Law, Innovation and Technology, 3*(1), 113–136.

Reynolds, J. (2014). Climate engineering field research: The favorable setting of international environmental law. *Washington and Lee Journal of Energy, Climate, and the Environment, 5*(2), 417–486.

Rhodes, J., & Keith, D. W. (2007). Biomass with capture: Negative emissions within social and environmental constraints: An editorial comment. *Climate Change, 87*(3–4), 321–328. doi: 10.1007/s10584-007-9387-4.

Richards, R. K. (2011). Deepwater mobile oil rigs in the exclusive economic zone and the uncertainty of coastal state jurisdiction. *Journal of International Business & Law, 10*, 387.

Sandin, P. (1999). Dimensions of the precautionary principle. *Human and Ecological Risk Assessment: An International Journal, 5*(5), 889–907.

Saxler, B., Siegfried, J., & Proelss, A. (2015). International liability for transboundary damage arising from stratospheric aerosol injections. *Law, Innovation and Technology, 7*(1), 112–147.

Schuiling, R. D., & Krijgsman, P. (2006). Enhanced weathering: An effective and cheap tool to sequester CO_2. *Climatic Change, 74*(1–3), 349–354.

Scott, K. N. (2005–2006). The day after tomorrow: CO_2 sequestration and the future of climate change. *The Georgetown International Environmental Law Review, 18*, 57–108.

Scott, K. N. (2012–2013). International law in the anthropocene: Responding to the geoengineering challenge. *Michigan Journal of International Law, 34*, 309–358.

Scott, K. N. (2013). Regulating ocean fertilization under international law: The risks. *Carbon and Climate Law Review, 7*(2), 108–116.

Sillmann, J., Lenton, T. M., Levermann, A., Ott, K., Hulme, M., Benduhn, F., & Horton, J. B. (2015). Climate emergencies do not justify engineering the climate. *Nature Climate Change, 5*(4), 290–292.

Slaughter, A., Tulumello, A. S., & Wood, S. (1998). International law and international relations theory: A new generation of interdisciplinary scholarship. *American Journal of International Law, 92*(3), 367–397.

Stewart, R. B. (2002). Environmental regulatory decision making under uncertainty. *Research in Law and Economics, 20*, 71–126.

Strand, S., & Benford, G. (2009). Ocean sequestration of crop residue carbon: Recycling fossil fuel carbon back to deep sediments. *Environmental Science and Technology, 43*, 1000–1007.

Stward, R. B., & Wiener, J. B. (1992). The comprehensive approach to global climate policy: Issues of design and practicality. *Arizona Journal of International & Comparative Law, 9*, 83.

Sunstein, C. R. (2003). Beyond the precautionary principle. *University of Pennsylvania Law Review, 151*(3), 1003–1058.

Tanimura, E. (2013). Geoengineering research governance: Foundation, form, and forum. *Environs: Environmental Law & Policy Journal, 37*, 167.

Tedsen, E., & Homann, G. (2013). Implementing the precautionary principle for climate engineering. *Carbon & Climate Law Review, 7*(2), 90.

Trouwborst, A. (2007). The precautionary principle in general international law: Combating the Babylonian confusion. *Review of European Community & International Environmental Law, 16*(2), 185–195.

Victor, D. G. (2006). Toward effective international cooperation on climate change: Numbers, interests and institutions. *Global Environmental Politics, 6*(3), 90–103.

Victor, D. G. (2008). On the regulation of geoengineering. *Oxford Review of Economic Policy, 24*, 322–336.

Victor, D. G., Morgan, M. G., Apt, F., & Steinbruner, J. (2009). Geoengineering option – A last resort against global warming, the essay. *Foreign Affairs, 88*, 64–76.

Virgoe, J. (2009). International governance of a possible geoengineering intervention to combat climate change. *Climatic Change, 95*(1–2), 103–119.

Watson, A. J., et al. (2008). Designing the next generation of ocean iron fertilization experiments. *Marine Ecology Progress Series, 364*, 303–309.

Wiener, J. B., & Rogers, M. D. (2002). Comparing precaution in the United States and Europe. *Journal of Risk Research, 5*(4), 317–349.

Williamson, P., Wallace, D. W., Law, C. S., Boyd, P. W., Collos, Y., Croot, P., . . . Vivian, C. (2012). Ocean fertilization for geoengineering: a review of effectiveness, environmental impacts and emerging governance. *Process Safety and Environmental Protection, 90*(6), 475–488.

Winter, G. (2011). Climate engineering and international law: Last resort or the end of humanity? *Review of European Community & International Environmental Law, 20*(3), 277–289.

Wright, T. (2009). Toward effective multilateralism: Why bigger may not be better. *The Washington Quarterly, 32*(3), 163–180.

Zedalis, R. J. (2010). Climate change and the national academy of sciences' idea of geoengineering: One American Academic's perspective on first considering the text of existing international agreements. *European Energy and Environmental Law Review, 19*(1), 18–32.

F. Electronic articles

Armen, C., & Redgwell, C. (2015). *International legal and regulatory issues of climate geoengineering governance: Rethinking the approach* (Climate Geoengineering Governance Working Paper Series No. 021). Retrieved from http://geoengineering-governance-research.org/perch/resources/workingpaper21armeniredgwe ll-theinternationalcontextrevise-.pdf

Baum, S. (2015, June 5). Is stratospheric geoengineering worth the risk? *Bulletin of the Atomic Scientists*. Retrieved from http://thebulletin.org/stratospheric-geoengineering-worth-risk8396

Berge, Hein F. M. ten, Meer, Hugo G. van der, et al. (2012). Olivine weathering in soil, and its effects on growth and nutrient uptake in ryegrass (Lolium perenne L.): A pot experiment. *PLOS One.* doi: 10.1371/journal.pone.0042098

Blackstock, J. J., et al. (2009). *Climate engineering responses to climate emergencies.* Retrieved from http://arxiv.org/pdf/0907.5140

Bracmort, K., Lattanzio, R. K., & Barbour, E. C. (2010, August). *Geoengineering: Governance and technology policy.* Congressional Research Service, Library of Congress. Retrieved from www.fas.org/sgp/crs/misc/R41371.pdf

Davidson, P., Burgoyne, C., Hunt, H., & Causier, M. (2012). Lifting options for stratospheric aerosol geoengineering: Advantages of tethered balloon systems. *Philosophical Transactions: Series A, Mathematical, Physical, and Engineering Sciences, 370*(1974), 4263–4300. doi: 10.1098/rsta.2011.0639

Dykema, J. A., Keith, D. W., Anderson, J. G., & Weisenstein, D. (2014). Strato-spheric controlled perturbation experiment: A small-scale experiment to improve understanding of the risks of solar geoengineering. *Philosophical Transactions of the Royal Society of London A: Mathematical, Physical and Engineering Sciences, 372*(2031), 20140059. doi: 10.1098/rsta.2014.005

Gough, C., & Upham, P. (2010). *Biomass energy with carbon capture and storage (BECCS): A review.* Tyndall Centre for Climate Change Research, WorkingPaper147.Retrievedfromwww.tyndall.ac.uk/publications/tyndall-working-paper/2010/biomass-energy-carbon-capt ure-and-storage-beccs-review

Hammitt, J. K., Wiener, J. B., Swedlow, B., Kall, D., & Zhou, Z. (2005). Precaution-ary regulation in Europe and the United States: A quantitative comparison. *Risk Analysis, 25*(5), 1215–1228. doi:10.1111/j.1539–6924.2005.00662.x

Hubert, A., & Reichwein, D. (2015). *An exploration of a code of conduct for responsible scientific research involving geoengineering.* IASS working paper. Potsdam: Institute for Advanced Sustainability Studies (IASS). Retrieved from www.insis.ox.ac.uk/fileadmin/images/misc/An_Exploration_of_a_Code_of_Conduct.pdf

Keohane, R., & Nye, Jr., J. S. (2001). *Between centralization and fragmentation: The club model of multilateral cooperation and problems of democratic legitimacy.* KSG Working Paper No. 01–004. Retrieved from SSRN: http://ssrn.com/abstract=262175

Kohler, P., Hartmann, J., & Wolf-Gladrow, D. A. (2010). Geoengineering potential of artificially enhanced silicate weathering of olivine. *Proceedings of the National Academy of Sciences of the United States of America, 107*(47), 20228–20233. doi: 10.1073/pnas.1000545107

Kosugi, T. (2010). Role of sunshades in space as a climate control option. *Acta Astro-nautica, 67*(1–2), 241–253. doi:10.1016/j.actaastro.2010.02.009

Latham, J. (2002). Amelioration of global warming by controlled enhancement of the albedo and longevity of low-level maritime clouds. *Atmospheric Science Letters, 3*(2–4), 52–58. doi:10.1006/asle.2002.0099

Latham, J., Bower, K., Choularton, T., Coe, H., Connolly, P., Cooper, G., . . . Wood, R. (2012). Marine cloud brightening. *Philosophical Transactions of the Royal Society A: Mathematical, Physical and Engineering Sciences, 370*(1974), 4217–4262. doi: 10.1098/rsta.2012.0086

Lehmann, J., Gaunt, J., & Rondon, M. (2006). Bio-char sequestration in terrestrial ecosystems – a review. *Mitigation and Adaptation Strategies for Global Change, 11*(2), 403–427. doi: 10.1007/s11027-005-9006-5

Lovelock, J. E., & Rapley, C. G. (2007). Ocean pipes could help the earth to cure itself. *Nature, 449*(7161), 403. doi:10.1038/449403a

Matthews, H. D., & Caldeira, K. (2007). Transient climate – carbon simulations of planetary geoengineering. *Proceedings of the National Academy of Sciences, 104*(24), 9949–9954. doi: 10.1073/pnas.0700419104

OECD. (1994). *The measurement of scientific and technical activities.* Organisation for Economic Co-Operation and Development. doi:10.1787/9789264063525-en.

Parson, E. A., & Keith, D. W. (2013). Science and regulation. end the deadlock on governance of geoengineering research. *Science, 339*(6125), 1278–1279. doi: 10.1126/science.1232527

Petersen, A. (2014). *The emergence of the geoengineering debate within the IPCC. Case study.* Geoengineering our climate working paper and opinion article series. Retrieved from https://geoengineeringourclimate.com/2014/09/09/the-emer gence-of-the-geoengineering-deba te-within-the-ipcc-case-study/

Prather, K. A., et al. (2013). Bringing the ocean into the laboratory to probe the chemical complexity of sea spray aerosol. *Proceedings of the National Academy*

of Sciences of the United States of America, 110(19), 7550–7555. doi: 10.1073/
pnas.1300262110

Proelss, A. (2012). International legal challenges concerning marine scientific research in the era of climate change. *2012 LOSI-KIOST Conference on Securing the
Ocean for the Next Generation*, Seoul, Korea. Retrieved from www.law.berkeley.
edu/files/Proelss-final.pdf

Reynolds, J. (2015). Why the UNFCCC and CBD should refrain from regulating
solar climate engineering. *Working Paper Series: Geoengineering Our Climate?*
Retrieved from https://geoengineeringourclimate.com/

Robock, A. (2008). Whither geoengineering? *Science, 320*(5880), 1166–1167.
doi:10.1126/science.1159280

Robock, A. (2000). Volcanic eruptions and climate. *Reviews of Geophysics, 38*(2),
191–219. doi: 10.1029/1998RG000054

Robock, A. (2008). 20 reasons why geoengineering may be a bad idea. *Bulletin of the
Atomic Scientists, 64*, 14–18. doi: 10.2968/064002006

Robock, A., Bunzl, M., Kravitz, B., & Stenchikov, G. L. (2010). Atmospheric science: A test for geoengineering? *Science, 327*(5965), 530–531. doi: 10.1126/
science.1186237

Robock, A., Marquardt, A., Kravitz, B., & Stenchikov, G. (2009). Benefits, risks,
and costs of stratospheric geoengineering. *Geophysical Research Letters, 36*(19),
L19703. doi: 10.1029/2009GL039209

Robock, A., Oman, L., & Stenchikov, G. L. (2008). Regional climate responses to
geoengineering with tropical and arctic SO_2 injections. *Journal of Geophysical Research: Atmospheres (1984–2012), 113*(D16). doi: 10.1029/2008JD010050

Schiermeier, O. (2012). *Dumping iron at sea does sink carbon.* Retrieved from www.
nature.com/news/dumping-iron-at-sea-does-sink-carbon-1.11028

Tilmes, S., Muller, R., & Salawitch, R. (2008). The sensitivity of polar ozone depletion to
proposed geoengineering schemes. *Science, 320*(5880), 1201–1204.

Wigley, T. (2006). A combined mitigation/ geoengineering approach to climate stabilization. *Science, 314*(5798), 452–454. doi: 10.1126/science.1131728

G. Technical reports

Abaza, H., Bisset, R., & Sadler, B. (2004). *Environmental impact assessment and
strategic environmental assessment: Towards an integrated approach.* UNEP/Earth-
print. Retrieved from www.unep.ch/etu/publications/textONUbr.pdf

Bodle, R., Oberthür, S., et al. (2013). *Options and proposals for the international
governance of geoengineering* (No. (UBA-FB) 001886/E). Dessau-Roßlau: Umweltbundesamt. Retrieved from www.umweltbundesamt.de/sites/default/files/
medien/376/publikationen/climate_chang e_14_2014_komplett_korr.pdf

European Environmental Agency. (2011). *Air pollution impacts from carbon capture
and storage (CCS)* (EEA Technical Report No 14/2011, 23). Retrieved from
www.eea.europa.eu/publications/carbon-capture-and-storage

Fisheries and Oceans Canada. (2010). *Ocean fertilization: Mitigating environmental
impacts of future scientific research* (Canadian Science Advisory Secretariat Science
Advisory Report No. 2010/012). Retrieved from www.dfo-mpo.gc.ca/csas-sccs/
publications/sar-as/2010/2010_012_e.pdf

IGBP, IOC, SCOR. (2013). *Ocean acidification summary for policymakers –
third symposium on the ocean in a high-CO_2 world.* International Geosphere –
Biosphere Programme, Stockholm, Sweden. Retrieved from www.igbp.net/

download/18.30566fc6142425d6c91140a/1385975160621/OA_spm2-FULL-lorez.pdf

McLaren, D. (2011). Negatonnes – an initial assessment of the potential for negative emission techniques to contribute safely and fairly to meeting carbon budgets in the 21st century. *Report for Friends of the Earth, UK.*

Rickels, W., Klepper, G., Dovern, J., Betz, G., Brachatzek, N., Cacean, S., & Güssow, K. (2011). *Large-scale intentional interventions into the climate system? Assessing the climate engineering debate.* Scoping report conducted on behalf of the German Federal Ministry of Education and Research (BMBF), Kiel: Kiel Earth Institute.

Royal Society. (2001). *The role of land carbon sink in mitigating global climate change,* 8. Retrieved from https://royalsociety.org/~/media/Royal_Society_Content/policy/publications/2001/9996.pdf

Smolker, R., & Ernsting, A. (2012). *BECCS: Climate saviour or dangerous hype? 1 &* 6. Retrieved from www.biofuelwatch.net

Sohi, S., Lopez-Capel, E., Krull, E., & Bol, R. (2009). *Biochar, climate change and soil: A review to guide future research.* CSIRO Land and Water Science Report. Retrieved from www.clw.csiro.au/publications/science/2009/sr05-09.pdf

UK House of Commons, Science and Technology Committee. (2006). *Scientific advice, risk and evidence based policy making* (No. HC900-I). London: The Stationary Office. Retrieved from www.publications.parliament.uk/science

UK House of Commons, Science and Technology Committee. (2010). *The regulation of geoengineering – fifth report of session 2009–10* (No. HC221). London: The Stationary Office. Retrieved from www.publications.parliament.uk/pa/cm200910/cmselect/cmsctech/221/221.pdf

World Economic Forum. (2006). *Global risks 2006.* Retrieved from www.circleofblue.org/wp-content/uploads/2015/01/WEF_Global_Risk_Report2006.pdf

H. Electronic newspapers

Backer, P. (2009, July 14). Poorer nations reject a target on emission cut. *The New York Time.* Retrieved from www.nytimes.com/2009/07/09/world/europe/09prexy.html?_r=0

Desert Research Institute. (2016, March 25). Autonomous cloud seeding aircraft successfully tested in Nevada. *Science Daily.* Retrieved from www.sciencedaily.com/releases/2016/03/160325093945.htm

Hale, E. (2012, May 16). Geoengineering experiment cancelled due to perceived conflict of interest. *The Guardian.* Retrieved from www.theguardian.com/environment/2012/may/16/geoengineering-experiment-cancelled

Latham, J. (2007, February 15). Futuristic fleet of "cloudseeders". *BBC News.* Retrieved from http://news.bbc.co.uk/2/hi/programmes/6354759.stm

Neslen, A. (2015, December 14). EU says 1.5°C global warming target depends on 'negative emissions' technology. *The Guardian.* Retrieved from www.theguardian.com/environment/2015/dec/14/eu-says-15c-global-warming-target-depends-on-negative-emissions-technology

Society of Chemical Industry. (2008, July 22). Adding lime to seawater may cut carbon dioxide levels back to pre-industrial levels. *Science Daily.* Retrieved from www.sciencedaily.com/releases/2008/07/080721001742.htm

I. Blogs, online fora and other webpages

Berkum, E. van. (2012, August). *CO₂ in horticultural greenhouses.* Retrieved from http://blog.maripositas.org/horticulture/ocap-organic-carbon-dioxide-for-assimilation-of-plants

CBD. (2007). *Biofuel electronic forum – Impacts.* Retrieved from www.cbd.int/forums/biofuel/impacts.shtml

Earth's oceans: An introduction. Retrieved from www.enchantedlearning.com/subjects/ocean/

FAO. (2006). *Deforestation causes global warming.* Retrieved from www.fao.org/newsroom/en/news/2006/1000385/index.html

Farber, D. (2015, December 14). *Does the Paris agreement open the door to geoengineering?* Retrieved from http://legal-planet.org/2015/12/14/does-the-paris-agreement-open-the-door-to-geoengineerin/

Fløistad, B., & Lothe, L. (2010). *The possibility of an Arctic treaty.* Retrieved from www.arctis-search.com/The+Possibility+of+an+Arctic+Treaty

Garcia, S. M. (1995). *The precautionary approach to fisheries and its implications for fishery research, technology and management: And updated review.* Rome: Fisheries and Aquaculture Department. Retrieved from www.fao.org/docrep/003/W1238E/W1238E01.htm

Global CCS Institute & Biorecro. (2011). *Global status of BECCS projects 2010.* Retrieved from www.globalccsinstitute.com/publications/global-status-beccs-projects-2010

IMO. (2013). *Marine geoengineering including ocean fertilization to be regulated under amendments to international treaty.* Retrieved from www.imo.org/MediaCentre/PressBriefings/Pages/45-marine-geoengieneering.aspx

IPCC. *Organization.* Retrieved from www.ipcc.ch/organization/organization.shtml

Kuo, K. (2012, June 18). *Geoengineering trial cancelled: More regulation needed.* Retrieved from https://theconversation.com/geoengineering-trial-cancelled-more-regulation-needed-7297

Lovett, R. (2008, May 3) *Burying biomass to fight climate change.* Retrieved from http://science.org.au/nova/newscientist/108ns_006.htm

Major Economies Forum on Climate and Energy. (2015). *About.* Retrieved from www.majoreconomiesforum.org/

Morgan, M. G., & Ricke, K. (2010). *Cooling the earth through solar radiation management: The need for research and an approach to its governance.* Retrieved from http:// www.irgc.com

Mortensen, C. (2012). *Biomass vs. environmental justice issues.* Retrieved from www.eugeneweekly.com/2009/08/20/news.html#2

NOAA. *Ocean.* Retrieved from www.noaa.gov/ocean.html

OCEANA. *Ocean pollution and climate change.* Retrieved from http://oceana.org/en/our-work/climate-energy/ocean-acidification/learn-act/what-is-ocean-acidi fication

Ogiwara, S., Awashima, Y., Miyabe, H., & Ouchi, K. (2001). Conceptual design of a deep ocean water upwelling structure for development of fisheries. *Fourth ISOPE Ocean Mining Symposium Oil & Gas Field Technical Terms Glossary.* Retrieved from www.oilgasglossary.com/mobile_offshore_drilling_unit.html

Parties to the Basel convention. Retrieved from www.basel.int/Countries/StatusofRatifications/PartiesSignatories/tabid/1290/

Rayner, S., & Prins, G. (2007). *The wrong trousers: Radically rethinking climate policy.* Climate Feedback, Nature Blogs, Retrieved from http://blogs.nature.com/climatefeedback/2007/10/the_wrong_trousers.html

Rayner, S., et al. (2009). *Oxford principle.* Retrieved from www.geoengineering. ox.ac.uk/oxford-principles/principles/

Republic of Philippine National Disaster Risk Reduction and Management Council. (2014, January 14). *SitRep no. 92 effects of typhoon "Yolanda" (haiyan).* Retrieved from http://reliefweb.int/sites/reliefweb.int/files/resources/ NDRRMC%20Update%20re%20Sit%20Re p%2092%20Effects%20of%20%20 TY%20%20YOLANDA.pdf

Rotterdam Climate Initiative. (2016). *CO_2 capture, transport and storage.* Retrieved from www.rotterdamclimateinitiative.nl/uk/projects/co2-capture,-transport-and-storage?portfol io_id=282

Schlossberg, J. (2013). *Biomass battle casts spotlight on environmental justice.* Retrieved from www.energyjustice.net/content/biomass-battle-casts-spotlight-environmental-justice-bio mass-monitor

Sea Web. (2014). *Ocean issue briefs – large scale ocean circulation.* Retrieved from www.seaweb.org/resources/briefings/circulation.php

SPICE. (2010). *The SPICE project.* Retrieved from www.spice.ac.uk/about-us/ aims-and-background/

UK Health and Safety Executive. *General hazards of carbon dioxide.* Retrieved from www.hse.gov.uk/carboncapture/carbondioxide.htm

UN News Centre. (2013). *Asia-pacific nations at UN call for urgent global approach to mitigate climate change.* Retrieved from www.un.org/apps/news/story.asp?NewsID= 46125&Cr=climate+change&Cr1=#.Um4lf3AyLjY

UNECE. *Geographical scope.* Retrieved from www.unece.org/oes/nutshell/region. html

UNEP. *Water, soil and air.* Retrieved from www.unep.org/climatechange/mitigation/Bioenergy/Issues/WaterSoilAir/tabid/29468/Def ault.aspx

UNSC. (2007, April 17). *Security council holds first-ever debate on impact of climate change on peace, security, hearing over 50 speakers.* Retrieved from www.un.org/ press/en/2007/sc9000.doc.htm

U.S. Environmental Protection Agency. (2010). *Ozone science: The facts behind the phase-out.* Retrieved from www.epa.gov/ozone/science/sc_fact.html

U.S. Environmental Protection Agency. (2011). *Health and environmental effects of ozone layer depletion.* Retrieved from www.epa.gov/ozone/science/effects/index. html

U.S. Government Accountability Office. (2011). *Technology assessment: Climate engineering technical status, future directions, and potential responses* (No. GAO-11-71).

The Wingspread Consensus Statement on the Precautionary Principle, Wingspread conference on the precautionary principle, January 26, 1998. Retrieved from www. sehn.org/wing.html

World by Map. (2015). *The length of the coast for the countries of the world.* Retrieved from http://world.bymap.org/Coastlines.html

Index

Note: Page numbers in *italics* indicate a figure and page numbers in **bold** indicate a table.